THE

HISTORY

OF THE

PENAL LAWS

ENACTED AGAINST

Roman Catholics;

THE OPERATION AND RESULTS OF THAT SYSTEM

OF

LEGALIZED PLUNDER, PERSECUTION,
AND PROSCRIPTION;

ORIGINATING IN RAPACITY AND FRAUDULENT DESIGNS,
CONCEALED UNDER FALSE PRETENCES, FIGMENTS OF REFORM,
AND A SIMULATED ZEAL FOR THE INTERESTS OF

TRUE RELIGION.

BY

R. R. MADDEN, M.R.I.A. &c. &c.

" Jubet supponere terræ
Vipereos dentes, populi incrementa futuri."
Ovid. Metam. Lib. 3.

London:

THOMAS RICHARDSON AND SON,
172, FLEET STREET ; 9, CAPEL STREET, DUBLIN ; AND DERBY.

——

1847.

DEDICATORY LETTER

TO

WM. B. MAC CABE, Esq.

AUTHOR OF "A CATHOLIC HISTORY OF ENGLAND," ETC.

———

MY DEAR MAC CABE,

It is customary for authors to parade at the commencement of their works, their intimacy with great men or influential people, and to make the eminence or notoriety of such persons, the auspices of their success. The object of this work, its affinity with your pursuits, the spirit in which the undertaking of it was imposed on me, are of a nature that induce me to think the dedication should be in keeping with them, that it should be inscribed to a good man, truthful, upright, and steadfast in faith, and therefore to one of the best men I have the happiness to know: even to yourself, my dear friend and school-fellow, I dedicate this volume.

R. R. MADDEN.

Introduction.

IT is hoped that the following pages may be deemed worthy of the examination and study of thoughtful men, be they Roman Catholics or Protestants.

They relate to events, the consequences of which are still felt, and the true character of which it is indispensable for an honest politician to know, for a wise statesman to be in a condition to master, and for a sincere christian to comprehend.

This work is not published with the intention of wantonly reviving bad and bitter feelings, of recalling evils that are irremediable, and crimes that have triumphed for a season over truth and justice, that have passed apparently unpunished, or left behind them no seeds of mischief.

The Penal-Law enormities abound with the latter. In the hope that a fearless and impartial history of this code might tend to wiser, kindlier, and more just legislation for the future, that good men might learn to respect the conscientious convictions of those who differ from them in faith, as to matters affecting the things of another world, and unfitted to be made subjects of party contention, or the objects of political control by the state, the task of undertaking this work, was pressed on the author by the late Thomas Davies.

The tendency of such a work he hoped would be to separate the interests of religion from those of mere pretenders to it, and to show the great care and caution that was required in making laws, so that neither the ferocious passions of fanaticism, nor the fell designs of sordid hypocrisy, were ministered to or encouraged.

With such views the work was undertaken, and the moral that the lamented friend of the author would have drawn from it, the reader, it is hoped, will find in its pages.

They are not written for the purpose of establishing any peculiar theory, nor of pleasing any particular party. The author knows that the faith and discipline of his Church are never to be confounded with the mistakes, the errors, or the offences of churchmen, and therefore he boldly and candidly exposes them when they have failed in their duty, or brought scandal upon the faith. He has dealt with equal freedom towards those who failed not only in their duty to man, but in their fealty to God and to His Church.

Impartiality is aimed at in this work, and with the honest desire to slur over no important fact, to conceal no interesting circumstance, and to evade no grave event, it is hoped that such impartiality is attained; and that where a work is written, which eschews, as if it were a poisonous ingredient, the spirit of controversy, the Roman Catholic may learn why " the Reformation" made progress in these countries, and the Protestant may reflect upon the means employed to advance, uphold, and perpetuate it.

These pages are committed to the press, at a time when the author is about to take his departure for a far distant country; so distant, that the public opinion in these countries can only reach him in faint echoes and by few intervals. Should his work be favourably received, its popularity will probably have passed away, before the letter of a friend can tell him of its success; and should its fate be otherwise, then he can patiently bear the misfortune; because he has the conviction that he has laboured in the cause of truth, and has done his utmost to make it known and render it respected.

THE HISTORY

OF THE

Operation of the Penal Laws

ENACTED

AGAINST ROMAN CATHOLICS.

CHAPTER I.

THE REFORMATION.—THE EVILS THAT LED TO IT, AND THE
OCCURRENCES THAT PRECEDED IT.—THE EXECUTION OF JOHN
HUSS AND JEROME OF PRAGUE.—THE CAREER OF SAVONA-
ROLA.—THE PROGRESS OF LUTHER AS A REFORMER.—THE
USES AND ABUSES OF RELIGION CONFOUNDED IN THE STRUGGLE
WITH ROME.—REPORT OF THE CARDINALS IN 1538, ON THE
EVILS AFFECTING THE CHURCH, AND THE MEANS OF REMOVING
THEM.

THE evils that beset the Church at the close of the 15th
century were deplored, denounced, and over and over again
rung into the ears of Alexander the 6th, from the year 1488
to 1498, A.D., by a Dominican monk, who brought all the
intrepidity, fervour, and ability of the Augustinian friar of
Wirtemberg to the contest with ecclesiastical abuses, but
who brought also to it fidelity to his church and heroism in
defence of its holy doctrines, that the latter unfortunately
did not manifest. The struggle Savonarola was engaged
in was a reformation—Luther a revolt. The efforts of the
former failed. He had to do with an Alexander the 6th,
not with a Paul the 3rd.

1

Had Paul been Pontiff when Savonarola laboured, preached, and prayed for the regeneration of the Church, the later efforts to establish a religion with new doctrines would perhaps have been unsuccessful.

Savonarola endeavoured to force on the attention of Alexander the necessity of a reform; he pointed out the evils that would overwhelm the Church if that reform were not made. His remonstrances were ill received, perhaps ill understood. The Pontiff depreciated the author of one of the holiest books that was ever written in defence of religion, "Triumphus Crucis," and of another, "Simplicitatis vitæ Christianæ," which is only inferior to it, and to another of a similar scope and tendency, "The Imitation of Christ." He treated that holy man as an enemy of religion, who was an enemy only of Satan and of his agents in this world, who are the oppressors of their fellow-men, despots, wrong-doers, and workers of all evil. He favoured the enemies of Savonarola, and encouraged their enmity till their victim was persecuted to the death. But Paul the Third, when attempts were made to call in question the orthodoxy of his writings, gave honourable testimony to their piety when he rebuked the maligners of the martyr's memory.[*] He would look with a suspicion of heresy on whosoever would dare to accuse Savonarola.[†] This intrepid champion of religion and of liberty perished on the scaffold, and his memory is hardly known in Europe, to laymen at least, except as that of a fanatic and an impostor. Nevertheless, he was one of the greatest men of his time—great in point of Christian heroism; in respect to the intrepidity of his efforts to battle with grievous abuses, to stay the torrent of evils that beset his Church; and above all things, great in the maintenance of his unshaken religious principles, in the midst of his boldest efforts for reform, and most formidable struggles with ecclesiastical abuses. Like all men who achieve or attempt great things, he was an enthusiast, and like many of them at the close of his career, his enthusiasm exalted his sentiments almost beyond the height of reason.

He was, if not the founder, at least the first propounder

---

[*] Hist. des Hommes Illustres de l'ordre de I. Dom. Tom. 8. p. 647.

[†] "Quin potius suspectum de hæresi illum habituri sumus quicumque Hieronymum impugnare audebit."—Ap. Brovi, p. 520, col. 1.

in his age of that doctrine to which mankind sooner or later will be brought to look for the regeneration of mankind, which teaches that the true interests of the christian religion and of civil liberty are identical. That great doctrine is embodied in all the preachings and teachings of Savonarola. He never spoke nor wrote in the discharge of his high functions, that it did not seem to be a part of his apostolic mission so to speak and write that his words and writings might tend to make men such as their Maker would have them to be,—good and happy, free from all slavery, from that of sin, of despotism, and of gold. He died on the scaffold in defence of the holiness of religion, and of the rights of the poor against the rich oppressors of his country, the 23rd of May, 1498, about twenty years before Luther's efforts against the abuses of the Church and the vital doctrines of it came into operation.

In the reigns of Edward the Third, Henry the Second, John, and Henry the Seventh, events had taken place in England that had left the seeds of schism in the Church. In 1342, in the reign of Edward the Third, disagreements occurred between the latter and the court of Rome, which well nigh led to a separation. The frequent missions of a pecuniary kind of the agents of the Pontiff into England in former reigns, and the disposal of Church livings both in England and in Ireland to foreign ecclesiastics, had been at times the occasion of remonstrances and complaints on the part of the clergy; some new representations of the latter on this subject, were taken advantage of by the king to defeat all commissions for similar objects, and nearly all papal ecclesiastical appointments in his dominions.

From the teachings of the Apostles, and the councils of the Church presided over by its pontiffs, the Catholic believes the fundamental doctrines of his religion have proceeded, and these cannot be added to nor taken away from, to the consummation of all things. It is not from the court of Rome, nor from the temporal power of him who rules it, they proceed; and if that court ceased to exist, and if that temporal power were taken away, it is a matter of faith that the Church would still subsist in its integrity.

The spiritual power of the Church, says Bossuet, *is independent of all the kings of the earth.* What a blessing would it be for Christendom, if entire faith had been put, and continued so to be, in that axiom.

The origin of the Reformation in England is, however, to be largely attributed to lust and avarice, and in Germany to resentment and ambition. There were mingled with the motives of its prime movers in the latter country, incidents of an old date and provocations of a new one, which had a mighty influence on the great revolt which commenced in 1515. At so early a period as the separation of the Western empire from that of Rome, the popes had been obliged to keep a strong hand upon some of the Eastern Churches, and to plunge into an arduous contest with some of the European princes respecting the nomination and investiture of bishops, the presentation to abbeys and priories.

These circumstances, embittering the minds of unsubmissive men, were among the many causes of the schism in the East, and of grave disorders, jealousies, and animosities in some continental countries, especially in Germany, centuries before the era of the Reformation. But the events that the Council of Constance gave birth to in 1415 and 1416, A. D., the trials and executions of John Huss and Jerome of Prague, nourished a religious flame in Bohemia and other parts of Germany, which for one hundred years we find breaking out at short intervals in various places on various pretexts and under various leaders, now smouldering for a brief season, now issuing forth in flame, and furnishing ample proof that the fate of Huss and his companion had sunk deep into the minds and hearts of the people of Germany, and produced the very opposite effects that were expected from these measures of severity. They had not intimidated boldness, nor reformed error, nor reclaimed impiety; they had exasperated many and disgusted all. At the expiration of a century, they furnished Luther with a motive for making war on the power and authority of Rome, in the persons of its agents charged with the publication of Papal bulls in Germany. " Les foudres et les feux du concile de Constance n'empecheront pas, qu'elle ne renaisse de cendres de Jean Huss, et de Jerome de Prague, en la personne de Luther."*

---

* Varilla Revolut. en mat. de Relig. Tom. 1. p. 2.

Charles the Fifth could have checked (humanly speaking) Luther in his career, without employing measures of extreme severity, had it suited his policy to have done so; but for thirty years he allowed the Reformation to take its course, and when he would have stopped it he could not. The Duchy of Milan was of more importance to him than the Church of Rome. Philip the Second thought more of the latter than of his Dutch dominions. He desired to put down the Reformation in the Low Countries by measures of inordinate severity, and he could not; but he practised horrors enough in the attempt to bring on an insurrection, and the frightful executions of his forty-eight Calvinist subjects in the Low Countries, only tended to root the persecuted religion in the soil, and to lose the latter to the crown of Spain.

While Catholics denounce innovations and innovators, it behoves them to reflect with profound humility on the state of religion which had led to those innovations, or furnished a pretext for them; to deplore the evils of luxury and rapacity, which prevailed in the court of Rome at that period; the negligence of pastors, the laxity of discipline, the secularization of the spirit of religion and of the professors and the ministers of it. No Catholic can or ought to deny that some of the clergy of that period had grievously suffered in character from connection with the state; that many of the members of the monastic orders had ceased to live in accordance with their vows; that in various places ecclesiastical government greatly needed a reform, and that several of the religious orders required to be brought back to the original intentions of their founders, to a new sense of the piety, self-denial, humility, and poverty which early characterized them, and to make the Church of God what it was in primitive times.

"Who shall grant me," cried St. Bernard, "to see, before I die, the Church of God such as she was in primitive times?" He did not live to see that happy change. On the contrary, the evils went on augmenting. "From the period of the Council of Vienna," says Bossuet, a great prelate, charged by the Pope with the preparation of the matters which ought to be treated of there, "laid it down as the basis of the work of that holy Assembly, that *it was essential to reform the Church in its chief and in its members.*

The grand schism which arose a little later caused more than ever the same sentiment to be expressed, not only by individual doctors of the Church,—a Gersen and a Daillé, and other great men of their time,—but also by Councils, and especially in the Council of Pisa and in that of Constance.* It is well known what happened at the Council of Basle, where the reformation was unfortunately deferred, and the Church replunged into new dissensions. The Cardinal Julien represented to Pope Eugenius IV. the disorders of the clergy, especially those of Germany. *Those disorders* (said he) *excite the hatred of the people against the whole ecclesiastical order ; and if they are not corrected, care is to be taken that the laity do not fall on the clergy in the manner of the Hussites, as they loudly menace us.* He predicted, that if the clergy of Germany were not promptly reformed, that when the Bohemian heresy should have been smothered, another would arise still more dangerous ; for the clergy (said he), it will be affirmed, are incorrigible, and have no wish that a remedy should be applied to their disorders," &c........" The little of respect left for the sacred office of the priesthood will end in being lost. The whole blame of those disorders will be cast on the court of Rome, which will be regarded as the cause of all existing evils." ...."I see (continued he) that the axe is laid to the root ; the tree bends, and, instead of supporting it whilst it could be done, we help to cast it down."............." God has taken away the perception of our perils, as He is accustomed to do with those whom He intends to punish. The flames are kindled before us, and we run on till we rush into the midst of them."

" It is thus," says Bossuet† in the fifteenth age, " the greatest man of his age deplored the evils, and foresaw the sad consequences of them, and seemed to predict those which Luther was about to bring on the Christian world, commencing with Germany ; and he was not deceived when he imagined, that reform being contemned, and the hatred against the clergy redoubled, an enemy was about to be produced, more formidable to the Church than the Bohemian one." It is evident, then, that great abuses had crept into some of the religious houses and episcopal

---

* Histoire des Variations, Vol. i. Liv. 1. p. 2.
† Ibid. p. 4.

palaces, and that those of cardinals were not exempt from them.

The acquisition of great wealth, the worldly cares which the extensive possession of landed property brought with it, the cupidity excited in the breasts of princes by the reputed riches of the Church ; the consequent attempts to discredit the clergy, to lessen their influence, to hurt their authority, to defame, and then to plunder them, followed in return by acts unworthy of the clerical character to defeat such attempts, — acts sometimes of violence, sometimes of intrigue ; at other times of misapplication of spiritual power— all these things were evils of which the existence was well known in Rome, and especially to Paul III., of the removal of which there is incontestable evidence that there was, on his part, a sincere desire and a firm intention to enter on the undertaking.

There is a very remarkable treatise in the author's possession, printed at Cologne, in small 4to, in 1538, consisting of thirteen pages of matter in the Latin tongue. The title is, "Concilium delectorum Cardinalium et aliorum Prelatorum, de emenda Ecclesiæ S. D. N. D. Paulo ipso juvente, conscriptum et exhibitum Anno 1538."

It purports to be a representation of the abuses in matters of religion which required reform, the result of an enquiry instituted by Pope Paul III. It bears the signatures of Gaspar. Card. Contarenus. Johannes Petrus. Card. Theatinus Jacobus Card. Sodeletus. Reginaldus Card. Anglicus. Freder. Archiepis. Solernitanus. Hier. Arch. Brundusinus. I. Mathœus Epis. Veronensis. Gregor. Abbas S. Georgii Venet. Frater Thomas Mag. Sac. Palatii.*

Their report or representation treats of the various abuses requiring reformation, and the remedies proposed for them, which are specified in twenty-eight articles, preceded by a preamble of three pages. Sarpi gives the names of the subscribers in full.

The state of religion previously to the Council of Trent, is set forth more clearly in this representation of the abuses that time and the negligence of pastors had introduced, not only into religious houses but into the Court of Rome, than in any other document illustrative of the condition of the Church at that period. The substance of the several arti-

---

* Hist. du Concile de Trente. Liv. i. p. 78.

cles of this Report is given in the following pages. The origin of the Report is described in a work valuable for much of its historical data concerning the Council of Trent, though a very disingenuous production, written by an insidious enemy of his religion in the habit of a monk—the History of the Council of Trent, by the Friar Paoli Sarpi. The following are his words :—" To give an effectual contradiction of those rumours (of the Pope's disinclination to call a Council for the purpose of reform), and to remove the evil opinion formed of his intentions, the Pope, Paul III., resolved to begin the reform with himself, and with the cardinals and his court.* *For this object* he chose four cardinals and five other prelates, whom he so much esteemed that he made cardinals of four of them; commanded them to make a collection of the abuses which ought to be reformed, and to indicate the remedies which ought to be applied. In obedience to his commands they made a written Report, setting forth *that all abuses were occasioned by the too great facility with which the Popes lent their ears to flattery, and departed from the laws and the commandments which Jesus Christ had given, to draw no profits from spiritual functions.*† After which, coming to detail, they set down twenty-seven abuses (twenty-eight) in the administration of ecclesiastical affairs, and in the particular government of Rome."

He then very briefly notices the articles in question, and speaks of the Report as "A work worthy of being read, and which he would have translated word by word, if it had not been too long." It is to be observed, that this dishonest writer, in stating that the Report of the cardinals and prelates attributed all the abuses to the faults of the Popes, falsified the terms of the document he referred to.

Its authors certainly reprehended the court of Rome with a high hand, but they did not attribute all the evils which had fallen on the Church to the acts or conduct of the pontiffs. They attributed the chiefest of those evils to the dignitaries of the Church who composed the court of Rome, to the crime of simony with which they especially charged them : "Ex hoc fonte, Sancte Pater, tanquam ex

---

* Histoire du Concile de Trente, Liv. 1. p. 79.
 † In the original, this passage is not in Italics. I have thus put it for the purpose of directing attention to that portion of his observations, which are particularly unjust.

equo Trojano, irrupere in Ecclesiam Dei tot abusus et tam gravissimi morbi," &c.

Sarpi falsified history in treating of the Pope's commission given to the cardinals to draw up this representation, as a measure dictated solely by a desire of saving appearances, and of silencing the enemies of his holiness. Sarpi must have well known that the commission in question was given by Pope Paul with a *bonâ fide* desire of forcing on the attention of his court the necessity of a reform there, commenced and undertaken by themselves, when a council was about to be called, one of the avowed objects of which was the reformation of manners and discipline in religious houses and amongst the subordinate clergy. This proceeding of Paul III. was one of the noblest acts that can be imagined; the choice of the persons he commissioned to carry it into execution was worthy of it, and their Report was in all respects worthy of the great trust reposed in them.

I doubt if in ecclesiastical annals any instance of a similar kind is to be met with, of a number of the chief dignitaries of a Church engaged in a business of this kind, examining the evils that had fallen on religion, without regard to the worldly interests of their order; tracing those evils to the fountain head, and fearlessly and frankly, where reprehension was due, reprehending the highest authority of the Church, even that under which they acted; laying bare the most grievous faults of their own body, and, lastly, lifting the veil from every irregularity and disorder in life or discipline in the subordinate ministers of that religion, whose fame was evidently dearer to them than any earthly consideration.

It was very base of Sarpi to withhold commendation from such an act as that of Paul III., and the execution of his orders in respect to it. *A false religion could not possibly have afforded such a step, nor have survived such an exposure of the abuses of its discipline and of the faults of its ministers.*

The following is, in substance, the representation made to Paul III. of the abuses requiring the most prompt reform.

Art. 1.—The first abuse is the total want of care and circumspection " in the ordination of priests, and especially of presbyters;" persons being every where ordained, disqualified by their condition, age, and education. "Hence arose innumerable scandals, contempt of ecclesiastics, not only diminished veneration for divine worship, but even almost the extinction of it."

ART. 2.—" The collation to ecclesiastical benefices, especially curacies, but above all the nomination to bishoprics, constituted another grievous abuse, from which it arose that benefices had been conferred on persons not even of the flock of Christ nor of the Church."

ART. 3.—The custom of entailing pensions on benefices in favour of those who collated to them, an abuse which would not cease to be so if "the Pontiff, who was the universal dispenser of all the goods of the Church, burdened benefices with reservations of their emoluments only for pious and charitable uses, which interferes with the decent maintenance of pastors."

ART. 4.—The abuse of exchanging benefices by simoniacal compacts, in which lucre was the only object of the parties to them.

ART. 5.—The abuse of bequeathing benefices, of renouncing bishoprics and benefices in consideration of a reservation of some part of their revenues.

ART. 6.—The infraction of the ancient law of Clement, that the sons of presbyters shall not possess the benefices of their fathers. The custom of converting spiritual things to private uses having occasioned scandals; and no cause had more contributed to the enmity to the clergy, from which so many seditions had arisen, and others were arising.

ART. 7.—The abuse of disposing of benefices before the deaths of the incumbents.

ART. 8.—The evil of uniting two or more benefices, and what is worse, bishoprics: "Non tantum duobus, sed pluribus, et quod pejus est, in episcopatibus."

ART. 9.—" An abuse in the Church of great moment," is the custom of conferring on cardinals, not only one, but many bishoprics; "and chiefly so, because the office of cardinal and the office of prelate are incompatible."

ART. 10.—" The abuse which first, and before all others, should be corrected," was that of the non-residence of prelates and beneficed clergy in their sees and parishes.

ART. 11.—The non-residence of cardinals at the court of Rome was also an evil that needed to be removed.

ART. 12.—" It was a great abuse, and by no means to be tolerated, that the universal Christian world should be scandalized by the impediments which bishops in the government of their flocks put in the way of punishing and correcting criminals. For, in the first place, by many modes evil doers escaped, and especially clergy, from the jurisdiction of their ordinaries. Then, if they be not exempt from it, they fly immediately to confession, or to means of corruption, by which they obtain impunity ; and what is worst is, that it is obtained by means of money. These abuses, most holy Father, we conjure you, by the blood of Christ, who redeemed His Church and washed it with the same blood, those abuses which have perturbed Christianity, let them be taken away !"

ART. 13.—" Another abuse to be corrected is in the religious orders, many of which have become so defiled, that their example has become a scandal to the laity and noxious to the latter. We think all conventual orders should be abolished, (' Conventuales ordines abolendos esse putamus omnes,') not, however, to inflict injury on any, but to prohibit the reception of any novices, (' Non tamen ut alicui fiat injuria, sed prohibendo ne novos possent admittere.') So that, without injury (to the existing orders), they shall be suppressed, and good religious may be substituted for them. Now, we think it would be best if all youths, who are not professed, should be sent away from their monasteries."

ART. 14.—The abuse of the indiscriminate liberty given to friars to exercise the functions of preachers and confessors, without episcopal examination of their fitness for such offices, and sanction for the performance of their duties.

ART. 15.—" We have stated, most holy Father, that it is not lawful by any compact to derive lucre from any use of the keys whatsoever : in this matter the words of the Saviour are express, ' *Freely you have received, freely give.*' This matter not only concerns your Holiness, but all who are partakers of this power. The same applies to legates and nuncios."

ART. 16.—" Another abuse troubles Christendom, that of nunneries which are under the care of convents of monks, where, in many monasteries, public sacrilege is committed, to the very great scandal of the citizens."

ART. 17.—"It is a great and pernicious abuse in the public schools, especially of Italy, that in them many philosophers teach impiety. Even in the temples of religion they hold most impious disputations, and if some of them are of a pious nature, they are treated before the people in a most irreverent manner."

ART. 18.—The abuse of permitting monks, for the sake of lucre, of retaining the monastic habit who have apostatized from their vows.

ART. 19.—"Another abuse is the existence of questing-crafts, called of the Holy Spirit and of St. Anthony, by which the country people and the simple are deluded and involved in many superstitions: these, we think, ought to be put an end to."

ART. 20.—Another abuse is the facility with which dispensations have been given to marry to persons who have been ordained.

ART. 21.—The abuse of dispensations in cases of affinity or consanguinity. Marriages within the second degree should not be tolerated, except on very grave public grounds. In other degrees to be withheld also, except for justifiable reasons; and never for money, except by the imposition of a fine after absolution for pious uses.

ART. 22.—The abuse of absolving persons guilty of simony, and still profiting by it. "Alas, how widely spread is this pestilential vice in the Church of Christ! So much so, that persons are not ashamed to commit the crime of simony, and forthwith to ask absolution for it. They even buy it, and thus retain the benefice they have purchased."

ART. 23.—The abuse of granting the clergy permission to bequeath the things of the Church, or to convert the patrimony of the poor into private uses or the enlargement of houses.

ART. 24.—The abuse of the confessional, with the use of portable altars, which tends to bring sacred things into disrespect. Indulgences should be granted only at stated times of the year, and in some important place. Commutation of vows should be less frequently sanctioned.

ART. 25.—The impiety of changing the last wishes of a

testator, with a view of diverting property from the heir at law on any pretences of charitable purposes.

ART. 26.—The scandal given by priests officiating in the temple of St. Peter unfit for the sacred functions, and robed in vestments utterly unfit for divine service, and that, too, "in the city of Rome, which is the Mother Church and the mistress of other Churches."

ART. 27.—"In this city [of Rome] even courtesans go about on mules as matrons, who are sought at noon day by high personages and of the court. In no other city have we seen this corruption besides this, which is accounted of all the example. They inhabit also fine houses. This vile abuse ought to be corrected."

ART. 28.—The abuse in this city of feuds between citizens, fomented by some cardinals, instead of being appeased by them. And, lastly, the state of the hospitals in Rome, asylums of orphans and widows, calls for the care of his Holiness and his cardinals.

The statement of the evils which afflicted the Church, terminates with a moving appeal to his Holiness, "that as he had taken the name of Paul, he would imitate the charity of the apostle who was chosen to be the bearer of the name of Jesus to the Gentiles. He, it was to be hoped, was chosen to prevent the name of Christ being forgotten by them, to have it restored by the clergy, renewed in the hearts and works of the laity, so that the sick might be healed, the sheep of Christ gathered in one fold, the impending wrath of God and his revenge, justly merited, turned away from the nations of the Christendom."

The preceding extracts, it may be repeated, are taken from the original published Report. "The Pope, (says Sarpi,) caused this Report to be examined by several Cardinals, and proposed the matter in full consistory. Nicholas Schomberg, commonly called Cardinal of Capua, contended in a long discourse that the reform was not seasonable. He said that such was the malice of men, that. if one attempted to prevent them doing evil, they would take a delight in doing still greater evil; and that there was less inconvenience from suffering a known disorder, which being in existence, gives less scandal than the introduction of another, which being new became more apparent, and consequently more subject to censure. That it would give the

Lutherans reason to boast of having forced the Pope to make this reform, in which the abuses would not only be taken away, but also other good customs, and thus the affairs of religion would be put on a worse footing. That the Lutherans would proclaim they had reason to make their complaints, which would increase their obstinacy. On the other hand, Cardinal Caraffa a Theatine, contended that the reform was necessary, and could not be deferred without offence to God. That it was a general rule of Christianity, as evil could not be done that good might come of it, one ought not moreover to refrain from a good work that was obligatory, on account of the evil that might arise from it."

Sarpi is too disingenuous a writer to place entire reliance in his reports of the discourses he refers to. Of the substance of such discourses he may give some idea. If the spirit of that discourse of Cardinal Schomberg was such as Sarpi has described it, the arguments were those which Milton makes Satan and his agents have recourse to, to "make the worse appear the better reason," and those adduced by Cardinal Caraffa, were such as we might expect to proceed from inspirations of a very different nature and origin, and directed towards an end of a very different character. The opinions in the consistory were much divided, and the Pope finally ordered the sentiments of the Prelates to be kept secret. Action on the Report in the meantime was postponed. The Cardinal Schomberg, Sarpi states, sent a copy of the document in question into Germany, "and some persons believed it was done with the consent of the Pope, who wished it to be known that he was intent on the reform." The copy was printed and widely circulated in Germany, and many pieces were written against it in German and in Latin.[*] "This was in the year 1538, and the printed copy which is in the author's possession is dated the same year."

Pallavicino, in his history of the Council of Trent,[†] makes mention of the appointment, by the Pope Paul, of this commission of inquiry of the four cardinals and five prelates in the year 1537, and in general terms of their recommended reforms. He speaks of the Cardinal Schomberg as a man, " religionis studiossisimus et Germanicorum ingeniorum

---

* Hist. du Con. de Trente, Liv. 3. p. 79.
  † Hist. Con. Trid. Vol. i. p. 137.

peritissimus." With reference to the scandals given in
Rome, referred to in the 27th Art., he observes, "Num
amplius hoc enorme spectaculum Romam deturpat."

With respect to the 13th article, which represents the
religious orders as a scandal to the laity and noxious to
them, much might be said. This article is very singular,
and calculated to make a false impression, if the circumstances of the times are not taken into account, and likewise
the extreme jealousy that existed on the part of the secular
against the regular clergy. The former were disposed to
throw all the blame of the abuses of the time on the friars;
the latter were no less disposed to retort on the lives and
luxurious habits of the secular clergy and the court of
Rome. There is a striking instance of this in the observation of the celebrated Dominican bishop Bartholomew das
Martires, at the Council of Trent. That eminent and holy
prelate pressed on the council the necessity of commencing
its proceedings with the reform of the clergy and dignitaries
of the Church. One of the latter objected to their Eminences the cardinals being considered in need of any
reform. Bartholomew das Martires said, it was exactly
their eminences who stood most eminently in need of
reformation.

"Illustrissimi Cardinales indigent ut mihi quidem vide-
tur, illustrissima Reformatione." "And the first thing I
would wish them deign to change in themselves, is the
manner in which they treat the bishops. For it appears
to me that the veneration with which I honour them would
be more human than divine, more in appearance than
reality, if I did not wish that their conduct should be as
pure as their dignity is eminent." He himself was the
means of effecting a great reformation in the way the cardinals were permitted to treat the bishops. It was always
the custom for bishops to stand with their heads uncovered
in consistories at Rome, while the cardinals sat down. He
once attended a consistory in Rome, and was very indignant that aged bishops had to stand while the cardinals
sat down. On retiring from the assembly he spoke warmly
of the impropriety of such conduct to Cardinal Alexandrin,
afterwards Pius V., both on the part of those who so acted,
and of those who permitted it. He urged the cardinal to
speak to the pope on the subject. The cardinal refused,
for he dreaded a refusal on the part of the pope, who, he

observed, may be offended by the demand. "Then I will speak myself," said Bartholomew.—"You may, but 'you will not succeed," answered the cardinal. "Dices sed nihil proficies."

On the morning of the next consistory he called on the pope, and after praising him for the zeal with which he laboured to carry out reforms about the persons and residences of church dignitaries—"But, holy father, your work is not yet perfect: how happens it that you permit bishops to stand bareheaded while the cardinals sit covered?" The pope pleaded the antiquity of the custom. "Banish, I pray you, most holy father, banish far from the Roman court those customs which are called ancient but which are contrary to the laws of the church. The dignity of cardinals comes from human institution—that of the bishop from Jesus Christ himself. Yes, most holy father, the bishops, as bishops, are brothers of your holiness; therefore your own self-respect ought induce you to treat them as such." The pope was moved. "Go," said he, "to the council, and see how I will treat them." He opened the council by expressing his regret that popes, like secular kings, had the disadvantage of hearing not what was useful but pleasing to them. The truth is kept from them and they are ignorant of what they ought to know. This I say, because I have just now received an important advice regarding the manner in which we treat bishops in this assembly. The Archbishop of Braga has spoken to me on the subject. I have easily conceived, from the solid reasons he alleged to me, that the same zeal which makes us firm in preserving good things ought to animate us to destroy bad. Therefore we are for the future resolved that the bishops shall sit and be covered in this assembly. His holiness at the same time made a sign to the bishops to sit down and put on their caps.

The recommendation of the cardinals was not the first of the kind nor the last acted on. The council of Lateran, in the time of Innocent III., prohibited the institution of new religious orders: "Ne nimia religionum diversitas gravem in ecclesia Dei confusionem inducat firmiter prohibemus, nequis de clero novam religionem inveniat," &c.

The Spanish sovereign, by the advice of the royal council of Castile, in the latter part of the seventeenth century, made an application to the pope, requesting that no persons might be admitted into any convent under sixteen years of age, nor *ordained* under twenty. It is somewhat singular in this recommendation of prohibiting the reception of novices in the monasteries, the coincidence between it and a similar suggestion of the Duke of Wellington in Portugal, in 1812, when the immediate suppression of the religious orders, and the seizure of their property was in the contemplation of the Portuguese government, and was pressed on him by his own.

It might be argued, perhaps, from the words of the thirteenth article of the representation, that good religious may be substituted for them, namely, the bad ; that the step recommended, of prohibiting the admission of novices, was only meant to be enforced while the existing disorders remained unremoved in religious houses. The use of the monastic orders to religion could not be unknown to the eminent men who drew up this representation : it was the abuses of those bodies they were desirous of abolishing. It would seem as if the wants of the church at different epochs were providentially to be met by the appearance of some new religious order : at one time, when sloth and luxury prevailed amongst the clergy, by the appearance of a body of priests devoted to a life of toil and poverty ; at another time, when the word of God was seldom preached to the people, by the institution of an order of preachers ; and so on, at different periods, different wants being supplied in the church by new associations, each of which were made especially the depository of some peculiar truth or tenet.

A general of the Dominican Order of great learning, the Rev. P. Russell, has favoured the author with some observations on this subject, suggested by the perusal of the preceding pages, in manuscript, well worthy of attention. Relaxation had assuredly crept into many religious communities at the close of the fifteenth century, but not into all. At this very period religious houses (such as Bemfica, near Lisbon) were nurseries of saints as well as of most learned men. Though it was in the schools of the religious orders that the giant and daring mind of Luther waxed strong, yet it ought to be remembered that there also were trained the best and most skilful champions that encountered the host he marshalled against the church. By giving a rapid sketch of the moral and intellectual condition of one religious order at this period, I shall be furnishing

2

data for my readers to judge whether the cardinals acted wisely and justly in giving that suggestion. The Council of Trent was held shortly after this advice was given. Its benches were thronged with holy prelates and learned divines belonging to all the religious orders. But I will speak only of the Dominicans or Friars Preachers. There were fifty of that order, either bishops or theologians, at the council, when Dominick Soto arrived there as representative of his general.* To name even the most illustrious would occupy too much space. Melchior Cano was one of them, the author of " the Book of Gold," in which, according to Pallavicini, he has treated before all others and better than all others, de Locis Theologicis. He was the first to join beauty of style and eloquence with irresistible force of argument. The two Sotos were there, Dominick and Peter, equally learned and pious. The vast learning of Dominick, displayed in his writings, gave rise to a common proverb, " Qui scit Sotum, scit totum." Peter was chosen under Mary and Philip to re-establish studies in the University of Oxford. He took with him, according to Sanders, in his History of the English Schism, Spanish and German friars of his order. Among the Spaniards was the holy and learned Bartholomew de Carranza, subsequently Archbishop of Toledo.

Leonardo de Marinis, Dominican Archbishop of Lanciano, attended the Council of Trent as the pope's legate. He is described by the Abbe Ughel as naturally eloquent, most prudent, adorned with virtues, affable in his address, staturâ simul et decorus aspectu. In all difficult and disputed questions his opinion had great weight, so solid and lucid were the reasons with which he supported it. All that is contained in the twenty-second Lesson of the Council, about the sacrifice of the mass, was written by him. The council greatly admired the beautiful order with which he treated the subject. His singular prudence and tact in the management of difficult affairs, were displayed in various missions to the principal courts of Europe under five successive popes, Julius III. Paul IV. Pius IV. Pius V. and Gregory XIII. He was particularly used by St. Pius V. in reforming twenty-five dioceses, and in exhorting the princes of Europe to arm against the threatened encroachments of the Turks.

* Touron, vol. 4, p. 209.

Francisco Foriero, a Portuguese Dominican, was one of the most remarkable men in the Council ; remarkable for his holiness, for his varied and profound knowledge, and for his eloquence. Being appointed to preach to the Council, his first sermon gave the Fathers so high an opinion of his fervent piety and learning, that they wished him thenceforward to preach for them once a week. He was appointed to succeed Louis of Grenada, as Provincial of the Dominicans of Portugal. What holy and learned men must have grown under the direction and example of such Superiors ! He was a great Latin, Greek, and Hebrew scholar. " He made an exact and literal translation, from the Hebrew, of the Books of Job, David, Solomon, and all the Prophets. His design in this great work was to confirm the authority of our Vulgate, and to show that the author had, with great fidelity, given the natural sense of the text." " He as yet lives," says Sixtus of Sienna, in his Bibliotheca Sancta, "in this year, 1566, and he happily continues his labours, and perseveres day and night in explaining the Holy Scriptures." Unfortunately, his varied occupations from 1560 to 1571, prevented him from publishing his learned works, and Providence permitted that an accident should destroy the greatest part of his manuscripts. His cell took fire : when it was quenched he expressed a hope that "his Job " was at least safe. It had been saved,—the only monument of his past labours,—and he was satisfied. Louis of Sousa mentions that this precious manuscript, so dear to its author, was actually in his [Louis] possession, and that it would be soon published.

Foscharari, Dominican Bishop of Modena, was called "Father of the Poor ;" *he often pledged his ring and pastoral staff* to raise money to relieve their distresses ! Pallavicini says, that his firmness in maintaining the necessity of episcopal residence as of divine right, exposed him to calumny. Ughhel, in his Italia Sacra, says, that not only did the Fathers of the Council venerate him for his extraordinary virtue, but the most skilful theologians acknowledged his pre-eminence in learning. They all called him "An Ark of Sciences." Arcæ scientiarum a doctis omnibus tulit cognomen. Suffice it to say that he was appointed from the first congregation on the 15th of January, 1562, to revise and approve all the discourses that were to be preached before the Council. He was subsequently solicited to put in order every thing which had been defined in the different sessions, and to draw up the canons which had to be signed by the Council. He put every thing in the state we now have it. But I must quote a passage about him written by Bartholomus de Martyribus, worthy alike of both men.* "Among the Bishops of Italy who are here, there are two of our Order; one of whom, who is of Modena, is eminent for his learning and sanctity. We know each other but a few days, and we are as great friends as if we lived together for ten years.........I conjure you to have an extreme care of the poor, still greater if possible than what I recommended you on my departure : for I confess that the love of this virtue is greatly increased in me by the exam- ple of the holy Bishop of Modena, who is the ornament of our Order. His revenue amounts only to a thousand ducats, and he does more charity in his diocese than I can, I think, do in mine. I do not know how he contrives to live. As for me, I believe that God does miracles in favour of those generous persons who are so liberal for the love of Jesus Christ. He told me that he is himself astonished how, with such narrow means, he can incur such large expenses. Therefore I again conjure you to be not only liberal but magnificent, and, if I may say it, saintly pro- digal towards the poor!.......Pardon me, my father, if I recommened you this with so much ardour. I speak to myself in speaking to you ; and I exhort myself in exhort- ing you ; that being excited by the example of this holy bishop, I may, at least, follow him whom, I think, I ought to have preceded," &c., &c.

What a blessed emulation! So great an opinion had the Council and the Pope of the capacity of these three Dominicans, Francisco Foriero, Leonardo de Marinis, and Œgidius Foscharari, that to them was committed the composition of the remarkable work called "the Catechism of the Council of Trent." "Its style is elegant, its arrangement beautiful, its lucidness marvellous, its solidity admirable, its piety most prudent and spiritual. So that it may be called 'a perfect abridgment of Christian Theo- logy.' " So says an eminent French bishop. It is a work that all ought to read—Catholics to be well instructed, and Protestants to learn the *real* doctrine of the Catholic

* Touron, vol. iv, page 288, and Echard, vol. ii. page 185-86.

Church. There is, I must remark, a dispute among the learned, whether another divine did not share the honour of their labour, or whether the final polish was not given to the style by one of the most elegant Latin scholars of the day, Muzio Calini. But from what I have read of the great taste and scholarship of Francisco Foriero, I believe that he was fully capable of clothing his thoughts in language of classic elegance.

Bartholomew de Martyribus, Archbishop of Braga, was there,—the model of Christian prelates, the friend and director of St. Charles Borromeo, and the greatest ornament of the Council. St. Pius V., was at this time establishing the character that merited for him the Papal dignity. He was one of the greatest and holiest men that ever sat in St. Peter's chair. He was fully equal to the exigences of the times. The Church required a great but a true reform—Pius V. fulfilled the delicate and arduous mission. He commenced with the city of Rome. His own palace and family felt first his correcting hand. Modesty and piety soon reigned in it, for he wished it to serve as a model to all, and that he should be more authorised to correct all public disorders. He then proceeded through every ramification of ecclesiastical and civil office, correcting every abuse and establishing everywhere regularity and justice. He made many salutary regulations for the clergy, secular and regular. He introduced "a most illustrious reformation" among the cardinals,—permitting creditors to use legal means to recover from them their debts, and, if necessary, to seize on their property and furniture. But he did not confine his zeal for the correction of abuses to Rome. He extended it to all Christendom. He appointed visitators to examine if the bishoprics, chapters, colleges, and monasteries were well governed, and to send him an exact report of all things. Leonardo de Morinis, after resigning his archbishopric, was one of those selected to be apostolic visitator, and absolutely made the prescribed inquiries or reforms in twenty-five dioceses. He sent legates to every court, and zealous missionaries to every afflicted church. His spirit was felt everywhere, and the face of things began to change. His reign shows what a spirit of vitality there is in the Church, and that it was a legitimate reformer, and not a sacrilegious destroyer, that was required. He stirred up all the Princes of Europe to band against the Turks ; and to his zealous and importu- nate exhortations and active co-operation, was generally attributed the success of the famed battle of Lepanto. It broke the Ottoman power, and rolled back the tide of con- quest that was about to sweep over Europe. His virtues are summed up by his biographer, Touron, in these words : " He had all the virtues of a solitary, of an apostolic man, of a bishop, of a cardinal, and of a pope. He was neither less religious in his episcopacy, nor less penitent under his purple, nor less humble on his throne, than in his cloister." All Europe wept for him ; and Selim II., who considered him the most terrible enemy of the Ottoman power, ordered public rejoicings at his death for three days in Constantinople.

At that time lived the sainted and persecuted Arch- bishop of Toledo, the Dominican Bartholomew de Cavanza. He attended the beath-bed of Charles V., and was cast by Philip II. into Philip's state prison, the Inquisition, and kept there for seven years, though Philip was remonstrated with, and the Inquisition was threatened with censures. The Council of Trent examined his works, and declared him innocent ; but his enemies were too powerful, *and the revenues of his diocese were two hundred thousand crowns.* So much for the power of the Church over the Inquisition, and for the influence of the Dominican Order in its govern- ment.

At this period lived "*the Protector of the Indians,*" the noble-minded, the indomitable Bartholomew de las Cazas. Who has not heard of him? Echard says that he first visited America in the year 1493, when he was only nine- teen years old. Then it was, probably, that his young heart first felt those tender sentiments of compassion and charity for the Indians, which, during the seventy-three subsequent years of his life, he never ceased to manifest. He lived to the patriarchal age of ninety-two. He returned in 1502 to San Domingos, and saw with horror and indigna- tion the treatment received by the Indians from the Spa- niards. He instantly denounced the atrocity and injustice of the oppressors ; he sought to vindicate for the Indians the common rights of humanity. He was seconded by kin- dred spirits—the Order of Preachers—of which he became a member. Their example added fire to his zeal. He heard them fearlessly proclaiming from the pulpit, that the laws of God and human nature were outraged by the atrocious cruelties and unbridled despotism of the Spaniards. He saw Montesino obliged to mount that same pulpit before an incensed audience, to express an apology for his violence and to retract his propositions. Las Cazas heard him apologize to God if he offended him, and then, chaining the oppressors to the spot by his commanding eloquence, pour forth upon them God's judgments if they did not spare the defenceless and cease to do murder. Montesino fled for redress to the Court of Spain, and Las Cazas undertook to publish the ordinance which Montesino brought back in favour of the Indians; and "to secure its execution, and to oppose himself as a wall of brass to the violences and cruelties of which he continued to be witness. What he resolved in the ardour of his zeal, he executed with unwavering constancy during the fifty years he lived. Neither human respect, nor labour, nor fatigue, nor danger, was able to check him or to quench the zeal that consumed him." So says Touron. He seemed inspired by Heaven to be the assertor of the rights of injured and insulted humanity. Four times he crossed the Atlantic, and broke, with the intrepidity of a Paul, on the false peace of royalty. He wrung the hearts of despots with tales of oppressive cruelty and misery, and hesitated not to awaken their dread by denunciations of Divine vengeance. He was appointed "Protector of the Indians," and much as mortal man could do to save and relieve them, he did. For dearly he loved them, "eos in visceribus gestabat," Echard says.

About this period lived St. Louis Bertrand, the apostle of the new world. He accomplished in the West Indies and Mexico, all that St. Francis Xavier achieved in Japan. God distinguished them both by similar supernatural gifts and similar success.

And Louis of Grenada, author, among other ascetic and learned works, of the Memorial of a Christian Life, was at this time Provincial of the order of preachers in Portugal. "He was a christian man, a religious man, a great man, and a perfect orator," says Touron.

Crowds of others I could name that adorned at this period the Church by their holiness and learning in this *one* order. But enough has been said to show that the zeal of the cardinals, or some unhappy spirit of rivalry, made them forget or disregard, while they justly denounced real abuses, the past and existing services, the exemplary piety and vast learning that distinguished members and communities of the religious bodies in every part of the christian world. The Church saw what they were blind to; though she admitted that some scandals existed and that discipline was relaxed, she refused to abolish those orders that supplied very many of her best doctors, very many of her holiest prelates and priests, and nearly all the pioneers of christianity in the East and the West, in Japan and America. And indeed it was an indiscreet advice, as it is always a ruinous and lazy one, "to burn the house in order to get rid of the cobwebs."

In conclusion, the facts adduced by Bossuet, Baronius, and Pallavicini, illustrative of the ardent desire for a reform that existed within the Church for the acknowledged abuses that had crept into the administration of its affairs and its discipline, ought to be borne in mind much more than it is by the advocates of separation from that Church. The urgent necessity that is admitted for a salutary reform of the grievous abuses that existed in ecclesiastical affairs and in the administration of them, from the head to the lowest members of the Church, ought to make Catholics *humble*. On the other hand, those who belong to the Church they believe to have been reformed, it would be well also for them *to be humble, charitable, and tolerant.* There are many admissions in the best writings of their best authors calculated to make them so.

The enlighted Roscoe, in his Life of Leo the Tenth, characterizes the suppression and spoliation of religious houses, as "the abolition of the odious and absurd institutions of monastic life, by which great numbers of persons were restored to the common purposes of society, and fresh vigour was infused into those states which had embraced the religion of the reformers," &c.* And what has been the result of this reformation in the opinion of Roscoe? He says, "in calling to mind the Penal Laws and Criminal Codes of the Lutheran and Calvinistic nations of Europe, it must be admitted, that the important object which the friends and promoters of rational liberty had in view, had hitherto been but imperfectly accomplished, and that the human mind, a slave in all ages, had rather changed its master than freed itself from its servitude."†

* Bohn's Ed. Vol. ii, p. 242.   † Ibid. p. 242.

CHAPTER II.

SCHILLER, in his ' History of the Thirty Years' War,' and Roscoe, in his ' Life of Leo the Tenth,' look on the Reformation as a necessary and inevitable consequence of the discovery of printing and of the revival of learning in Europe. The Roman Catholic religion is treated (especially by the former) as a religion inimical to liberty and the dignity of enlightened intellect, and that therefore the diffusion of knowledge, arising from the multiplication of books by means of machinery, could not fail to prove fatal to it. This argument passes for one that is not to be controverted ; nay, with some Roman Catholics, who know everything *but their own religion and its history*, it passes for one that is not pleasing to them, but cannot be replied to.

Chateaubriand tells us, that " it would shake his faith in revealed religion, if it could be demonstrated to him that Christianity was incompatible with liberty, because that system would be opposed to the dignity of the human race, and its worship could not emanate from heaven, and be capable of smothering noble and generous sentiments, of clipping the wings of genius, and of placing intelligence under the ban, instead of using it as a means of elevating the soul to the height of a fitting love and contemplation of the works of the Deity."

He denies the flippant falsehood that is so widely circulated, that the Protestant religion is more favourable to the cause of liberty than the faith of Catholics.

The Catholic religion is not inimical to liberty. Its name has been abused, and its principles perverted, to serve the purposes of tyranny in many countries, because there is nothing too high and too holy not to be profaned and desecrated by ambitious wicked men. But if an angel came from heaven to refute that calumny which has just been referred to, on the Catholic religion, it might almost be feared that the messenger would be ill received by the people of Protestant countries. The latter have been so long deceived by time-serving literary men and self-seeking theological writers, by parasites and hypocrites interested in cajoling them, that they have become accustomed to delusion and kindly disposed towards their deceivers.

· The people of England especially suffer themselves to be easily convinced that there is no religion but theirs which is compatible with liberty, and that liberty ought to be the exclusive property of Protestant nations. ·"Yet it is not true," says Chateaubriand, "that the Protestant religion is more favourable to liberty than the Catholic religion." The sense of property that is associated with everything in some countries, even religion, leads people to monopolize all the the blessings of it, as precious gifts necessarily belonging to the Church of their favoured land. Chateaubriand, however, thought Christianity a religion of liberty, and his creed one that was favourable to freedom. "Christianity," he said, "had for him two manifest proofs of its divine origin —its morality tended to break down the tyranny of the passions, and its policy aimed at the abolition of slavery. It is, then, a religion of liberty."

Are Chateaubriand's manifest proofs of its divine origin *necessarily* to be sought out of the Catholic Church ? Did its Basils, its Anthonys, its Francis's, its Vincents, in their lives and actions fail to manifest the power of its morality over the passions ? Did its Las Casas, its Juan de Dios, prove false to its policy of protection against persecution, of redemption from slavery, of deliverance from abused power ?

It is the fashion, however, to say that in the Roman Catholic religion there is a slavish spirit which subjugates the intellectual powers. Its writers on all historical and scientific subjects are therefore suspected (or, rather, it is pretended they are to be suspected) of covertly aiming at the restriction of learning, the establishment of arbitrary power, or of leaning to the doctrine of the divine right of kings. A saint of the Roman Calendar, a monk, moreover, and of the Dominican order, "a popish friar,"* a theologian,

---

* The Dominican friar, whose tendencies, in the true sense of the word, were of so democratic a character, was not of "the dregs of the

however embued with all the doctrinal learning of his Church, and likewise with all the philosophy of former ages, as well as that of his own time, wrote a treatise on government, which the admirers of Locke and Bolingbroke may wonder to see cited in the same pages in which their names are found, and in illustration of the same subject which has been treated by them.

The treatise I refer to is that of St. Thomas of. Aquinas, and is called, "Opusculum de Regimine Principum," ad Regem Cypri.* The object, he declares in his preface, is to describe the duties of the kingly office, guided by the authority of the Sacred Writings, the doctrines of philosophers, and examples of past rulers. When it is borne in mind, that the unpalatable truths, scattered so abundantly through this treatise, were written for the perusal of a king, and for his guidance, we ought not only to admire the noble daring of the writer, but the public virtue of the earliest defender of the full rights of the people. The following passages are literally translated, and afford a fair specimen of the political opinions of a saint, whose knowledge of the subject of which he treats might serve to make the reputation of half-a-dozen sages of modern times:

" The intention of every ruler," says St. Thomas, "ought to be to secure the prosperity of the body which he undertakes to govern. But the welfare and prosperity of the community consists in the preservation of that unity which is called peace. Every disturbance of it endangers the utility of the social life ; nay, more, a distracted community renders society burdensome to itself. It should then be the chief object of the rulers of the multitude to procure that unity which constitutes peace. When a government, therefore, is most efficacious in promoting that object, it is most useful. Hence we call that most useful which conduces most to this end. It is manifest, that the union

people;" his "Order" was not the "lower" nor the lowest one. He was of a kingly race; and if a man of genius need to be beholden to genealogists, it would appear there was no dearth of the "sangre azul" of royalty in the veins of this monk. "He was grand-nephew of the Emperor Frederic I., cousin of the Emperor Henry VI., cousin-german of the Emperor Frederic II. on his father's side; while on his mother's side he was descended from the Norman princes who had chased the Arabs and the Greeks out of Italy, and conquered the Two Sicilies."—See Lacordaire's "Memoire des Freres Precheurs," p. 123.

* Edit. Fol. Antwerpiæ, 1612.

which is most effective, is that which is (so maintained) by one rather than many............Wherefore the government of one is more useful than that of many.".............[This proposition he proves at some length from religion, reason, and analogy with natural phenomena: "In toto universo unus Deus factor omnium et rector............in membrorum multitudini unum est quod omnia movet, scilicet cor, &c. ....omne enim naturale regimen ab uno est."]*

"But as the government of a king is the best, so the government of a tyrant is the worst............For power in unity is more efficacious than power divided or dispersed. As, therefore, power *operating good* is useful, and more unity renders it still more *potent for good*, so the mischief is greater if the power which effects evil is unbroken and undivided............Wherefore, in a *just government* the more unity (of action) the more useful is the rule, as the rule of a king is better than that of an aristocracy, and that of an aristocracy rather than that of the many. So, on the other hand, *in an unjust government*, the more the governing power is removed from unity, the more mischievous. Wherefore, the tyranny (of one) is more pernicious than an oligarchy, but an oligarchy is more pernicious than a democracy."

And further, "the government becomes unjust which despises the common good, and seeks the private advantage of the ruler. The more, therefore, it recedes from the public weal, the more unjust is that government. It recedes more from the public weal in an oligarchy in which the welfare of a few is sought, than in a democracy, where the good of the many is the object. But further still does it recede from the common good in a tyrannous government, in which the good of one alone is sought. *Therefore a tyrant's rule is the more unjust.* But, like the manifest order of divine providence which prevails in the government of the universe, all good in human affairs arises only from one perfect cause; but what is evil in them is separately produced by each particular defect. For there is no beauty in a body, unless there is a corresponding disposal of all the members; but deformity is the result when any part is not in keeping with another; and thus deformity from many causes and in different ways arises, but comeliness in one way only, and from one perfect cause. And thus it is in

---

* De Regimine Principum S. Thomæ Aquinatis, cap. i. p. 160.

all things, good and evil.   Providence determines in this matter also, that the good arising from one cause should be powerful, but evil from many causes should be weak. Hence it is, therefore, that a just government should be of one, in order that it should be strong.   But if it declines into an unjust one, it is better that it should be of many, that it may be weaker, and that the rulers may embarrass and thwart each other.   Therefore 'inter injusta' *demo-cratic* government is more tolerable, but tyranny truly is worst of all.

"If a ruler govern a multitude of free men for the common good of the multitude, the Government will be good and just, such as becomes free men.   But if the Government be conducted not for the common good of the multi-tude, but for the private good of the ruler, the Government will be unjust and perverse.   Whence the Lord threatens such rulers through Ezechiel, saying, 'Woe to the shepherds who fed themselves,' as if seeking their private personal advantage; 'should not the flocks be fed by the shepherds?' That is, as shepherds ought to seek the good of the flock, so rulers ought each to seek the good of the multitude subject to him.   If, therefore, the Government by one becomes so unjust as that he seeks only his private advan-tage, and not the good of the multitude subject to him, *such a ruler is called a tyrant*, a title derived from strength, because he oppresses by power ; *he does not govern by justice.* But an unjust Government when conducted not by one but by many, if by a few it is called oligarchy, to wit, when a few through the influence of their wealth oppress the peo-ple, differing only in number from a tyrant.   But if the unjust Government be in the hands of many, it is then called a democracy, that is, the dominion of the people, when, to wit, the populace by the power of their multitude oppress the rich.   For thus a whole people would be as one tyrant.   In like manner a just Government ought to be distinguished.   If it be administered by any numerous body, it is called *politia*, as when a military body govern in a city or province.   If it be administered *by a few virtuous men*, the Government is called an aristocracy ; and if a a just Government belong to one, he is properly called a king.   Whence the Lord says by Ezechiel, 'My servant David will be king over all, and he will be one pastor over all these.'   Hence it is manifestly shown, that what constitutes a kingly Government is, that he who governs should be *one*, and that he should be *a pastor seeking not his own good, but the common good of the multitude.*"*

, "If a tyrant be avaricious, he amasses wealth at the expense of his subjects. If he be sanguinary, he makes no account of shedding blood. Hence it is said in Ezechiel, ' her princes in the midst of her, are like wolves ravening for prey to shed blood.' Therefore there is no security, all things are unsettled when the law is abandoned, nothing can be steady or relied on which depends on the will or rather caprice of an individual. They burden their subjects not only in material things ; they are inimical even to their intellectual advantages, (spiritualia bona,) because their object is to rule, not to benefit. They also thwart every undertaking of their subjects, suspecting that the prosperity of their subjects would be prejudicial to their unjust domination. The good are greater objects of suspicion to tyrant rulers than the base. They therefore labour to prevent their subjects from becoming virtuous, lest assuming a spirit of magnanimity, they should refuse to endure unjust domination. They also prevent a union of friendship from growing strong among their serfs, and thus cause men to distrust one another, so that nothing by union can be effected against the Government. *Hence they sow discord and nourish it when existing ;* hence they prohibit those things which promote union among their subjects, such as marriages, festive intercourse, and other things by which confidence and familiarity are produced among men. They also strive to prevent them becoming powerful or rich, because, judging of their subjects according to the standard of their own malice, they fear that their subjects, imitating themselves, might use their power and wealth to inflict injury ; whence Job says of the tyrants, ' The sound of their terror is always in their ears, and when all things are peaceful, no one plotting evil against them, they often suspect treachery.'.........

"It is also natural, that men brought up under terror, should degenerate into persons of slavish dispositions, and should become very timid and incapable of any manly and daring enterprise, (virile opus et strenuum,) an assertion which is proved by the conduct of countries that had been

* Cap. 1. p. 161,

for a long time under despotic government. Solomon says, 'when the impious are in power men hide away,' in order to escape the cruelty of the tyrants, nor is it astonishing, for a man governing without law and according to his own caprice, differs in nothing from a beast of prey ; hence Solomon designates an impious ruler over an impoverished people, a roaring lion and a ravenous bear.* Because therefore the government of one is to be preferred, which is the best, and because this government is liable to degenerate into tyranny, which has been proved to be the worst, hence the most diligent care is to be taken so to manage the establishment of a king over the people, that he cannot fall into tyranny.

"The first thing necessary for the election of a king is, that a man who by nature and disposition is totally averse to tyranny, be advanced to the sceptre by those whose duty it is. Wherefore Samuel, praising the providence of God with reference to the institution of royalty, says, 'He sought for Himself a man according to His own heart.' The next thing necessary is, that the Government of the kingdom be so disposed of, *as to remove from the king* who has been elected, *all occasions of falling into tyranny.* Also, let his power be so confined or moderated, that he cannot without difficulty fall into tyranny.......In fine, we must endeavour to foresee the opportunities he may have of changing from a mild to a tyrannical government. And indeed it is much better, if the tyranny be not excessive, to endure it for a time, than by a revolt to implicate oneself in many dangers, which may be more grievous than the tyranny itself. For it may happen, that those who revolt may not succeed, and by thus provoking the tyrant, subject themselves to more cruelty than they had before endured. But even supposing that any individual succeeded against the tyrant, thence most injurious dissensions among the people frequently arise, for the multitude may divide into party factions, either at the moment in which they are warring with the tyrant, or after they have subdued him. It sometimes also happens, that he, through whose means the tyrant has been expelled by the multitude, while in power seizes on the sovereign authority ; and fearing to suffer from another what his predecessor suffered from him,

* Ibid, Cap. 3. pp. 161-62.

oppresses his subjects with far greater severity. It is of frequent occurrence in royalty, that the latter possessor is more cruel than he that went before, for he not only allows the grievances inflicted by his predecessor to continue, but also increases them from the malice of his own heart.*

"It seems better that proceedings be taken against the cruelty of a ruler, by no other than the public authority. For, first, if it belongs of right to the public to choose for themselves a king, it belongs, consequently, to them either to dethrone him if he abuse his authority, or to set limits to his power.......Thus the Romans banished from the kingdom, on account of his tyranny and that of his children, Tarquin the Próud, whom they themselves had advanced to sovereignty, and in consequence instituted the lesser authority of the consuls. Thus also Domitian, who succeeded the very mild emperors, Vespasian, his father, and Titus, his brother, was killed by the senate, whilst he was exercising tyranny, and all his unjust decrees were repealed. Whence, blessed John, the evangelist and beloved disciple of our Lord, was recalled to Ephesus, by a decree of the senate, from the island of Patmos, to which, by order of Domitian, he had been banished.......

"But if, in short, no human power can withstand tyranny, we must have recourse to God, who is our helper in our distresses and tribulations, for it is in his power to turn the cruel heart of a tyrant into meekness, according to those words of Solomon. 'The heart of the king is in the hand of the Lord, whithersoever he will he shall turn it.' (12 Par. alias Wisd. xxi. 1.) He turned into clemency the cruelty of king Assuerius, who was contriving the death of the Jewish people. It is he who converted the cruel king Nabuchodonosor, and made him bear testimony to his divine power. 'Therefore,' says he, 'I Nabuchodonosor do now praise, and magnify, and glorify the King of heaven: because all his works are true, and his ways judgments, and them that walk in pride he is able to abase.' (Dan. iv. 34.) But those tyrants, whom he judges unworthy of conversion, he can either destroy or reduce to nothing, according to Ecclesiasticus, x. 17. 'God hath overturned the thrones of proud princes, and hath set up the meek in their stead.' For he, on beholding the affliction of his

* St. Thomas was not a contemporary of Louis Philip, but of a king of Cyprus about 600 years ago.—R. R. M.

people in Egypt, and hearing their groans, plunged the cruel Pharao with his whole army into the sea ; for it is he who, having cast the above-mentioned proud Nabuchodonosor not only from his throne, but also from the society of men, changed him into a beast. Nor is his hand shortened so that he could not now liberate his people from their tyrants ; for he promises, by the mouth of the prophet Isaias, that he will give his people rest from the labour, and confusion, and hard servitude in which they have been plunged, and in xxxiv. 10. of Ezechiel, he says, ' I will deliver my flock from their mouth,' that is, of those pastors who feed themselves. But that people may deserve to receive this benefit from God, they ought to refrain from sin.

" The government of tyrants cannot be long lived, since it is hateful to the public ; for that cannot be of long continuance, which is repugnant to the wishes of the many. The present life never passes without adversity, wherefore an opportunity cannot be wanted for revolting against a tyrant ; and when a favourable opportunity occurs, then also is found some one to profit by it, for the people will very willingly follow him who revolts. And the revolution will scarcely be void of effect, since it is accompanied with the good will of the public. Wherefore the dominion of a tyrant can scarcely be prolonged for any length of time. This is also very evident to any person who considers whence or how it is that the dominion of tyrants is preserved ; for it is not preserved by love, since the friendship of the subject multitude for the tyrant is evidently either very slight or none at all.

" Tyrants cannot trust the loyalty of their subjects, for among the populace, virtue is not found to exist to such an extent as to hinder them from shaking off the yoke of extraordinary oppression.........

" Wherefore it follows, that the rule of tyrants is to be supported by fear alone ; and their whole aim is to have themselves feared by their subjects. But fear is a weak foundation, because those who are kept under obedience by fear, never let any opportunity escape, in which they can hope for impunity, of rebelling against their rulers, and that too with proportionably greater ardour, as by fear they were restrained, just like water, shut up by force, which gushes out the more impetuously when a passage has been opened for its escape. Nor is fear itself free from danger, since from too great a fear many fall into despair; but despair of safety precipitates people boldly to attempt any thing.*

" Wherefore a tyrant's government cannot be of long continuance. This is apparent, no less from example than reason, to any one who takes the trouble of reflecting on the actions of the ancients and the events of modern times."

The doctrine, that tyranny is oftener found in the government of many than that of one, and therefore that the latter is to be preferred, is advocated, if not successfully, at least with great ability, in the fifth chapter of his treatise.

" When we must select between two things, to each of which danger is attached, we ought to take that from which the smallest evil follows. But from monarchy, even though it should be converted into tyranny, less evil results than from the government of many nobles, when it is corrupted. For dissension, which for the most part arises from the government of many, is opposed to the well-being of peace, which is the principal thing in a social multitude, and which at least is not destroyed by tyranny; only something that is the good of individuals is threatened, unless there should have been an excess of tyranny which would attack the entire community. Therefore the government of an individual is preferable to that of many, although evils should spring from both. Besides, it seems that we ought to avoid that from which great evils can oftener arise; but greatest evils for the multitude follow more frequently from the government of many than from that of one. Because it oftener happens that out of many, some one falls off from the intention of the common good than if there were one only. But if any one out of many governors should turn away from the intention of the common good, the danger of dissension hangs over the multitude of their subjects; because it follows, that when dissension exists among the heads it should exist also among the members. But if one should have the government, he would for the most part regard the common good; or if he should divert his attention from it, it does not immediately follow that he intends the oppression of his subjects, which is an excess of tyranny, and holds, as

---

* Had Bacon those *words* in remembrance when he said in his Essay on Seditions: " For they are most dangerous discontents where the fear is greater than the feeling; grief has bounds, but fear has none!"

was already shown, the highest step in bad government. Therefore the dangers which spring from the government of one, are more to be guarded against. Nay, it does not less often occur that the government of many is turned into tyranny than that of one, but perhaps more frequently. For it often happens, in the government of many, that when any dissension arises, one vanquishes the others and usurps to himself the government of the people."*

Finally, the resumé of all the reasoning in the treatise just quoted, is to be found in his Summa Theologiæ, a work of unequalled excellence. In that work we find the following proposition, in plain intelligible language, which Paley never could have ventured to put forth in the same explicit terms, and yet which is the doctrine of the rebel lords and prelates who became "the patriots" of 1688.

" A tyrannical government is unjust, being administered not for the common good, but for the private good of the ruler. Therefore the disturbance of this rule is not sedition, unless when the overthrow of tyranny is so inordinately pursued, that the multitude suffers more from the disturbance than from the existence of the Government. Magis autem tyrannus sæditiosus est, qui in populo sibi subjecto discordias et seditiones nutrit, ut tutius dominari possit ; hoc enim tyrannicum est, cum sit ordinatum ad bonum proprium præsidentis cum multitudinis nocumento."†

Away then with the trash of the political theologians, which is poured forth in solemn, specious, sanctimonious language in the pulpit, in the press, and in public assemblies, on the subject of the tendencies of the Church of the great body of the christian world, and of the teaching of the master spirits of it of bye gone ages. Nothing unfavourable to the moral or material interests of mankind will be found in either. They will stand the scrutiny of modern lore and science, as they have stood the test of time and persecution. They are happily separable from the acts, the policy, and the abuses of the State power of Italian Potentates.

* Cap. v. p. 163. Ibidem.
+ Vol. xvii. page 186. Ed. fol. Ven. 1787.

CHAPTER III.

THE FIRST FRUITS OF THE SPIRIT THAT ANIMATED THE REFORMERS.

THE evils that beset the Church at the period of Luther's assumption of the character of a Reformer, the glaring abuses that needed reformation, have been freely pointed out in the preceding chapter. More freely, perhaps, than many may deem it was necessary thus to deal with them.

In the same spirit, however, which has truth and truth only for the aim and end of its pursuit, the following observations are made on the character of those who set themselves up to remove the scandals that had been brought on religion by ministers unworthy of it.

Happy would it have been for religion had these scandals to it only been dealt with, and had those who set about the removal of them been men of holy lives, of high purposes, and actuated solely by pure motives of piety towards God and of love towards their fellow-men.

The Reformers of the 16th century carried on their work as if they were animated by a spirit of deadly hatred to a large portion of mankind, and of jealousy and ill-will towards one another. The wise counsel of Joseph to his brethren—" be not angry on the way," was in no esteem with them. Abraham's saying to Lot—" let there be no contention between us, between your shepherds and my shepherds, we are brothers," was too primitive for them. These pastors acted as if their principal duty was to wrangle and jangle with one another, and these contentions were looked upon by them as the fair fruits of the spirit of free enquiry.

They walked not in the paths of peace, but in the highways and bye-ways of polemical strife, in various directions, and each one said, "viam veritatis véni," and scolded his brother-traveller for stopping short on the road, or taking a different rout to his own.

The Reformers of Germany treated the ministers and

members of the Church from which they seceded, with
unparalleled acrimony; but before we are in a condition to
appreciate their denunciations, it is requisite we should
know how they maltreated and vilified one another.

"The bold rough man" of Germany, as Luther is
termed, called his majesty of England a "Thomistical
tub," but the latter had imprudently begun throwing mis-
siles at the windows of the wedded monk's character for
chastity, when his majesty's own repute for morality was
lodged in a glass house, penetrable to the smallest pebble,
to say nothing of the argumentative paving stones that
polemical disputants were then wont to fling at each other.
To begin with the first supreme head of the Church of
England: we find our royal theologian, the bluff king, thus
reviling Luther for his marriage: "An abominable crime,
for which, if you lived in a state only governed by learned
pagans, the object of your obscene passion would have been
buried alive; and as to you, they would have cut you to
pieces with rods, till you expired under the blows."[*]

The peculiar amenities of Luther's style of argument are
happily exhibited in his various references and apostrophes
to Henry:

"Thou liest, thou sacrilegious and foolish king."[†]

"I speak to a lying scoundrel."

"You, Henry, not even a king without sacrilege."

"This doating illiterate beast."

"This trifling impertinent king."

Luther to Pope Paul:

"Gently, my dear little Paul; have a care, my ass, of
stumbling. Have a care, my Pope ass. Go no further, my
dear little ass, lest thou fall, and break a leg. For there
has been this year so little wind ahead, that the ice is
mighty slippery."[‡]

The language that follows is so indecent as to be unfit
for perusal.

Luther's mode of improving things and persons at Rome:

"Well, were I master of the empire, I would order all
those profligate rogues, the pope and cardinals and their
families, to be fagotted up together and carried to Ostia, seven

---

[*] Coch. Apud Ruff. Epist. i. Cum Lib. i. Hen. 8vo. de Sacram.
p. 340.

[†] Luther's Works, Wittenburgh Ed. Vol. ii. p. 331, 337.

[‡] Ibid. vol. vii. fol. 452,

miles from Rome, where there is a puddle called by the Latins the Tyrrhene Sea. 'Tis a bath of wonderful virtue against all diseases and infirmities of the papal kind. In this bath I would gently dip them : and if they stayed there but half-an-hour, I would engage my word—*nay, my Lord Christ's too*—that they would be cured of all their distempers."[*]

One of Luther's latest energetic efforts to promote the new religion, was what Bossuet terms a "trumpet blast" to stir up the people to take arms against Catholics,—his "Theses," composed in 1540, but republished by him the year before his death in 1545, wherein open war is declared against the Emperor Charles V. and the League of Smalcalde. The Pope he compares to a mad wolf,—

" Against whom the whole world takes up arms at the first signal, without waiting for commands from the civil magistrate. And if, after he has been shut up in an enclosure, the magistrate sets him at liberty, you may continue," said he, " to pursue this savage beast, and with impunity attack those who prevent his destruction. If you fall in the engagement, before the beast receives its mortal wound, you have but one thing to repent of,—that you did not bury your dagger in his breast. This is the way to deal with the Pope. All those who defend him must also be treated as a band of robbers under their captain, be they kings, be they Cæsars."[†]

Luther of Calvin treats in these terms :

" Calvin, I know, is violent and wicked : so much the better, such men are needed to promote our affairs."[‡]

Calvin of Luther observes :

" In fact, Luther is very much given to vices. God grant him to refrain from the intemperance which binds him all round."[§]

In his last admonition to the Westphalians, he says :

" The Lutherans, both in language and belief respecting the Real Presence, are, in my opinion, more preposterous than the papists."

Luther of Zuinglius says :

"Zuinglius died, and he is condemned because he wished,

* Luther's Works. tom. vii. fol. 474.
† Ibid. p. 407.   Ap. Hist. des Variat. par Bossuet.   Paris, 1760, Tom. i. p. 402.
‡ Epist. Luther ad Jacob. Presb.
§ Calvin's Theology, Book ii. p. 126.

as a thief and a seditious man, to promulgate his errors by force of arms."[*]

And of Zuinglian divines he speaks as " Fools, asses, antichrists, deceivers, and men of an asinine understanding."

" Satan reigns in them, so they can now only engender errors and scatter lies."[†]

Zuinglius of Luther remarks:

" He is an impostor, who changes and rechanges the Holy Scriptures..........If you saw him among his disciples, you would think he was surrounded by a phalanx of devils."[‡]

" A foul corruptor and horrible falsifier of God's word."[§]

Luther of Erasmus declares:

" I will certify everywhere that Erasmus is not a Lutheran, but an Erasmian; that is to say, a speculator, a waverer," &c.[||]

Erasmus of Luther states:

" I cannot but feel indignant at seeing, that with those who endeavour to support him he goes to extremities: if he is treated mildly, far from being soothed, he throws himself headlong into new excesses, as if he had no other design but to pass from one extreme to the other..........Oh, you who appeal to the pure word of God, be of accord among yourselves, before you give law to the universe....... I was greatly deceived in thinking matrimony had humanized him."[¶]

Bucer of Calvin asserts:

" Calvin is a mad dog. This man judges others as he loves or hates them."

Calvin to Chatillon writes: " May Satan's deity daily give you peace."

Of Osiander (the brother-in-law of Cranmer) Calvin writes to Melancthon that he had conceived a horror of his profanity: " That as often as he found good wine at an entertainment, he praised it by applying to it those words which God of Himself had spoken: '*I am Who am;*' and again: '*Here is the Son of the Living God.*' "[**]

---

* Op. Luther. Tom. ii. p. 36.   † Ad. Hospin. 1529.
‡ Zuinglius, De Sacramento, Tom. ii. p. 881, 454, 388.
§ Lib. de Sacram.
|| Luther ad Armsdorf.
¶ Erasmus ad Melancthon. lib. iii. Letters 19 and 24.
** Epist. Calvin ad Melanc. apud Hist. des Variat. Tom. i. p. 409.

Calvin, who had been at the banquets where these blasphemies, which horrified him, had gone down with his fellow reformers, says of Osiander: "He was a brutal man, a wild beast not to be tamed." He adds: "The first time I saw him I detested his profane spirit and infamous morals, and always looked upon him as the shame of the Protestant party." Yet Melancthon praised him, and he and Luther took pleasure in his society. The former wrote to Camerarius: "Osiander has very much amused Luther and all of us."

Elsewhere Calvin of Osiander simply speaks as "an atheist."

Stancharus of Calvin asks: "What devil has possessed you, Calvin, to declaim with arms against the Son of God?"

Beza of Hesushius concerning the Eucharist says: "He is an ass."[*]

Beza of Stancharus says: "He is a heretic."

Stancharus of Melancthon to Calvin: "The antichrist of the North, whom you, Calvin, have the impudence to adore—I mean that grammarian, Melancthon."[†]

Luther of Carlosdat enquires: "What harm did the Roman Mass do to you? He must be a madman or an atheist who thus makes a burla of religion."[‡]

Melancthon of Carlosdat discourses as, "A turbulent man, more a Jew than a Christian."

Hospinian of Luther asseverates: "This man is furious. He never ceases to attack the truth against justice, and against the voice of his conscience."[§]

Œcolompadius of Luther: "He is puffed up with pride and arrogance; he is seduced by Satan."[‖]

In England we have Bishop Jewel declaring, "The tenets of Zuinglius are diabolical."

Archbishop Tillotson, describing the qualities of a messenger charged with a divine mission, speaking of such as might belong to a gladiator or a performer of feats of strength: "When antichrist sat securely in the quiet possession of his kingdom, Luther arose, a bold, rough

---

* Stanch. In Calv. De Medit. 4.
† De Medit. in Calvin.
‡ Op. Luther. Tom. vii, Fol. 275.
§ Discussion Amicale sur l'Eglise Anglicane.
‖ Discussion Amicale sur l'Eglise Anglicane.

man, but a fit wedge to cleave asunder so hard and knotty a block," &c.*

And, further, we have Dr. Robertson reconciling us to the ferocity of disposition and foul-mouthed vituperation of the first reformer, as "habits and tendencies which are only different from others that we deem decent, as they are regarded at periods distant from each other."......

"Even the impetuosity and fierceness of Luther's spirit, his confidence in asserting his own opinions, and the arrogance as well as contempt wherewith he treated all who differed from him, which, from usages of greater refinement, have been reckoned defects in the character of that reformer, did not appear excessive to his contemporaries."......

"Nor were they offended at that gross scurrility with which his polemical writings are filled, and the low buffooneries which he sometimes introduced into his gravest discourses."†

Omnia pro tempore nihil pro veritate.‡ The morality of Dr. Robertson's reasoning needs no other comment.

"The instrument of Providence" in England, the King Henry, in the thirty-seventh year of his bloody reign, made a speech to his parliament, wherein he reproached the fathers and preachers of the new spirituality, with their broils and wranglings.—"What love or charity is there among you, when one calls another heretic and anabaptist, and he calls him again a papist, hypocrite, pharisee? I must needs judge the fault and occasion of this discord to be partly by negligence of you, the fathers and preachers of the spirituality. For I hear against you that you of the clergy preach one against another, teach one contrary to the other, railing one against another.§ Some are so stiff in their old mumpsimus, and others so busy and furious in their new sumpsimus, that almost all men be in variety and discord, and few or none preach truly and sincerely the word of God."

So much for "the instrument of Providence" in the sixteenth century, in respect to their opinions of each other.

Dr. Robertson refers to the following passage in the

* Tillotson's Sermons, xxix. p. 258.
† History of Charles V., Vol. v. p. 152.
‡ St. Optat. Milevilam Advers. Parmen.
§ Stow Op. Historical Collection, p. 43.

last Will and Testament of Luther, which he says "has a certain elevation of sentiment in it."*

" I am known in heaven, on earth, and in hell, and have authority enough to expect that credit should be given to my single testimony, since God has entrusted the Gospel of his Son to me, though a damnable sinner. And truth has owned me for its teacher, in contempt of the pope and Cæsar, and of the hatred of all the devils in hell. Why then should it not be sufficient to say, Mr. Martin Luther wrote this will, God Almighty's notary, and the witness of the Gospel ?"

These awful words (for nothing is more awful than blasphemy combined with levity) were written by Luther, when serious thoughts and humbled pride might have been expected in one who was on the brink of eternity.

CHAPTER IV.

CHANGES IN THE RELATIONS OF THE CHURCH OF ENGLAND WITH THE SEE OF ROME ;—THE SUPPRESSION AND SPOLIATION OF RELIGIOUS HOUSES IN ENGLAND, IN THE REIGN OF HENRY VIII.

THE difficulties that Henry VIII. met with in the court of Rome in obtaining a divorce from Queen Catharine, led to his first act of hostility to the holy see. In the twenty-second year of his reign, he issued a proclamation prohibiting the purchase of any faculties or dispensations from Rome. The proclamation had not been long issued before an opportunity was afforded of punishing the prelates and clergy who were obnoxious to him. Henry having ordered his attorney-general to proceed against the ecclesiastics, for their submission to the legatine court, contrary to the statutes of provisors, the convocation, instead of appealing to the pope, whose authority they perceived to be rapidly declining, unwisely determined to throw themselves on the mercy of their sovereign. They accordingly paid him a fine of £.118,840 for a pardon,† in addition to which, they

* Life of Charles V., vol. 2, p. 68. note.
† Lord Herbert's Life of Henry VIII. p. 321. 2 Fox, p. 273.

were compelled (though with much reluctance, and with the explanatory clause, "as far as the law of Christ allows,") "to acknowledge that the king was the protector, and supreme head of the church and clergy of England." On the 14th of November, 1532,* the nuptials of Henry and Anne Boleyn were privately solemnized, notwithstanding he was then under citation to Rome, to answer the appeal of Catharine, his marriage with whom was, in the summer of the same year, declared to be illegal by Cranmer, Archbishop of Canterbury.

Events had occurred in former reigns which had furnished Henry with a plea for his proclamation.

In the reign of Henry III. his representatives at the Council of Lyons, had complained that the benefices of the Italian clergy in England amounted to the yearly value of 60,000 marks, a sum which the pope declared was much beyond the real amount, and which Hume says, " exceeded the annual revenue of the crown itself."

The successor of Henry, Edward I. enacted the first statute against papal provisors.

Edward III. in the twenty-fifth, twenty-seventh, and thirty-eighth year of his reign, passed still more rigorous laws against papal presentation to benefices and citations to Rome. And in the latter part of Edward's reign, Wickliffe and his followers inveighed against all foreign interference in the English church ; and during the minority of Richard II., what was, perhaps, in some degree, the effect of new doctrines, was exhibited in still stronger enactments, and by one of these the acceptation of a living by any foreign provision, was punished with forfeiture of land, and goods, and banishment.†

Henry's reform, though it nominally went only to the renunciation of the authority of the pope, involved in reality the total abandonment of the Roman Catholic religion ; for even Luther, in his latter days, admitted that in taking away the headship of the church, a torrent of contradictory doctrines had been let in, which had swamped its Christian character of peace and unity.

The results of Henry's assumption of the government of the church, were soon such as might have been expected, a succession of incongruous, ludicrous, and unavailing acts,

* Ibid. 340. Ap. Brown's Penal Laws, p. 23.
† Brown's Penal Laws, p. 20.

done with a view of obviating the absurdity of his claims to the supremacy.

And though constantly expressing his wishes, and publishing his commands for a general conformity of religious opinions, the new head of the church unfortunately thought it far from necessary to establish any such conformity in his own mind; the vagaries of which, he nevertheless expected his subjects implicitly to receive as the groundwork of their faith. Hence his law of the six articles were amended by his "Institution of a Christian man," which in its turn soon gave way to his "Erudition;" and so much in fact did the religion of the nation depend on the will of this absolute and capricious monarch, that in 1541 a law was passed, confirming by anticipation, "all tenets which shall hereafter be enacted by the king's consent."*

He endeavoured, by other means, to establish the usurped supremacy, and those means were more consonant to his brutal character,—the scaffold and the gibbet,—the shedding of the blood of many of the most virtuous persons, some of the noblest in the land, and one of the most eminently good and great men in his dominions.

Three priors of the Carthusian Order, interrogated before Cromwell in April, 1535, touching the supremacy, were condemned forthwith, and hanged in their monastic habits.†

Two other priests were executed on the same charge at the same time outside London; one a secular priest, Aylo; the other a Bridgetine monk, named Reginald. The quarters of the principal prior were hung up at the door of his convent, the Observantines of St. Francis, to terrify his brethren, whose Order was the most powerful and influential in England.

Three other Carthusians were seized, tortured, half hanged, cut down, and then beheaded, and their quarters dispersed in the principal high roads.‡

The Countess of Salisbury, an aged lady upwards of seventy-six years of age, the last of the Plantagenets, the daughter of George, Duke of Clarence, brother of Edward IV., consequently a near relative of the monster king, the

---

* Brown's Penal Laws, p. 25.
† Historia del Scisma del Reino de Inglaterre. Madrid: 1589. Page 63.
‡ Historia de Scisma, page 65.

mother of Cardinal Pole, whose crime was to have corresponded with her son then in exile, (having refused to take the oath of supremacy), was condemned for treason and executed. The old lady was dragged to the block. She refused to lay her head down ; she said, " it had committed no treason and should never bow to tyranny :" " the executioner struck at her with his axe, and as she ran about the scaffold with her grey locks streaming down her neck and shoulders, he pursued her with repeated blows, till at last he brought her down."

Dr. Forest, a Franciscan friar, confessor to Queen Catherine, for denying the supremacy, was "executed upon a pair of new gallows set up for that purpose in Smithfield ; he was hanged by the middle and arm-pits, and under the gallows was made a fire, wherewith he was burned and consumed."[*]

John Beck, Abbot of Colchester, for denying the king's supremacy, was executed at Colchester.[†]

Dr. Fisher, Bishop of Rochester, and Sir Thomas More, for refusing to take the oath of supremacy, were beheaded in 1535.

Sir William Peterson, priest, and Sir William Richards, a priest, were both hanged at Calais for refusing the oath of supremacy.[‡]

Seven persons for denying the king's supremacy, were hanged and quartered at Tyburn, to wit :—the Prior of Doncaster ; Lawrence Cook, a lay-brother of the Charterhouse ; Giles Horn, gentleman ; Clewer Philip, gentleman ; Edward Bolhelm, priest ; Darcy Jennings, and Robert Bird.[§]

German Gardiner, and one Lark, a priest of Chelsea, were executed for the supremacy.[‖]

Sir David Jenison, " for the supremacy," was drawn through Southwark and executed there.[¶]

Henry had been about two years "under God the Supreme Head of the Church in England " in virtue of his own will, and in consequence of the Papal opposition to his unbridled sensuality, when by his foreign wars and private profligacy, having wasted his revenues and exhausted his exchequer, he fixed his attention on the possessions of the

* Stowe, p. 577. † Ibid.
‡ Ibid, p. 579. § Ibid, p. 581.
‖ Ibid, p. 588. ¶ Ibid, p. 581.

monastic establishments, and determined on their appropriation.

Leland coolly asserts, that "the suppression of monasteries was Henry's favourite object, for removing the instruments and restraining the enormities of popular superstition, and for communicating the Scripture to the laity in the vulgar tongue."*

Henry's only anxiety was for appropriating the lands and the moveables of the convents.

Dr. Heylin refers to a statute passed in his reign, prohibiting the circulation of the Scriptures in the mother-tongue, which act was only repealed in the reign of Edward VI.

"The evils resulting from the unrestrained perusal of the Scriptures in English, by the illiterate vulgar, before their pastors had come to an agreement, or even formed any settled opinion in their own minds, respecting the principal articles of faith, were so apparent as to occasion a clause in the 34 and 35 H. VIII. c. 2, commanding that ' the Bible shall not be read in English in any church, and that no women, or artificers, 'prentices, journeymen, servingmen of the degree of yeomen or under, husbandmen, nor labourers, shall read the New Testament in English.' This singular prohibition will at least evince that the equality of the sexes was not one of the favourite tenets of those days."†

In a Speech of Henry to the Parliament, in the thirty-seventh year of his reign, he says to his faithful commons, " I am very sorry to hear how irreverently that most precious jewel, the Word, is disputed, rhymed, sung, and jangled in every ale-house and tavern, contrary to the true meaning and doctrine of the same."

Heylin cites a very remarkable, and (it may be truly styled) prophetic speech in the House of Peers, of the martyred Dr. Fisher, Bishop of Rochester, in opposition to the intended suppression of the monasteries, from which the following extracts are taken.

" My noble lords, this is the place where your glorious and noble progenitors have preserved the kingdom from oppression. Here is the sanctuary where in all ages, but in this of ours, our Mother-church found still a sound protec-

* History of Ireland, vol. ii., p. 157.
† Brown's Penal Laws, note xviii.

tion. I should be infinitely sorrowful that from you, that are so lovely branches of antiquity and Catholic honour, the Catholic faith should be so deeply wounded."......

" The Commons shoot their arrows at our livings, which are the motives that conceit us guilty. Is all the kingdom innocent, and we only faulty, for that there is no room left for other considerations far more weighty ? The diligence, devotion, and liberality of our forefathers, endowed their Mother-church with fair and large revenues, making it still their greatest care to keep her upright, able still in freedom : and will you consent that, like a servile bondmaid, she now sinks lower, to a naked thraldom, and by degrees be forced from her mansion ?"

" These (enemies) strike not at the withered branches, but at the tree on which religion groweth. Certainly all are not guilty. Admit that some, as they enforce, be vicious, must it be concluded there is none good amongst us, or able to reform their proper vices ? Will you assume a power till now unheard of, to give away their rights by new made statutes ? If you will seek and sift our constitutions, you shall there find as strict injunctions as you can make for reformation. But I suppose it is not that that is aimed at : pretence of restoration tends to ruin, else such beginnings would find no favour. My lords, consider well your actions : be advised. *This cause seems ours, it will be yours, if that the Mother-church do feel injustice. Your turns are next to feel oppression.* When faith begins to fail, then all must perish."......

" The church's wealth occasioned this first moving. If that were poor, our vices would be virtues, and none would be so forward to accuse us. Our smaller houses are desired from us : not that their value doth deserve the motion, *but that the greater may succeed their fortune, which soon will follow if the gap be opened.*"......

" Some giddy brain, whose fading fortunes lead him to hope to raise himself out of our ruins, betrays his judgment with a show of justice ; which seeks in truth but merely innovation, which must succeed unless you oppose it. Wherefore, my lords, call back that ancient virtue that so long hath sat in these your places. Now is the time to show your worth. The Church implores it, the Church which you acknowledge for your mother. *If liberty take* *place of faith—farewell religion. The Turk may then direct us how to guide in rapine, blood, and murder.*[*]

The solemn warning of the virtuous and venerable prelate was contemned.

" Farewell religion," farewell, a long farewell indeed in England to peace and unity, to the comforts and happiness of a contented people. Worse than Turk or Arab rules the land, with a robber's aim directs its councils and resigns to his passions the guidance of his course, " in rapine, blood, and murder."

Henry confined his first measure of monastic reform, to the suppression of the houses with small revenues. Stow states that by an act of parliament, all religious houses in the kingdom of the value of £200. and under, with all their lands and goods, were granted to the king and his heirs.

The preamble of the act for the suppression of the lesser houses, was couched in the following terms :

" Forasmuch as manifest synne, vicious, carnal, and abominable living is daily used and committed, commonly *in such little houses, and abbeys, and priories, and other* religious houses of monks, canons, and nuns, *where the congregation of such religious persons is under the number of twelve persons,* whereby the governors of such religious houses and their convents, spoyle, destroye, consume, and utterly waste, as well their churches, monasteries, priories, principal farms, granges, lands, tenements, and hereditaments, as the ornaments of their churches, and their goods and chattels, to the high displeasure of Almighty God, slander of good religion, and to the great infamy of the king's highness and the realm, if redress should not be had thereof. And albeit that *many continual visitations hath been heretofore had by the space of* 200 *years and more, for an honest and charitable reformation of such unthrifty, carnal, and abominable living,* yet nevertheless, little or none amendment is hitherto had, but their vicious living shamelessly increaseth and augmenteth, and by a cursed custom so rooted and infected, that a great multitude of the religious persons in such small houses, do rather choose to rove abroad in apostacy, than to conform themselves to the observations of good religion ; so that without such small houses be utterly suppressed, *and the*

[*] Historical Collections from Protestant Historians concerning changes in Religion, &c., p. 153.

religious persons therein committed to great and honourable monasteries of religion in this realm, where they may be compelled to live religiously for reformation of their lives, the same else will have no redress nor reformation in that behalf. In consideration whereof, *the king's most royal majesty being supreme head on earth under God of the Church of England, daily studying and devising the increase, advancement, and exaltation of true doctrine and virtue in the said Church,* to the only glory and honour of God, and the total extirpation and destruction of vice and sin, having knowledge that the premises be true, as well as the accounts of his late visitations, as by sundry credible informations, CONSIDERING ALSO THAT DIVERS AND GREAT SOLEMN MONASTERIES OF THIS REALM, WHEREIN (THANKS BE TO GOD,) RELIGION IS RIGHT WELL KEPT AND OBSERVED, be destitute of such number of religious persons, as they ought and may keep, hath thought good that a plain declaration should be made of the premises, as well to the lords spiritual and temporal, as to other his loving subjects the commons, in this present Parliament assembled. *Whereupon the said Lords and Commons, by a great deliberation, finally be resolved,* THAT IT IS, AND SHALL BE, MUCH MORE TO THE PLEASURE OF ALMIGHTY GOD, AND FOR THE HONOUR OF THIS HIS REALM, *that the possessions of such houses now being spent and wasted for the increase and maintenance of sin, should be used and committed to better uses, and the unthrifty religious persons so spending the same, to be compelled to reform their lives.*"

This preamble was followed by enactments giving the whole of the property to the king and his successors, to use "according to their own wills, to the pleasure of Almighty God, and to the honour and profit of this realm." This act gave the king also the sacred vessels and ornaments of the altars, the gold, silver, and jewels thereunto belonging.

Henry had appointed "one Thomas Cromwell" his vicar general, principal visitor of the religious houses throughout the kingdom. "Thomas Cromwell," says Sir Richard Baker, (p. 408.) "was the son of a blacksmith at Putney, who, being raised to high dignities, was lastly made vicar general under the king in all ecclesiastical affairs, and sat divers times in the convocation house amongst the bishops as head over them."

Cranmer's instructions to the subordinate visitors were

4

contained in eighty-six articles, enjoining enquiry into the
government and behaviour of the religious of both sexes,
which commissioners, we are informed on Protestant
authority,[*] " the better to manage the design, gave encouragement to the monks not only to accuse their governors,
but to inform against each other, compelling them also to
produce their charters and evidences of their lands, as also
their plate and money, and to give an inventory thereof.
And hereunto they added certain injunctions from the
king, containing most severe and strict rules ; by means
whereof many, being found obnoxious to their censure,
were expelled, and others, discerning themselves not able
to live free from exception or advantage that might be
taken against them, desired to leave their habitations ; and
having by these visitors thus searched into their lives,
(which, by a ' Black Book' containing a world of enormities, were represented in no small degree scandalous,) to
the end that the people might be the better satisfied with
their proceedings, it was thought convenient to suggest,
that the lesser houses, for want of good government, were
chiefly guilty of those crimes ; and so they did, as appears
by the preamble of the Act made for their dissolution in
the 27th Henry VIII., which parliament consisting, for the
most part, of such members as were packed for the purpose
through private interest, (as is evident from divers original
letters of the time.) Many of the nobility, for the like
respects also favouring the design, assented to the suppression of all such houses as had been certified of less value
than two hundred pounds a-year, giving them with their
lands and revenues to the king : yet with this addition,
*that the possessions belonging to such houses should be converted
to better uses. But how well this was observed we shall soon
see: these specious pretences being made use of for no other purpose than by opening this gap to make way for the total ruin of
the greater houses,* wherein, notwithstanding, it is by the said
act acknowledged that religion was well observed."

Stowe (at page 572 of his ' Chronicles') tells us, that
" Cromwell and others, being sent forth to visit the abbeys
and nunneries in England, put forth all religious persons that would go, and all under the age of twenty-four,
and after closed up the residue that would remain, so that

they should not come out of their places. All religious men that departed, the abbot or prior gave them for their habit a priest's gown and forty shillings in money. The nuns had such apparel given them as secular women wear, and had liberty to go whither they would. They took out of the monastery their reliques and chiefest jewels, (to the king's use they said)."

He states (page 560) the first religious house the king seized on was " the hospital of St. James, near Charing Cross, with all its property, compounding with the sisters of the house, who were to have pensions during their lives ; and building in place of the said hospital a goodly mansion, retaining still the name of St. James."

It is related in Dugdale's ' Antiquities of Warwickshire,' (page 801.) that Cromwell and his visitants employed menaces, violence, and calumny of the most atrocious kind, to effect the rapacious object of their master. The canons of Leicester were threatened with adultery and other horrid crimes. The nuns of Godstow were told by Dr. Loudon, " he would dissolve the house, by virtue of the king's commission, in spite of their teeth." The monks of Charterhouse were committed to Newgate, where with hard and barbarous usage five of them died, and five more of them lay at the point of death, as the commissioners signified. Under the pretence of robbing the treasures of the church, they charged the abbot of Glastonbury with the crime, " and he and two of his monks being condemned to death, were drawn from Wells upon a hurdle, and then hanged upon the hill called the Tore, near Glastonbury." Hugh Farrington, abbot of Reading, and two priests, Brigg and Owen, were hanged and quartered at Reading. The same Richard Whiting, abbot of Glastonbury, and John Thorn and Roger James, monks, treasurer and sub-treasurer of the church, were executed adjoining their monastery.* " The abbot's head was set upon the abbey-gate, and his quarters disposed of to Wells, Bath, Ilchester, and Bridgewater. Nor did the abbots of Colchester and Reading speed much better." Some priors and other ecclesiastical persons, who had spoken against the king's supremacy, were likewise condemned to death and executed.†

It is worthy of remark, that religion, which had taken

* Stowe, p. 577.
† Historical Collections out of Several Protestant Historians, p. 27.

refuge in the convents and nunneries of the monastic orders from the palaces of prelates and the neglected temples of the secular clergy, was represented by the ecclesiastical commissioners as wholly desecrated, outraged, and abused in the monasteries. The number of the suppressed houses, Stowe says, was about 376 ; the value of the lands above £.32,000 a-year ; the moveable goods, as they were then sold at Robin Hood's, amounted to more than £.10,000. Of the religious persons who were turned out of convents, some went to other great houses, some were turned adrift on the world. " It was a pitiful thing to hear the lamentations that people in the country made for them ; for there was great hospitality kept amongst them, and, as it was thought, more than 10,000 persons, masters and servants, lost their living by the pulling down of those houses."*

The cruelties practised on individuals in 1536, the outrages committed on religion, the evils inflicted on the poor by the spoliation of those houses, are largely commented on by all the writers on those events, of the period in question.

But it is to be remembered this was only the plundering and pulling down of the small monasteries ;—the spoiling of the great houses, the shrines and altars of all orders of religious men and women, of the white friars first, of the black friars next, then of the grey friars, and so on with all the abbeys throughout the land, was prudently reserved for a second blow at the monastic orders. Two years had not elapsed after the first partial spoliation of religious houses, when the confiscation and suppression of all the monastic establishments in England was decreed and carried into effect.

In the first spoliation of 1536, we find the number of suppressed houses estimated at 376, their inmates at 10,000, which would give 26 inmates to each house.

In the second general suppression and confiscation in 1538, Baker (page 411,) states, the number of suppressed convents was 645, colleges 90, hospitals 110, chantries and free chapels 2374. Total of religious establishments abolished 3219.

The sum of £.142,914, the estimated amount of the revenues of all the suppressed convents, at the present time would be equivalent to about £.2,858,000.

* Stowe.

· " The whole of the rents of the estates of the church, including those tithes which were confiscated and transferred to lay parsons, amounted to, perhaps, a third part of the whole rental of the kingdom."*

O'Mahony, the Jesuit, in his work, " De pure Regni Hiberniæ," says, it is difficult to estimate the number of churches and religious houses destroyed, but thinks it might have been 10,000, more or less—" ut cumque tamen fuerit de numero sive 10,000, sive plura vel pauciora templa et monasterias devastata, corvorum nidos esse penitus disturbandos, ne postea iterum ad cohabitandum convolarent.": This estimate, however, of the number of churches and religious establishments, suppressed in both countries, is probably exaggerated.

The following account is that on which most dependance is to be placed.

The annual revenue of all the convents in England was estimated at £.142,914 sterling. The number of large convents, which yielded these revenues, was 555, exclusive of the knights hospitallers.† The revenue of the Benedictines yielded nearly one-half of the whole amount; that of the Augustines a fourth; that of the Cistercians an eighth.

The acts of impiety, sacrilege, and revolting profanity, that were done in those religious houses, " great and solemn monasteries," in which, according to the preamble of the first law of spoliation, " Thanks be to God, religion was right well kept and observed ;" the unholy acts that were committed by the creatures of Cromwell, his plundering protegees, with his sanction committed, were of unparalleled turpitude. They not only plundered churches, convents, altars, shrines, and libraries ; they defaced, destroyed, levelled, tore down, pulled to pieces, all that could be wrecked or injured by them. They ransacked the female convents, sacked their cells, and their sanctuaries, terrified the unfortunate inmates, threw some of them into prison, and turned the others into the streets.

The libraries of the monasteries were not more sacred than the shrines and altars of their churches, in the eyes of the licensed robbers, the subordinate agents of Cromwell. The splendid missals and illuminated manuscripts

* Second Part Cobbett's Prot. Reform. Introd.
† Tanner's Notitia ap. Lingard, vol. 4, p. 486.

of the convents were rifled of their clasps and covers for the sake of their gold and silver ornaments.*

The king and his vicar-general carried their warfare on the monastic establishments, against the very grounds and gardens of the monasteries. It was thought unpolitic to leave any mementos, on the land, even of the taste and refinement of the late owners of the plundered convents. Nay, the walls of the pillaged houses and churches it was deemed expedient to cast down.

"The work of demolition, however, went on slowly, the venerable piles which had withstood the rage of men at various epochs, engaged in civil war, and the ravages of time, still resisted the efforts of the sacrilegious hands employed for their ruin, by the Vandal vicar of the monster king." A new agent of destruction was had recourse to. The mighty structures, the massive walls, the majestic roofs, the sanctuaries, the altars, and the shrines, which the piety of the ancestors of the destroyers had erected in the bye-gone ages of faith, were brought to the ground, or left in utter ruin. The work of destruction was instantaneous, but enough of the remains are still left to perpetuate the barbarity of the acts of Cromwell and his master.

There are many things analogous in the suppression of the monastic orders in England and in Portugal, but the plunderers of the religious houses in Portugal did not thirst after the blood of the victims of their cupidity. They spoiled, deceived, and violated their engagements with them it is true, but they did not put them to death on the scaffold, they did not hang, embowel, and behead them; they were satiated with the spoil of their churches, their convents, and their estates. At the period of Elizabeth's persecution and spoliation, some of the victims of his rapacity and cruelty found an asylum in Portugal. Englishmen in Portugal should bear this in mind, and evince their remembrance of it by their generosity to the unfortunate monastic victims of the liberalism of 1834.

The sufferings endured by the ladies of the Bridgetine nunnery near Brentford, called Sion House,† have been

---

* This villanous example, in recent times, was followed by the rapacious liberals of Spain and Portugal. The author, in both countries, has seen the most valuable works taken from the pillaged convents, thus despoiled of their covers, in grocers' shops, sold by the Arroba weight of 32lbs.

† The Sion House nunnery was founded by Henry V. in 1414, A. D.

recorded by one of its members, the sister of the well known Jesuit, Father Nicholas Sanders. Several of the community were of noble families, and of noble qualities, as they evinced by their courage and constancy in very grievous trials. Their convent was not only suppressed, but several of the inmates were treated with brutality and cruelty, and some of them cast into prison and kept there. In a subsequent reign they were dragged from tribunal to tribunal, where they were charged with obstinacy and contumacy for the purpose of getting money from their relatives, who had to pay the heavy monthly fines imposed on them for recusancy. In a work of Dr. Sanders, on the persecution in England, translated into Spanish, there is a narrative of the sufferings and wanderings of the ladies of Sion House, written by Elizabeth Saunders, after the dispersion of the community, in the reign of Henry VIII., and her own long imprisonment.*

This lady states, that at the visitation at Sion House, by the king's commissioners, the nuns were treated with great harshness ; their property was taken, several of the community were imprisoned, the rest turned adrift on the world.

Miss Saunders was imprisoned at Windsor, and, probably on her brother's account, was treated with great rigour. She was frequently exposed to annoyances of the most odious kind, to language offensive to modesty, and conduct insulting to it. When the further changes in religion took place, after Henry's death, she was constantly importuned to go to the sermons of ministers, and punished for refusing to do so, brought before the magistrates, and judicial tribunals at the end of each term of six months, on charges of refusal to attend sermons and the new service, in her prison, and for each monthly offence condemned to pay a fine of 80 ducats, till the sum at length amounted to 500 ducats, which sum being unable to pay, she was condemned to perpetual imprisonment. This is worthy of notice, for though the crime of non-attendance at church was only nominally punished with a fine of £.20 monthly for each offence, the actual penalty, in case of poverty, was imprisonment for life. But the worst of all her sufferings, worse

The yearly revenue was £1944 11s. 8½d.; now worth upwards of £.38,000. This house was granted to the Duke of Northumberland.
* Relacion de algunos Martyrios, &c. &c., p. 42,

even than those arising from want, on many occasions, of the common necessaries of life, to her and the other ladies confined in the same prison, were those which they were subjected to by the guardians of the prison, and the agents of the authorities in the shape of impious discourses and indecorous behaviour. After a long confinement, Miss Saunders effected her escape, but had not been long at liberty when her conscience reproached her with having fled, and she returned to her prison. Her spiritual director had the good sense to convince her of her error, he assured her it was lawful to fly from an unjust imprisonment; and the wife of the jailor having consented to favour her escape, she fled a second time, and was kindly received by a wealthy gentleman of Berkshire, Mr. Francis Yates, who kept her closely concealed for some weeks, when the authorities came to the house, seized Mr. Yates, and threw him into prison, where he died. She, however, contrived to elude the search that was made for her, and succeeded in effecting her escape to France, and joining some of the members of her community at Rouen, where they had then established themselves.

After some time they were banished from France, fled to the Low Countries, and established themselves in Flanders; but the persecuting spirit of Elizabeth's government followed them there, and its influence caused them again to have to seek another place of refuge; they made their way to Portugal, with the intention of proceeding to Spain, where an asylum had been offered to them, but in the former country they were hospitably received, and the kindness they met with from the Portuguese, induced them to establish themselves in that country. Thus the survivors of the community of Sion House, after many wanderings and persecutions in many lands, arrived in Lisbon, in 1594, (Castro, in his Mappo de Portugal says, fifteen in number,) and were enabled, by the noble liberality of a Portuguese lady, Donna Isabella de Azevedo, to found their first convent in Lisbon, in the street of Mocambo, which house was destroyed by the great earthquake. Another country establishment was founded for them at Maravillas, near Lisbon, by a dignitary of the church, Archdeacon Cabral.

Their present house in the capital, called St. Salvador de Sion, the convent of the Inglesinhas, was founded in

1651. The community now is chiefly Portuguese, there are a few English ladies belonging to it; the existence of this convent is connived at by the government, the inmates have nothing more to be robbed of.

It would seem that the greater was the reputed sanctity of any establishment, the greater claims it had to veneration or respect, either on account of its antiquity, its holiness, its connection with the piety of the worthies of the land of bye-gone ages, the greater disposition was evinced to plunder, to profane, or to demolish it. And this Vandal sentiment was exhibited in the treatment of the inmates of such houses. If there was one of the monasteries in England, whose inmates might have expected some consideration at the hands of Englishmen, however bent they might be on their work of rapacity—the house of Glastonbury, "the first land of God," in England, it might be thought, would have experienced some considerate regard. The sympathy of King Henry and his Vicar-general, was shown to its inmates by hanging the Prior and two of his community.

Of this earliest of the religious houses of England, there is a very curious account in the work of Richard Broughton, the theological antiquarian, printed clandestinely in 1658.*

Broughton cites various authorities to show that a Cenobite community existed at Glastonbury long before the origin of the Benedictine monks, or the mission of Augustine.†

This monastery, Protestant antiquaries thus speak of : " The first land of God, the first land of Saints in England ; the Tomb of Saints ; the Mother of Saints ; the Church founded and built by the Lord's disciples ; the famous Abbey of Glastonbury, the beginning whereof is very ancient, fetched even from that Joseph of Arimathea, who interred the body of our Saviour. Wherefore Polydore Virgil doth rightly call Glastonbury the parent and mother monastery of all England."‡

To the great house of Glastonbury, the monastery of Bangor, in Wales, yielded only in point of antiquity and celebrity.

* " A True Memorial, &c.," by Richard Broughton, priest.
† Antiquities of Glastonbury.—Winton.—William of Malmesbury.—Cambden.—Treculphus.
‡ Theatre of Great Britain, Ap. Broughton.

"That famous college, our monasterie at Bangor, in which there were 2100 christian philosophers, that served for the profit of the people in Christ, living by the labours of their hands, according to St. Paul's doctrine."[*]

This house was founded, Broughton states, "about the year of Christ's nativity 200, or sooner."

St. Bernard termed it the head of the chiefest monasteries in the world.

The Abbey of St. Augustine, at Canterbury, the Apostle of England, was gutted, his shrine torn to pieces. The materials of the Abbey were used, we are told by Cobbett, "in building a menagerie for wild beasts," and a palace for the brutal king.

The magnificent shrine of St. Thomas-a-Becket, was likewise spoiled.

The tomb of Alfred, in Hyde Abbey, at Winchester, was profaned and plundered, as well as that of St. Grimbold.

The suppression of the convents led to discontents throughout the country. Large expectations had been held out to the people, that the property of the convents would render it unnecessary to burden them with future imposts. But the royal plunderer could only purchase the acquiescence of his courtiers and nobility, in his rapacious measures, by sharing the spoil with them.

When complaining to Cromwell of the rapacity of the applicants for grants, he exclaimed, "By Our Lady, the cormorants, when they have got the garbage, will devour the dish." Cromwell reminded him that there was much more yet to come. "Tut, man," said the king, "my whole realm would not staunch their maws."

Four years had hardly passed over, before his majesty found himself as much embarrassed as he had been, before the confiscation of the property of the monasteries.

The people were burdened with new imposts. Insurrections broke out in various counties. The insurgents exclaimed against the plunderers of the monasteries.

"Hume (says Cobbett) affects to pity the ignorance of the people, (as our stock-jobbing writers now affect to pity the ignorance of the country-people in Spain), in showing their attachment to the monks."

The military adventurers, the courtiers, and the money-

---

[*] "A True Memorial, &c.," page 40.

dealers, became the inheritors of the wealth of the plundered monasteries, and the spoiled churches, shrines, tombs, and altars.

The grants of the royal robber to the needy courtiers, and the greedy rabble of minions, legal, military, and political intriguers, who waited on providence and hung about "the king's vicar-general and vicegerent in spirituals," "were so enormous," in the language of Burke, "as not only to outrage economy, but even to stagger credibility." These are the men to whose ill-gotten property, the spoil of the churches, the partition of the precious metals of the chalices, the patens, the pixes and censers, the lamps and crucifixes, and the broad lands of the abbeys, of the priories, the chantries and free chapels, and nunneries,—these are the "new made men," the male Naiads of the fountains of honour, with "prodigies of profuse donation," to whom our modern aristocracy owe "their derivative merit." The Garters, and Ulsters, and Norroys, the proclaimers and blazoners of heroic virtues and chivalrous exploits of the herald's office, have not done all that was needful for the honour of the ancestral arms of the families of those men. They have given them Griffins, and Dragons, Lions rampant, and Tigers spotted, Wild Boars, Hawks, and Pelicans; they should have superadded to the ravenous beasts and birds explanatory devices, such as a bloody hand on a silver Crucifix, a Chalice and a Crucible, a sledge-hammer and an image of the Virgin, a Trooper rampant and a Friar couchant, a Knight in armour trampling on the reliques of a Saint, a Baron with a reeking sword, and a flaming torch at the door of a convent, a glaived hand clutching the rent-roll of an abbey, and a Soldier of fortune tolling stalls for the sale of cabbages in the garden of a convent.

These devices might convey some information respecting "grants from the aggregate and consolidated funds, of judgments iniquitously legal, and from possessions voluntarily surrendered by the lawful proprietors, with the gibbet at their door; the merit of those to whom they were granted, and from whom they are derived, that of being prompt and greedy instruments of a levelling tyrant who oppressed all descriptions of his people, but who fell with particular fury on every thing that was great and noble."*

* A letter from Edmund Burke to a noble lord, 1796. p. 28.

Another result of the change in religious matters in the reign of Henry VIII., was the horrid effusion of blood that followed its course, and the sanguinary character that was given to the laws of England.

At some periods the savageness of Henry's disposition was chiefly shown in the burning of heretics. Such records as the following, (a small portion of those of a similar kind,) are worthy of his annals.

Three men and one woman were burned in Smithfield "for the Sacrament."

A man and woman, Dutch Anabaptists, were burned in Smithfield.*

Three Anabaptists were burnt near Newington.†

Dr. Barnes, D.D., Thomas Gerrard, a priest, and William Jerome, vicar of Stepney Heath, charged with heresy,‡ were drawn to the stake and burned; and three doctors of divinity, Powell, Abel, and Fetherstone, were hanged, drawn, and quartered.

Elizabeth Barton, the maid of Kent, and a number of persons implicated with her in a charge of blasphemy, were executed in 1534.

But it was subsequent to his assumption of the spiritual power, that his murderous jurisprudence reached the acmé of its cruelty and injustice. The people who had been involved in the ruin of the monastic institutions, the rents of whose lands recently held from the latter had been greatly augmented, whose hard earnings were now swept away by a rapacious proprietary, clamoured against the latter and the royal patron of the new possessors of the soil.

The change of property was an unfortunate one for the people. The friars were not absentee landlords, there were no middle-men between them and their tenants. They had no spendthrift heirs, they left no litigious inheritors to squabble for their estates, to throw them into chancery, or to bring them to the hammer.

The property of the monasteries was administered not only for the benefit of their inmates, but for that of the people in the districts in which they existed. The poor were co-proprietors with the friars, and the convents were endowed not only for religious but charitable purposes.

When the royal spoiler, whom Leland does not scruple to

---

* Stowe, p. 392.   † Ibid, p. 579.
                    ‡ Ibid, p. 581.

call "an instrument of providence to introduce the first beginnings of reformation in this kingdom,"* plundered those religious houses on a false pretence, he destroyed the establishments which provided for the poor, the aged, the sick, the halt, and the blind of his dominions.

The monastic landlords had sympathies with the people. In the troubles of the latter they had recourse to the monasteries. And to have recourse to them, and a claim for counsel, protection, or support, it was requisite to be known to those resident landlords, to have a good name in their vicinity, to be in fair repute with their neighbours, to be known to the priests, and not to the agents of police.

Hume admits, "the suppression was very much regretted by the people......Complaints were heard in every part of the kingdom." There was "a great decay of the people... ...a diminution of former plenty......usury and avarice began to dominate in England."†

The same author tells us all the lands of England, in the reign of Henry VIII., had been rated and estimated at three millions.

In three hundred years they were estimated at more than twelve times that amount. In 1804 the rack rental of England and Wales was thirty-eight millions.‡

The destitute people, driven from their homes, wandered over the country in quest of food. Licenses to beg were at last had recourse to, to restrain mendicancy and vagrancy. The most horrible violations of humanity and justice were the results. The people were made poor, and they were treated as malefactors. Scourgings, imprisonments, the stocks, and bread and water,—these were the punishments that became the penalty of poverty, and of the crime of seeking alms without the sanction of authority, without the license duly sealed and registered, that conferred the privilege of begging on the poor.

The statute against vagabonds of the 22nd Henry VIII. made it incumbent on justices of the peace to seek out all poor and impotent persons who lived on charity, and appoint certain limits for them to beg in, and to enrol the names of all licensed beggars. The penalty of transgress-

* History of Ireland, Vol. ii, p. 157.
† Hist. of England, vol. i. p. 197.
‡ Cobbett's Reform.

ing such appointed limits was confinement in the stocks for two days on bread and water.

" V. If any such impotent person be vagrant, and go a begging, having no such letter under seal as above specified, then the constable, and other inhabitants within the place where he shall beg, shall cause every such beggar to be taken and brought before the next justice of the peace, or high constable of the hundred, who shall command the said constables, or other inhabitants of the town or parish that bring him, that they strip him naked from the middle upward, and cause him to be whipped within the town where he was taken, or within some other town where they shall appoint (if they in their discretion think it convenient to punish such beggar so) ; if not, then to command him to be set in the stocks in the same town or parish where he was taken, by the space of three days and three nights, and have only bread and water : And then the said justice or high constable, before whom he was brought, shall limit him a place to beg in, and give him a letter under seal, as aforesaid, and swear him to repair thither immediately, after his punishment executed.

" VI. If any person, man or woman, whole and strong of body, and able to labour, be taken begging in any part of this realm, or having no estate, nor using any merchandise, craft, or mystery to get a living, be vagrant, and can give no account how he does lawfully get his living ; then it shall be lawful for the constables or other officers of every town, parish, and hamlet, to arrest such vagabonds and bring them to any justice of the peace of the same shire or liberty, or else to the high constable of the hundred, rape, or wapentack, within which they are taken, or before the chief officer of a corporation (if they be taken there) : And every such justice, high constable, or head officer, by their discretions, shall cause every such idle person so brought before him, to be had to the next market town, or other place where they think fit, and there to be tied to the end of a cart, and to be whipped through the said market-town or other place till his body be bloody ; and after such whipping, the justice of the peace, &c., before whom such person shall be brought, shall enjoin him upon oath to return without delay the next way to the place where he was born or dwelled, by the space of three years.

" VII. And every such person so punished, shall have a

letter sealed with the seal of the hundred, rape, or wapentack, city, borough, &c., where he is punished, witnessing the same, and containing the day when, and place where, and the place to which he is limited to go, and by what time ; within which time he may lawfully beg, showing his testimonial, or else not. And if he perform not according to his testimonial, then to be taken where he begs, and whipped ; and every time he shall offend against this statute, in every place to be taken and whipped till he come to the place where he was born or dwelled, by the space of three years ; and there labour for his living.........

" IX. Begging scholars of *Oxford* or *Cambridge*, not authorized under the seal of the said universities by the commissary, chancellor, or vice-chancellor of the same, all shipmen, pretending losses of their ships and goods at sea, begging without sufficient authority, and all other idle persons going about the country or abiding in any city, borough, or town, using unlawful games and plays, or pretending to have knowledge in physic, phisonomy, palmistry, and other crafty sciences, making the people believe that they can tell their fortunes ; shall, upon examination had before two justices of the peace (*Quor. unus*), if by proof they be found guilty of such deceits, be punished by whipping two days together, after the manner before rehearsed. And if they offend again, then to be scourged two days, and the third day to be put upon the pillory, from 9 of the clock till 11 before noon of the same day, and have one of their ears cut off ; and for the third offence to have like punishment of whipping, standing on the pillory, and have their other ear cut off ; and that the justices of the peace shall have like authority within liberties as without, being within their shires."*

In the reign of Henry VII. England was a land of plenty. The manners of the humbler classes were those of a happy, industrious, independent people.

In the reign of his successor the land was one of poverty, depravity, and crime. After the suppression, the latter kept pace with the destitution consequent on that measure. The savagery of the king kept pace likewise with that destitution. " The number of executions in the latter part of his reign was incredible."† Harrison, in his ' Description

* Abridgment of the Statutes, p. 286.
† Baker's Chron.

of Great Britain,' (vol. iv. p. 280.) states, that 72,000 persons were hanged in the kingdom in the reign of Henry VIII., " thieves and rogues, besides other malefactors."

Well might Sir Walter Raleigh say of the monster king : " If all the patterns of a merciless prince were lost in the world, they might be found in this king."

The pious Cromwell, who had sanctioned this unholy work, "who superintended the scattering into the air of the ashes of St. Thomas a Becket," had got about thirty of the estates belonging to the suppressed monasteries. He was created Earl of Essex. His impious career was, however, brought to a close by his loving master in 1540. He was charged with heresy* and treason ; his ill-gotten riches, however, constituted his crime, and to get at these it is probable the monster who was the supreme head of the Church, had decreed his death. Cromwell died like a sycophant and a slave, meanly and dastardly. This is the man whose memory the historian Hume delights to honour; from whose pitiful letter of supplication to the tyrant he quotes the concluding words : " I, a most woful prisoner, am ready to submit to death when it shall please God and your majesty ; and yet the flesh incites me to call to your grace for mercy and pardon of mine offences. Written at the Tower, with the heavy heart and trembling hand of your highness's most miserable prisoner and poor slave,—Thomas Cromwell.———Most gracious prince, I cry for mercy, mercy, mercy."

But Hume was a philosopher, a political economist, and a deist ; and he says, " Cromwell deserved a better fate." All the judicial murders on account of religion to which he was accessary—that of the aged mother of Cardinal Pole, of priests and laymen, of More and Fisher, must have been evidences of his merit, in the sight of the historian who disbelieved Christianity, and looked on all religions (and especially the creed which united the suffrages of the largest number of Christians) as futile superstitions.

* In the first twenty-three years of Henry VIII. thirty heretics were committed to the flames; and in the last sixteen of his reign twenty-one more. Of these, sixteen were Anabaptists, one for denying the king's supremacy; the greater part of the remainder for offences against the law of the six articles.

Between thirty and forty others were executed ostensibly on convictions founded on new statutes; but in reality for their adherence to the old religion. (Brown's Penal laws, p. 10.)

In the following summary will be found an account of the several measures and acts, connected with matters of religion, passed in the reign of Henry VIII.

In the twenty-second year of his reign, Henry issued a proclamation prohibiting the purchase of any faculties or dispensations from Rome. This was the beginning of his defection.

In the twenty-third year of his reign, the clergy submitted themselves to him, being found guilty of acts against the Statute of Premunire,* and gave him the title of " Supreme Head of the Church "—" so far as it was according to God's Word."

In the twenty-fourth year of his reign, an act was passed prohibiting appeals out of the realm to the Court of Rome, on pain of incurring a premunire.

In the twenty-fifth year of his reign, an act was passed against paying pensions, Peter's-pence, or any other dues to Rome.

In the twenty-sixth year an act was passed which legalized the king's claim to the title of the supre-

---

* " By these penalties of Premunire, so frequently alluded to in the penal statutes, we are to understand the punishment of Papal provisors, contained in 16 R. II. c. 5: namely, that they shall be ' mys hors de la protection nostre dit Seigneur le Roy, et leurs terres et tenementz, biens, et châtieux, forfaitz au Roy nostre Seigneur; et q'ils soient attachez, par leur corps, s'ils porront estres trovez, et amesnez devaunt le Roy et son conseil, pour y respondre es cases avaunditz, ou que processe soit fait devers eux par premunire facias, en manière come est ordeiyne, en austres estatutz, des provisours et austres qui seuent en autry courte en derogation de la regalie nostre Seigneur le Roy.'

" The various parts of this severe and most indefinite species of punishment, which has been subsequently extended over our statute-book down to the 12 G. III. c. 11, are thus summed up by Sir Edward Coke: ' From the conviction the defendant shall be out of the king's protection, and his lands and tenements, goods and chattels, forfeited to the king: and his body shall remain in prison at the king's pleasure; or (as other authorities have it) during life.' To which he adds, that a man thus attainted, may be slain by another with impunity, because it was provided by 25 Edward III. st. 5, c. 32, that any man do to him as to the king's enemy. This notion, indeed, unfounded as it is, had so generally prevailed as to require the interference of the legislature; who by 5 Eliz. c. 1, enacted, that it shall not be lawful to kill any person attainted on a premunire, ' any law, statute, opinion, or exposition of law to the contrary notwithstanding. But though the offender's life is thus protected, his civil rights are completely annihilated; for he can neither bring any action, even for the most atrocious private injury, nor can any one with safety give him comfort, aid, or relief."— Brown's Penal Laws. Note to p. 24.

5

macy, and the abolition of the Pope's authority in England.*

In the twenty-seventh year an act was passed for the suppression of the lesser houses, and confiscation of their property.

In his twenty-eighth year Cromwell was made Vicar-general and chief visitant of religious houses.

In 1538, an act was passed for the suppression of all religious houses, and confiscation of their property.

In the thirty-first year of his reign, the Book of the Six Articles was set forth, and the property of all monasteries was vested in him.

In 1547, in the fifty-sixth year of his age, the monster, execrated by his people, died.

---

* "If any resiant within this land, shall, by writing, ciphering, printing, preaching or teaching, or by any deed or act, obstinately or maliciously, extol or defend the authority of the Bishop of Rome, (heretofore usurped within this land), or shall invent any thing for the extolling of the same, or attribute any authority to the said See, or to any Bishop of the same, such offenders, their aiders, &c., and every of them, (being thereof lawfully convicted according to the laws of this land), shall incur the penalties of a premunire, provided by the Statute of the 16 R. II."

CHAPTER V.

THE REFORMATION AND ENACTMENTS OF PENAL LAWS IN ENG-
LAND IN THE REIGN OF EDWARD VI., FROM 1547 TO 1553.

IN A.D. 1547, Edward VI. ascended the throne. Sixteen
executors had been appointed to carry into effect the will of
Henry, and govern the kingdom, till Edward, then under
ten years of age, should reach the age of eighteen. The
Earl of Somerset contrived to monopolize all the power of
the other executors in his hands, and in his quality of Protector, in a short time his authority was absolute. Cranmer, an ambitious ecclesiastic, who had embraced the
opinions of the foreign Reformers, was the confidential
agent and adviser of the Protector.

A roving ecclesiastical commission to go into all parts of
the kingdom, was appointed for the settlement of questions
appertaining to religion, and especially to take into consideration the complaints against the Six Articles of King
Henry, and the Commissioners were accompanied with
preachers to instruct the people, and enlighten their ignorance, and to dissuade them from the invocation of saints,
prayers for the dead, from images, the mass, and dirges for
the dead, all which observances or rites had been spared
by Henry.

In his will, the recommendation of his soul to God, was
accompanied with a declaration of his belief, in which he
particularly specified the merits of our Saviour's Sacrifice,
efficacy of the Sacrament of His Body and Blood, the intercession of the Blessed Virgin, the offering up of Masses at a
convenient Altar at Windsor, the daily offices for the dead,
and charitable donations to the poor, to pray for the remis-
sion of his sins and his soul's good.

The primate Cranmer, and Somerset the protector, had
taken oaths to fulfil the duties imposed on them by their
trust as the late king's executors. Henry had solemnly
enjoined that his son should be brought up in the religion
he professed, the Catholic Faith; his executors violated

their oaths, for they caused the young king to subvert all
its leading doctrines.

Cranmer and Somerset, in reality, were the sovereign
rulers of the state. The former had long carried on an
active communication with the reformers in Germany, and
especially with the Calvinists in Switzerland, who begun at
this time to acquire an influence in England, and to exercise it in a very fierce and fanatic spirit. Somerset, it is
generally admitted, espoused the plans of the reformers, for
the purpose of profiting by the plunder of the Church.

The executors made many changes in the laws, and some
in the constitution, very detrimental to popular liberty, *for
in the old Catholic times, the spirit of democracy was largely
blent with the religious sentiment.* One of the first acts of
the reformers on Edward's accession, was to abolish the
ancient custom of "*asking the people* if they were willing to
have and obey the king."

Various measures were passed for re-modelling or rather
re-constructing the religion of the country; an act of
Henry's, prohibiting the reading of the scriptures in the
English tongue, was repealed, and all former acts recited in
it concerning doctrine, and imposing penalties in those
which involved matters of belief, were abrogated. An act
however was soon passed to restrain the liberty conferred
by the preceding measure.

"An act (entitled) against such as speak against the
Sacrament" was passed, and it would appear not too soon,
for the reformers had proceeded from improving the modes
of administration, to the most scandalous and scurrilous
abuse of the holy Sacrament.

There was another act for receiving the Communion
in both kinds, with some exceptions, in case of sickness, &c.

The next grand measure of the reformation in the boy king's
reign, was the enforcement of a statute, the 27th of Henry
VIII., by which all Chantries, (endowments and foundations
united with parochial and other Churches for masses for
the dead,) Colleges (for similar objects, but exceeding the
former in their revenues and costliness of their structures,)
Chapels, Hospitals, Gilds, and Fraternities, and their possessions, were given to the king.*

* Heylin.

The act which struck deepest at the root of the religion of the country, was an act for the election of bishops, in which it was ordained that bishops should be made by the king's letters patent, and not by the election of Deans and Chapters; and that all ecclesiastical processes should be made in the king's name only, with the bishop's attestation to them, and sealed only with the king's seal.

This was taking away the divine institution of the episcopal office and order, and making the king's command the substitute for it. The bishops, in fact, were changed into ecclesiastical state servants, for doing the king's will and promulgating the king's mandates.*

An act was passed prohibiting the use of flesh-meat on Fridays, Saturdays, Ember-days, Lent, and other reputed fish days, on pain of ten shillings fine and ten days' imprisonment for each offence; the reason given in the preamble being, that "Parliament, considering that due and godly obedience was a means to virtue, and to subdue men's bodies to their soul and spirit; and considering withal that fishers may thereby be more set at work, and that by eating of fish much flesh may be saved and increased, ordain," &c.†

Various commotions had at this time taken place in consequence of the reviling of the Sacrament, the casting it out of the churches in some places, the tearing down of altars and images, in one of which tumults one of the authorities was stabbed, in the act of demolishing some object of popular veneration in a Church. The act restoring the fasts was passed at this time, to appease the indignation of the people.

The whole kingdom, in short, was in commotion, but particularly Devonshire and Norfolk. In the former county the insurgents besieged Devon; a noble lord was sent against them, and being reinforced by the Waloons, a set of German mercenaries brought over to enable the Government to carry through their plans, his lordship defeated these insurgents, and many were executed by martial law.

---

* This is what statesmen of England in our own days are bent on accomplishing in Ireland, by other means than those of terror and persecution, which were tried in former times and found to be ineffectual. Shame upon those who shall ever lend themselves to the success of such a policy.

† Heylin, p. 57.

Great numbers of the clergy were imprisoned, and many were executed in both counties; several laymen also were persecuted and prosecuted for adhering to the old religion. In Devonshire the noble commander had a priest hanged from the steeple of his own Church. In Norfolk the executions were still more numerous.

The next act of Parliament for the making of a new religion, was a statute confirming the public liturgy, in the framing of which (from Calvin's letters in 1549, 1550, and 1551,) it appears that he was very desirous to have taken part; "but Cranmer knew the man," he had been in Geneva, and for some time refused his co-operation.

Martin Bucer, however, and Peter Martyr, zealous Zuinglians, were brought over to forward the great work, and the labours of these gentlemen were more likely to undo all that was done, than to do anything that was likely to subsist. At length, to remedy the frightful disorders arising from disputations about the administration of the Sacrament, a rubric was resolved upon, and this rubric was a new subject of contention, more rancorous than that which it was introduced, for the removal of.

Another law was enacted, permitting priests to marry. The sacrament of auricular confession was one of the last tenets of the Catholic religion denounced and relinquished in this reign. The doctrine of the Real Presence was the last of all subverted; it kept its ground for some time, when all the other dogmas of the religion which had subsisted for upwards of a thousand years had been abandoned. The vitality of a divine principle was in it; it outlived all the other dogmas of the Faith planted in England by St. Augustine.

Calvin's repeated remonstrances, addressed to the king, to Cranmer, and the protector, against the moderation of the English reform, were at length attended to; he drove the latter to greater extremities, both in pulling down and establishing. It was at his instance that the former Book of Common Prayer was set aside, new Articles composed, and a new book of Common Prayer set forth, and Hopkins's parodies of the Psalms of David, "done into English metre, and fitted unto several tunes," began, after the Genevan fashion, to be sung in churches; and as the Puritan faction grew in strength, so did the hatred augment to all that was beautiful in art or poetry connected with Church service.

Hopkins's barbarous hymns "thrust the Te Deum, the Benedictus, the Magnificat, and Nunc Dimittis quite out of the Church."[*]

Calvin's influence gradually prevailed in England ; his agents, who were numerous, represented all that Henry had done as merely preparatory to the grand work of the Reformation. These views were still further enforced by a German disciple of Zuinglius, John Alasco, a Pole, who had brought over with him a great number of his countrymen and Germans, who obtained the privilege of a Church for themselves, distinct in government and form of worship from the Church of England.

The influence of Calvin completed the subversion of the vital doctrines of the Roman Catholic Church, and of the establishment of all the sects which sprung up from its ruins in England. The Earl of Warwick was the first of the aristocracy who inveighed publicly against the super- fluities of episcopal habits, the expense of vestments and surplices, and ended with denouncing altars and "the mummery" of crucifixes, pictures, and images in churches.

The earl had an eye to the church plate and the precious jewels that ornamented the tabernacles and ciboriums. Many courtiers soon were moved by a similar zeal for reli- gion—a lust for the gold, silver, and jewels of the churches. In a short time, not only the property of churches, but the possessions of rich bishoprics and sees, were shared amongst. the favourites of Cranmer and the protector, as were those of the see of Lincoln, "with all its manors save one ;" the bishopric of Durham, which was allotted to Dud- ley, Earl of Northumberland ; of Bath and Wells, eighteen or twenty of whose manors in Somerset were made a present to the Protector, with a view of protecting the remainder.

The religious houses, shrines, altars, and tombs, dese- crated and destroyed in the reign of Edward VI., were innumerable. The general spoliation of the churches, of the secular clergy, and the chantries, colleges, and free chapels ; the taking down of altars, and confiscation of their ornaments and furniture proceeded rapidly. The hospital of a nunnery near St. James's Park furnished the

* Heylin, p. 107.

materials and a site for the goodly manor which merged
into the royal palace of St. James's.

Three episcopal houses, and a parish church, dedicated
to the Blessed Virgin, in the Strand, says Dr. Heylin, were
demolished by the Protector, and furnished a site and part
of the materials for the splendid palace of the Duke of
Somerset. His Grace had determined to demolish St. Margaret's church, in Westminster, for the sake of the materials
for the new palace, but the parishioners in a great multitude resisted the sacrilege with staves and clubs, with
bows and arrows. Upon this, the Protector desisted, and
fell upon St. Paul's; he demolished the cloister, a chapel in
the church-yard, also the charnel-house that stood on the
south side of it, with the chapel lumber and monuments
therein, which were all beaten down, the bones of the dead
carried into Finsbury-fields, and the stones converted to
the building, and the vacant places filled up afterwards
with dwelling-houses. Moreover, the church of St. John's
of Jerusalem, near Smithfield, was undermined and blown
up with gunpowder, and the stones applied to the spacious
building. Likewise Barking chapel, near the Tower of
London, and the College Church of St. Martin's-le-Grand,
nigh the shambles, and St. Ewen's, within Newgate; also
the parish church of St. Nicholas, in the shambles, were
quite pulled down. Such were the materials of the Duke's
palace, called Somerset-house.

The economical disposition which distinguished one of
the apostles, who sold his master for thirty pieces of silver,
(that first political economist, whose breast was afflicted at
the expensiveness of vain ceremonies and solemnities connected with religious observances), who asked—"What
need all this waste," when one poor chalice might have
served the turn, characterized also the conscientious Cranmer and Somerset, the guides and guardians, spiritual and
temporal, of the young king.

The copes in which the priests officiated at the Holy
Sacrament, usually made of cloth of gold or silver, richly
embroidered of velvet or satin, the ponderous lamps of
silver, the crucifixes of the same metal, the precious
chalices, ciboriums, pixes, and patens, were great eye-
sores in the sight of the saints of the new school of sanctity,
who professed to worship God in spirit and in truth, and all
simplicity of mind and plainness of external service.

"But that the consideration of profit (says Dr. Heylin) did advance this work as much as any other, (if perchance not more), may be collected from an inquiry made two years after ; in which (inquiry) it was to be interrogated— ' What jewels of gold or silver crosses, candlesticks, censers, chalices, copes, and other vestments, were then remaining in any of the cathedrals or parochial churches, or otherwise had been embezzled or taken away.'......' The leaving,' adds Dr. Heylin, ' of one chalice to every church, with a cloth or covering for the Communion-table, being thought sufficient. The taking down of altars by command, was followed by the substitution of a board called the Lord's Board, and subsequently of a table, by the determination of Bishop Ridley.' "*

The free chapel of St. Stephen, the chapel royal of the Court, with its curious cloister, built by John Chambers, the king's physician, were fitted up and employed for a House of Commons. The church and college of St. Martin's, near Aldersgate, were made a present by the boy king to the church of Westminster. Both were pulled down by those persons they had been given to, the materials sold by the Dean and Chapter, and a tavern built on the site of the east part of the premises.

Westminster Abbey, in its turn, says Heylin, was disposed of. Seventy of its manors in Gloucestershire, the Dean and Chapter were obliged to make a present of to Lord Thomas Seymour, in addition to his manor of Sudely, "humbly beseeching him to stand their good lord and patron, and to preserve him in fair esteem with the Lord Protector."

The nobility and gentry, following the rapacious example of the Government, seized on the revenues of the benefices to which by law they were only entrusted with the presentations. Bishop Latimer, in his published sermons, pp. 31, 71, 91, and 114, complains of the abuse.

The gentry of that time invaded the profits of the Church, leaving the title only to the incumbent......many benefices were let out in fee-farm, or given unto servants for keeping of hounds, hawks, and horses, and for making of gardens......The poor clergy being kept to some sorry pittance, were forced to put themselves in gentlemen's houses,

* Dr. Heylin, Ap. Historical Collections, p. 88.

and there to services, clerks of the kitchen, purveyors, and receivers.

The booty of the spoiled Church in the reign of Edward VI., when the bishoprics even ceased to be respected, and the Gilds, Fraternities, and Chantries, devoted to charitable and pious purposes were totally abolished, Dr. Heylin informs us, "did not prove so great as was expected."

Private persons embezzled the plundered property, and ornaments of gold and silver, and rich vestments and tapestry, "so that although some profit was heretofore raised to the king's exchequer, yet the greater part of the prey came to other hands.* Insomuch that many private persons' parlours were hung with altar cloths, their tables and beds covered with copes instead of carpets and coverlets, and many made carousing cups of the sacred chalice, as once Belshazzar celebrated his drunken feasts in the sanctified vessels of the temple. It was a sorry house not worth the naming which had not something of this furniture in it, though it were only a fair large cushion made of a cope or altar cloth to adorn their windows, and to make their chairs appear to have somewhat in them of a chair of state.

"Yet how contemptible were those trappings in comparison of those vast sums of money which were made of jewels, plate, and cloth of tissue, either conveyed beyond the seas or sold at home, and good lands purchased with the money, nothing the more blessed to the posterity of them that bought them, for being purchased with the consecrated treasures of so many Churches."†

"As for the fruit, (says Dugdale,) that the people reaped from all the hopes built upon those specious pretensions of reform, it was very little; for subsidies from the clergy, and fifteenths of all laymen's goods were soon after exacted; and in Edward's time, the Commons were constrained to supply the king's wants by a new invention; to wit, taxes on sheep, clothes, goods, debts, &c., for three years, which grew so heavy, that the year following they prayed the king for the mitigation of it."

Somerset, the principal actor in this reign in the struggle with the old Church, was an ambitious, remorseless man; avaricious and prodigal.

* Historical Collections.
† Ibid. p. 99.

In 1549 he was the means of bringing his own brother to the block, who had quarrelled with him on account of the public spoil ; and in his turn Somerset was brought to the same end, in 1552, by the intrigues of a jealous rival, the most zealous promoter in his time of the destruction of altars and abolition of images, vestments, and church ornaments, — Dudley of Northumberland, previously Earl of Warwick. This nobleman, in his turn, having promoted the Reformation by the spoliation of chantries, colleges, and bishoprics, and having made an attempt at the crown for his daughter-in-law, Lady Jane Grey, was brought to the block to which he had consigned his fellow labourer in the Reformation.

It is difficult, in the history of great crimes and their retributions, to avoid anticipating events.

At the end of the reign of Edward VI. the same state of things was found in existence, as at the conclusion of the former reign. The treasury was involved in debt, notwithstanding all the plunder of the churches, which was to have enriched the state and its ruler.

The anxiety of Somerset for the good of the people's souls and bodies ; his denunciations of the religious houses he pillaged, as " nurseries for vice and luxury ;" his complaints of the plundered friars as " cherishers of all evil vices, robberies, rebellious thefts, whoredoms, blasphemies, and idolatry," furnish evidence of the extraordinary extent to which the brazen impudence of unblushing rapacity and barefaced hypocrisy were carried in those times.

The official reports on monastic abuses of the foreign reformers—the liberal statesmen of Spain and Portugal, in our own times, addressed to their respective sovereigns in justification of the seizure of the Church property of those countries—in respect to hypocrisy, cannot be compared with those of our own reformers.

In 1553 the illfated Duke of Somerset, Cranmer, and Northumberland died.

The following summary affords a view of the chief Penal Acts of Edward's reign :

" It is provided by the 1 Ed. VI. c. 12. that all persons maintaining the supremacy of the pope, or denying that of the king, or his successors, shall, for the first offence, forfeit all their goods and chattels, and suffer imprisonment at the king's pleasure ; for the second, shall forfeit the profit of their lands and promotions, and be imprisoned for life ; and for the third, shall be deemed guilty of high treason, the penalties of which are also incurred by those who, by writing or printing, offend against this statute......

"For the establishment of a conformity of religious opinions, a book of Common Prayer having been provided, it was ordered by the 2 and 3 Ed. VI. c. 1. that if any minister preach or speak in degradation of anything therein contained, or refuse to read this, or wilfully use any other manner of mass, openly or privately, he shall suffer for the first offence forfeiture to the king of the profit of one of his benefices, and imprisonment for six months; for the second, imprisonment for one year, and deprivation of all spiritual promotions ;' and for the third, imprisonment during life. If, however, the offender should have no spiritual promotions, he shall for the first offence be imprisoned for six months, and for the second for life. Those persons who deprave the said book, or cause any one to use any other form of prayer, or interrupt him in the use of this, forfeit for the first offence ten pounds, or not paying it in six weeks, shall have three months' imprisonment; for the second, twenty pounds, or not paying it within the same period, six months' imprisonment ; and for the third, shall forfeit all their goods and chattels, and be imprisoned during life.

"By the 3 and 4 Ed. VI. c. 10, Missals, &c., in English or Latin, other than such as are set forth by the king's authority, are abolished for ever ; and persons having them or any images, &c., taken from, or yet standing in any church or chapel, in their possession, who do not destroy, or cause them to be delivered to the bishop or his commissary, to be openly burned or destroyed, shall forfeit for the first offence twenty shillings, for the second four pounds, and for the third shall suffer imprisonment at the king's will......

"The 5 and 6 Ed. VI. c. 1, confirms a former act of Henry VIII., relative to conformity of religious opinions, and adds, that whoever is present at any other form of prayer than that directed to be used in the said statute, shall suffer imprisonment for the first offence for six months, for the second for one year, and for the third during life."*

* Brown's Penal Laws, pp. 51, 52.

CHAPTER VI.

MARY commenced her reign with prudence and moderation, and with generosity to the opponents of her rightful
claims to the throne. Happy would it be for her memory,
if she had continued in this wise and merciful course !

During her brother's reign, she had resisted all attempts
to cause her to renounce her religious sentiments, and adopt
those of the court. This fidelity to her religion passes for
besotted bigotry. Her liberation of the bishops and clergy
unjustly imprisoned in the late reign, is denounced as treason to the interests of the new true religion.

All that was evil in Mary's nature was derived from her
brutal father ; all that was good in it (and there was much
more in it than Protestant historians choose to admit) she
derived from her noble mother, Catharine of Arragon.

In a letter to the Protector, in 1549, Mary boldly vindi-
cated the right of toleration for her religious opinions at a
time when very great perils beset her. " I pray you, my
lord," she said, " and the rest of the council, no more to
disquiet and trouble me with matters touching my conscience, wherein I am at a full point, with God's help, whatsoever shall happen to me ; intending, with His grace, to
trouble you little with any worldly suits," &c.

But this letter only caused her renewed annoyance ; the
Lord Chancellor and Bishop Ridley were sent to remon-
strate with her on her nonconformity to the new religion,
and threaten her with the king's displeasure,—to which
she answered, that " her soul was God's ; and touching her
faith, as she would not change, she would not dissem-
ble." The messengers informed her the king intended not
to constrain her faith, but to restrain the outward profession of it.

The princess, however, was constrained in her faith, and
kept rather as a state prisoner, than in the enjoyment of

liberty, in the king's palace. The ambassador from the imperial court no sooner heard of this violence, than he sent a threatening message to the Protector, plainly intimating that war would be the result, if his master's relative, the Lady Mary, was denied the free exercise of her religion. The Lady Mary was then allowed to hear Mass privately in her own apartments. The bigots had not the courage to encounter the wrath of the foreign prince whose ambassador bullied them.

" From her attempt to escape for protection to her cousin, the Emperor Charles V., it is evident that Mary must have considered a summons to give a last proof of her attachment to the faith of her ancestors as no very improbable event, or at the least that she apprehended some violence in her person from the zeal of her brother and his Protestant counsellors. On the renewed interference of this powerful monarch, the liberty of conscience which was demanded in her behalf, was only obtained by a threat of immediate recourse to hostilities, and even then it was wrung with much difficulty from the young king, who burst into tears on being thus compelled to allow the continuance of his sister in that abominable and idolatrous mode of worship, which he believed himself called on to extirpate by a most rigid severity, which should be no respecter of persons."*

However, after the death of the imperial ambassador, these zealots arrested and prosecuted two of the chaplains of the princess for officiating in her apartments. This outrage was the subject of a new complaint of this poor lady, addressed to the protector, and another to the king. To the former she said : "Notwithstanding, to be plain with you, howsoever ye shall use me or mine, with God's help I will never vary from mine opinion touching my faith ; and if ye or any of you bear me the less good will for that matter, or lessen your friendship towards me only for that cause, I must and will be contented, trusting that God will in the end show His mercy to me : assuring you I would rather refuse the friendship of all the world than forsake any point of faith."

This is bigotry with some of our historians. There are few persons, however, who are not blinded by prejudice,

---

* Brown's Penal Laws.

who will not deem it courage, constancy, and noble resolution.

Still the persecution continued: Mary retired to Hunsdon, in Herefordshire, and there she was followed by Bishop Ridley, who obtained a reception at her abode, and repaid her hospitality by expressing a desire to preach before her the following Sunday. To which she answered, " the doors of the parish church adjoining should be open to him, that he might preach there if he chose, but neither she nor any of her servants would be there to hear him." "Madam," said he, " I hope you will not refuse to hear God's word :" to which she answered—" That she could not tell what they called God's word, it not having been accounted such in the days of her fathers." After which, some altercation having taken place, she dismissed him thus—" My Lord, I thank you for your kindness to visit me, but for your offer to preach before me, I thank you not."

The Bishop departed, but not before he reproached himself to her gentleman in waiting, for having tarried in the house, " and not having shaken the dust from off his feet in testimony against that house in which the word of God could not find admittance."......" Which words he spoke with such an insolency of spirit as made the hair of some of them which were present stand of an end, as themselves afterwards confessed."[*]

Though Bishop Ridley, on this and other occasions, had pandered to the intolerance and tyranny of the Protector, and for his unfeeling conduct to this unprotected and maltreated Princess, deserved no favour at her hands, there is no excuse for her burning him at the stake when she came to the throne. But still it is well to bear in mind how she had been persecuted by those men whom she persecuted to the death in her turn—and to remember also the characters of some of those martyrs who suffered in her reign, and who are ranked by Fox in the list of the great confessors of the christian faith.

In 1554, shortly after her accession, Mary married Philip, son of Charles V., of Spain ; and this marriage with a Catholic Prince excited a furious clamour against her. An unsuccessful insurrection, headed by Sir Thomas Wyat, gave the queen an opportunity of resenting the indignities she had suffered since her marriage. The sword of justice

_ * Historical Collections, p. 115.

was converted into one of vengeance. The wounded pride
of a woman, whose husband was openly abused and brutally
reviled; whose own personal qualities, her defects, and even
infirmities likewise, were the common subjects of scurrilous
jibes with the adversaries of her religion and of her claims
to the throne; transformed itself into a headlong zeal for
the interests of her faith, which blinded her reason,
inflamed her passions, and stained her hands with the
blood of a great many of her subjects.

Mary's first act in reference to religious matters, was an
act of toleration; at her coronation a tumult had taken place,
in consequence of a preacher having prayed for the dead,
and denounced the persecutions in the previous reign, being
insulted in the pulpit, and compelled to leave it. The
Council the next day wrote to the Mayor to take measures
for the prevention of similar disorders, and reminded his
Worship and the Aldermen of the Queen's determination
uttered to them at the Tower; "That albeit her Grace's
conscience was settled in matters of religion, yet she gra-
ciously meant not to compel nor to restrain other men's,
otherwise than as God should, as she trusted, put into their
hearts a persuasion of the truth which she was in, through
the opening of his Word unto them by godly, virtuous, and
learned preachers."*

This, however, was soon followed by a proclamation of her
Majesty, of a very different character, prohibiting seditious
writings, preachings, and teachings. "Books, ballads, rhymes,
and other lewd treatises, concerning doctrines in matters
now in question." The arrival of the Pope's Legate, Cardinal
Pole, was followed by the reconciliation of the nation
through its Parliament, with the Pope. The Parliament
humbly petitioning on their knees, the Legate's intercession, that his Holiness would be pleased to pardon the
nation's crimes, of which they heartily repented, and
remove the censures they had incurred, promising that all
the laws they had made offensive to his Holiness in the
Catholic religion should be repealed.

Absolution was granted to them by the Legate in the
name of the Pope, and on the Thursday following, the
bishops and clergy presented themselves at Lambeth, "and

* Heylin, p. 21. Ap. Hist. Coll. p. 122.

kneeling reverently before the cardinal, obtained pardon for all their perjuries, schisms, and heresies.

A remarkable convocation of the bishops and clergy of Canterbury, was held during the Parliament, from which body a petition to the Sovereign emanated. The author of the Historical Collections, speaks of this document as not being easily met with, and never having been before printed. "The petition prays Her Majesty to take into her gracious consideration, that, though bound by the Canons of the Church to use all lawful means for the recovery of those goods, rights, and privileges, &c., which had been lost in the late schism, and to regain the same for the Church as in her first and right estate; yet in regard to the manifold sales, transfers, and alienations of Church property, which had taken place, that it would be difficult, if not impossible, to recover the same, and might lead to breaches of the public peace, they besought Her Majesty to intercede with the Lord Cardinal, to settle and confirm the said goods and possessions to the existing holders of them."

This proceeding was evidently the result of a compromise between the holders and purchasers of the plundered church property and the Court. Her Majesty is said to have been violently opposed to it, but at length was induced to give it a reluctant consent.

The prayer of the petition was attended to, and wisely acquiesced in by the Legate. Mary, however, declared her determination to renounce all the lands and possessions of the spoiled Church, which had been vested in the Crown. Three Acts of Parliament were passed, repealing all the Statutes since the 28th of Henry, in regard to religion, and restoring all things to their former state, with the exception generally of the suppressed religious houses.

Several churches were restored, and *some* monasteries, in London. A Benedictine, a Franciscan, and Dominican convent, and at Brentford, the Bridgetine nunnery called Sion House.

The Reformers, in the mean time, libelled, lampooned, and denounced all the measures of the Queen and her government. Their preachers openly inveighed against them in the pulpit. Plots and conspiracies were the only fruits of "Gospel liberty" that were now exhibited. The clerical incendiaries were seized and imprisoned. But vengeance,

6

and not security, became the motive which prompted the further measures taken against them, and, as in our own day, the Sovereign was spoken of there, as the woman Jezabel.

Bonner, Bishop of London, was the Cromwell of Mary— the ready instrument of an intemperate zeal, and a principal actor in all the sanguinary measures of those times. The judicial murders of Hooker, Ridley, Latimer, Ferrers, Rogers, Sanders, and Taylor; of Cranmer—even the perjured, blood-stained Cranmer,—their deaths are attributed to the violent councils and revengeful feelings of this cruel and overbearing churchman. Bonner, it is to be borne in mind, had come out of persecution to persecute. He had been imprisoned and maltreated during Edward's reign. It was a time of deadly hate, of religious hate, which is devoid of all charity and mercy. "Schisma et secta, exacerbationes animorum indices quibus sit ut Christianus a Christiano tanquam a leproso et maledicto abhorreat."

The principal victim in this reign, had been the prime persecutor in the former. Archbishop Cranmer's first preferment in the Church, arose from a base prostitution of his clerical character at the onset of his ministry, namely, a public opinion pronounced in favour of the divorce of Henry VIII. from Catherine of Arragon, for which service he was made the King's Chaplain, *and placed in the family of Thomas Boleyne, Earl of Wiltshire and Ormond*, for purposes, some writers state, most unworthy of his calling, and from that time, was employed to write in favour of the divorce. True to the king's lust, he wrote a book on this subject, and then set out for Cambridge to dispute upon the question, and for this service was made Archdeacon of Taunton.

In 1530, he was sent to Rome to procure the Pope's consent to the divorce; he did not obtain it, but on his return he obtained a wife in Germany, married, or was compelled to marry, the sister of Osiander, one of the great eccentric luminaries of the German Reformation. On his return to England in 1533, he was nominated Archbishop of Canterbury, for the purpose of pronouncing the divorce, which he accordingly did, and from that time both he and his master, the sensual monarch, and the pander priest, abjured the Pope's supremacy, and thus founded the Church of England. Three years after he had pronounced the divorce between Henry and Queen Catherine, he was again called on to prostitute his clerical functions, by divorcing his brutal master from Anne Boleyn.

On Henry's decease, as one of the Regents of the kingdom, and godfather both of Edward VI., and the Lady Elizabeth, he had the power to persecute the Church he had abandoned, and to instil his principles into the minds of his god-children. In 1549, he was appointed a Commissioner, and found a congenial employment in the proceedings against Bishop Bonner. On Mary's accession, he was put on his trial for high treason, in setting his hand to the instrument of Lady Jane Grey's succession, and for the spiritual offence of openly justifying the religious proceedings of the late king. He was convicted of treason, and pardoned, and anew proceeded against for heresy. In 1554, he was brought before the Commissioners at Oxford, and having refused to subscribe to the doctrines of the Roman Catholic Church, was barbarously condemned. A new trial was instituted in 1555, which terminated also in his condemnation.

He then signed a formal recantation, wherein he renounced the Protestant religion, and re-embraced the Roman Catholic one. But this proceeding had no effect on the inexorable Mary, his execution was determined on, and her obduracy can never be sufficiently abhorred and lamented by all enlightened Catholics, worthless as the man was whose doom depended on her decision.

At his execution his behaviour commenced with weakness and confusion, and ended in a heroic endurance of his sufferings worthy of a nobler character. On the scaffold on which he was placed previously to fixing him to the stake, he made a profession of faith, in which he renounced his recent recantation, and declared all he had written against the reformation was in the hope of saving his life, and in token of his sincerity he thrust the hand which signed that recantation into the flames.

The contrast is striking between the conduct, the character, and the constancy displayed in the life and death of Sir Thomas More, and Archbishop Cranmer. When More was called on by the British Tarquin to renounce the authority of the supreme head of his church, and to subscribe the act of abjuration with an oath, he refused to comply with the king's mandate; and when his friends represented to him that " he could not entertain a different opinion from that of the great council of the nation :" " I have for my opinion," replied More, " all the Church, which is the great Council of Christians."

His wife even pressed him to obey the king, in order to save his life. " How many years," said he to her, " do you think I might still live ?" She said, " perhaps more than twenty." " Ah, my wife," replied this great man, " would you have me exchange eternity for so few years ?"

His enemies render unwilling homage to the noble courage he displayed in his martyrdom ; they confess that he lived at court without pride, and died on the scaffold without weakness ; and well has he been called by Protestants, " the Socrates of Christianity in a barbarous age ;" and by Macintosh, " the best of men."

Cranmer's judicial murder is a very different sort of martyrdom from that of Sir Thomas More. The latter, it is confessed by the enemies of his faith, did honour to his creed by his death, and his life was a testimony to its truth.

Cranmer's career was a reproach to the character of a religion professing to have justice and mercy for the great landmarks of its christianity, and his death left it doubtful whether he loved best his religion or his life.

In More's case the offer of a pardon produced the rejection of the proffered terms, and this rejection caused his martyrdom. In Cranmer's case the hope of pardon produced a recantation of his opinions, and then the failure of that hope occasioned a new recantation of the recent abjuration of his old belief, and rendered the honours of martyrdom preferable to the obloquy of an unavailing submission to the fiat of sanguinary power. Cranmer died for his character, and More for his church ; the former lived for his king, the latter for his God : both were scholars, but the learning of the high churchman went to pander to the passions of a tyrant who was a slave to his sensuality, while the wisdom of the Catholic layman had no other scope but to serve religion and save his king from his own vices.

Cardinal Pole, it is admitted by the historians who are advocates of the Reformation, fruitlessly endeavoured to check the persecuting spirit of Mary's mischievous advisers, and frequently protested against the inefficacy and impolicy of such means of maintaining truth or vanquishing error. There is a detailed account given of the arguments he adduced on one occasion, and amongst these it is worthy of notice, that the grounds on which he recommended moderation were, that all the causes of the reformation were not to be sought out of the religion that was attacked by the reformers, but that many of them were attributable to the relaxation of discipline on the part of the clergy, and the scandal that their conduct brought on the church. This is worthy of notice, as throwing some additional light on the subject of the authenticity of a representation on the state of religion in the pontificate of Paul III., bearing his signature, which has been noticed elsewhere. The only blot on the character of this great and good man, is that which attaches to his conduct when he stooped to become the agent of Henry VIII., and attempted, by unworthy means, to obtain answers from the universities on the subject of the divorce favourable to that project. He acknowledges in one of his letters to Henry, that having found "it more difficult to obtain subscriptions at home than abroad, he overcame the difficulty with the aid of menacing letters."*

The total number of persons who suffered on account of religion, and of matters connected with religion, in the reign of Mary, as stated by historians who are desirous of making her crimes equal those of her more sanguinary sister, is estimated at 300, including five bishops and twenty-one clergymen; 277 of the whole number are said to have suffered by fire. This estimate is probably exaggerated, but the number of these barbarous executions is more than sufficient to load the memory of queen Mary with obloquy and disgrace.

"After every allowance," says Lingard,† "it will be found that, in the space of four years, almost 200 persons perished in the flames for religious opinion, a number at the contemplation of which the mind is struck with horror."

Of those barbarities committed in the name of the law, and on the plea of promoting religious interests, it can only be said they are such detestable proceedings that no

* Lingard, Vol. iv. p. 484.
† History of England, Vol. v. p. 100.

language can be found strong enough to express the horror they inspire. . "Hæc sanè tam sunt fœda, tam turpia, tam detestanda, ut quis color iis obduci possit non videam."*

CHAPTER VII.

PENAL ENACTMENTS OF ELIZABETH, AND MEASURES TAKEN IN HER REIGN IN RELATION TO RELIGIOUS AFFAIRS IN ENGLAND. FROM 1558 TO 1603.

THE daughter of Anne Boleyn was educated in the principles of "the Reformation," which her mother had patronized, and these were confirmed by feelings of personal animosity to her half sister Mary, and also by the machinations of the party opposed to the religion of the latter, who treated Elizabeth with all the deference due to one, destined, as they hoped, to make the opinions they entertained predominate in the nation. Elizabeth was a woman of a vigorous, masculine understanding, with the education of a man; without the feelings of her own sex, but with some of the most odious of its failings; she was sagacious, shrewd, skilled in some branches of scholastic learning, headstrong, heartless, vain, and jealous.

She was crowned according to the order of the Roman Pontifical, by the Bishop of Carlisle, after having caused the solemn obsequies of her sister, the late queen, to be performed in Westminster Abbey, with a mass and all the Catholic ceremonies of a state funeral. But even then a change of religion was determined on. Dr. Heylin imagines that this determination was the consequence of her persecution, that her legitimacy and the pope's supremacy could not stand together.

There was some little apparent wavering in her conduct with respect to religion, at the beginning of her reign, though she had openly declared to her confidential friends her preference for the reformed religion. She soon recalled the exiled Protestants, released all who were confined on account of religion, ordered the Lord's prayer, creed, and gospels to be read, and the litany recited in English in

* Episcopius.

the churches, and forbade the host to be elevated in her presence.

Bossuet says,* "the step she had taken with regard to Rome, immediately upon her coming to the throne, countenanced the opinion that has obtained publicity, that she would not have departed from the Catholic religion had she found the pope more conformable to her interests. But Paul IV. would give no favourable reception to the civilities she had caused to be tendered to him, as to another prince, without a further knowledge of her dispositions, from the resident of the late queen, her sister."

It is said at this time, on the subject of the invocation of saints, the real presence, the use of external ceremonies, and even the spiritual supremacy of the pope, her opinions were rather in favour of the Catholic religion than against it.

Dr. Heylin states, that Elizabeth had appointed Sir Edward Karne, her agent at Rome, to inform the Pope of Mary's death, and her wish to live on amicable terms with his Holiness. The Pope (Paul IV.) at first, it is said, showed indignation at Elizabeth's assumption of the regal power without his sanction, and altogether seemed ill-disposed towards the queen; but at length, judging a course of mildness the best he could pursue towards a headstrong woman, he sounded the agent, with respect to her intentions towards her religion.† Karne declined to give any assurance of her not changing its forms, till his Holiness had first pronounced her mother's marriage with Henry VIII. valid.

"The Pope," says McGeoghegan, "saw clearly the best plan he could adopt would be to come to no decision, rather than do what could be productive of no good."

Was this plan of procrastination the best he could adopt? Was the plan successful in the case of Henry, when he sought a divorce from Catherine of Arragon, in order to marry Elizabeth's mother? Did not the state of suspense in which Henry was kept, tend more to his breach with Rome than an immediate decision might have done, even though it were adverse to his demands? Did not the suspense in which both sovereigns were left, afford the enemies

---

* Histoire de Var.
† Burnet, Bossuet, Heylin.

of Rome time and opportunity to turn those sovereigns against the papal authority, and mature the plans of those engaged in the great revolt? But, whatever reluctance Clement VII. justly felt to countenance adultery, to sanction lust, to inflict the cruelest of all injuries on a lawfully wedded and faithful wife, the circumstances were altogether different in the case of Elizabeth.

She was elevated to the throne without opposition; she had given no offence to religion or scandal to morals; and for the sake of peace and quiet in her dominions, and with the view of maintaining amicable relations with her, the court of Rome might have ratified her people's choice, when there was no child of the deceased queen, or of her mother, prejudiced by Elizabeth's accession to the throne.

Elizabeth's council, it is stated, was constituted with a view to the reformation of religion : but while the negociations with Rome were pending, and the deliberations of that council going on, she prohibited by proclamation all preachings and wranglings about religion, and even shut up some of the churches to prevent violent reforming theologians from dealing damnation on all who differed from them. Elizabeth's change was a bit by bit reform, carried on stealthily and closely till the Book of Common Prayer, which had been committed to Dr. Parker and others for remodelling, was set forth anew, and within three months of her coronation the mass was abolished, and the liturgy in English established by act of parliament.

The two latter objects were effected (it is said by Sir. R. Baker*) by a majority of six votes only. The next month the queen's supremacy was proclaimed, and the oath of supremacy tendered to the Catholic bishops. All who refused it were deprived of their sees, and other prelates appointed by her, and the month following images were removed from the churches, and were publicly broken and burnt. Thus " the Reformation" progressed, and the consequence of these changes was in a short time a general confusion in matters of religion.

The same means which Henry employed to get his supremacy legalized, Elizabeth employed to get hers confirmed by a statute,—she packed a parliament.

* Chron. p. 472.

Dr. Heylin states, that certain lords and gentlemen had the management of elections in their several counties, "amongst whom none appeared more active than the Duke of Norfolk, the Earl of Arundel, and Sir William Cecil." When the question of supremacy was propounded to parliament, "it seemed to be a thing abhorrent even in nature and polity, that a woman should be declared supreme head of the Church of England." There is a very remarkable speech of Bishop Heath, who had filled the office of chancellor, in opposition to the measure, given in full, and published from a manuscript copy of it, in the "Historical Collections." (p. 162.) There never was an argument on this subject so ably put as that of Bishop Heath. It is impossible to follow it, step by step, in its logical positions and deductions, without being persuaded of the mischievous results of this measure.

"First," he said, "by relinquishing and forsaking the Church or See of Rome, we must forsake and fly from all General Councils:

"Secondly, from all canonical and ecclesiastical laws of the Church of Christ:

"Thirdly, from the judgment of all other christian princes:

"Fourthly, and lastly, we must forsake and fly from the holy unity of Christ's Church, and so, by leaping out of Christ's ship, we hazard ourselves to be overwhelmed in the waves of schism, of sects, and of divisions."

The four General Councils, on which he relied as received by the Roman Pontiffs, were the Nicene, the Constantinopolitan, the Ephesian, and Chalcedon Councils. But all opposition to the measure was in vain; the packed parliament passed the measure,—the queen was declared supreme head of the Church of England. From that time she freely exercised her supremacy, making and unmaking doctrine. A convocation that was held at this time made a declaration of their judgment on certain points, for submission to parliament, expressive of their opinions, that the Sacrament of the Eucharist was still to be retained; the Real Presence to be declared, in the consecrated Host, but no longer having the substance of bread and wine, and to be held a propitiatory sacrifice for the quick and the dead; that the government of the Church was in the successors of

Peter, and that ecclesiastical jurisdiction belonged only to the legitimate pastors of the Church.

These Articles were presented to the Upper House, but were made of no account. The bishops, who were now reduced to the number of fifteen, made a stand against the Liturgy. They were called on by the Council to conform, but all refused with one exception, the Bishop of Llandaff; whereupon they were deprived of their sees. Many of the clergy also refused, and were stripped of their benefices.

"It was at this time," says McGeoghegan, "that the bishops displayed a firmness truly apostolic."[*]

It is curious to observe how much more strenuously the prelates and superior clergy, in the reign of Elizabeth, resisted the renunciation of the Pope's authority, than they had done in the reign of Henry. Did this arise from their experience of the evils of the usurpation?

By the deprivations of these prelates and pastors, a sufficient number of qualified persons to supply the sees and cures was not to be found. Hence arose the monstrous evils connected with the existence of an ignorant, insolent, dissolute clergy, which all the historians and other writers of the time speak of.

The first acts of the new prelates and pastors, it is said by the Queen's injunctions, were the removal of all the images and crosses out of the churches. Those taken out of the London churches were burned in St. Paul's church-yard, Cheapside, and other places in the city, and in some of them the copes, vestments, and cloths of the altars.[†]

This bewilderment of public opinion in England, in respect to all religious matters, consequent on three great changes within a compass of twelve years, was such as might be expected. Henry assumed the supremacy of the Church, the enjoyment of first fruits and tithes, renounced the Papal authority, suppressed convents, appropriated their funds, but maintained the mass, the seven sacraments, the prayers for the dead, and invocation of Saints.

Edward abolished the mass, authorized a book of Common Prayer in English, demolished altars, shrines, and images of saints, changed the ordinances respecting the Sacrament of the Eucharist, spoiled the churches of the

* Histoire d'Irelande, Tom. 2. Cap. 40.
† Heylin, p. 131.

secular clergy, and reduced the seven sacraments to two.

Mary restored all things to the Church of Rome, except the plundered property and confiscated estates of the Church and convents not vested in the Crown, and reduced the ecclesiastical jurisdiction to Papal obedience.

Elizabeth resumed the supremacy, first fruits, and tithes, suppressed the mass, auricular confession, the consecration of the host, renounced all the leading doctrines of the Church of Rome, sought to establish uniformity of Protestant doctrine, and one unvarying book of Common Prayer, by means of a code of laws, the bloodiest and most barbarous that ever was enacted in any Christian land.

Pope Pius V. had long strenuously endeavoured to conciliate the friendship of Elizabeth, and induce her to return to the old religion ; but finding all his efforts were in vain, in 1570 he issued a bull of excommunication against her, and from that time Elizabeth may be said to have commenced her frightful career of blood, for the promotion of her views, of religious reformation. It would seem at that time as if Divine retribution had sent this schism over Europe for the scourge of the people of every realm where it came, by fomenting strife, encouraging fanaticism, exciting hate, and driving men to dip their hands in blood, with the name of God upon their lips and the fury of devils in their hearts. Knox and his disciples were blowing the coals of persecution in Scotland, violent commotions were then raging in that country.

In France there was a war of religion, carnage in the provinces, and a massacre in the metropolis. In 1572, nearly 12,000 Protestants, it is said, were butchered in cold blood in the latter country.

In Germany, the Reformers in various places were at daggers drawn.

In the Low Countries, the war between the Spaniards and the Dutch, had more in it of the bitter character of a religious war, than of a struggle for the acquisition of liberty, or the maintenance of despotic power.

In Ireland, where all battles are fought that affect great interests in England, where the decisive battle of civil and religious liberty was fought in 1829, the bloody battle of the Reformation was raging likewise upwards of three hundred years ago.

In England itself, such discord and distractions arose as had never before been in that country ; a complete change in the course of a few years, was effected in the habits and dispositions of the people. The epithet of merry, was no longer applicable to that country. There was neither peace nor plenty in the land. Poverty and crime began to make rapid strides. The sports of the people were cried down by the evangelical preachers. Other spectacles and pastimes began to be made familiar to them, the burnings in the market-places of crucifixes and images, frequent executions, and violent contentions in sacred places between preachers and teachers of contrary opinions in religious matters. These barbarities and unseemly excesses were chiefly the work of the returned clergy from Geneva, and the foreign disciples of Calvin who had been received in England, and with singular fatuity on the part of the Reformers, had been suffered to build up their independent Presbyteries along side the Episcopal Church, " as if it was practicable to set up a republic within the precincts of a monarchy."

In the latter part of Elizabeth's reign, the Calvinists gave as much trouble to Elizabeth, as they and the Anabaptists had done to Luther ; enough of trouble and tribulation of spirit, to cause all thinking men of both persuasions to question whether their acts have been beneficial or otherwise to mankind. The Calvinist, or Puritan faction, was espoused and protected by the most dissolute, grasping, and vicious man in England, the Earl of Leicester, the paramour of "the Virgin Queen." This man, at one time, engrossed nearly all the offices in the State, and preferments in the Church. Heylin says he was insatiable in his avarice, and sacrilegious beyond all other men of his time in his rapine. Such was the man "the Saints of the latter days," the Puritans, extolled to the seventh heaven. But though they courted this influential profligate, many of them reviled the Queen herself, and preached, prayed, and wrote pamphlets against her. One of their ministers openly prayed "that God would either turn her heart, or put an end to her reign."*

.They wanted to set up a new form of Ecclesiastical policy, and were prepared in the execution of their scheme,

* Heylin, p. 244.

to rebel against her. Many of these men held high offices in the Church. The deaths of the clergy by the plague, and deprivations, the result of that after-pestilence of Elizabeth's Ecclesiastical jurisdiction, her *unfrocking* so many bishops, and disgowning so many pastors, twelve deans, twelve archdeacons, fifteen masters of colleges and halls, fifty prebendaries of cathedrals, and about fourscore beneficed clergy, had left the parochial churches without incumbents, till the vacancies were filled up by actors from the platform of Geneva. The laws that were passed for the establishment of the new religion, were sanguinary, cruel, and oppressive. One of these acts made it treason for any man to maintain the power and jurisdiction of the Bishop of Rome.* It was ordained likewise that no man should be admitted to Orders, or take degrees in Universities, be a bencher of the Inns of Court, or an attorney, without taking the oath of supremacy, on pain of felony. To embrace the Roman Catholic religion, or in the legal slang of the Penal Code, "to be reconciled to the Church of Rome," was likewise made treason. A proclamation was set forth, commanding all who had children abroad, to call them home by an appointed day. This was to compel parents to Protestantize their children.

Another act made it high treason for any priest ordained since the first year of her reign, by a Roman Catholic bishop, to return to, or to be found in England, and felony for any person to harbour, succour, or assist a priest, knowing him to be such.

Another act made it a capital offence to oppose the Queen's supremacy.

It was made a crime, punishable with fine and imprisonment, (perpetual at the Queen's pleasure by another act), to hear mass, or be taken at religious worship in any popish house or chapel.

By another act it was made a capital offence to call the Queen "a heretic, an infidel, schismatic, or usurper:" to name her successor, except it should be a *natural* son or daughter of her Majesty :† under pain of loss of goods and perpetual imprisonment, it was forbidden to carry any thing of devotion from Rome, such as an Agnus Dei, a cru-

---

* Fifth of Elizabeth. Stowe, p. 678.
† Historia del Scisma de Inglaterra por Padre Ribadeneyra, Madrid, 1588, p. 184.

cifix, an image, or any object blessed by the Pope : under penalty of death, it was prohibited to receive or possess any bull, or brief, or Papal rescript, or form of absolution from heresy, or of reconciliation with the Church of Rome.

By the statute of 1575, it was declared felony to defame the Queen in any book or writing of any kind, or to encourage insurrection. This was a general way of felonizing any act, or expression of opinion, that her ministers might object to. Under this comprehensive statute, two nonconforming clergymen were hanged for a polemical treatise.*

In 1581 several new acts of increased severity against the Catholics passed through parliament. It was enacted first, that persons withdrawing or attempting to withdraw others from the Protestant faith, or suffering themselves to be withdrawn from it, should, with their aiders and abettors, suffer the penalty of high treason : secondly, that the punishment of saying mass should be increased to the payment of 200 marks and one year's imprisonment ; of hearing mass to 100 marks, and imprisonment for the same period : thirdly, that the fine of absence from church should be fixed at £.20 a month, and in cases of absence for an entire year, the recusant should find two sureties for his good behaviour of £.200 each ; and every priest acting as tutor or schoolmaster in private families without a licence from the ordinary, to be punished with a year's imprisonment, and the employer to be fined £.10 a month.†

In 1588 these laws were executed with greater rigour than ever, and others of still greater severity were enacted. Previously to this period, when the appearance of the Spanish Armada was daily expected : "impressed with these fears (of the Catholics in England) several of the ministers began to look on the massacre of St. Bartholomew as a useful precedent."‡ The expedient of a counter plot to be fabricated for the purpose of implicating in it the principal Catholics was suggested, but Camden says that Elizabeth rejected the proposal : " Illa autem crudele

---

* "Darcie, in his ' Annals of the Reign of Elizabeth,' relates, that a Frenchman, on witnessing the numerous executions, cried out, in amaze, ' *Deus bone ! quomodo hic vivunt gentes? suspenduntur Papistæ, comburuntur Anabaptistæ.*' Good God! how do the people make a shift to live here, where both Papists are hanged and Anabaptists burned."—Brown's Penal Laws, notes.

         † Lingard, Vol. v. p. 378.
         ‡ Ibid, Vol. v. p. 495.

consilium aversata." This is the only trait of humanity
we find recorded of her throughout her long reign, it would
be a bad act to deprive her memory of the benefit of it.
When her ministry could not shed the blood of their Catholic countrymen in a general massacre, they indulged their
wicked appetites for persecution, by procuring a return of
all persons suspected on religious grounds, from the magistrates of the capital, and throughout the country strict
search was made for recusants. "Crowds of Catholics of
both sexes, and of every rank, were dragged to the common
jails throughout the kingdom, and the clergy declaimed
from their pulpits with vehemence against the tyranny of
the pope and the treachery of the papists."* The penalty
of recusancy deprived numbers of gentlemen of their
estates. The perpetual fine of £.20 a month on recusants, must have required an ample fortune to discharge, "and whenever they were in arrear the queen was
empowered by law to seize all their personal property, and
two-thirds of their real estate, every six months." For this
purpose returns of the name and property of the recusants
in each county were repeatedly required by the council,
and the best expedient of the sufferers was to prevail on
the queen, through the influence of her favourites, to accept
an annual composition. Yet even then they were not
allowed to live in quiet. They were still liable to a year's
imprisonment, and a fine of 100 marks each time they
heard mass: "On each successive rumour of invasion they
were confined at their own charges in the jail of the
county: they were assessed, as often as it appeared proper
to the council, in certain sums towards the levy of soldiers
for the queen's service: on their discharge from prison
they were either confined in the house of a Protestant gentleman, or if they were permitted to return to their homes,
were made liable to the forfeiture of their goods, lands,
and annuities during life, for the new offence of straying
more than five miles from their doors."† Recusants in
meaner circumstances, at first, were imprisoned till the
jails became so crowded that the counties complained of
the expense, and then the queen relented so far as to permit the magistrates to release them. Some were accord-

---

* Lingard, Vol. v. p. 495.
† Ibid. Vol. v. p. 515.

ingly liberated on a promise of good behaviour; "some
had their ears bored with a hot iron, and others were publicly whipped."* It was afterwards enacted that a recusant not possessing twenty marks a year, should conform
within three months after conviction or quit the kingdom;
but the actual penalty was death three months after the
promulgation of the law, for the crime was declared "felony
without benefit of clergy if they were afterwards found at
large." At one sessions in Hampshire 400 recusants were
presented, and at the assizes of Lancashire 800.

"In pursuance of those laws commissioners were sent
into all parts of the realm to inquire out priests,† and such
as were reconciled by them."‡

"In the execution of which commission a priest was
taken in the Lord Morley's house, and the Lady Morley,
with the children and divers others, were also taken hearing the same mass."

"There was also taken at the same time another priest
at the Lord Guilford's, in Trinity Lane, for saying mass;
and for hearing the said mass the Lady Guilford, with
divers other gentlewomen, were taken."

"And likewise at the same time were taken two priests
in the Lady Brown's house, in Cow Lane, for saying mass;
with the lady herself and divers others for hearing it, all
which persons were indicted, and had the law executed
according to the statute."§

The number of ladies of high rank who were cast into
prison, charged with this high crime and misdemeanour,
was very great. Lingard gives one instance of a lady
going mad with terror, after her apprehension; and of another dying in jail from the effects of the fright she had
been seized with, at the time of her seizure.

"On the trials of the Catholics the court frequently dispensed with the examination of witnesses: by artful and
ensnaring questions, an avowal was drawn from the prisoner that he had been reconciled,‖ or he had been ordained beyond the sea, or that he admitted the ecclesiastical supremacy of the pope, or rejected that of the queen.

* Lingard, Vol. v. p. 516.
† Historical Collections, p. 235.
‡ Stowe, p. 678.
§ Ibid.
‖ Lingard's History of England, Vol. v. p. 515.

Any one of these crimes was sufficient to consign him to the scaffold."

The trial by jury, it is well worthy of observation, provided not the slightest protection to prisoners wherever the crown prosecuted, nor indeed was there any safeguard for innocence in any legal forms, or in any tribunals, either judicial or magisterial.

It is well worthy of observation, that in all times of despotism in England, Ireland, and Scotland, trial by jury has proved a delusion, a mockery, and a snare, and the judges of the land have been the partisans of tyranny.

There is much in the history of those times, which ministers of state, secretaries for the home department, even in our days, might read with advantage. They would learn by its perusal, that the persecution which brought such disgrace on the British nation, was less the consequence of a blind zeal for religion, than the result of the fanaticism of fear. Elizabeth was kept for the last twenty-five years of her reign in a constant fever of fear, affrighted with reports of plots and conspiracies to take away her life, fabricated by the ministers, and chiefly by Walsingham, for the promotion of their own private ends, with the view of causing their services to be deemed important and indispensable to the queen. A fierce hatred to Mary, Queen of Scots, on the part of Walsingham, contributed not a little to keep up that system of government which was carried on by the agency of spies, informers, seal breakers, stealers of private thoughts, and misinterpreters of unguarded expressions to familiar friends,

Walsingham was a burglar of state, who broke through all moral obligations and social restraints, and swindled himself into the secrets of foreign princes, sometimes with false keys to the cabinets of their ministers.* But people will say, the times are gone by for acts like those to be committed. Are they gone by? The ghost of Lord Malmesbury may be called to answer that question; and if his spirit will not come "from the vasty deep," the ambassador who buried the constitutions of Naples, Spain, and Portugal, whom Lord Castlereagh called "a very clever man in his line," he might be summoned to give expression to his experi-

---

* Memoires de Walsingham, Traduits de l'Anglois. Amster. 1700. p. 577.

ence, of "the means to an end," that have been had recourse to in modern diplomacy to find out secrets of state, or to get at the thoughts of courtiers and politicians. "Walsingham entertained fifty-three agents and eighteen spies in foreign courts," we are told by his biographer.[*] Letter work formed a large part of the employment of those functionaries. "Few letters escaped him," says his biographer, "and he could read them without its being perceived by the seal that he had done so;" and his eulogist adds :—"This great man had so much patience that his valet never saw him angry. He learned his great arts of government from Lord Burley, of whom he had been an official slave ; and his favourite maxim was founded on one of the lessons of Cecil : qu'il ne coute jamais trop pour scavoir ce que se passe."[†] "He was more astute (*plus fin*) than the Jesuits, who sometimes were the dupes of their equivocations and mental reservations ; yet *he never told a lie*, but he always knew how to inter the truth with discretion." The author was unmindful of the truism : "Qua non est plena veritas est plena falsitas." It was a proverbial saying of his, that "a man should never say anything which he could not draw back from without danger, or could not gallantly sustain in case of contradiction."

Faithful to his maxims, Walsingham rifled letters, broke seals and forged them, received fabricated letters from his spies, many of which he must have known to be forgeries, and carried them to the queen, and sometimes had to defend the dishonourable means by which he acquired them. The great conspiracy of priests for the destruction of the queen, which he invented so early as 1577, he did not bring to "a premature explosion ;" he dragged it on for nine years, meshing his clerical victims year after year till the plot was sufficiently ripe, in 1586, to bring his crowned victim at Fotheringay Castle to the block.

The plot which was got up in 1577, to effect the ruin of the Jesuit missionaries of Rheims, was principally worked by foreign agents. One of Walsingham's spies at Rome, of the name of Eliot, ingratiated himself into the confidence of the English Jesuits at Rheims, lived amongst them as a zealous Catholic, travelled into Italy, and eventually ac-

[*] Memoires de Walsingham, Traduits de l'Anglois. Amster. 1700. p. 574.

[†] Ibid. 572.

companied from Rome to Paris several of their body who were going on the mission into England. At Paris he furnished the English Ambassador with the names and a personal description of all these gentlemen, and on their arrival in England they were arrested. These particulars are given in a letter of one of his victims, in the Memoirs of Missionary Priests. In England he soon distinguished himself as a priest-catcher, an informer, and a perjured witness.*

Tertullian says, it was a common custom with Pagan persecutors to deny that they ever punished people for their religion, or for ought except their crimes against society or the state.

Eusebius says, it was the practice of the persecutors of the Christians, to accuse them, on account of their religion, of the most atrocious crimes against society, such as murdering and eating children.

It is said by the eulogists of Elizabeth, that no executions took place in her reign on account of religion, but solely on account of conspiracies against the state, and plots against her life. Of the plots and conspiracies in her reign, we have only to read the memoirs of her minister Walsingham, to be convinced of most, if not all of them, being fabrications of that subtle schemer and his agents, though the accounts are given with a very different design. Boldness of assertion on the part of historians, and effrontery in the statement of great falsehoods made palatable and plausible, go very far with the public in most countries. The people who are only acquainted with the writings of those who deal thus with the history of those times, are kept in utter ignorance of their character.

The best answer that can be given to the audacious assertion referred to, is the substance of an indictment on

---

* This swearing and priest-catching avocation was a regular profession from 1577 to 1684, for upwards of a century. In 1601, Mr. Tichborne, a Jesuit, a gentleman of an ancient family in Hampshire, arrived in England on the mission. It was not long before he was apprehended, by means of one Atkinson, an apostate priest, who meeting him in the streets of London, and recognizing him, cried out, " a priest, a priest, stop the priest;" and pursued him with this hue and cry, till he was run down as if he had been a mad dog and seized upon by his pursuers. Mr. Tichborne, to stop Atkinson's cry and carry off the matter said, what was quite true, he was no more a priest than himself; but he was imprisoned, arraigned, condemned, and executed, merely on account of his priesthood.—Memoirs of Missionary Priests.

which one of the missionaries, the celebrated Robert South-well, was tried, condemned, and executed.

" Middlesex,

" The Jury present on the part of the Queen, that Robert Southwell, late of London, Clerk, since the first of May in the thirty-second year of her majesty's reign, made and ordained priest by authority derived from the See of Rome, not having the fear of God before his eyes, and slighting the laws and statutes of this realm of England, traiterously, and as a false traitor to our said Lady the Queen, was in this kingdom, and remained contrary to the form of the statute in such case set forth and provided, and contrary to the peace of our said Lady the Queen, her crown, and dignities."*

Stowe, as concisely and complacently as usual, in his Chronicle of the Deaths of Missionary Priests in this reign, alluding to Father Southwell's murder merely says,

" February 20th, 1594-5.

" Southwell, a Jesuit, that long time had lain prisoner in the Tower of London, was arraigned at the King's Bench bar. He was condemned, and the next morning drawn from Newgate to Tyburn, and then hanged, bowelled, and quartered."

Of the numerous priests martyred in England in Eliza-beth's reign, several of the cases recorded, are those of per-sons prosecuted solely on account of professing the Roman Catholic religion, and officiating as priests. The general practice however was, on the pretence of punishing sedition, to kill the clergy, for their creed. Thus without exciting horror in foreign nations, the Government was able to inflict unheard of barbarities on the ministers of the obnoxious religion in the name of law—atrocities that have not been exceeded in cruelty in the annals of missionary enterprise and suffering in any country.

It would be a folly to attempt to deny that there was some ground of apprehension of projects formed in Spain and France against Elizabeth ; and that some writers in

* History of Missionary Priests, p. 331.

those countries had written works, in which the right of removing tyrants and persecutors by any means, however summary, from their thrones, was coolly discussed, nay in some of them was advocated.*

But none knew better than Walsingham, that the missionaries who were sent over from the continental colleges to England, were strictly enjoined to abstain from all interference in secular affairs. Ballard's conduct does not make him an exception to the rule. He did not come into England in the character of a missionary, but in that of a political agent, without the consent, and contrary to the advice of his order at Rheims.

Walsingham's machinations were not limited to the concoction of one plot, but a congeries of conspiracies against the missionary priests, the Catholic laity of note in England, and the Catholic princess Mary Queen of Scots.

It was feared in 1586, that Philip meditated a descent on England. Walsingham boasted to his mistress that "he had given the Spanish sovereign a bone to pick, which would fully occupy him for two years."† In plain terms, he had agents in his dominions sowing discord and dissensions, and laying the foundation of insurrections in his provinces. He justly dreaded that Philip would follow his example in England; indeed, that course is plainly suggested in Campanelli's Monarchia Hispanica, "talis que inimicitiæ semina semel sparsa, latius evagarentur neque unquam enecarentur."‡

The destination of Philip's immense armament, was a mystery which all the astuteness of Walsingham had been employed to clear up. "It did not suffice him, (says the author of his memoirs,) to know that the design was known to the Pope; the difficulty was to know the contents of a letter in the hand writing of Philip transmitted to the Pope. Walsingham found the means of surmounting the difficulty, which to all others would have been insurmountable. He maintained at Rome a spy who was a Venetian priest, who having gained an officer of the chamber of the Pope, found

---

* Burnet, in his " History of His Own Times" states, that some days before the death of Charles the First, Cromwell, in discoursing on the subject of his trial, referred to Marianna's work, De Institutione Principes, for a sanction of the doctrine that it was lawful to kill a bad king.

† Mem. of Walsingham.
‡ Mon. Hist. p. 205.

means to obtain the original letter, and to take a copy of it, which was sent to Walsingham."

But another writer of more authority, the editor states, had asserted "that the Pope, Sixtus the Fifth, jealous of the power of Philip the Second, and resolved to try all means to recover Naples, which Spain had taken away from the Ecclesiastical States, exhorted Philip to push on his grand design, for the accomplishment of which he promised him his benediction, whilst he gave information of all that passed to one Carr, whom Elizabeth kept in Rome, and who played his part so successfully, that he gained the confidence of the Pope and of the Ministers of Spain, without ever failing in his fidelity to the Queen his mistress, to whom he rendered services very signal and important. However it was, he adds, the discovery was very advantageous to England, and fatal to the Queen of the Scots, to whom it cost her head."

The author proceeds to detail the extraordinary pains taken by Walsingham, to persuade the Queen that this expedition was solely got up to subvert the reformed religion, and to place a Catholic Sovereign on the throne, which Sovereign was the unfortunate Mary, her prisoner. He therefore incessantly demanded her execution, and "to place the necessity for it in its full light, he (Walsingham,) was obliged to make a long written representation (of his views,) which still exists, says his biographer,* in the Cotton Library at Oxford, and which may be regarded as the chef d'œuvre of this great man."

That Walsingham was informed of all Mary's secrets, he adds, was certain, for "the servants of this princess, in whom she had most confidence, carried him all her letters. He caused them to be deciphered by one named Philip and another named Gregory ; he re-sealed them so well, that neither Queen Mary nor her correspondents were aware that the seals had been broken, or the letters had been retarded."

"Video et Taceo," was the ordinary maxim of Walsingham,† words which her majesty his mistress had already taken for her device. "There is nothing new under the sun in affairs of state."

If some good was effected by the timely discovery of the

* Mem. de Walsing.
† Ibid.

destination of the Armada, an immensity of mischief was
done by all those plots and conspiracies that sprung up
under Walsingham's direction, grounded probably on unguarded communications, intemperate expressions, the
language of passion and complaint, on the part of those
who were injured in purse or person by the persecuting
spirit of those days.

There may have been emissaries of Philip in England;
at that time Ballard might have been one of them, though
it is more probable that he was originally the dupe of
Walsingham's agents; but to involve all of his class and of
his communion in England, who received spiritual assistance
from the missionary body, in a series of treasonable conspiracies, was a proceeding that must for ever stamp the
character of Walsingham and Cecil with infamy of the
deepest dye.

A Welshman, a Dr. Parry, who had been in the service
of the Queen, had resided for several years abroad in the
capacity of a spy at foreign courts, " to collect and transmit secret intelligence for the use of the minister,"[*] (Lord
Burleigh,) had returned to England, married a rich widow,
ran through her fortune, attempted to rob and murder an
acquaintance, was saved from the doom he merited by the
influence probably of his patron, and again had resumed
his employment of a spy. About this time he obtained a
seat in Parliament, and when the bill was introduced
declaring it treason for a priest to come into England, and
felony to harbour one, " Parry boldly rose in his place and
denounced the bill as a measure savouring of treasons, full
of blood, danger, and despair to English subjects," &c.
His virtuous boldness astonished the house; he was immediately arrested, however, by order of the speaker, and
the next day was released by the Queen's command. Burleigh and his villain quarrelled; Parry was dissatisfied with
the smallness of his allowance, and his employer with the
small importance of his discoveries. He then proceeded to
France, embraced the Catholic creed at Lyons, and revealed
to the Jesuit who reconciled him his intention to kill the
Queen, if he was only satisfied of the legality of that act,
for the benefit of religion in the sight of God. Mr. Creigh-
ton, the Jesuit referred to, assured him it was not lawful to

* Lingard, Vol. v. p. 412.

commit murder. He proceeded to Venice, made a similar revelation to another Jesuit with the like result.

He fled from Italy to Paris, revealed his project to another priest named Morgan, who, according to his statements, approved of the scheme. He became again scrupulous, and was advised, he says, to consult Parsons, the Jesuit, and Dr. Allen of Rheims. The first he refused to see, but the latter, when he did see him, he felt too much disconcerted to open his mind to him, but he did so to some other priests, who disapproved of the design. He then applied to the nuncio at Paris, for an introduction to the Roman secretary of state, who gave him a letter to a cardinal. Furnished with this document he returned to England, with the view of reinstating himself in the good graces of her majesty. He accordingly informed her, that he had been solicited to assassinate her by a priest, and encouraged to do so by some others of his profession. He was so well received by the queen, that " he had the impudence to ask an employment about the court."* He showed her majesty a letter he had received, he said, from a cardinal, approving of his design. The queen was satisfied of the honesty of the man's intentions towards her. Walsingham and Burleigh allowed him, of course, to go at large. He proceeded in his work; entrapped, as he thought, a young gentleman of distinction, of the name of Neville, in another plot of his fabrication, to assassinate the queen.† Neville then was in the employment of Walsingham, and his occupation abroad was to watch the motions of the Jesuit, Parsons.

But Burleigh was an enemy of Neville. The latter was of the family of the Earl of Westmoreland, and claimed the inheritance of the last Lord Latymer, whose estate was in the possession of Lord Burleigh's eldest son. Parry, knowing the fact, inflamed the mind of Neville against Burleigh, and at the same time it would appear, from the proceedings of the parties, that Neville was instructed to blacken the character of Parry to the queen.

Thus Walsingham,—to whom
—   —   —   —   " it was most sweet,
When in one line two crafts directly meet"—

* Walsingham's Memoirs, p. 574.
† Lingard, Vol. v. p. 145.

having caused Parry to inveigle Neville, as he thought, into his schemes, had got Neville in his turn to ensnare Parry, and denounce him as a traitor.

Lingard says: "It appears to have been a trial of skill between two experienced impostors, which should be able to entangle the other in the toils. Parry's conduct, when taken before Walsingham, showed that he counted entirely on the queen's protection, and depended more on it than her minister's patronage. Walsingham allowed him, however, to be hanged. He was sacrificed partly for his arrogant and intractable behaviour, but chiefly for his unfitness for the business of importance. Walsingham was then engaged in the development of his schemes for involving Mary, Queen of Scots, in the charges of foreign conspiracies, which he was feeding and fomenting by his continental agents. This unfortunate wretch, Parry, died protesting the innocence of his intentions towards her majesty. He said on the scaffold: 'No evil thought ever came into his mind against her; she knoweth it, and her own conscience will tell her so.' In his letter to the queen he ends thus: '*Remember your unfortunate Parry, chiefly overthrown by your hand.*' "[*]

This passage was suppressed (says Strype) by the ministers in the printed copies. In his speech on the scaffold he declared that her majesty was cognizant of his intrigue with Neville.

The next year, 1585, one of the missionaries of Rheims, Father John Ballard, was taken up on a charge of conspiring to kill the queen. He had come into England under a feigned name, and, it was sworn to, in a military uniform. It appears that, from the time of his arrival in England, he was accompanied wherever he went by a young gentleman of Derbyshire, of the name of Babbington, "of worth, of good abilities, and knowledge," who had been on the continent, and affected there a great zeal for Catholicity and the interests of the Queen of Scots. Finding that Ballard (says the author of 'Walsingham's Memoirs') was bent on achieving the alleged exploit of his mission, "Babbington became jealous that another should have the infamous glory of killing a heretic sovereign, disapproved of Father Ballard's plot, and formed another, in

* Lingard, Vol. v. p. 416.

which he engaged many persons of consideration, of whom some were about the person of the queen."*

At this time, according to the author of the 'Memoirs,' he was a spy in Walsingham's employment. The author previously tells us, that it was one of Walsingham's perfections "to turn parties to his advantage, as well as his mistress's, and thus maintain them without advancing one faction or depressing another."

But another of his perfections was to get rid of parties who were inimical or useless to him by any means, however villanous they might be, within his reach. The young Derbyshire gentleman gave him an opportunity of putting some of these means in practice, in the getting up of a conspiracy of which he was to be made a victim. Babbington, however, was too young a man, too light in his behaviour and limited in mental capacity, to be trusted alone to carry into effect the widely-extended plans of a ministerial conspiracy against the Scottish queen.

It appears that a principal agent, in 1586, in this foul business, was a Roman Catholic priest of the name of Giffart. He was made to avow himself one of the conspirators who had been sent over from the continent to kill the queen. He betrayed his pretended accomplices, discovered everything that he had been instructed to disclose by Walsingham, and produced a number of letters alleged to be those of the conspirators, and also of Mary, Queen of Scots.

This miscreant Giffart was employed to corrupt the servants of the imprisoned Mary, and to open a correspondence with her two secretaries. His successful mission furnished Walsingham with the documents which brought Mary to the block.

Ballard was arrested, but Babbington was left at large ; he sought and obtained, what will surprise the reader, says Lingard, an asylum in the house of the secretary himself, with a promise of license to depart the realm that he might watch the conduct of the traitors abroad.

The author of 'Walsingham's Memoirs' says, he was so closely observed as to have no means of eluding those who watched him. "Under pretext," he says, "of discovering the conspiracy, Babbington had an audience of the queen,

* Walsingham's Memoirs, p. 575.

and, in consequence of it, liberty to go where he chose, accompanied by a man given for his protection, but really to prevent his escape."[*]

This villany must have been peculiarly atrocious; even Burleigh disapproved of Walsingham's conduct in this business, and the latter was obliged to justify himself for procrastinating by such means the complete discovery of the plot.

One of the confidential servants of Mary, Queen of Scots, was a spy of Walsingham's.[†] Her secretary mistrusted this man, and cautioned her against him; but Mary refused to listen to this warning, so that she was exposed to the treachery of a servant in her abode, and a pretended friend without, Babbington.

Through the medium of the infamous Giffart, a communication was made to her of an intended invasion, an insurrection, and an attempt on the life of Elizabeth; and a letter was either received from her addressed to Babbington, or a forged letter purporting to be written by her, approving of the projects; and this document was shown by Walsingham to Elizabeth. In the meantime, by a refinement in official wickedness worthy of this minister, Babbington, the agent and the tool of Walsingham, was sacrificed by the latter. He and thirteen others, including Ballard, were tried, condemned, and executed; and seven of the duped conspirators acknowledged the justice of their sentence.[‡]

It is painful to find an English liberal writer of eminence —Brown, the author of the History of the Penal Laws,— adducing as a gratifying proof of the humanity and mildness of the government of Queen Elizabeth, the *alleged* fact that in her reign only two persons, Anabaptists, were burned for heresy, while in the reign of Mary, he adds, the number of heretics executed for heresy, according to Fox, was 170, and to Hume, 77. But Mr. Brown, by mere accident of course, forgets to notice the executions in the reign

---

* Memoirs of Walsingham.
† Ibid.
‡ On the eleventh of November 1586, Mary Queen of Scots received a letter from Elizabeth, commanding her to submit herself to trial for a conspiracy against the Queen of England's life. The issue it is needless to mention. Walsingham's machinations and Elizabeth's diabolical policy triumphed. Another judicial murder was committed, that weighs heavily on the memory of both.

of Elizabeth, for Catholicism. The hangings, beheadings, bowellings, and quarterings, for that crime, though, in many cases, nominally for high treason.

The horrid effusion of blood in the reign of Elizabeth, on account, or rather on pretence of religion, far exceeded that which took place in the two preceding persecutions.

In her reign of forty-five years, more blood was spilt on the scaffold on charges of violation of the Penal Laws, than ever was shed in Portugal by the Inquisition of that country, during the whole term of its existence, little short of three centuries.*

Doctor Milner says, he "had collected the names of 204 persons, executed on that sole account, (religion), chiefly within the last twenty years of Elizabeth's reign.† Of this number 142 were priests, three were gentlewomen, and the remainder esquires and yeomen. Amongst them fifteen were condemned for denying the Queen's supremacy, 126 for the exercise of the priestly functions, and the rest for being reconciled to the Catholic faith, or for aiding and abetting priests. Besides these, I find a particular account, together with most of the names, of ninety priests and Catholic lay persons, who died in prison in the same reign ; and of 105 others who were sent into perpetual banishment. I say nothing of many more who were whipped, fined, or stripped of their property, to the utter ruin of their families."

"In one night, fifty Catholic gentlemen in the county of Lancaster, were suddenly seized, and committed to prison on account of their non-attendance at church. About the same time, I find an equal number of Yorkshire gentlemen lying prisoners in York Castle on the same account, most of whom perished there. Those were every week, for a twelvemonth together, dragged by main force to hear the established service performed in the Castle chapel. An account was published, by a contemporary writer, of 1200 Catholics who had been in some sort or other victims of this persecution, previously to the year 1588, that is to say, during the period of its greatest lenity."

The following account of some of the executions in her reign, is extracted from the "Historical Collections from

* The Inquisition of Portugal was established in the reign of John the Third, in 1535, and abolished in 1820.
† Letters to a Prebendary, Seventh Letter, p. 95, 96.

Protestant Historians, concerning the changes in Religion,"* and Stowe's Chronicle.

Two laymen and one priest were hanged, bowelled, and quartered, for denying the Queen's supremacy.†

Six priests were drawn from the Tower to Tyburn, and there hanged, bowelled, and quartered.‡

Four priests more were found guilty of high treason, in being made priests beyond the seas, and by the Pope's authority, and had judgment to be hanged, bowelled, and quartered: they were all executed at Tyburn.§

Two other priests were condemned for treason, for being made priests at Rheims, in France, were drawn to Tyburn, and there hanged, bowelled, and quartered.‖

As likewise two other priests were condemned and executed for the same cause.¶

Six priests more were executed, for being made priests beyond seas; and four secular men for being reconciled to the Roman Catholic Church; and four others for relieving and encouraging the others.

Moreover, thirteen secular men were, upon the same account, hanged in several places; and a gentleman for conveying a cord to a priest in Bridewell, whereby he let himself down and escaped.**

Another priest was hanged, headed, and quartered, at Kingston: and after this, two more for being made priests at Paris: and a secular man for being reconciled to the Church of Rome.†

There was another priest hanged for being made priest beyond the sea; and two secular men for relieving him. The priest was hanged, quartered, and bowelled, in Fleet-street, at Fetter-lane end.‡

Three priests more, with four others for relieving them, were executed: one of whom was Swithin Wells, gentleman.§

Another priest was convicted for being a priest, and reconciling a haberdasher, who was likewise convicted of high treason, for being so reconciled, and of felony for

---

* Hist. Coll. p. 236.
† Stow, p. 684, 685.
‡ Ibid. p. 695.　　　　§ Ibid. p. 698.
‖ Ibid. p. 719.　　　　¶ Ibid. p. 720.

** Ibid. p. 750.　　　　† Ibid. p. 750.
‡ Ibid. p. 761.　　　　§ Ibid. p. 764.

relieving the said priest. The priest was executed in St. Paul's Church-yard.*

Likewise another secular priest and a Jesuit, hanged, cut down alive, and then bowelled and quartered.†

One priest more, hanged, bowelled, and quartered, for being made priest beyond the seas. His head was set upon the pillory in Southwark, and his quarters in the highway, towards Newington and Lambeth.‡

A layman was hanged, bowelled, and quartered, for being reconciled to the Church of Rome ; and five priests more, were hanged and quartered for coming into this realm ; and with one of them, a gentleman was likewise executed, for relieving and lodging them in his house.§

Another priest, after seven years' imprisonment, was hanged and quartered for the same cause. Also the same day, and in the same place, was hanged a gentlewoman, for relieving a priest.‖

In Dr. Challoner's "Memoirs of Missionary priests," &c., it is stated that in Elizabeth's reign, from 1577 to 1603, the number of persons who suffered death on account of religion, in England, was 186, of whom 125 were priests. The author professes to take his statements from cotemporary accounts, and from manuscripts kept in the archives of the English convents. The names of the persons who suffered death, who were priests, are marked with an asterisk.

EXECUTIONS.

1577, Cuthbert Maine,* at Launceston.
1578, John Nelson,* at Tyburn.
   "   Thomas Sherwood, at ditto.
1581, Everard Hanse,* at ditto.
   "   Edmund Campion, Jes.* at ditto.
   "   Ralph Sherwyn,* at ditto.
   "   Alexander Briant, at ditto.
1582, John Paine,* Thomas Ford,* John Shert,* Robert Johnson, at Tyburn.

* Stow p. 764.   † Ibid. pp. 766-769.
‡ Ibid. p. 788.   § Ibid. p. 790.
‖ Ibid. p. 795.

1582, Thomas Cottam,* William Felby,* Luke Kirby,*
    Lau. Johnson, at Tyburn.
" W. Lacy,* R. Kirkman,* J. Thomson,* burned at
    York.†
1583, Richard Shirkill, and W. Hart,* executed at York.
" John Bode, M.A., at Andover.
" J. Slade, Schoolmaster, at Winchester.
1584, J. Bell,* and J. Finch, at Lancaster.
— " R. White, Schoolmaster, at Wrexham.
" Dr. Lancaster, at ditto.
" W. Carter, Printer, G. Haydock,* J. Fen,* T.
    Hemerford,* J. Munden,* and J. Nutter,* at
    Tyburn.
1585, T. Alfield,* T. Webbey, at Tyburn.
" H. Taylor,* M. Bowes, Gent., at York.
1586, E. Transon,* N. Woodfen, alias Wheeler,* at
    Tyburn.
" Margaret Clitheroe, Gentlewoman, at York.
" R. Sergeant, alias Long,* W. Thompson, alias Black-
    burn,* at Tyburn.
" R. Anderton, W. Marsden,* at the Isle of Wight.
" F. Ingelby, J. Finglow,* at York.
" J. Sandys,* at Gloucester.
" J. Law, J. Adams,* R. Dibdale, at Tyburn.
" R. Bickerdike, Gent., and R. Langley, Esq., at York.
1587, T. Pilchard,* at Dorchester.
" E. Sykes,* at York.
" R. Sutton,* at Stafford.
" S. Roushem,* at Gloucester.
" J. Hambley, at Chard.
" G. Douglass,* and A. Crow, at York.
1588, W. Deane,* H. Webley, at Mile-end Green.
" W. Gunter,* at the Theatre.
" H. Moore, Esq., R. Morton,* at Lincoln's Inn
    Fields.
" T. Holford, or Acton,* at Clerkenwell.
" J. Clarkson,* T. Felton, Gent., at Hounslow.
" R. Lee,* E. Shelley, Gent., R. Martyn, R. Flower,
    J. Rock, and Margaret Ward, Gentlewoman, at
    Tyburn.
" W. Way,* at Kingston.

† Memoirs of Missionary Priests.—Introduction.

1588, R. Wilcocks,* Edward Campian,* C. Buxton,* and
    R. Widmerpoole, Gent., at Canterbury.
" R. Crocket,* and E. James,* at Chichester.
" J. Robinson,* at Ipswich.
" W. Hartley,* near the Theatre.
" J. Weldon,* Miles-end Green.
" R. Sutton, Schoolmaster, at Clerkenwell.
" R. Williams,* at Holloway.
" E. Burdon,* and J. Hewet,* at York.
" W. Lampley, at Gloucester.
" N. Garlick,* R. Ludlam,* R. Simpson,* at Derby.†
1589, J. Amias,* and R. Dalby, at York.
" G. Nichols,* and R. Yaxley,* at Oxford.
" T. Belson, Gent., H. Pritchard, W. Spencer,* and
    R. Hardesley, at York.
1590, C. Bales,* at Fleet Street.
" N. Horner, at Smithfield.
" A. Blake, Gray's Inn lane.
" M. Gerard,* and F. Dickinson, burned at Rochester.
" E. Jones,* executed in Fleet Street.
" A. Middleton,* at Clerkenwell.
" E. Ducke,* R. Holliday,* J. Hogge, and R. Hill, at
    Durham.
1591, R. Thorpe,* and T. Watkinson, Yeoman, at York.
" M. Scot,* and G. Beesley,* in Fleet Street.
" R. Dickenson,* and R. Milliner, at Winchester.
" W. Pike, at Dorchester.
" E. Jennings,* and S. Wells,* at Gray's Inn Fields.
" E. White,* Polydore Plasden,* B. Lacy, Gent.,
    J. Mason, and S. Hodson, at Tyburn.
1592, W Patteson,* at Tyburn.
" T. Portmore,* at St. Paul's.
" R. Ashton, Gent., at Tyburn.
1593, E. Waterson,* at Newcastle.
" J. Bird, Gent., at Winchester.
" A. Page,* at York.
" J. Lampton,* at Newcastle.
" W. Davis, at Beaumaris.
1594, J. Speed, at Durham.

† In the year above mentioned, 1588, Father Robert Parsons, in his
" Relacion de Algunos Martyrios en Inglaterra," published in 1590, p.
21, gives a list of twenty-eight Catholic priests martyred, all educated
in the Irish Seminaries of Rheims and Rome, and twelve laymen.

1594, W. Harrington,* at Tyburn.
"   Cornelius John, alias Mohun, Jes.* T. Bosgrave,
         Gent., J. or T. Carey, P. Salmon, at Dorchester.
"   J. Bost,* at Durham.
"   J. Ingram,* at Newcastle.
"   G. Swallowell,* a converted minister, at Darlington.
"   E. Osbaldiston,* York.
1595, R. Southwell,* Jes., A. Rawlins,* at York.
"   H. Walpole,* at York.
"   J. Atkinson, and W. Freeman,* at Warwick.
1596, G. Errington, Gent.,. W. Knight, W. Gibson, and
         H. Abbot, Yeoman, at York.
1597, W. Audleby,* at York.
"   T. Warcop and E. Fulthrop, gent., at York.
1598, J. Britton, gent., at York.
"   P. Snow,* R. Grimston, at York.
"   J. Jones, alias Buckley,* at St. Thomas' Watering.
"   C. Robinson,* at Carlisle.
"   R. Horner,* at York.
1600, C. Wharton,* at York.
"   J. Rigby, gent., at St. Thomas' Watering.
"   T. Sprott,* and T. Hunt,* at Lincoln.
"   R. Nutter,* and E. Thwing, at Lancaster.
"   T. Palasor, * J. Norton, gent., and J. Talbot, gent.,
         at Durham.
1601, J. Pibush,* at St. Thomas' Watering.
"   M. Lambert,* alias Harkworth, R. Filcock,* Jes., and
         Anne Line, gentlewoman, at Tyburn.
"   H. Thurston,* and R. Middleton,* at Lancaster.
"   N. Tichburn, gent., and T. Hackshot, at Tyburn.
1603, W. Richardson,* alias Anderson, at Tyburn. This
         was the last martyrdom in this bloody reign.

Thus the total number of Catholics put to death in the
reign of Elizabeth, from 1577 to 1603, amounted to 204,
according to Milner, of which number, he says, 142 were
priests. "The True Memorial," makes the number 186,
and that of priests, 125. Lingard states, that in a period
of fourteen years, from the defeat of the Armada, in July,
1588, to the decease of Elizabeth, "sixty-one clergymen,
forty-seven laymen, and two gentlewomen, suffered capital
punishment for some or other of the spiritual treasons and
felonies which had been lately created."

8

"The author of a tract entitled 'The execution of justice in England, for the maintenance of publique and Christian peace, without any persecutions for questions of Religion, published in 1581, and re-printed in Somers's Tracts, speaking of the execution of the Catholics, in the reign of Elizabeth, observes, 'And, to make the matter seem more terrible, they recite the particular names of all the persons, which by their own catalogue exceeds not, for these twenty-five years' space, above the number of three-score.' Camden, however, (though certainly an apologist for the errors of Elizabeth), admits that within ten years fifty priests were executed and fifty-five banished."[*]

"As to the names and numbers of the other Catholics, as well as of the clergy as of the laity, who under the same reign, were either deprived of their livings, or suffered loss of their estates, imprisonments, banishments, &c., it is impossible to set them down all.[†] Dr. Bridgwater, in a table published at the end of the 'Concertatio Ecclesiæ Catholicæ,' gives the names of about 1200 who had suffered in this manner, before the year 1588, that is, before the heat of the persecution. In this list there are three archbishops, including two of Ireland; eighteen bishops, consecrated or elect; one abbot; four whole communities of religious; thirteen deans; sixty presbyters; five hundred and thirty priests; forty-nine doctors of divinity; eighteen doctors of law; and fifteen masters of colleges: eight earls; ten lords; twenty-six knights; three hundred and twenty-six gentlemen; and about sixty ladies and gentlewomen. Many of these died in prison, and several under the sentence of death. We shall here add, by way of conclusion of this first part, the names of those who were not executed, whose sufferings for religion are briefly touched on in our Memoirs.

"Ailworth, an Irish gentlemen, died in jail.
Arundel, Sir John, cast into prison.
Arundel, Earl of, sentenced to death,—died in prison.
Barnet, Mr., condemned to die.
Bennet, John, priest, imprisoned, tortured, banished.
Bishop, William, imprisoned, afterwards banished.
Bosgrave, Soc. Jes., sentenced to death,—banished.
Caufield, Bennet, friar, imprisoned,—banished.

* Brown's Penal Laws, Note.
† Memoirs of Missionary Priests.—Contents.

Catholic prisoners in York Castle, dragged to Protestant sermons.

Chaplain, William, priest, died in prison.

Clifton, Thomas, priest, condemned to perpetual imprisonment.

Cooper, John, perished in the Tower.

Collins, John, bookseller, condemned to die.

Cornish Gentleman, (query, Tregian), cast in a præmunire.

Cotesmore, Thomas, priest, perished in prison.

Crowther, Thomas, priest, died in prison.

Dymock, Esq., Champion of England, died in prison.

Feckenwell, Abbot of Westminster, died in a prison.

Fenn, Robert, priest, imprisoned, racked, banished.

Harrington, John, priest, died in prison.

Hart, John, priest, cruelly used in jail,—banished.

Hatton, Richard, priest, condemned to perpetual imprisonment.

Holmes, Robert, priest, perished in the Tower.

Hunt, Eleanor, sentenced to death for harbouring a priest.

Jenks, Rowland, condemned to lose his ears.

Jetter, John, priest, died in prison.

Lancashire Gentleman imprisoned

Lomax, James, priest, perished in prison.

Maskew, Bridget, condemned to be burned.

Mettham, Thomas, priest, S. J., died in prison.

Norton, Mrs., sentenced to death for relieving a priest.

Orton, —, sentenced to death,—banished.

Pounds, Thomas, Esq., suffered greatly for religion.

Pole, Edward, priest, died in prison.

Priests, seventy banished in 1585.

Priests, several banished in 1603.

Priests, thirty committed to Wisbech Castle.

Pugh, John, condemned to die.

Pugh, Henry, gentleman, cruelly tortured.

Rishton, Edward, priest, sentenced to death.

Shelley, Mrs., died in the Marshalsea.

Sherton, Martin, priest, died in prison.

Steile, James, priest, cruelly treated,—banished.

Tesse, Anne, sentenced to be burned for persuading a minister to turn Catholic.

Vaux, Lawrence, Warden of Manchester, died in jail.

Wakeman, Roger, priest, died in jail.

Watson, Richard, priest, cruelly treated in jail.

Wells, Mrs., died in jail under sentence of death.

Williamson, Thomas, priest, sentenced to perpetual imprisonment.

Wiseman, Mrs., condemned to death.

Yates, Edward, Esq., of Berkshire, with six other gentlemen, cast into prison.

Tregian, Francis, Esq., of Cornwall, stripped of a plentiful estate, and condemned to perpetual imprisonment."[*]

This last case is taken out of the alphabetical order of Dr. Challoner's list, for the purpose of referring more particularly to it in the following chapter.

CHAPTER VIII.

THE PROGRESS OF PERSECUTION IN ENGLAND IN THE REIGN OF ELIZABETH. NOTICE OF THE MARTYRDOM OF FATHER CUTHBERT MAINE, SOC. JES., AND OF THE SUFFERINGS OF FRANCIS TREGIAN.

THE case of Father Cuthbert Maine, and of Francis Tregian, furnishes data from which a correct general idea may be formed of the persecution that was carried on against the Catholic clergy and laity in those times.

The account of the sufferings of the two persons referred to, may serve, in an especial manner, for a general portraiture of the terrible oppression practised in this reign, and the heroism with which its most iniquitous acts were encountered.

The fate of Mr. Francis Tregian, of Valveden, or Golden, near Truro, in the county of Cornwall, is closely connected with the history of Father Cuthbert Maine, of Douay College, the first missionary priest who suffered in England, in 1577. Gentlemen of England, read this brief notice of the sufferings and the virtue of one of your order in those times, when Elizabeth was baptizing your creed in blood, and persecuting to the death, the best, the noblest, and the most virtuous people of the land.

The author of "The Memoirs of Missionary Priests," states, that his notice of the proto-martyr of the English

* Memoirs of Missionary Priests.

Missionaries, is taken from a short account of him in English, *published in* 1582, and a more ample account of him in a Latin manuscript of Douay College, written by an intimate friend of the martyr. The substance of this memoir is to the following effect.

Mr. Maine was born near Barnstaple, in Yalston parish, Devonshire; he was brought'up in the Protestant religion at Oxford, became convinced there of the errors of his faith, but "withal a persuaded Catholic, continued yet . in the same College for some years,"[*] and there took out his degree of Master of Arts. He corresponded with Mr. Edmund Campion, the Jesuit, who was then on the Continent, and was invited by the latter to Douay. The letter with this invitation, fell into the hands of the Bishop of London, who immediately sent to Oxford to have Maine and others arrested. Maine, however, escaped to Douay, where he was ordained, and after some time, was sent in 1576, on the mission into England, by the President of the College, afterwards Cardinal Allen. On his arrival in his own country, he was received into the house of a virtuous Catholic gentleman of distinction, *Mr. Francis Tregian, of Valveden,* or Golden, five miles from Truro, in Cornwall; where he passed in those evil times for the steward of this gentleman.

In June, 1577, the Bishop of Exeter, being on his visitation at Truro, was requested by the Sheriff of the County and others, to aid them in searching Mr. Tregian's house, "where Mr. Maine did lye." The Sheriff, the Bishop's Chancellor, and divers gentlemen and their servants, came to Mr. Tregian's house on pretence of seeking for a criminal who had fled into Cornwall. Mr. Tregian answered the Sheriff that the fugitive was not there, "and swore by his faith, that he knew not where he was, further adding, that he thought it great discourtesy to have his house searched, for he was a gentleman, and they bore ho commission from the Queen for this proceeding." The Sheriff swore by all the oaths he could devise, that he would search the house, or kill, or be killed in the attempt, "holding his dagger, as if he would have stabbed it into the gentleman."

The house was searched. The first chamber they went

* Memoirs of Missionary Priests, p. 11. et seq.

into was that of Mr. Maine, which being fast shut, "they bounced and beat," till it was opened by Mr. Maine, who was in the garden when he first heard the uproar, and might have escaped had he chosen to do so.

The Sheriff seized him by the breast, and said to him, "What art thou?" He answered, "I am a man." Whereat the Sheriff being very hot, asked, "If he had a coat of mail under his doublet? And so unbuttoning it, he found an Agnus Dei about his neck, which he took from him, and called him traitor and rebel, and many other opprobrious names." They carried him, his books and papers, to the Bishop, by whom he was examined, but nothing against him appears to have been elicited by his examination. He was then taken to Launceston, where he was imprisoned, cruelly treated, and kept chained to the posts of a bed with large gyves about his legs.

"He remained in prison from June to Michaelmas, at which time the judges came their circuit. The Earl of Bedford was also present at Mr. Maine's arraignment, and did deal most in the matter."

* This was not the first service of the Earl, of this description.

The charges brought against Mr. Maine at his trial were—

1. That he had published, in Mr. Tregian's house, a bull from the Pope, of a treasonable nature. (This charge was fabricated on the mere fact of the discovery of a papal bull among his papers; a copy of the one of the Jubilee, which had been published the preceding year.)

2. That he maintained the usurped power of the Pope, and denied the Queen's supremacy.

3. That he had brought into England an Agnus Dei, and had given it to Mr. Tregian.

4. That he had said Mass in Mr. Tregian's house.

There were no sufficient proofs of the truth of any of the charges, but the judges, in bad times, ever pander to tyrannic power; and faithless to the interests of justice, corrupt, overbearing, and merciless, were true to their character on this occasion. "Judge Manhood, who behaved himself very partially in the whole trial, directed the jury to bring the prisoner in guilty of the charges in the indictment,"* saying, "THAT WHERE PLAIN PROOFS WERE WANTING, STRONG PRESUMPTIONS OUGHT TO TAKE PLACE."†

The jury had been chosen for the purpose of conviction, (there were political Recorders, and partisan Sheriffs in those days), "because he was a Catholic Priest." After "the twelve good men and true," or as we call them in our times, "*jurors of the right sort,*" had given in their verdict of guilty, and Judge Manhood had pronounced sentence of death, Mr. Maine lifted up his hands and eyes to heaven, and said, with a calm and cheerful countenance,—"Deo Gratias."

He was to have been executed within fifteen days, but his execution was deferred till St. Andrew's day, *Judge Jefferies being dissatisfied with the proceedings of his colleague.*

There was an appeal to all the judges, but they disagreed ; it was sent to the Council however, and the latter concluded that the prisoner should be executed "FOR A TERROR TO THE PAPISTS." The *worthy* Sheriff of Cornwall, who was knighted for his late services, procured the death warrant to be signed, which he sent into the country to the Justices.

Three days before Mr. Maine's trial, a servant had come to him and told him to prepare for death, for he was to be executed within three days at farthest. Mr. Maine took the notice kindly, he said—"If he had any thing to give the man, he would rather bestow it on him than any body else, for he had done more for him by his information, than any one had ever rendered to him."

He gave himself up from that time to prayer and meditation, and with the exception of the intermission of a few hours snatched from what seemed to be the business of his life—devotion, his remaining days and nights were spent in prayer. Many gentlemen and justices came to him on the morning of his execution, and brought with them two ministers to reason with him.

He replied to their arguments and confuted them; but the justices and gentlemen falsely affirmed that the ministers were much more learned than the prisoner. His life was offered to him that morning, if he would renounce his religion, which he calmly refused to do. He was then pressed to acknowledge the Queen's supremacy, assuring him of his life if he would make this declaration; upon

* Memoirs of Missionary Priests.
† Lingard confirms this statement of the Judge's charge.

which he took a bible out of the hands of one of the gentlemen, made the sign of the cross upon it, then kissed it, and said—" *The Queen never was, nor is, nor ever shall be the head of the Church of England.*"

He was then drawn to the place of execution, about a quarter of a mile distant. At setting out, when they were placing him on the sledge, " some of the justices moved the sheriff's deputy that he would cause the prisoner's head to be laid over the edge, so that it might be trailed against the stones in drawing, and MR. MAINE OFFERED HIMSELF THAT IT MIGHT BE SO, but the sheriff's deputy would not suffer it. The name of this deputy one longs in vain to know. Did his descendants prosper? Did his humanity bring a blessing on his children? Or. is it only merit like that of the noble Earl, who was the great terrorist of those times, which has been embalmed in the indignant eloquence of Edmund Burke, and damned therein to everlasting fame, that brings with it its reward.

When the prisoner was brought to the place of execution, (the market-place of Launceston), where they had erected a very high gibbet, on being taken from the sledge, he knelt down and prayed. When they had placed him on the ladder, and the rope was put round his neck, he would have spoken to the people, but the justices would not suffer him. They desired him to say his prayers, which he did very devoutly: and as the hangman was about to turn the ladder, one of the justices spoke to him in these terms,— " Now villain and traitor, thou knowest thou shalt die, therefore tell us truly whether Mr. Tregian and Sir John Arundel, did know those things thou art condemned for ; and what also thou dost know of them ?"

Mr. Maine answered mildly, " I know nothing of Mr. Tregian and Sir John Arundel, but that they are good and godly gentlemen ; and as for the things I am condemned for, they are only known to me and to no other." Then as they were casting him off the ladder, he knocked his breast, saying, " In manus tuas," &c.

Some of the gentlemen would *have had him cut down immediately, and quartered whilst he was alive,** but the sheriff's

---

* The State Trials, Milner's Treatise, and the Memoirs of Missionary Priests, leave no doubt whatever of the fact, that similar barbarities were frequently practised at the executions of Catholics in this reign.

deputy would not consent, he let him hang till he was dead. The Latin manuscript of Douay states, that he was cut down alive, but falling from the beam, which was of an unusual height, he fell heavily and struck his head against the side of the scaffold where he was to be quartered, and consequently was almost dead, and insensible of the butchery which then ensued. His head was cut off, and when the other mutilations were performed, his quarters were disposed of, and sent to Bodwin, Tregny, Barnstable, and Launceston Castle; his head was set on a pole at the highway of Wadebridge. Stowe, the stoic annalist of the atrocities of those times, in his chronicle of this year, thus coolly writes of the judicial murder of Mr. Maine. "Nov. 9th, 1577; Cuthbert Maine was hanged, drawn, and quartered, at Launceston, in Cornwall, for preferring Roman power."

Let us see what the author of the "Memoirs of Missionary Priests," says of the fate of the unfortunate Cornwall gentleman, who was cast into prison for having the charity to succour and shelter a persecuted priest of his persuasion.

"Mr. Tregian,* the gentleman who had entertained him, (Maine), lost his estate, which was very considerable, for his religion, and was condemned to perpetual imprisonment; and several of his neighbours and servants were cast in a præmunire, as abettors and accomplices of Mr. Maine. Sir John Arundel was also persecuted and cast into prison on this occasion."†

Doubtless, Gentlemen of England, you will imagine that a man of such respectability, with such "a plentiful estate," as Mr. Francis Tregian, of Golden, could not have long remained in prison for exercising that old English virtue on which your ancestors prided themselves, and especially towards a man in misfortune and a native of his own country! For this, you will say, was in "the golden days of good Queen Bess," and she would not have suffered one of the lords of the land of Old England, to lie

* Memoirs of Missionary Priests, Vol. i. p. 20.
† Lingard, in speaking of Mr. Tregian says, he was cast in a Premunire, his large estate was taken by the Queen, but he was mistaken in stating that "the unfortunate gentleman languished till death in a prison."—History of England, 4to. Edition, Vol. v. p. 376.

for any length of time in a dungeon, and keep his plentiful estate from him, except for the short period of
his imprisonment, with the view of deterring others of
meaner quality from harbouring traitors in the guise of
Popish priests! Doubtless, Gentlemen of England, you
will presume that intercession was made for him in high
quarters, by his rich friends in Cornwall, and the result of
such intercession with a gracious Queen, and one of glorious memory, was his restoration to liberty, his family,
and his estate. And yet you would be utterly mistaken.
In the work referred to, no further mention is made of the
unfortunate old gentleman. Lingard speaks of him, but is
mistaken in saying that he died in confinement. Yet the
sequel of his story may be told from a record of the cruelty
of Elizabeth, and of the virtue of her victim, written on
stone, on the tomb of Francis Tregian in a foreign land,
where by accident it was discovered by the author of this
work.

In the church of S. Roque, in Lisbon, the church of the
suppressed convent of the Jesuits, there is, on the left hand
side of the aisle, not far from the principal entrance, a sepul-
chral stone, set in the wall in a vertical position, covering the
tomb of Mr. Tregian. The inscription states, that AFTER
AN IMPRISONMENT OF TWENTY-SEVEN YEARS, on account of his
fidelity to his religion, after great sufferings and the loss of
all his property, he terminated his days in Lisbon, in 1607,
"WITH A GREAT FAME FOR SANCTITY." And that after seventeen
years his remains had lain in that church, in 1605 his
body was found entire and uncorrupted, and was re-interred
the following year where it now lies.

Father Maine was arrested in 1577. Tregian was committed to prison the same time. He was imprisoned
twenty-seven years, consequently his liberation must have
taken place in 1604, about a year after the death of the
persecuting Queen, and it appears that he only survived his
liberation three years.

The following is a copy of the inscription on his tomb:

✝

"Aqui esta em pè o Corpo de Dom Francisco Tregian,
Fidalgo Ingres, mui illustro o qual depois de confisca dos
seus estados è grandes trabalhos padecidos en 28 annos de

presam polle defesa de fè Catolica em Inglaterra, na perse-
cucao da Rainha Isabella, anno de 1607, a 25 de Decem-
bro, morreo na esta Cidade de Lisboa, con grande fama de
Santidade, avendo 17 annos, que estava sepultado nesta
igreja de S. Roque da Compania de Jesus, no anno de
1625, aos 25 April, se achava seu corpo inteiro e incor-
rupto è foi collocado neste lugar pellos Ingreses Catolicos
residente, neste Cidade, os 25 de April, de 1626.''

No more was to be learned there of Francis Tregian ;
but in another country the history of his sufferings was
brought to the knowledge of the author. In the catalogue
of the National Library, in Madrid, he found mention made
of a Life of Tregian, entitled, "Vida de D. Fran. Tregeon,
Fr. F. Plunquetus, (auctor), Sevilla." Two days in vain
were spent in ransacking the library for this work, but
unfortunately the book was not to be found. In Lisbon,
however, a copy of it was discovered by him in the hands of
the President of the English College, taken from a reprint
of the work which existed a few years ago in the library of
the convent of Jesus, and by the kindness of that gentleman, the author was permitted the use of it.

The title is, " Heroum Speculum de vita D. D. Francisco
Tregeon. Edidit F. Fran. Plunquettus Hibernus, ordinis
S. Bernardi, nepos ejus maternus Olispone, 1655."

This little work, notwithstanding its barbarous Latinity,
is highly interesting. We learn from it that Tregian was
connected with the Arundel family, was married to a
daughter of Viscount Stourton, and was a frequenter of the
Court of Elizabeth.

He had the misfortune to become, unconsciously, the
object of one of those attachments for her courtiers, which
persons of comely looks and portly persons, about the
palace, were but too often the victims of. Elizabeth's passion for Tregian, was one of head-long violence,—" Amoris
peste corripitur." She would have him lodged near the
palace, and when the "incendium amoris " was at its
height, she endeavoured to persuade Tregian to allow her
to create him a Viscount, which he constantly refused.

At length the vehemence of her passion led to scenes of
violent advances on one side, and of virtuous resistance on
the other, which terminated on the part of her Majesty, in
hatred of the man who dared to repel the favour of a

Queen, and a determination to be revenged of him. Letters, by the Queen's special orders, were despatched to the authorities in Cornwall, to have Tregian and all his family arrested, and these order were carried into execution with barbarous rigour, the 8th of June, 1599.

In prison, in chains, subjected to all kinds of indignities, separated from a beloved wife and children, cut off from all communication with friends and relatives, twenty-seven years of cruel sufferings were endured by him with all the bravery of spirit, dignity of mind, and resignation, that became a christian gentleman. Prayer was his only occupation and recreation. In his daily form of prayer, to which it would be impossible to find any thing superior in point of elevation of language and of thought—his earnest supplication to God is to take away from him all sense of fear, all feelings of pusillanimity, so that he might bear all that the malice of his enemies might do against him, as it became a christian man to endure persecution.—" Deus Immortalis! Solamen peccatorum abige a me procul omnem pusillanimitatis speciem nec me obruat servilis metus."......

The cruelties inflicted on him were of the most revolting kind ; at times he was immured in a filthy dungeon, on one occasion for three months, on a charge of attempting his escape, after suffering personal violence at the hands of his jailers.   At length, after a persecution of twenty-seven years and upwards, he was set at liberty, deprived of all his property ; for this had been confiscated soon after his imprisonment.

The ambassador of Philip III. of Spain, was commissioned by his master to offer this unfortunate gentleman an asylum in his dominions ; the offer was gratefully accepted, and he was received at Madrid with all the honour and respect due to his virtue and his former position in society. A liberal monthly allowance was made by the king for his subsistence, in a manner suitable to his rank. Shortly after his arrival, he was seized with illness. Change of air was recommended by the physicians, and Lisbon was the place he was advised to proceed to. There his life was spent in holiness and works of mercy, and especially in relieving the unfortunate Irish refugees, who at that time crowded Lisbon.

He died as he lived, in the odour of sanctity, in his sixtieth year, the 25th of September, 1608.

His remains (adds his biographer) were interred in the Jesuit's church of St. Roch's, in a marble sepulchre, and after seventeen years, when that tomb was opened, his body was found in a perfect state of preservation.

D. D. Philippa, and D. D. Jacob Plunket, to whom a portion of the shroud, which retained its original appearance, had been sent to Ireland as a relic, presented the same to his widow. A host of miraculous cures, alleged to have been made by similar relics taken from his remains when his tomb was opened, are detailed in the biography, which occupy no small portion of the narrative. These, at least, are evidences of the fame of his holy life.

In these times of hero worship, of war and warrior idolatry, the eclat of the virtue of Francis Tregian, the man "of a great fame for piety," of unshaken fidelity to his religion, of constancy invincible in sufferings, and triumphant over them, has now little chance of renown. The merit of the christian chivalry, moreover, of Cuthbert Maine will sink to the dust, it may be, in our days, in comparison with the glory of great military prowess, no matter how acquired. There may be some persons, however, who would prefer the simple record of the merit of exalted virtue on the tomb of Francis Tregian, or the remembrance of the dignified bearing and christian chivalry of Cuthbert Maine, to all the trophies that are destined to adorn the statues and the sepulchres of successful soldiers. There may be some who will not laugh to scorn the idea of the virtue of the old Cornish gentleman, and the valour of the other intrepid soldier of the Cross being on a par with any qualities which belong to military heroes.

The day will come when the memories of the persecuted missionary priests of England will be honoured in their own land, and the exploits of the heroes who are now the gods of our idolatry, will be remembered, perhaps, with less admiration than theirs. Even now in the Church that persecuted theirs, there are enlightened members, christian men, who would set a higher value on the fame of those martyrs than all the glory that ever gathered over the eagles of Napoleon, that fell to the share of Picton and Davoust, or was gained by the sabre of Murat; who would deem all worldly honour of small account compared with that of having bravely borne the banner of that Cross which the pious Maine died on the scaffold under the folds of, and the man of great fame for sanctity, the venerable Tregian, sunk beneath, after his long sufferings in a foreign land.

We read with horror of the excesses in the mass, of the monsters of the French revolutionary tribunals, and we turn with complacency from the details of each individual case of savagery at home. The case which is the subject of this chapter was one only, of barbarity and injustice, perpetrated in a single instance. This was only the judicial murder of one man—the killing only of one priest. This was not a *noyade*—a fusilade of priests—a file of clergymen shot down in flank, raked by artillery in a narrow passage, like the clerical *aristocrats* of Avignon. This was not a French revolution massacre of the ministers of religion in the mass! No: but it was one of a hundred and twenty-five butcheries of priests in a period of twenty-five years—a period which we speak of as the brightest in the annals of English history.

We blush for the barbarities of Frenchmen and of Spaniards: we lament their blindness and national faults and follies; let us reserve our shame and sorrow for the horrors of our own history. We need not recur to the pages of French or Spanish historians, for details of crimes committed by monsters in the human form. We find them in our own. Our Burleighs, our Walsinghams, and their subordinate agents have left us in no ignorance of such enormities.

> "Oh, what are these?
> Death's ministers; not men, who thus deal death
> Inhumanly to men, and multiply
> Ten thousand fold the sin of him who slew
> His brother: for of whom such massacre
> Make they but of their own brethren—men of men."*

.* Milton's Paradise Lost.

CHAPTER IX.

THE PROGRESS OF PERSECUTION IN ENGLAND IN THE REIGN OF ELIZABETH. NOTICE OF THE MARTYRDOM OF FATHER EDMUND CAMPION, SOC. JES., AND OF FATHER RALPH SHERWINE, OF THE SAME ORDER.

EDMUND Campion, a native of London, pursued his academical studies in St. John's College, Oxford, with much credit, and left it with the reputation of an eminent classic scholar.

After having taken deacon's orders he travelled into Ireland, made himself somewhat acquainted with the history of that country, and wrote a work on it pretty much in the spirit of all the writings of his countrymen at that time, in relation to Ireland.

Bishop Nicholson says, Campion's two books of the History of Ireland were written in 1570, and furnished the materials chiefly for Hollingshed's Irish Annals. His writings were commended by the latter "for the clearness of their style, though he complains of their brevity." "Stannihurst" (Nicholson states) gives this character of his intimate friend Campion. "He was a rare clerk, upright in conscience, deep in judgment, and ripe in eloquence." But not even the literary character of Campion, nor the consideration which one man of letters ought to meet with from another, could save the memory of this murdered man from the base malignity of the literary bishop. He ridicules the idea of his death being designated a martyrdom, and calls him "an apostate and a traiterous Jesuite." Literature has no humanizing effect on bigots and hypocrites; of its influence over the minds of such persons, it cannot be said "Emollit mores, nec sinit esse feros."

While Campion was in Ireland, the high repute of Douay College attracted his attention to its objects and missions. The exclusion of Catholics from the universities, the imprisonment and proscription of the clergy, had left England destitute of pastors; and as the old priests were fast dropping off, there was no means of filling up their places, so that the people must have been soon left destitute of spiritual assistance, if some means were not taken to prevent that evil.

Dr. William Allen, afterwards Cardinal Allen, conceived the idea of instituting seminaries abroad, for training up priests for the home mission, and with the authority of Pius V. he founded an English seminary in Douay, in 1568, which was the parent of all the other English, (and I believe) Irish institutions of a similar kind and for similar objects on the continent.

The British government, however, prevailed on the Dutch authorities to withdraw their sanction from this institution. The English seminary at Douay was transferred to Rheims, in 1578, after having sent fifty-two priests on the mission. The same year it sent twelve more, and the year following twenty others. Other colleges for the education of youth, and training up of students for the home missions, sprung up at Salamanca, in 1582 ; at Seville and Valladolid, in 1589 ; Alcala at the close of the sixteenth century ; St. Omer's for the education of youth, in 1594 ; Paris, an Irish college, that of the Lombards, (originally for Italians) in 1676, rebuilt in 1681, and abandoned about a century later for the present establishment in the Rue d'Irlande ; Rome, an English college, in 1576, and subsequently an Irish and a Scotch one. At Lisbon an English college for secular ecclesiastics, instituted in 1628, by Ralph Stiefield, a Staffordshire gentleman, condemned to death in Elizabeth's reign for his faith, but eventually banished. Another Dominican one in Lisbon for Irish students, in 1639 ; another named St. Patrick's College for secular priests ; and Seminaries likewise in Bourdeaux, founded in 1603, and also in Nantes and Toulouse.

The hatred of Walsingham of the seminaries abroad for English Priests was so great, that amongst other attempts to effect their ruin, it is stated by Ribadaneira, in his History of the Schism,* and by Dr. Champney, that he (Walsingham) once by his emissaries, procured to have the wells poisoned which supplied the college of Rheims with water,

---

* Historia de Scisma, &c.

with the view of destroying the priests and students ; and that another time he caused poison to be given to Dr. Allen, the first president of that community. But the Providence of God defeated these and many others of his plots. This seminary of Rheims, and the similar one in Rome, Ribadaneira states, previous to Walsingham's death, had sent 380 Missionary Priests (chiefly Jesuits) into England.

Mr. Campion proceeded to Douay, entered on his studies there for the priesthood, and became bachelor of Divinity. He then entered the Society of Jesus, went to Rome in 1573, was sent to Bohemia, where he was ordained, and abode there seven years, faithfully labouring in that mission. He returned to Rheims in 1580, was prevailed on by Dr. Allen to make England the scene of his future labours, and set out for that country accompanied with the well-known Jesuit, Father Robert Parsons.

When Parsons and Campion arrived in England, the queen's proclamation against priests from foreign countries had been recently published. Before they separated, each of them committed to paper the motives which had induced him to visit England, and committed to a respective friend this explanatory paper, with an injunction not to publish it unless the writer was arrested. One of the parties confided in betrayed his trust, or mistook its nature; he published the paper of Campion under the title of a letter addressed to the Lords of the Council. " In it," says Lingard, " the missionary asserted that he was solely come to exercise his spiritual functions, and had been strictly forbidden to meddle with worldly concerns or affairs of state, and requested permission to dispute on religion before the queen, the council, and the two universities, and declared that all the Jesuits in the world had made a holy league to brave every danger, suffer every kind of torment, and shed their blood, if it were necessary, for the restoration and propagation of the Catholic faith."*

The latter part of this declaration was of very questionable prudence. It is difficult to conceive a man of Campion's character, setting his signature to a cartel of this kind not altogether free from bravado. It is more easy to believe that the person who betrayed his trust in publishing

* Lingard's History of England, Vol. v. p. 379.

this paper, and addressing it in the form of a letter to the lords of the Council, had taken further liberties with it.

These were the two first missionaries sent from Rome into England, both were Jesuits.

On Mr. Campion's arrival in London, he preached his first sermon to a numerous audience of persons of distinction, at which the author of the memoir in Challoner's Collection, says he was present. His eloquence was remarkable; he preached daily, and sometimes thrice daily, and many Protestants, "of good disposition," were admitted to hear him. He addressed a work to the universities on the subject of the late changes in religion, which called forth sundry pamphlets, but no answer worthy of his notice. He was, however, led into an engagement to dispute the controverted points between Catholics and Protestants, with the doctors of the latter, which caused some uneasiness. The doctors became alarmed for their credit, they caused the council to alter the proposed questions, from matters of controversy in religion, to the political question of the queen's position in respect to the church, which proceeding left them in security.

"Thereupon it was given out by divers speeches and proclamations, that great confederacies were made by the pope and foreign princes, for the invasion of the land, and that the Jesuits and seminary priests were sent in, forsooth, to prepare their ways, and such like trumpery, to beguile and incense the simple against them. Then all exquisite diligence was used for the apprehension of others, but more particularly of Father Campion, whom they called the Pope's Champion."*

He contrived, however, to elude his opponents till he had been near thirteen months on the mission, when he was betrayed by one of Walsingham's spies, George Elliot, and found secreted in the house *of Mr. Yates of Lyford in Berkshire,* along with two other priests, Messrs. Ford and Collington. Elliot and his officers made a show of their prisoners to the multitude, and the sight of the priests in the hands of the constables, "was a matter of mockery to the unwise multitude." This was a frequent occurrence in conveying captured priests from one jail to another, or from London to Oxford, or vice versa, and it would seem

* Memoirs of Missionary Priests, Vol. i. p. 43.

instead of finding sympathy from the populace they met with contumely, insult, and sometimes even brutal violence. This is singular, and not easily accounted for; of the fact there can be no doubt. Mr. Campion and his companions were sent to London. The legs of the former were tied under the horse's belly, his arms were bound behind his back, and by the instructions of the council a label was affixed to his hat with the words in large capitals, " *Campion, the seditious Jesuit.*" Matters were so ordered that the journey was made by very short stages, in order to bring them through towns on the market days, to have them exposed to large numbers of people, "whom in such matters the policy (of the council) seeks most to please." In London vast multitudes gathered round the prisoners, "the mob gazing, and with delight beholding the novelty, but the wiser part lamenting to see our countrymen fallen to such barbarous iniquity as to abuse in this manner a religious man, so honourable in all nations."*

On the 22nd of July he was delivered up to the lieutenant of the tower. Here, after sundry examinations, terrors, and threats by the Lord Chancellor and others of the Queen's Council, "HE WAS DIVERS TIMES RACKED, to force out of him by intolerable torments whose houses he had frequented, by whom he was relieved, whom he had reconciled, when, by what route, and for what purpose he came into the kingdom, and by what commission,"† &c.

Before we proceed farther, it is necessary to ascertain what was the nature of that racking, of which the memoirs of the missionary and his associates make such frequent mention.

"The following," says Lingard,‡ "were the kinds of torture chiefly employed in the Tower:

"1st. *The rack* was a large open frame of oak, raised three feet from the ground. The prisoner was laid on his back under it, on the floor: his wrists and ancles were attached by cords to two rollers at the ends of the frame: these were moved by levers in opposite directions, till the body rose to a level with the frame. Questions were then put, and if the answers did not prove satisfac-

---

* Memoirs of Missionary Priests, Vol. i. p. 44.
† Memoirs of Missionary Priests.
‡ History of England, Vol. v. note u. p. 650.

tory, the sufferer was stretched more and more, till the bones started from their socket.

"2nd. *The scavenger's daughter* was a broad hoop of iron so called, consisting of two parts fastened together by a hinge. The prisoner was made to kneel on the pavement, and to contract himself into as small a compass as he could. Then the executioner, kneeling on his shoulders, and having introduced the hoop under his legs, compressed the victim close together till he was able to fasten the extremities over the small of the back. The time allowed for this kind of torture was an hour and a half; during which time it frequently happened that, from excess of compression, the blood started from the nostrils—sometimes, it was believed, from the extremities of the hands and feet.*

"3rd. *Iron gauntlets*, which could be contracted by the means of a screw. They served to compress the wrists, and to suspend the prisoner in the air from two distant points of a beam. He was placed on three pieces of wood, piled one on the other, which, when his hands had been made fast, were successively withdrawn from under his feet. Father Gerard, one of the racked Jesuits, speaking of his torments, says: 'I felt the chief pain in my breast, belly, arms, and head. I thought that all the blood in my body ran into my arms, and began to burst out of my fingers' ends. This was a mistake: but the arms swelled till the gauntlets were buried within the flesh. After being thus suspended an hour I fainted, and when I came to myself, I found the executioners supporting me in their arms: they replaced the pieces of wood under my feet, but as soon as I was recovered, they removed them again. Thus I continued hanging for the space of five hours, during which time I fainted eight or nine times.'†

"4th. The torture called *little ease* was so constructed that the prisoner could neither stand, walk, sit, nor lie in it at full length. He was compelled to draw himself up into a squatting posture, and so remained during several days."

The detailed account of our English tortures is taken from one of the most scrupulous writers in all his statements, and the best of all English historians. Yet it will

* Bartoli, p. 280.
* Ap Bartoli, p. 418.—Ap. Memoirs of Missionary Priests.

be read by a vast number of English readers without the horror it is so well calculated to inspire ; not because their feelings are blunted and insensible to the sufferings of their fellow creatures, but because they have been so blinded by the prejudices of their education, that they regard all truths which are injurious to the fame of a sovereign, whose reign they have been taught to consider a most glorious one, and whose efforts to establish the reformed religion most righteous ones, as misrepresentations of the enemies of both ; and with that comfortable persuasion and convenient conviction, they can hear of the tortures inflicted on their Catholic countrymen with composure, because with incredulity in respect to the accounts given of them. There are some of them, however, and not a few, who will shudder at the recital of the sufferings of the racked priests, the tortured gentlemen, the mutilated scholars, the swelling of their arms till the gauntlets were buried in the flesh, the stretching of the extremities over the small of the back, the compression of their bodies till the blood started from their nostrils, the suspensions in the air from the two distant points of a beam, the supporting of the fainting sufferers in the arms of the executioners, the replacing of them on the rack, and the hangings there for the space of five hours. And these things, will they say, have been done in England in the holy name of religion, by people who for worldly purposes having thrown off all its obligations of mercy and of justice, became as devils to their fellow men !

"At the first racking of Father Campion, they went no further with him" (than questioning him about his missionary movements in England, &c.) "but afterwards, when they saw he could not be won to condescend somewhat in religion, which was the thing they most desired, *they thought good to forge matters of treason against him*, and framed their demand accordingly ; about which *he was so cruelly torn and rent upon the torture*, that he told a friend of his, who found means to speak with him, that he thought they meant to make away with him in that manner. *Before he went to the rack, he used to fall down at the rack-house door upon both knees, to commend himself to God's mercy, and upon the rack he called continually on God, repeating often the holy name of Jesus*."*

* Memoirs of Missionary Priests.

The use of torture during Burleigh's and Walsingham's administration, there are numerous records of in the 'Memoirs of Missionary Priests.' They were not satisfied in the case of Catholic laymen with racking them ; they terrified and tormented the families of the accused, they examined the wife, the children, the nearest and dearest of their relatives, their servants and familiars.

Father Southwell, in a letter of his dated January, 1590, makes mention of two priests confined in Bridewell most cruelly used : "What was given them to eat was so little in quantity, and withal so filthy and nauseous, that the very sight of it was enough to turn their stomachs.   The labours to which they obliged them were continual and immoderate, and no less in sickness than in health ; for with hard blows and stripes they forced them to accomplish their task, how weak soever they were.   Their beds were dirty straw, and their prisons most filthy.   Some are there hung ·up for whole days by the hands, in such manner that they can but just touch the ground with the tips of their toes. In fine, they that are kept in that prison truly live in 'lacu miseriæ et in luto fœcis.'* This purgatory we are looking for every hour, in which Topliffe and Young, the two executioners of the Catholics, exercise all kinds of torments."†

Not the least of the sufferings endured by the Catholics were those occasioned by the sickness that prevailed from the beginning of the persecution, and continued for several years in the crowded prisons throughout the country.   A pestilential malignant fever broke out in the Court House at Oxford Assizes, on the 6th of July, 1577, during the trial of a Catholic bookseller of the name of Jenks, the first of the victims of that inhuman persecution which stained the annals of England.   This man was condemned to imprisonment, the pillory, and the loss of his ears ; but the iniquitous sentence was hardly pronounced, before several of the ministers of injustice were seized with a deadly sickness. This was the first conviction of a Catholic for a matter of religious opinion, and the vengeance of heaven was signally displayed on this occasion : the two judges, the sheriff, the under-sheriff, most of the jury, and many of-the spectators,

---

* Ps. 39.
† Memoirs of Missionary Priests.—Memoir of South.

were seized with violent pains in the head, with nausea and extreme prostration of strength, followed by delirium, and, in the majority of cases, death ensued in thirty hours. The disease spread, and did not abate much before the middle of August.*

A malignant fever, not less fatal, occasioned by the filth and crowded state of the prisons, likewise prevailed in the principal jails throughout the kingdoms. In York Castle twenty Catholics of family and fortune perished of this infectious disease about the beginning of 1578; and a similar fate befel the Catholics in Newgate in 1580.† It is stated by several writers, that the pestilential disease which seized on the judges and others in the Court House of Oxford, was brought there by the prisoners from the crowded jail.‡

Father Campion, throughout his torments, manifested no ill will towards his tormentors. His keeper, after one day's torture, asked him how he felt his hands and feet. He replied: "Not ill, because I feel not at all." Not content with these tortures, they slandered him in his fame, they put foul falsehoods in the mouths of the preachers and ministers against him; sometimes they said he had conformed, at other times that he had confessed upon the rack all his secrets, and even that he had committed suicide in prison. "After they had brought him almost to the brink of death by the rack," they set their divines at him to dispute on religious matters three several times; and when the tortured priest defended his faith, and was supposed sometimes to press too hard upon his adversaries, the officials of the prison, who were present, interposed with their tipstaves, and commanded him to be silent. There were some Protestants present, who were ashamed of such conduct and of their ministers, "and surprised exceedingly at the other's learning, meekness, patience, and humility."

Lingard says: "It was the second time Campion was racked, that he made disclosures which he deemed of no

---

* Lingard, Vol. v. p. 376.
† Ibid.
‡ In Fitzgerald's quaint Chronicle, "The Remembrancer of Memorable Events," this calamity is thus recorded: "three hundred people died at the Assizes of Oxford by the stench of the prisoners."

importannce, but which report had exaggerated and misrepresented."*

It was on account of this misrepresentation he wrote to one of his friends, saying, though he had mentioned the names of some persons by whom he had been hospitably received, "he had never discovered any secrets there declared, nor ever would, come rack, come rope." This letter was intercepted, and in consequence of the allusion to secrets, he was twice more racked, "till it was thought he had expired."

We are informed by Lingard, that Elizabeth had been desirous to see this celebrated man, — the frequently racked missionary priest ; and by her order he was brought one evening from the Tower, and introduced to her at the house of the Earl of Leicester, in the presence of the latter and her two secretaries. There the hard-hearted woman questioned her victim about his recognition of her title to the crown, and his opinion of the dispensing and disposing power of the Pope ; and when her majesty's curiosity was gratified, and some vague answers on the latter point were elicited, he was led back to his dungeon. Howell states that, between the torturings, he had been several times called to dispute on religion, sometimes publicly in the Church, and sometimes in private. They at length gave over their efforts to convert him, and proceeded with their machinations to prove him guilty of high treason against the state. They procured some swearers to come against him, who had never seen him before his imprisonment. The principal miscreants of this class were then—Sled and Munday—the Oates and Bedloe of that period. One of the chief lictors of that time was a ruffian named Toplift, a pursuivant and terrorist, fit to cope with any of the wretches of the French revolutionary tribunals. He assisted at rackings and executions, attended trials and examinations before justices, bullied the prisoners, and bantered them sometimes even on the scaffold. The French revolution did not produce a monster much more ruthless, ribald in his barbarity, or more atrociously wicked than this man.

The 14th of November, 1581, Father Campion and several other priests† were brought to trial. All were in-

---

* History of England, Vol. v. p. 380.

† The Memoir states seven, but Lingard says twelve priests and one layman named Coleton, who was acquitted. He states, that of the

cluded in the same indictment. The principal count charged Father Campion with conspiring beyond the seas to dethrone and put the queen to death, to stir up rebellion, and invade her realm from abroad.

When arraigned with the others, and commanded to hold up his hand, "*his arms being pitifully benumbed by his often cruel racking before*, and having them wrapped in a furred cuff, *he was not able to lift up his hand so high as the rest did, and as was required of him; but one of his companions, kissing his hands, (so abused for the confession of Christ,) took off his cuff, and so he lifted up his arm as high as he could, and pleaded not guilty, as all the rest did.*"

He pleaded in these solemn words: "I protest before God and His holy angels, before heaven and earth, before the world and this bar whereat I stand, which is but a small resemblance of the terrible judgment of the next life, that I am not guilty of any part of the treason contained in this indictment, nor of any other treason whatsoever." Elevating his voice, he added: "Is it possible to find twelve men so wicked and void of all conscience in this city or land, who will find us guilty together of this one crime, divers of us never meeting or knowing one the other before our being brought to this bar?"

Nothing more was done that day; the prisoners were removed, and on the 20th of November Mr. Campion and his companions were tried. Walsingham's gang of swearers, his oath-men of all work in the courts, were produced, and did all they were brought there to do; they swore away the lives of a number of innocent men, of whose innocence Walsingham could not have been in ignorance. The attorney-general plainly gave the jury to understand that it was the queen's will the prisoners should be condemned. The jury dared not for their lives do otherwise than obey the royal will. Their verdict against all, with one exception, was—*guilty*; and the sentence of the unjust judge was—death. They were sentenced to be hanged, drawn, and quartered. "That sentence," says the author of the ' Memoir,' "gave the world full proof of the sad fall of

twelve condemned to death, three only were then executed, because the Duke of Anjou, Elizabeth's Catholic suitor, was then in England, and hanging so many priests might have disgusted him, and that of the nine respited, six were subsequently executed.

secrets of some houses where he had been entertained, had been misconstrued on his trial, and had no reference to any treasons or conspiracies, but to the duties and functions of a priest, which had been in secret performed in such houses. They pressed him to declare his opinion of the bull of Pope Pius V. concerning the excommunication of the queen ; to which he made no reply. Then they asked him, did he renounce the Pope? His reply was, "*I am a Catholic.*" To which it was observed that "*his Catholicism was all treason.*" His only reply was putting up his last prayer to God, when a member of the new religion brutally interrupted the man about to die, and begged of him "to pray with him." On which, with a mild countenance, turning round his head towards the speaker, he said : "*You and I are not one in religion, wherefore I pray you content yourself.* I bar none of prayer, only I desire of them of the household of Christ to pray with me, and in my agony to say one creed." Some person cried out, "Pray in English." To whom he answered, "that he would pray in a language he well understood." His indefatigable tormentors lastly called on him to "ask the queen's forgiveness, and to pray for her." He meekly said : "Wherein have I offended her? In this I am innocent. These are my last words : in this give me credit. I have prayed, and do pray for her." Lord Howard asked him, "for which queen." He replied : "For your queen and mine." The cart was then drawn away, and one more judicial murder was perpetrated in England.

Melancthon, in one of his letters written at this period, says, that the reformers of his country called the murdered English priests "the devil's martyrs." We need not go back to the sixteenth century or to Germany for men who professed to be preachers and teachers of a purified christian faith, who gave utterance to similar language in respect to Campion and his fellow sufferers.

Thus died an English gentleman, a scholar, a pious clergyman, a most amiable man, persecuted to the death by a villain in the office of a minister of state. Thus perished on the scaffold a minister of the Gospel, a man of peace, whose holiness of life his gaolers even bore testimony to. Thus punished as a felon for his fidelity to his religion, cast into a loathsome prison, racked many times, dragged from his dungeon to the presence of the merciless woman who wore the crown, to gratify her curiosity ; again sent back to gaol, subjected to a trial that was "a mockery, a delusion, and a snare," condemned to a malefactor's death, to be hanged by the neck, to have his remains mangled on a scaffold,—thus died the Rev. Edmund Campion, in his forty-second year.

Father Ralph Sherwine was born in Radesley, Derbyshire. He matriculated in Exeter College, Oxford, and was admitted a fellow in 1568. Wood (Athen. Oxon.) says, that in 1575 "he left the University, with the reputation of an acute philosopher, and an excellent Greek and Hebrew scholar." He abandoned at the same time the Protestant religion, and went to Douay, where he was ordained in 1577. He proceeded to Rome shortly after his ordination, and remained there till 1580, when he returned to England by the way of Rheims. Shortly after his arrival, he was arrested and lodged in jail with shackles on his legs, which were left on for the space of a month.

He had not been long in confinement, when the gaoler received a message from the Knight Marshall, to inquire if there were any Papists in his prison who would dispute their religious principles, "and defend their cause by disputation ;" and if there were any such, that they should send him such questions as they would defend, and he would appoint the time and place for the disputation. This was a new mode of seeking a champion for a theological controversy.

Mr. Sherwine and two other priests, (afterwards condemned with him,) fell into the snare. They drew up questions, subscribed their names to them, and furnished evidence enough of their religious principles to hang a score of priests. "But the very day appointed for the disputation, Mr. Sherwine was removed to the Tower, where he was at sundry and several times examined and racked, and the latter time he lay five days and five nights without speaking to any one, all which time he lay as he thought in a sleep with our Saviour on the cross. After which time he came to himself, not finding any extremity in his torture."[*]

This absence of suffering after frightful torments, will appear to many incredible, nevertheless it is in entire accordance with the facts which the history of perse-

---

[*] Memoirs of Missionary Priests.

cution in all ages and countries discloses. It would seem that at such times, the spirit of man is in closer and more intimate communication with the Deity, than it is capable of arriving at in this world under any other circumstances, that all the senses are absorbed in divine love, and that it pleases God to render the martyr superior to the enmity of those who persecute Him in the persons of His confessors, insensible to pain, and incapable of resentment. The Englishman was racked divers times, but his tormentors did not shake his faith. They tried corruption, but it had no more success than torture. The Bishops of Canterbury and London, signified to him that if he would go to St. Paul's church and make a profession of the new faith, he should have a bishopric.

On Midsummer-day, 1581, he and his fellow-prisoners were summoned to the presence of the Lieutenant of the Tower, and inquiry was made of them if they would go to church and join in common prayer. They answered, that they would not. The Lieutenant warned them of a statute lately made, which they would render themselves liable to the penalties of, and eventually told them they would be indicted under it in two or three days.

Stowe bears out this account of the imposition of heavy fines for non-attendance at Protestant worship. "At the same sessions, 1581, were brought from the Fleet, sundry prisoners indicted for refusing to come to church, all which being convicted by their own confession, had judgment accordingly, to pay twenty pounds for every month of such their wilful absence from the church."

The piety of Mr. Sherwine, combined with his meekness and humility, excited the admiration of his keeper. He said his prisoner was "a man of God—the best and devoutest priest he ever saw." Mr. Sherwine was brought to trial with Father Campion, included in the same indictment, and condemned on the same perjured evidence for the same pretended conspiracy, of all knowledge of which he protested his entire innocence.

After his condemnation, writing to his friends, he said—"Delay of our death doth somewhat dull me, it was not without cause our Master said, '*Quod facis, fac cita.*' Truth it is, I hoped ere this, casting off this body of death, to have kissed the precious wounds of my sweet Saviour, sitting on the throne of His Father's own glory; which desire, as

I trust, descending from above, hath so quieted my mind,
that since the judicial sentence proceeded against us,
neither the sharpness of the death hath much terrified me,
nor the shortness of life much troubled me.   My negli-
gences are without number, I grant: but I appeal to my
Redeemer's clemency.   My sins are great, I confess : but I
flee to God's mercy.   I have no boldness but in his blood :
his bitter passion is my only consolation.   It is comfortable
what the Prophet hath recorded, that 'He hath written us
in his hands.'   Oh, that he would vouchsafe to write Himself in our hearts : how joyful then should we appear before
the judgment-seat of His Father's own glory : the dignity
of which when I think of, my flesh quaketh, not sustaining,
by reason of mortal infirmity, the presence of my Creator's
Majesty."

This is the language of a man whom the law declared a
traitor.   These are the sentiments of one, whom the villain
Walsingham caused to be " racked divers times," and to be
capitally punished as a felon.   It would be difficult in the
range of the most extensive reading, to point out a passage
of higher and of holier eloquence, than the preceding one
extracted from the letter of Mr. Sherwine.

What great and noble men, England at that time produced!   Men whose greatness and nobility of mind find no
place in our histories.   Oh no, the greatness and ability of
the murderous persecutors of those innocent men, the
merits of the fawning sycophants and servile ministers of
state, who pandered to the vices of a wicked, ferocious
woman, whom historians style the great and glorious
Queen ; these are the topics on which our Humes, our
Henrys, and Goldsmiths, were pleased to dwell.   The Lei-
cesters, the Burleighs, the Cecils, and the Walsinghams,
were the men, whom it was their delight to honour.

On leaving the Tower, the writer of the Memoir (who
states that he was present at the execution) says, that Mr.
Sherwine spoke some words to Charke, the minister, and
that some of the fellow-ministers of the latter said, " the
words he spoke could not come from a guilty conscience."

The day before his execution, he wrote a letter to the
Rev. John Woodward, his uncle, from which the following
passages are extracted :—

" My dear Uncle,   •

" After many conflicts, mixed with spiritual consolation and christian comforts, it hath pleased God, of His
infinite mercy, to call me out of this vale of misery.   To
Him, therefore, at all times and for ever, for all his benefits, be all praise and glory."

"Innocence is my only comfort against all the forged villany which is fathered on my fellow-priests and me. Well,
when by the High Judge, God himself, this false vizard of
treason shall be removed from true Catholic men's faces,
then shall it appear who they be that carry a well meaning,
and who, an evil murderous mind : in the mean time, God
forgive all injustice, and if it be his blessed will, convert
our persecutors, that they may become professors of his
truth."......" God grant us both his grace and blessing until
the end, that, living in his fear and dying in his favour, we
may enjoy one the other, for ever."

At the place of execution, (Tyburn), Mr. Campion had
precedence of him. He was executed before Mr. Sher-.
wine's face. When the body of the former was taken
down, and the butchery of beheading, bowelling, and quar-
tering, was finished, the executioner took hold of Mr. Sherwine, "with his hands all bloody," and said to him, thinking to terrify him, " *Come, Sherwine, take thou also thy
wages ;*" *but the holy man, nothing dismayed, embraced him
with a cheerful countenance, and reverently kissed the blood
that stuck to his hands, at which the people were very much
moved.*

" He asked if the people looked for any speech from him,
and many of the people, and some of the MORE HONOURABLE
SORT, answering, Yes, he commenced speaking ; but when
he was going on to give an account of his faith, Sir Francis
Knowles interrupted him repeatedly, and bid him confess
his treason against the Queen.   Mr. Sherwine replied with
great constancy, ' *I am innocent of any such crime.*'   The
man, ' dressed in a little brief authority,' repeated his insolent admonitions, and even the patience of the meek fol-
lower of Jesus seemed ruffled for a moment. He turned
to Sir Francis Knowles, and said—' Tush, tush, you and I
shall answer this before another Judge—where my inno-

cence shall be known, and *you will see that I am guiltless of this.*' "

In the concluding words, there is evidence of the struggle to repress the last emotions of nature in a passing moment of irritation. He does not end the sentence as the commencement of it would lead one to expect; he moderates its bearing, and leaves it to be understood, not that this man would be confounded before men and angels, but that he would be convinced of his error,—" You will see that I am guiltless of this."

There is something in this, that vouches for the sanctity of the victim, and the veracity of the person who recounts his martyrdom. The effect of this mild remonstrance is perceptible in the altered tone of Sir Francis Knowles.

" We know you are no contriver or doer of this treason, for you are no man of arms, but *you are a traitor by consequence.*"

The only answer to this miserable logic was—" If to be a Catholic were to be a traitor, then I am one." The same revolting ceremony was then gone through as in the case of Mr. Campion, and indeed as in almost all cases of the executions of clergymen in those times, of soliciting the presumed culprit to pray for the Queen, (this seemed to be the customary part assigned to the noble Lord Howard), and to inquire which Queen was prayed for. Whereupon Mr. Sherwine somewhat smiling, said, " Yea, for Elizabeth the Queen, I now at this instant pray my Lord God, to make her His servant in this life, and after this life co-heir with Jesus Christ."

One of the bye-standers cried out, " He means to make her a Papist." " God forbid otherwise," replied Mr. Sherwine. And then recollecting himself in prayer, he faced eternity with a meek and fearless countenance, and while fervently repeating the words, " Jesu, Jesu, Jesu—be to me a Jesus," he was set at liberty, released from life, which was to him a place of pilgrimage, preparatory only for an eternity of happiness.

Walsingham, in his conduct towards the persecuted missionary priests, manifested a savage spirit of hatred to the men and their religion, which nothing it would seem could soften.

In the memoirs of these martyred men, especially in the records of the years 1584, 1585, and 1586, we have frequent mention of Walsingham, of his examining culprit priests, and using them in a very brutal manner. One case is worthy of notice. Two clergymen, Messrs. Nicolls and Yaxley, were brought before him to be examined, the former a man of extraordinary learning, piety, and virtue. When he was examined by the Secretary, this " capital enemy of the Catholics" questioned and cross-questioned him with all the skill of a lawyer, but Mr. Nicolls limited himself to one reply, for himself and his companion, " We are Catholics, and for my own part I am, though unworthy, a priest of the Holy Roman Catholic religion."—" If you are a priest," said the Secretary, " then of course you are a traitor."

" A strange consequence, Sir," said Mr. Nicolls, " *since it is certain that they who first converted England from Paganism, were all priests.*"

" But they," said the Secretary, " did not disturb the nation as you do, nor stirred up seditions against their sovereigns."

To which the confessor replied, " If preaching the gospel of Jesus Christ, if instructing the ignorant in the Catholic faith, be disturbing the nation, or stirring up sedition, then are we equally guilty ; if not, both we and they are equally innocent ; nor can there be any treason in the case."

With this the two priests were *ordered* to Bridewell, where they were tortured, and hanged up in the air for the space of five hours together, to make them confess by whom they had been harboured or entertained.

The torments were in vain, they were tried, condemned, and executed, in company. Mr. John Munden, a Jesuit, a native of Dorsetshire, educated in the university of Oxford, being discovered to be a Catholic, was deprived of·his fellowship, went to Rheims, where he studied for some time, was finally ordained, and sent on the mission into England. He was arrested in 1583, and sent for examination to the secretary Walsingham. The secretary interrogated him closely about his return to England, the persons he had visited, the assistance he had received, and then took occasion to inveigh most bitterly against the seminary of Rheims, and the translation of the New Testament lately published there. He then put the questions, which were the common forerunners of death. Where Dr. Saunders was concealed? What he went to Ireland about? and what he, Mr. Munden, thought of his going there?

The reply was, that " he knew nothing of Dr. Saunders' business in Ireland, and could not say whether it was right or wrong. He could only answer for himself."

The secretary asked him, "what he would do in the event of the kingdom being invaded on account of religion? And what he thought of the deposing power?"

Mr. Munden said, "he must be excused from answering questions that were above his capacity, his studies were not of a nature to enable him to resolve such queries."

The secretary then asked him, "did he esteem Queen Elizabeth the true Queen of England?"

He answered, "Yes." "But," said Walsingham, "do you allow her to be queen as well de jure as de facto?" Mr. Munden hesitated to answer, as if he was deliberating on the motive for putting the question. *"How now, traitor," said Walsingham, "do you boggle at answering this?" and therewith gave him such a blow on one side of the head as perfectly stunned him, and made him reel,* so that for some days after he complained of a difficulty of hearing on that side. After this injury, and many other reproaches and affronts, the secretary sent for a pursuivant and ordered him to conduct Mr. Munden to the tower, and to take his horse and furniture for his pains.

In 1584 he and four others were hanged, drawn, and quartered, at Tyburn.

Here was a minister of the crown administering justice with a vengeance.

It is needless to trouble the reader with any other notices of the lives and martyrdoms of the confessors of the faith in England in this dreadful persecution of Elizabeth. The proofs that have been given of the piety and heroism of the sufferers, of the malignity, cruelty, and hypocrisy of the persecutors, are amply sufficient to afford a just idea of the character of the religion of the former, and the means that were taken for its overthrow by the latter. General descriptions of great catastrophes make less impression than particular instances illustrative of the character, the conduct, and the fate of the individual actors and sufferers in them.

CHAPTER X.

THE 29th of January, 1603, her majesty issued her last
proclamation against her Catholic subjects, a few weeks
only before her death. In that proclamation she commanded all priests, Jesuits, and others, and their adherents,
to quit the kingdom within thirty days, under the capital
penalty enjoined by law against those who received ordination by the authority of the pope. This was the crowning
act of persecution in the reign of the sanguinary daughter
of the brutal king. Cruelty and hypocrisy went hand in
hand in this last iniquitous measure. She spoke in it of
her clemency to the missionaries, of its being abused by
them, and of their having even "adventured to walk the
streets at noon-day," and carried themselves so "as to
breed a suspicion that she proposed to grant a toleration
of two religions; though God knew that she was ignorant
of any such imagination, and that no one had ever ventured to suggest it to her."*

"The golden reign of the good Queen Bess," terminated
in a few weeks after the promulgation of her last bloody
edict. She reigned forty-five years. "Her glories,"† we
find ample details of in Hume, and all his followers. Her
butcheries the historians make little or no account of.
She "made great wars" in Ireland to force her new fangled
faith on the people of that country, and she expended on

---

* Lingard, vol. 5, p. 607.

† In the 43rd of Elizabeth, "It was showed by Dr. Bennet," says
D'Ewes, "upon occasion of speech of the multitude of recusants, that
there were thirteen hundred, nay, fifteen hundred recusants in Yorkshire, which he vouched upon his credit, were presented both in the
ecclesiastical court and before the council at York." In the seventh
of James I., in the dispute touching a petition against Papists, it was,
say the Journals of the House of Commons, by occasion delivered,
that in England there were "three hundred convicted recusants in
a shire, at the queen's death now eight hundred."

them in one year (1589) the sum of £.600,000, which in the currency of the present time would be equal to about twelve millions sterling. She made small wars on the coast of Spain and Portugal, entered into on account of the reformed religion, and she expended on these between 1589 and 1593 the sum of £.1,300,000 sterling, equal to about twenty-six millions of our present currency; she made secret wars in the Low Countries, and in France, that is to say, she fomented rebellion in the former to favour the Protestant interest in Holland, and she clandestinely aided and abetted the Huguenots in France, to carry on a civil war against an ally with whom she was at peace, likewise to promote the interest of the Protestant religion in the French king's dominions. She sent an army into Scotland on a false pretence, but in reality to make enmity between the Catholic Queen of that country and her subjects; and when, by her emissaries, she stirred up those subjects into open revolt by her machination with the Calvinistic firebrands of Scotland, she caused the Catholic Queen to fly into her dominions, imprisoned her, and eventually cut off her head. All this was for the advancement of the reformation. What immense treasures must have been lavished on this object! What immense treasures might not have been spared to England—what shedding of blood might not have been avoided in England and Ireland—how many holocausts of priests and Catholic laymen hanged, drawn, bowelled, and beheaded, might not these countries have been saved the indelible disgrace of—how much burning, hate, and religious rancour might they not have escaped, if Elizabeth had left the people of her dominions to worship God according to the dictates of their own consciences.

It is said, that in 1573 " Elizabeth found means by economy, without imposing on her people any additional burdens, to discharge with interest, not only all the debts she had incurred, but those of Edward her brother, and of her sister Mary."*

But not a word is said of the way she got the means to do this; not one word of the church possession, vested in the crown by her father, which Mary had relinquished, and which she had resumed. These possessions were of im-

* Hume.

mense value, and were not only the property of the church, but the patrimony of the poor. And to the eternal disgrace of her rapacious reign, be it remembered, she completed the impoverishment of the nation commenced by her father, pauperized her people, resumed the plunder of the institutions which afforded the poor, the sick, the lame, the blind, the aged, a provision in their necessities ; and in return had eleven poor laws passed in her reign for a compulsory maintenance of the beggared English people.

These laws, which abolished charity, which created pauperism, which severed the bonds that united the rich and the poor, which degraded and debased the character of the burley honest independent yeomen of once " Merry England," were passed in " the golden days of the good Queen Bess."

It was not only to her Catholic subjects, as Catholics, she was a sanguinary tyrant ; she was a monster of cruelty to the poor of her own land. She made her people paupers, and when they were without food and homes, mendicants and vagrants, she inflicted savage punishments on them, branded them, imprisoned them, nay, in her latter days, when her feline nature was infuriated by the mad freaks of her hair-brained paramour, she hanged the poor without judge or jury, gave them the name of vagabonds, and consigned them to the gallows, and the penal settlements.

" In 1595, under the pretence that the vagabonds in the neighbourhood of London were not to be restrained by the usual punishments, she ordered Sir Thomas Wyllford to receive from the magistrates the most notorious and incorrigible of these offenders, and to *execute them upon the gallows according to the forms of martial law.*"*

These deeds were done in " the golden days of the good Queen Bess."

The glories of her reign are still rung in our ears, but the time will come when her memory will be loathed in the land she pauperized. Justice was never worse administered in England than in her reign.

The upright and respectable magistrates of the former reign were removed by Cecil, and replaced by men of inferior rank. Numerous complaints were heard of their tyranny, peculation, and rapacity. A justice of peace

---

* D'Ewes, p 661. Ap. Lingard, vol. 5, p. 628.

was defined in parliament, "an animal who for half-a-dozen chickens would dispense with a dozen laws."[*]

The higher tribunals were little better than the lower ; the judges were removable at pleasure, "and the queen herself was in the habit of receiving, and permitted her favourites and ladies to receive, bribes as the prices of his or their interferences in the suits of private individuals."[†]

Elizabeth, in fact, had no reverence for law or justice, and no love of virtue, if her contemporaries are to be believed. Faunt says her court was a place "where all enormities reigned in the highest degree ;"[‡] and, according to Harrington, "where there was no love but that of the lusty god of gallantry, Asmodeus." In her person she was repulsive and ungraceful. In her old age, when she imagined herself the most beautiful of women, Hentzner describes her at the age of sixty-five, "with false hair of a red colour, surmounted with a crown of gold ; her face wrinkled, her eyes small, her teeth black, her nose prominent, and her bosom uncovered, *as became a virgin queen.*" In her manners she was coarse, violent, and unfeminine, brutal in her anger; she swore like a trooper, and stormed like a virago on slight occasions at her courtiers and attendants.

Though possessed of natural abilities of a high order, some taste for letters and for music ; evidences of great intellectual power, enlarged views, are not to be found in her acts, with the exception of the clearness of perception and the discernment shown in the choice of her public servants. She was greedy of praise, or rather a glutton, who swallowed hyperbolical flattery as fast and as freely as a hungry traveller swallows poached eggs. She came to her paramours for praise with " a most ravenous appetite." She was arrogant, overbearing, jealous, and ridiculously vain ; meanly parsimonious, unprincipled, obstinate to a degree inconsistent often with the interests of the state, but at the same time irresolute to an extent bordering, as her ministers sometimes thought, on folly, and slow in comprehending all the bearings of a subject of great importance. Of her morals, the accounts given of them by the foreign ambassadors at her court to their respective sove-

---

[*] Rymer. Ap. Ling. vol. 5, p. 623.
[†] Lingard, Ibid.
[‡] Ibid. p. 622.

reigns and friends, present a picture exceedingly prejudicial
to the fame of " the virgin queen."

Lingard, who deals too gently with her vices, says, that
she disgraced herself by her conduct to one of her supposed
paramours—Leicester—in assigning an apartment to him
contiguous to her own bed-chamber ; " by this indecent act
she proved that she was become regardless of all sense of
shame." " Among his rivals," he adds, " were numbered
Hatton, Raleigh, Oxford, Blount, Simier, and Anjou : and
it was afterwards believed, that her licentious habits survived even when the fires of wantonness had been quenched
by the chill of age."*

Such was the person whom the Roman Catholics of
England and Ireland were called on to acknowledge as the
supreme head of the Church of Christ,—a vain, libidinous,
sanguinary woman ; and for opposing whose blasphemous
pretensions, they were horribly persecuted by her.

The following is a summary of the Penal Laws passed in
England during the reign of Elizabeth :

" The 1 Eliz. c. 1, confirmed all the acts levelled by
Henry against the see of Rome, which Mary had repealed,
and directed that all ecclesiastical persons, or other temporal officers, and all persons taking orders or degrees in a
university, shall take the oath of supremacy, under forfeiture of their spiritual and temporal promotions.   And all
who, in opposition to this oath, maintain the authority of
any foreign prince, or do anything for the advancement of
his jurisdiction, for the first offence forfeit all their property, real and personal ; or suffer imprisonment for one
year.   All ecclesiastical promotions, also, are void, as if the
party were dead ; whilst for the second offence they incur
the pains of a premunire, and for the third those of high
treason.

" The 1 Eliz. c. 2, sets aside the repeal of Edward's
statutes by Mary, and revives the acts of her brother ;
altering, however, the punishment of ministers who use
other forms of prayer, from forfeiting, for the first offence,
the profits of one benefice, to the forfeiture of all their
benefices for one year ; and doubling the imprisonment for
the first offence of those who have no benefices.   The forfeiture of those who disparage the Prayer Book is likewise

* Lingard, Vol. v. p. 621.

increased from ten pounds to a hundred marks, for the first offence ; and for the second, from twenty pounds to four hundred marks : the imprisonment, in case of failure of payment, being in both cases doubled. To these increased penalties, there is newly added a fine of one shilling for every offence, to be levied, for the good of the poor, on those who do not resort to church.

"The statute of 5 Eliz. c. 1, by which all persons maintaining the Pope's authority are, for the first offence, made liable to the pains of premunire, and for the second declared guilty of treason. In addition, also, to those persons already required* to take the oath of supremacy, schoolmasters and private teachers of children, barristers, sheriffs, and all persons taking office in the law, or its courts, are commanded to take the oath in open court, or in some public assembly. And, further, the lord chancellor is empowered to issue commissions, authorizing the tender of the oath to any person whatever ; which, if they refuse to take, they also are for the first offence guilty of premunire, and for the second of high treason.

"By 13 Eliz. c. 2, whoever shall bring into England, or publish there any bull, absolution, or reconciliation from Rome, together with their abettors, are subjected to the penalties of high treason, and those who aid them, to the pains of a premunire ; though, if they do not disclose their knowledge within six weeks, they also are guilty of misprision of treason. The bringing into the realm any Agnus Dei, crosses, or beads, consecrated by the bishop of Rome, or by his authority, and the receiving the same with intent to use them, unless the party discover the bringer within three days, incurs the pains of premunire : a punishment which is likewise inflicted on those justices, to whom such offences are discovered, who do not within fourteen days certify them to the privy council.

"By the statute of the 23 Eliz. c. 1, the committing any overt act in order to reconcile any of her majesty's subjects to the Church of Rome, and the being reconciled thereto, is declared high treason : and the knowing of such offences, and not revealing them within twenty days to some justice of the peace, misprision of treason. Persons, also, saying mass incur the forfeiture of two hundred marks, with im-

* By 1 Eliz. c. 1.

prisonment for one year, and until the fine be paid; and those who willingly hear it, suffer the same imprisonment and half the forfeiture.

"Persons who, being above sixteen years of age, do not resort to some place of common prayer, forfeit twenty pounds for every month, and if they forbear for twelve months, must be bound with sufficient sureties in the sum of two hundred pounds at least for their good behaviour, and so continue till they comply with the provisions of the law; and if any person keeps or maintains a schoolmaster thus abstaining, he shall forfeit ten pounds per month, and a schoolmaster not having a license from the bishop or ordinary, shall be disabled to teach, and shall suffer imprisonment for one year. If fines are not paid within three months, the offender shall be imprisoned until it be discharged, or till he himself shall conform.

"The statute of 27 Eliz. c. 2, provided that all Jesuits and other priests, ordained by the authority of the See of Rome, should depart the realm within forty days after the close of the then session of parliament; and that no such person should hereafter be suffered to come into or remain in any of the dominions of the crown of Great Britain, under the penalties of high treason. Those likewise who receive, relieve, or maintain any such ecclesiastical person, are adjudged felons, and shall suffer death without benefit of clergy. And those who know of such priests being in the realm, and who do not discover it to some justice of the peace within twelve days, shall be fined and imprisoned at the queen's pleasure. Any other of her majesty's subjects, likewise, who hereafter shall be brought up in any foreign popish seminary, who within six months after proclamation does not return into the realm, and within two days submit himself to the laws and take the oath of the first of the queen, shall be adjudged a traitor. Persons, directly or indirectly, contributing to the maintenance of Romish ecclesiastics or popish seminaries beyond sea, incur the penalties of premunire. And still further this statute enacts, that no one during her majesty's life shall send his child or ward beyond sea, without special licence, under forfeiture of one hundred pounds for every offence.

"The 29 Eliz. c. 6, inflicts still farther penalties on the Catholic religion, by providing that all lands and tenements granted since the beginning of the queen's reign, or hereafter to be granted by a popish recusant, whereby he and his family are maintained, shall be utterly void as against the queen's majesty. And every such offender shall pay into the exchequer twenty pounds for every month since his conviction, or in default thereof the queen may take all his goods, and two-thirds of his lands.

"In a succeeding session of parliament, the rigour of the laws against non-conformity was carried to the *ne plus ultra* of persecution ; all persons who, for the space of a month, refused conforming to the established religion, or who oppugned, or persuaded others to oppugn, the queen's authority in ecclesiastical causes, being condemned to banish themselves from their homes and from all that was near and dear to them, or to suffer the ignominious death which the law has justly denounced on felons and murderers. The statute which authorized these severities was the 35 El. c. 1, which enacts, that persons above sixteen years of age, obstinately refusing to repair to Church, or being present at unlawful conventicles, shall be committed to prison till they make declaration of their conformity ; or if they do not so conform within three months must solemnly abjure the realm, or refusing to do so, not repairing to the place appointed for their embarkation, or returning without special leave of her majesty, shall suffer as felons without benefit of clergy. To these penalties is added a fine of ten pounds on those, who, after notice, relieve or keep in their houses any person refusing to come to church for a month, except nearest relatives not having any other place of habitation. By the second chapter of the same statute,* popish recusants convict are ordered to repair to their dwellings, and within twenty days to transmit the place of their residence to the authorities. They are likewise prohibited from going more than five miles from their houses, under forfeiture of goods and chattels, and of all their lands for life. Those persons who do not possess lands to the clear yearly value of twenty marks, or goods and chattels worth above forty pounds, unless they conform within three months after conviction, must abjure the realm, or refusing so to do, or returning without leave, suffer death without benefit of clergy.

"Such," says Brown, in his 'History of the Penal Laws,'

* 35 Eliz. c. 2.

"were the successive provisions of Elizabeth for the suppression of the Catholic religion."

CHAPTER XI.

THE FATE OF THE PERSECUTORS IN THE REIGNS OF HENRY VIII.,
EDWARD VI., AND ELIZABETH.

WHEN the fate of the principal persecutors of the 16th century in England is recalled, it would seem as if the book of Lactantius, 'De Mortibus Persecutorum,' furnished the examples, "magna et mirabilia," of the divine retribution. The three sovereigns in whose reigns this persecution raged most furiously, were Henry VIII., Edward VI., and Elizabeth. The chief agents of it in the former reigns were Cromwell, the vicar-general; Cranmer, archbishop of Canterbury; Anne Boleyn, the lord protector Somerset, and Dudley, duke of Northumberland: all of whom perished on the scaffold.

Their sovereigns, Henry VIII. and his daughter, Elizabeth, did not die there, but in their deaths the hand is to be seen of that Providence which sooner or later overtakes oppression.

Cromwell, the vicar-general of Henry VIII., was a persecutor of the stamp of that sordid Decius whom Lactantius denominates, "execrabile animal qui vexaret Ecclesiam." Like all upstarts suddenly elevated, he played the tyrant when he was placed in power. His office of visitor of religious houses immediately preceding the reformation, afforded him an opportunity of gratifying the instincts of a base nature, of trampling on the fallen, of browbeating the unfortunate, of terrifying the defenceless and the timid. The son of the blacksmith of Putney lorded it over not only the doomed monks, but over the prelates of the Church; and, lo and behold! in the midst of his insolent triumph over the Church, its prelates and its pastors, the hand that raised him was made by God the instrument of his destruction. Henry delivered over his vicar-general to the tender mercies of his laws; and the bold persecutor, after importuning his merciless master in the abject terms of a crouching slave for his life, died by the hands of the executioner he had provided so largely with employment.

Lactantius thus describes the persecutor Nero :* "Execrabilis ac nocens tyrannus (qui) prosilivit ad excindendum cœleste templum, delendamque justitiam, ac primis omnium persecutus Dei servos"—He persecuted the Church, he put a multitude of persons to death—some eminent philosophers ; he killed his own mother ; and eventually he was regarded as a wild beast, treated as one, and torn to pieces by the rabble.

Henry persecuted, prosecuted, and killed judicially a great many of his people, several men of learning and sanctity, one great philosopher, and two of his own wives. He was regarded by his people as a ferocious monster ; but their spirit was so broken by oppression, there was not strength enough left in their desperation for an attempt at the wild justice of a crime like an act of national revenge.

Our Nero died in his bed, but the wrath of God was on him and his race ; root and branch it was swept away—his children were childless—his son did not reach the years of puberty—his daughters were barren—and though only one of them was married, the other was but in name "a virgin queen." "Hoc modo Deus universus persecutores nominis sui debellavit ut eorum nec stirps nec radix ulla remanerit."†

The indulgence of brutal passions broke down the constitution of Henry VIII.,—those passions to which the torrent of evils is attributable that the Reformation poured in on the British dominions. "Ille dies primus leti, primusque malorum causa fuit."

A voluptuary, gross, sordid, and sensual in his appetites, he gave himself up wholly in his latter years to the pleasures of guzzling and gormandizing, and he indulged in them without restraint.

"At last," says Lingard,‡ "he grew so enormously corpulent, that he could neither support the weight of his own body, nor remove without the aid of machinery into the different apartments of the palace."

We find the leviathan of luxury depicted to the life

* De Mort Persec.
† Lactan. de Mort. Pers.
‡ History of England, Vol. iv. p. 346.

in the portraiture by Lactantius of the monster Maxi-
minianus.

"Erat etiam corpus congruens statu celsus, caro ingens
et in horrendam magnitudinem diffusa et inflata."

He became at length so unwieldy and helpless, as to
be incapable even of signing his name to public documents.
His temper grew daily more irritable and ungovernable, his
brutality to those around him more insupportable. All
that was left of the man was a bloated carcass; the powers
of vitality and volition were reduced at last to mere animal
impulses and instincts. His intellect had become fat and
pursy like his person. His extremities were corroded with
inveterate ulcers, complicated diseases attacked him, and
from the crown of his head to the sole of his foot, there was
no soundness in him. Disquieted by his gloomy apprehensions for his son, tormented by his bodily ailments, a torment and a terror to his attendants, as his bodily powers
failed his ferocity waxed fiercer; he devoted his dying
moments to orders for arrests, prescriptions of supposed
enemies who had been his most faithful servants, and death
warrants for them, till it pleased heaven, in mercy to the
nation, to put an end to his reign of terror. Such was the
death of the first but not the worst persecutor in England;
his daughter Elizabeth did not leave his memory a just
claim to the odium of the latter title.

The reign of Edward VI., was the second stage of the
persecution. The reformation assumed the character of an
organized system of rapacity and hypocrisy. The poor boy
on whose young brow the crown pressed heavily, was taught
to consider the spoliation of religious houses, and the persecution of his subjects on account of their religious opinions,
as meritorious acts in the sight of heaven. He sunk under
the excitement of false zeal and fanaticism. The fever of
this unnatural excitement of perverted religious feelings
preyed on his fragile constitution. The hectic of this
fanaticism was passed off by the swindlers of Church and
State (Cranmer, Somerset, and Dudley,) who surrounded
him, for the healthy glow of a holy enthusiasm. The sickly
boy languished on the throne seven years, and languishing
he died of a distempered zeal for the interests of the new
religion.

There is no occasion to have recourse to accounts of his
being poisoned by any deadly drugs, in order to account for

his early death. The pestilential influence of evil counsel, the contaminated atmosphere of a court where rapacity and hypocrisy were the only paths to fortune and the fame of piety, the breath of the Seymours, the Dudleys, and of Cranmer, was sufficient to poison the wholesome springs of life, and to deprive them of all their freshness and salubrity. Somerset was a rapacious hypocrite, who acquired enormous wealth by the spoliation of religious houses, and the confiscation of the lands of the Catholic gentry, and appropriation of those of the hierarchy. Of his infamy it might be said as of that of Maximinus, " vincit officium linguæ, sceleris magnitudo." In the height of his prosperity he was overtaken by the vengeance of the Almighty, hurled from the bad eminence he had attained by many crimes, cast into prison and consigned to the scaffold, to which he had brought his own brother.

Such was the end of another of the persecutors.

In the succeeding reign of Mary, Dudley, Duke of Northumberland, (father of the infamous Leicester, the paramour of Elizabeth,) another fierce persecutor, perished on the scaffold. Like Somerset, his zeal was not excited by fanaticism, his persecution was a speculation, his interest in religion a craving for the temporalities of the Church, a lust for the gold and silver of the sacred vessels of the altar, and the lands of the religious houses. His rapacity in the provinces, recall the outrages of the Roman plunderer : " qui jamdudum provincias afflixerat auri argentique indictionibus factis quæ promiserat redderet, etiam in nomine vicennatum securum alteram afflixit."* He too filled the office of Protector, acquired great wealth and power, and in the intoxication of his prosperity, aspired to the crown for his daughter-in-law. But the cry of the oppressed had pierced the clouds, the crimes of the persecutor had called for retribution, and all the ambitious schemes, the plundering projects of the high and mighty Earl of Northumberland, in the twinkling of an eye were overturned. The spoil and the spoiler, the proud lord of the noble house of Percy, were suddenly swept away. He and his son and his daughter-in-law were brought to the block. On the scaffold he expressed his hearty contrition for his deeds, and stated that at all times he had privately

---

* Lac. de Mort. Persec.

adhered to that religion, which he had publicly denied and persecuted.

And thus died another persecutor, and the only one of his class who proclaimed his heart-felt sorrow for his previous enormities.

Cranmer, Archbishop of Canterbury, whose elasticity of conscience was one of the most remarkable of his qualifications for a reformer, in those days when changes in religious rites and doctrines were every day occurrences, had a great facility in taking and breaking oaths, in making his master's marriages valid and invalid, as royal lust or loathing caused the laws of God and of the realm to be interpreted by this accommodating prelate. Like Cromwell, his furious zeal was insolent and sanguinary, he lifted his hand proudly against the Church, and shed the blood of its members profusely.

Among the Pagan persecutors, there was one whose career is told by Lactantius in a few words, which would serve for Cranmer's course. "Valerianus quoque non dissimili furare correptus, impias manus, in Deum intentavit, et multum quamvis brevi tempore, justi sanguinis fudit."[*] But the man who shed so much innocent blood in England, or was instrumental to its being shed, poured out his own on the scaffold. The arch persecutor was himself judicially murdered in another persecution.

The reign of Elizabeth realized all that we read of the atrocious proceedings of the persecutors of ancient times. Of her victims, it might be truly said, she spared no rank or condition, and respected no worth or virtue.[†]

In all ages persecution follows the same course; commences with hypocrisy and ends with rapacity. Extravagant pretensions to religious zeal, are succeeded by signal violations of justice, arbitrary measures, summary arrests, imprisonments, torturings, and executions of high-minded citizens; then comes confiscations, plunderings, and prodi-

---

* De Mort. Perse. p. 526.

† "Torquebantur ab eo non modo de curiones sed primores etiam civitatum egregu et perfectissimi viri.........

"Dignitatem non habentibus pœna ignis fuit et exilio primo adversus christianos permiserat dates legibus ut post tormentâ damnati lentes ignibus urerentur.........

"At vero illud publicæ calamitatis et communis luctus omnium fuit, census in provincias et civitates semel missus, censitoribus ubique diffusis et omnia exagitantibus hostiles tumultus et captivitatis horrendæ species erant."—Lactan. de Mor. Per. p. 545.

gality, that no spoil can satisfy the wants of; and finally, general impoverishment that creates crime, and leads to savage and sanguinary legislation.   In each phase of persecution, we find the employment of spies, informers, and witnesses, paid by the state—a Government of exalted scoundrelism, based on the agency of subordinate mercenary villany, that sooner or later comes to a bad end. Cecil, Walsingham, and Leicester, however, did not suffer on the scaffold : they died as they lived, obdurately, the worst of all deaths, that of hardened men reckless of past crimes, and regardless of future consequences.

The Earl of Leicester, whose grandfather was executed in the reign of Henry VIII., and his father and brother in the reign of Mary, accumulated more plunder than fell to the share of any of the succeeding robbers of the Church, and committed perhaps more crimes than most of them in his private capacity.   The dissoluteness of his life exceeded that of all the profligates of his age, and yet he played the part of a man deeply interested in religious matters, and by some strange arts, contrived to unite the characteristics of a man of fashion, a gallant, and a devotee.

He married the widow of the Count of Essex, in the lifetime of his first wife, and in his weariness of his royal mistress, he introduced to her the young Earl of Essex, his son-in-law, who became one of her paramours.   He is accused of having murdered one of his wives.   His crimes were enormous, and Elizabeth for many years made no account of them; but at length the multitudinous enmities created at court by his arrogance and ambition, brought him into disgrace ; he retired to the country and died suddenly, some say of fever, and some assert of poison, which he had prepared for others, " Car il passoit pour habile en l'art d'empoisonner."*   Elizabeth wept when she heard of his death ; but in the midst of her grief, she issued an order for seizing on his effects for the amount of a debt he owed to the exchequer ; but his creditors put in innumerable claims, and his tender mistress derived little advantage from the disposal of the spoil of her paramour.   Thus perished another of the persecutors.

Sir William Cecil, Lord Burleigh, was unquestionably the greatest statesman of his age ; a man without remorse,

---

* Memoirs of Walsingham.

where an object of importance to the interests of his government was in question, or of that reformation, of which he was undoubtedly the main support in Elizabeth's reign. But however unprincipled his acts might be, there was great power of intellect displayed, not only in their conception, but in their execution.

He was a truly great man, in the ordinary sense of that term ; but in the true sense of it, he was neither good nor great. He was possessed of consummate worldly wisdom. His wickedness was not wanton, nor was it employed merely for his own advantage. If he could have obtained his ends by fair means, he would probably have preferred them to the use of foul ones. He had all the intellectual qualities of Talleyrand, and much of his peculiar disposition, without some of the worst and most sordid of the passions of the latter. On the other hand, he was answerable for a vast effusion of blood, that Talleyrand has not had laid to his charge. His maxims and his conduct were founded on that kind of morality of state, which considers virtue a felicitous compromise of opposed principles and extreme opinions, making every thing legitimate that is expedient, and every thing expedient that is advantageous to the policy of the individual or of the state.

He died in the full enjoyment of his honours tranquilly and decorously, with all the decent official gravity and composure with which he filled the highest offices of state, just as Talleyrand slowly, stoically, and aristocratically died. But Cecil had a heavy account to settle in eternity: he had the blood of hundreds of innocent men on his hands ; he had the murder of the Queen of Scots to answer for, of whom he had formerly been a confidential friend and adviser. And yet as far as history informs us of his last moments, he died without a pang of remorse ; seemingly without an idea that he had a single crime to answer for. This awful state of mind on the brink of eternity—this fatal unconsciousness of guilt, the result not of innocence, but of familiarity with great crimes, and their commission on a large scale by privileged governmental agents—this complacency for crime, divested of its external grossness, which statesmen and diplomatists are peculiarly liable to fall into from their constant intercourse with ambitious and intriguing men devoid of principle—is a condition not less to be deplored, than that of any of the persecutors, of whose dying moments we read in Lactantius.*

Walsingham, "scelerum inventor et malorum machinator," the colleague and competitor of Cecil, though possessed of talents, a keen observer, an able diplomatist, plausible and astute, was in all respects a very inferior man to the latter.

Cecil allowed him to do all the dirty work of his administration, and Walsingham did it not for the love of his country, not for sake of lucre, but out of pure attachment to his office, from a passion for intrigue, and a strange pleasure in devising, watching, and conducting the courses of plots, machinations, and conspiracies. Walsingham was incomparably the worst of all the wicked men in the employment of Elizabeth. He was the foremost and most mischievous of all the persecutors of his time.

He was an enthusiast in his devotion to the duties of his office; not the legitimate duties of it, but those secret ones that were paramount to the latter. He ruined his fortune in maintaining a staff of spies at foreign courts, and of informers and approvers at home; in getting up Popish plots, and implicating Catholic missionaries in charges of treason. He caused the shedding of more Catholic blood in England, than any minister of the persecuting Queen. He was wantonly cruel and brutal to his victims. There is every reason to believe that he was thoroughly convinced of the innocence of several of the missionaries whom he caused to be repeatedly tortured, before he had them convicted by unjust means, and executed.

To cause men to be condemned by packed juries, (however favourably the acts of a public functionary, who is guilty of this mockery of justice, may be looked on by his cotemporaries), is to commit atrocious wickedness; and men who thus trample on justice, who sanction or defend a fraud on the highest of all earthly institutions, will be known to posterity only to be execrated by it.

In the collection of the Political Maxims of Walsingham, (in the 29th chapter of his Memoirs), the following passage occurs, which transcends in villany anything that we read in the works of Machiavelli. "False witnesses serve not a little to confirm calumny. This infamous expedient is principally

* Lact. p. 528.

necessary against those who are accused of treason and of capital crimes. And as domestics are very proper for that, (expedient), it is of them also that use is made most often for matters of this sort."* These maxims, it is to be observed, are written for the instruction of Ministers of State, to teach them how to make their way to the favour of the Prince.

Little is known of the quarrel of Elizabeth with Walsingham, in his latter years: he died in disgrace and in bad circumstances, in 1590:

. His library, it is said, was sold to defray the expenses of his burial. His death was a miserable one; that of a disappointed courtier, who had placed his whole freight of happiness in the bark of politics, and when he least thought of danger, the wreck was total.

Dr. Challoner says, " he died miserably of an ulcer and imposthume in his bowels, which reduced him to that wretched condition, that whilst he was yet alive, his chamber became so insupportable, scarce any one could bear to come near him."† The same author adds, "He maintained so many spies abroad, and was at such expense to bring about his wicked enterprizes, that he not only spent what was allowed him by the Queen for that purpose, which was very considerable, but also his whole estate, leaving nothing to his daughter, who having renounced her religion, embraced, at her father's death, the Catholic faith."

Thus died another of the persecutors, with a seared conscience and a callous breast; another of the examples, " Magna et mirabilia," of the direst of all the visitations of the divine retribution.

The death of Elizabeth was more appalling than that of many of the pagan monsters, who perished by the sword, the dagger, or the poisoned bowl.

The proud woman, whose mind was filled by the parasites of her court, her ministers, and her paramours, with exaggerated notions of the gigantic powers of her intellect, and the extraordinary beauty of her person—even when the failings of the former began to be topics of general complaint with her ministers—even when the wrinkles of old age had furrowed her repulsive features—came to old age

* Memoirs, p. 552.
† Memoirs of Missionary Priests.

and to the verge of the grave before she discovered how grossly she had been abused.

The knowledge of the attachment of Essex to the Countess of Rutland, of the fact that she had been despised and deceived, her understanding imposed on, that her person was an object of loathing and disgust to her chief favourite, and as she had reason to know a little later, to all the parasites around her, was a death-blow to the pride and vanity of Elizabeth. She sickened under her disappointments.

In her ravings and revilings, she might have truly said to those around her—

" They have flattered me like a dog.—
.   .   .   .
Go to, they are not men of their words,—
They told me I was everything ; 'tis a lie,
I am not ague-proof."

In Lingard's account of her death, there are some passages which make us almost forget the crimes of the Queen, and think only of the abject wretchedness of this scorned, heart-sick woman.

The close of the career of the persecuting Queen, is thus described by Lingard :—

" She was destined to close the evening of her days in gloom and sorrow. From Essex's confession, she learned the unwelcome and distressing truth, that she had lived too long, that her favourites looked with impatience to the moment which would free them from her controul, and that the very men on whose loyalty she had hitherto reposed with confidence, had already proved unfaithful to her. She became pensive and taciturn ; she sat whole days by herself, indulging in the most gloomy reflections : every rumour agitated her with new and imaginary terrors ; and the solitude of her court, the opposition of the Commons to her prerogative, and the silence of the citizens when she appeared in public, were taken by her for proofs that she had survived her popularity, and was become an object of aversion to her subjects. Under these impressions, she assured the French Ambassador, that she had grown weary of her very existence."*

Sir John Harrington, her god-son, who visited her seven

* History of England, vol. 5, p. 609.

months after Essex's death, described her in a letter—
" Altered in her features and reduced to a skeleton. Her
food was nothing but manchet bread and succory pottage.
Her taste for dress was gone : she had not changed her
clothes for many days. Nothing could please her: she was
the torment of the ladies who waited on her person. She
stamped with her feet and swore violently at the objects of
her anger. For her protection, she had ordered a sword to
be placed by her table, which she often took in her hand
and thrust violently into the tapestry of her chamber.''[*]
About a year later, he returned to the palace, and was
admitted to her presence.—" I found her," he says, "in
a most pitiable state. She bade the Archbishop ask me if
I had seen Tyrone. I replied, with reverence, that I had
seen him with the Lord Deputy. She looked up, with
much choler and grief in her countenance, and said—' O,
now it mindeth me, that you was one who saw this man
elsewhere ;' *and hereat she dropped a tear, and smote her
bosom.* She held in her hand a golden cup, which she often
put to her lips ; but in truth her heart seemed too full
to need more filling."[†]

In January, 1603, she was troubled with a cold, and the
tempest that was raging in her breast and consuming her
vitals, showed its workings in her hurried movements and
flighty moods. She removed on a wet and stormy day,
from Westminster to Richmond. Her disorder was aggra-
vated, but she obstinately refused medical assistance.
Her dejection increased, and it was heightened, it was supposed, by circumstances attending the death of her friend,
the Countess of Nottingham.[‡]

The story of the ring sent by Essex to the Queen after
his condemnation, and retained by the Countess, rests on
the authority of Monsieur Maurier's statement to the
Prince Maurice, which he (Maurier) said had been made to
him by Lord Dorchester, the Ambassador of England at
the Court of Holland.[§]

In a curious tract, published in 1725, entitled, " The
Secret History of the most renowned Queen Elizabeth and

---

* History of England, vol. 5, p. 610.
† Ibid.
‡ Lingard rejects the account of the death-bed interview with the
latter, but perhaps on insufficient grounds.
§ Mem. de Walsing. p. 607.

the Earl of Essex, by a Person of Quality," there is a cir-
cumstantial account of this occurrence.

From the period of the Queen's last illness in January,
she never spoke "except on some unpleasant and irritating
subject." And one of these unpleasant subjects was, *the
war in Ireland.* Even then, Ireland was one of the chief
difficulties of England. Another of the unpleasant subjects
was, "the Earl of Tyrone," whose recent pardon was a
deep grief to her. Tyrone of the "bloody hand," was
a great embodiment of "chief difficulties." And yet there
was a time when the person of the stalworth chief of the
O'Neils, had its attractions for "the Virgin Queen."

"On the 10th of March," says Lingard, "she fell into a
state of stupor, and for some hours lay as dead. As soon as
she recovered, she ordered cushions to be brought and
spread on the floor. On these she seated herself, under a
strange notion that if she were once to lie down in bed she
would never rise again. No prayers of the Secretary, or
the Archbishop, or the Physician, could induce her to
remove, or to take any medicine.

"For ten days she sat on the cushions, generally with
her finger in her mouth, and her eyes opened and fixed on
the ground. Her strength rapidly declined, it was evident
she had but a short time to live."[*]

When Sir Robert Cecil, (the son of Burleigh), and some
other of the high officers of state, came to the dying Queen
on the 22nd of March, to know her pleasure with regard to
the succession, she started as from a dream, repeated some
former words of hers, of which she had been reminded—
"My throne is the throne of kings," and added—"I will
have no rascal to succeed me.—Who should succeed me
but a king?" Cecil asked for some explanation of the
words, "No rascal."—She replied, "a king should succeed her, and who could that be but her cousin of Scotland?"[†] The Archbishop again prayed by her side. She
became speechless, but twice beckoned to him to continue.
In the evening, the three lords came to her again, and
asked, was she still in the same mind? She raised her arms
in the air, closed them over her head, and died at three
o'clock the following morning. Thus miserably died, in

---

[*] Lingard, vol. 5, p. 612.
[†] Ibid.

the midst of regal pomp and splendour, sunk in the lowest
state of melancholy and despair, the unrelenting persecutor of her Roman Catholic subjects.

CHAPTER XII.

PENAL MEASURES AGAINST ROMAN CATHOLICS IN ENGLAND, IN
THE REIGN OF JAMES I., FROM 1603 TO 1625; AND ALSO
IN THE REIGN OF CHARLES I., FROM 1625 TO 1649.

WITH the death of Elizabeth, persecution unfortunately
did not die. James I. found " the Reformation" established. The Catholics, it might have been thought, had been
crushed sufficiently in the previous reign, to have rendered
unnecessary any new attempts to exterminate them. New
measures of severity, however, from time to time, as the
bigotry of the times became urgent, were wrung from the
timid king. He had neither moral nor political courage,
but it is very evident that his zeal for the Protestant
church had more to do with a hatred of the Puritans than
of popery, and that he had a hankering after all for the
old religion which his mother belonged to, and had been
persecuted by the fanatics of Scotland for adhering to.*
His sentiments regarding the doctrines of the Catholic
church, we find pretty plainly stated in a letter addressed
to his sons in Spain, in 1622.
" I have fully instructed them (the chaplains sent with
the young princes) so as all their behaviour and sense shall,
I hope, prove decent and agreeable to the purity of the
primitive church, and yet as near the Roman form as can
lawfully be done, for it hath ever been my way to go with
the church of Rome *usque ad aras*."†
In his first speech from the throne, in reference to the
Catholics, he said, " I hope that those of that profession
within this kingdom, have a proof since my coming, that I
was so far from increasing their burthens with Rehoboam,

* Hume states, that his principles would have led him to earnestly
desire a unity of faith and of the churches which had been separated.
† Hardwicke, State Papers. Ap. Brown, Penal Laws, p. 45.

as I have so much as either time, occasion, or *law* could permit, lightened them."

Concerning those who had been educated from their youth in the Catholic religion, and lived peaceably under his government, he further said, " I would be sorry to punish their bodies for the errors of their minds, the reformation whereof, must only come of God, and the true Spirit."[*]

The parliament, however, throughout the whole of this reign, manifested a spirit of hostility to the Catholics, as determined as it was unchristian and revengeful. " Tie up all that are now recusants ;[†] let Jesuits and seminaries condemned, be hanged ; those not condemned, be judged ;[‡] no band can hold them but a band of imprisonment, a band of banishment, or a band of death."[§] These were common-place words.

James soon found it necessary to propitiate the favour of his new subjects. " And to leave no doubt on their minds of the sincerity of his intentions, a law was passed in the first year of his reign, confirming the statutes of Elizabeth, and enacting, that the two-thirds of the estates seized should be retained after the convict's death, until all arrears of the penalties are paid, and then delivered over to the heir, provided he be no recusant. The one-third, however, left for his support, is not to be liable to seizure for the penalties. Persons going beyond sea, to any Jesuit seminary, or not returning within one year after the end of the next session of parliament, were rendered, as it respects themselves, incapable of purchasing or enjoying any lands or goods, &c. Women also, and children under twenty-one, are restrained from passing over the seas without licence from the king, or six of his privy council. . The penalty of one hundred pounds, levied by 27 Eliz. c. 2. on those who send any child, or other person under their obedience, out of the realm, during her life, is here made perpetual. Persons likewise, who keep school, otherwise than in some university, public grammar-school, or in the houses of noblemen or gentlemen, not

* Journal of the House of Commons, die Jovis 22 Martii, 1603.
† Mr. Brook, Debate on Priests and Masses, die Veneris 25 Maii 1610, Journals of the House of Commons, Vol. i. p. 433.
‡ Mr. Chancellor, ib.
§ Mr. Hook, Debate on report of a conference with the Lords, Veneris 7 die Februarii 1607. Journals of the House of Commons, Vol. i. p. 265.

being recusants, without leave from the bishop, together
with those who retain or maintain them, forfeit forty
shillings for every day they so wittingly offend.   The
one half of these fines is for the king, the other for the
informer."*

In 1604, the discovery of the gunpowder plot, "the
Popish plot," as it was called, involved the Catholics in
new troubles.

Hume attributes this treason to the wide spread disappointment of the Roman Catholics.   When James, who
was believed " to have entered even into positive engagements with them to tolerate their religion, so soon as he
should mount the throne of England,"† took the earliest
opportunity after his accession, to express his resolution
" to execute strictly the laws enacted against Catholics,
and to persevere in all the rigorous measures of Elizabeth."

James allowed his ministers to keep his word for him ;
vast numbers of recusants were presented, the houses and
noble mansions of Catholics were at the mercy of the miscreants, who hung about the public offices.   Their wives'
and daughters' religion was enquired into, and the recusancy
of women visited on their families with heavy fines.

Great disappointment, undoubtedly, was felt by his Catholic subjects, and some Catholics unquestionably were implicated in this conspiracy, and figured too as the authors
of it.   But that many Catholics were privy to it, and that
those who were put forward as the originators were the
real authors of it, are matters which admit of much doubt.

One of the most infamous public acts of James throughout his reign, was the pretence set up by him that his past
forbearance in the case of recusants did not prejudice his
claim to the exaction of the penalties of recusancy.   He
had merely granted time for the payment, in the hope of
the indulgence leading them to conform to the true religion.   To the dismay of the unfortunate Catholic gentry,
the fine for non-attendance on Protestant worship, of £.20
a month, was demanded, " and not only for the time to
come, but for the whole period of the suspension; a demand
which, by crowding thirteen payments into one, reduced

---

* Brown's Penal Laws, p. 53.
† History of England, vol. vi., ch. 47, p. 30.

many families of moderate incomes to a state of absolute beggary."*

To satisfy the wants of his needy countrymen, by whom he was surrounded, he transferred to them his claims on the rich recusants, with a *legal right* to proceed by law for the recovery of the several amounts. Among the sufferers was Robert Catesby, a son of Sir Robert Catesby, a gentleman of Warwickshire, once of considerable property. The father had been imprisoned frequently on charges of recusancy ; the son had abandoned his religion, again returned to it, and had taken part in Essex's conspiracy.

Hume says, the secret of the conspiracy, which had been communicated to above twenty persons, was religiously kept during the space of a year and a half. The secret was at length revealed ; an anonymous letter to Lord Monteagle, a Catholic, son to Lord Morley, warning him to keep away from the opening of parliament, apparently led to the discovery. This letter bears the evident internal evidence of a subtle purpose, far removed from the mere object of cautioning a friend to avoid impending danger. The letter contained unnecessary revelations of the nature of the agency, intended for the destruction of the king and parliament, such as the intimation of "a terrible blow," concealed authors, "a danger past," "no appearance of any stir," and "they shall not see who hurts them."

It was evident that gunpowder was to be the agent of this threatened catastrophe. The principal conspirators were said to be "Piercy, a descendant of the illustrious house of Northumberland ;" "Catesby, a gentleman of good parts and of ancient family ;" "Sir Everard Digby, as highly esteemed and beloved as any man in England, and who had been particularly honoured with the good opinion of Queen Elizabeth."† Also two Jesuits, Tesmond and Garnet, superior of his order in England.

Are these the kind of men to have originated a plot of the most diabolical character, the successful execution of which even could lead to no reasonable hope of triumphing over the Protestant feeling then dominant throughout the country ; and to have associated themselves, of their

---

* Lingard's History of England, vol. 1. ch. 1.
† Hume, Ibid. ch. 47, p. 34-35-37.

own motion, with a desperado of a reckless character in a rash, bloody, and merciless design? The master-hand of a subtle state villain, of the stamp of Walsingham, in a preceding reign, or of *a Cecil* in that of James, or of Shaftesbury in a succeeding one, is discoverable in the skilfully woven meshes of treason, in which the obnoxious Catholic gentlemen, then justly irritated at the perfidious conduct of the king towards them, were entangled.

Hume acknowledges that the mystery of the machination of this plot had never been cleared up.*

James, in his speech to the parliament in reference to the plot, spoke generously of the criminality of involving all the Catholics in the guilt of the conspirators. "Nothing," he said, " can be more hateful than the uncharitableness of the puritans, who condemn alike to eternal torments even the most inoffensive partizans of popery. For his part," he added, " that conspiracy, however atrocious, should never alter, in the least, his plan of government; while with one hand he punished guilt, with the other, he would support and protect innocence."†

The professed intentions of the monarch were not in accordance with the views of the parliament. Its deliberations were unhappily guided by the demon of revenge and of persecution.

The following notice of the enactments of it against Catholics are chiefly taken from Brown's " Penal Laws."

By one of their statutes,‡ it is enacted, that popish recusants conforming, within the first year, and once within every year afterwards, shall take the sacrament according to the rites of the church of England, in the parish church, or in the one next adjoining, under forfeiture for the first year of twenty pounds, the second of forty, and for every

---

* " A true and impartial Narrative of the Dissenters' new Plot; with a large Relation of all their old ones, by one who was deeply concerned therein;" (originally published soon after the Revolution, 1691, and reprinted in Somers's State Tracts, Collection 3, vol. 3. p. 56,) contains the following passage,—" The succeeding reign of King James would afford a very large field, and tempt to expatiate on their plots therein. As their *sham plot of the gunpowder treason*, thrown upon the Catholics to render them odious, albeit they have so frequently, when thereon interrogated, assured the world it was a mere trick of Cecil's, (their religion not permitting them to equivocate or lie), with others truly innumerable."

† Hume, c. 46, § 14.
‡ 3 James 1, c. 4.

other year, or having once received it and afterwards offending, of sixty pounds: one half to the king and the other to the informer. Churchwardens making monthly returns of the absence of recusants from church, receive, as a reward for their diligence, if the offenders (not having been before presented) are amerced, forty shillings, to be levied out of the goods of the recusant. If they neglect to return such absentees (together with the names of their children and servants) once in the year, to the quarter sessions, they forfeit twenty shillings. The king is also empowered to refuse the forfeiture of twenty pounds, imposed by 23 Eliz. c. 1. and to take the two parts of the lands, according to the 29 Eliz. c. 6. But this choice is softened by a proviso, that the mansion house shall be left to the offender as a part of his lands. Bishops or any two justices of the peace, are likewise empowered to require any person above eighteen, (other than noblemen,)* convicted of, or even indicted for recusancy, in not repairing to church, or who have not received the sacrament twice in the last year, and persons unknown, who passing through their liberties, refuse to deny that they are popish recusants, or have not so received the sacrament, to take the oath of supremacy and allegiance, abjuring the temporal authority of the pope, and the spiritual exercise of it against the king's interests.

Those who refuse the oath are to be imprisoned till the next assizes, or quarter sessions, where it is again to be tendered, and if they then refuse it, they incur the pains of a premunire, except women convicts, who are to be committed to the common jail till they will take the oath. Gentlemen also, with persons of higher degree, or captains or lieutenants, who go abroad to serve any foreign prince, are required to give bond, with two sureties, in twenty pounds at least, that they will not be reconciled to the see of Rome; and persons who so depart, without taking the oath, are declared felons. The better to provide for the execution of this, and the preceding prohibitory and penal statutes, the sheriff, as in cases of ap-

---

* If any person (not noble) happen to be at the Assizes or Quarter Sessions, though not brought in upon process for recusancy, and the oath be tendered him, and he refuse it, he shall incur a Premunire, though it were never tendered him before.—12 Coke, 131.

prehending thieves and traitors, is empowered to break into a house to take a recusant; and the lords of the council, or any six of them, (of which the chancellor, treasurer, or principal secretary is to be one,) to require the oath of any nobleman or noblewoman, who, by a refusal to take it, incur the pains of a premunire.

The next chapter of the same statute* extends still further the system of discovering offenders by holding out rewards and immunities to such as will inform against them. A discovery of the heinous offence of bestowing shelter and a morsel of bread upon the poor hungry outcasts of the earth, whom the strong arm of the law was pursuing even unto death, for adhering to the dictates of conscience in the midst of persecution and of proscription, the statute provided a reward for.

By this act it is provided, that any one discovering a recusant, or other person receiving or entertaining a popish priest, persons hearing mass, or the priest saying the same within three days after the offence, so that he or they may be amerced and attainted, he shall not only be free from danger, if he be an offender therein, but shall have a third part of the forfeiture of the recusant's goods, provided it exceed not one hundred and fifty pounds, (in which case he shall have fifty), and a warrant to the sheriff to levy the same.

The act further ordains that no recusant shall come into the court or house where the king or his heir apparent shall be, unless by warrant in writing from the privy council, under forfeiture of one hundred pounds. Popish recusants convict, and persons who have foreborne repairing to church for three months, are ordered also to depart the city of London, and ten miles round it, within ten days, under a like forfeiture. Those, however, who exercise any trade, mystery, or manual occupation, or who have no other dwelling, are allowed to remain where they have resided for the last three months previous to the session of parliament, provided they give up their names and residences to the lord mayor, or to the next justice of the peace. The provisions of 35 Eliz. c. 2, are confirmed, but the power of granting licences to recusants to go beyond

* 3 James I. c. 5.

five miles from their habitations, is repealed, and in lieu thereof, it is provided, that three of the privy council may give such licence, for a time therein specified. Four justices of the peace next adjoining the recusant's abode, with the consent, in writing, of the bishop of the diocese, or of the lieutenant, or deputy lieutenant of the county, under their hands and seals, may likewise grant a similar permission, specifying the cause of the licence, and how long the party is to be absent, travelling, attending, and returning : he first making oath, that he has truly specified the cause of his journey, and that he will make no needless stay.

Popish recusants are also forbidden to practise the common or civil law, as counsellors, advocates, attorneys, proctors, or clerks ; or physic, even as an apothecary ; or to be a judge, steward, or other officer of any court or corporation ; or to bear charge as a captain, lieutenant, corporal, sergeant, or ancient-bearer in the army ; or any office or charge in the navy, castles, or fortresses of the king, his heirs or successors, or, in short, any public office whatever, under forfeiture of one hundred pounds for every offence ; the one half to the king, and the other to the informer.

This provision, indeed, was extended to those who marry a wife who is a popish recusant ; it being enacted, that no such person shall exercise any public office or charge in the commonwealth, by himself or deputy, except he and his children above nine years of age, together with his servants, repair to church at least once in every month, to hear divine service ; and such of them as are of meet age to receive the sacrament, at such times as the law prescribes, and except he bring up his children *in the true religion.*

Women recusants, married to husbands, not being convict, after the death of such husbands, incur the same forfeiture of lands and dower as other recusants, and are totally disabled from acting as executrix, or administratrix, and from enjoying any part of his goods and chattels. All persons, indeed, convicted of recusancy, until they come to church, and take the oath of 3 James I. c. 4., are so completely incapacitated to defend their civil rights, that any persons sued by them may plead the disability of the

plaintiff, as if he or she were actually excommunicated by
sentence of the ecclesiastical court.*

A recusant, who shall be married otherwise than according to the rites of the Church of England, is deprived of
the privilege of holding any lands, &c., belonging to his
wife, as tenant by the courtesy of England ; whilst a woman
so marrying, is not allowed to take dower, widow's estate,
or any portion of the goods of her husband, by any custom
or privilege whatever. And lest the recusant should be
fortunate enough to avoid this deprivation of his rights, by
choosing a woman who has no lands, it is further enacted,
that for thus marrying against the intent and meaning of
this act, he shall forfeit one hundred pounds. A similar
penalty is provided for the not having their children bap-
tized within a month after their birth, according to the
rites of the Church of England, in some public church or
chapel in or near the place where they are born.   Nor
were the Parliament content with thus debarring them,
under heavy penalties, from being married, or having their
children christened, according to their own ritual ; or with
prescribing to them a form, which they held at the least to
be of none effect. The necessary consequence of this pro-
cedure must have been destructive to the interests of
morality. But they stopped not their persecutions here,
but pursued their victims to the grave, nor suffered them
to rest even there in peace. For it is enacted by the same
statute, that no popish recusant, unless he be actually
excommunicated, shall be buried in any other place than in
a church or church-yard consecrated according to the
ecclesiastical laws of this realm, under a forfeiture of twenty
pounds, to be levied on the persons causing them to be so
unlawfully buried.

Children sent out of the realm without licence, incur the
incapacities of inheriting lands, &c., recited in 1 James I.
c. 4. until they return, and within six months after their
arrival conform and take the oath of 3 James I. c. 4.

The presenting, collating, and nominating to any benefice, or donative whatever, is likewise taken from recusants,

---

* A popish recusant convict it disabled, as an excommunicated person, to be a witness in any cause between party and party.—Bulstrode,
155. The same point seems admitted, 1 St. Tr. 268. 3 St. Tr. 245.—
Cawley, 216. But this seems to be a construction over severe.—2 Haw-
kins's Pleas of the Crown, 33.

and given to the two universities.   Nor are they even
allowed to act as executors, administrators, or guardians of
any child, but in the latter case the wardship is given to
the next of kin, to whom the lands cannot lawfully descend,
who shall resort to church, and receive the sacrament three
times a year.   And such of the king's wardships as shall
be granted or sold to any popish recusant, shall be void and
of none effect.

The next object of this very extensive statute, is to prevent the bringing from beyond sea any popish missals,
psalters, legends, &c., in any language, or any superstitious
book in English, under a forfeiture of all such books, (which
are to be burned ;) and of forty shillings for each individual
offence.   And any two justices, and all magistrates of corporations, are empowered, from time to time, to enter the
houses and lodgings of popish recusants, or those whose
wives are Papists, and if they find any crucifix, beads,
popish relic, or book, which they shall think unmeet for
such recusant to have, they are presently to be defaced and
burned.   A strange species of inquisition this, by virtue of
which a man, the most ignorant, may have the right of
invading the privacy and domestic sanctuary of his neigh-
bour, of rummaging his property, and of destroying every
thing, which to his wisdom may seem unmeet for him to
possess.   Another clause contains a proviso, if they find
any crucifix or other relic of value, that it is to be defaced
at the next quarter Sessions, and then returned to the
owner.

The final provisions of this act refer to the arms and
munition in the possession of recusants, which may be taken
from them, by order of four justices at the sessions, leaving
to them such part only as they shall think necessary for
the defence of their houses and persons.

The parliament having moved an address, praying a
more rigorous execution of the laws against the Papists,
and an abatement of those against Protestant clergymen,
who did not observe the rites and ceremonies of the established church ; they were refused their petition, and commanded, by the king, not to interfere in such matters.*
Before their dissolution, however, they passed a law,†
enacting, that no person of, or above eighteen years of age,

* Hume, c. 46. § 20.   † 7 James I. c. 2.
12

shall be naturalized, or restored in blood, unless within a month previous to the exhibiting the bill, they shall have received the sacrament, according to the rites of the Church of England, and taken the oaths of allegiance and supremacy in the parliament house, before the bill be twice read.

By the sixth chapter of the same statute,* all officers, civil, ecclesiastical, and military, doctors, &c., are compelled to take the oath of allegiance.

It is also enacted, that if any married woman convicted as a popish recusant, shall not conform within three months, and receive the sacrament, she shall be committed to prison, there to remain till she shall conform. The husband, however, has the choice of two methods of redeeming his helpmate from durance; the one, that of paying ten pounds per month; the other, of forfeiting to the king the one-third of his lands, so long as she shall remain a recusant; during the continuance of which penalty, and no longer, she may continue at large.

"Pending the negotiations for the marriage of prince Charles, and the Infanta, sister to Philip IV. of Spain, to forward which James had even proceeded so far as to issue public orders for the release of all popish recusants imprisoned,† the commons‡ presented a very violent memorial to the king, complaining of his indulgence to the professors of the Catholic faith, which, together with the hopes they entertained from the Spanish match, encouraged their insolence and temerity, and induced them to expect the complete toleration, if not the final re-establishment of their religion. It concluded, by entreating that his majesty would cause all the children of popish recusants to be taken from their parents, and committed to the care of Protestant teachers, and that the penalties to which the Catholics were by law subjected, might be levied with the utmost severity. To this the king answered, that he commanded them as he had before done, not to intermeddle with matters of such high importance to his state and dignity.§ On this they presented a fresh remonstrance, asserting their right to interfere with advice in all matters of government.‖ The king, in a spirited reply, told them, they were not entitled to interfere with anything that concerned his

* 7 James I. c. 6.
† Hume, c. 64, § 5.   ‡ 1 Rushworth, 41.
§ 1 Rushworth, 43.   ‖ Ibid. 44.

prerogatives, and that they had no rights but what they derived from the grace and permission of himself and his predecessors.* The commons, in their turn, entered a protest in vindication of their privileges ; and the king, having torn this instrument from their journals before the council,† terminated the sitting of the parliament, and soon afterwards‡ dissolved it by proclamation. On this occasion, he published a vindication of *his* conduct, and committed Coke, Seldon, Pym, and other leading members of the house to prison, as a punishment of their's."§

In 1623, a dispensation had been granted by Pope Gregory XV., for the marriage of the prince Charles with the Infanta of Spain.

To obtain the papal sanction for this mixed marriage, James entered into articles of agreement with the courts of Rome and Madrid, by one of which the exercise of the Catholic religion for the Infanta and her household was guaranteed ; by another, the education of any children by this marriage till ten years of age. " Besides this public treaty," says Hume, " there were separate articles *privately sworn to* by the king, in which he promised to suspend the Penal Laws enacted against Catholics, to procure a repeal of them in parliament, and to grant a toleration of the Catholic religion in private houses."‖

Hume, in reference to this promised toleration, sworn to, be it remembered, by James, further adds, " it was inscribed only to amuse the Pope, and was never intended by either party to be executed."¶

There is a cool debonnaire recklessness of all consideration, and profligacy in regard to literary morals, that distinguishes Hume, and renders him particularly worthy of such a task, as that of palliating a solemn violation, deliberately intended, of an agreement sworn to by a sovereign.

The humour of the parliament and of the people at this time, jumped with the spirit of puritanism. All affected a holy horror of popery. The most unprincipled men had to cloak their vices under the veil of sanctimony, and the only

---

* 1 Rushworth, 52. † Ibid. 54.
‡ January 6th, 1621, Original Proclamations in the Inner Temple library.
§ Brown's Penal Laws, p. 73.
‖ Hume's Hist. ¶ Ibid. p. 155.

test of piety, was depth of hate for the religion and the professors of Catholicism.   Lawyers and statesmen of the highest eminence, found it necessary to be hypocrites, to seem to be bigots, in order to pass for sage judges and profound politicians.   There was no justice, no liberty, no virtue, beyond the pale of the Church, which they made their ladder to place or power.

Sir Edward Coke, when presiding on the trial of Mrs. Turner, told her in his address, that she was guilty of the seven deadly sins ; she was a whore, a bawd, a sorcerer, a witch, a papist, a felon, and a murderer.   The learned and philosophic Bacon, (who as Attorney-General conducted the prosecution,) on the trial of Somerset, earnestly impressed on the minds of the peers, that poisoning was unheard of in these kingdoms, but as a popish trick.*

Throughout this reign the condition of the Catholics was deplorable.   Hume would have it believed that it was much ameliorated.   The king desired to ameliorate it, but he had not the courage nor the power to do so.   In every political crisis, in every public excitement, we find the parliament constantly calling out for new edicts against Catholics.

In 1610, the murder of the French king by Ravillac afforded a pretence for executing the penal laws with renewed vigour.

No matter what was the nature of any calamity that occurred, at home or abroad, the cry was raised, " Down with Popery !" "The Penal Laws in execution !"   The old war-whoop of the time of Tertullian, "Away with the Christians to the lions !" was new worded ; and eventually the cry of the persecutors, curtailed in matter, had all the bitterness of its original malice concentrated in that single yell of "No Popery !" which is known even in our times.

James died in 1625, after a reign over England of twenty-two years.   His death occasioned neither sorrow nor satisfaction.

The penal enactments in the reign of James I. (as they are set forth in Cawley's "Penal Laws") were five :

"An Act for the due execution of the statutes against Jesuits, seminary priests, recusants," &c. (1 Jac. cap. iv.)

* Brown's Penal Laws.

"An Act for the better discovering and repressing of popish recusants." (3 Jac. cap. iv.)

"An Act to prevent and avoid dangers which may grow by popish recusants." (3 Jac. cap. v.)

"An Act to cause persons to be naturalized or restored in blood, to conform and take the oath of allegiance and supremacy." (7 Jac. cap. ii.)

"An Act for the reformation of married recusant women, and administration of the oath of allegiance to all civil, military, ecclesiastical, and professional persons."

Charles I. came to the throne in 1625. In the previous year his marriage with the French princess, Henrietta, had been "conciliated," (to use Hume's phrase,) and an article inserted in the treaty, which conferred on the Catholic princess the right of educating the children by this marriage till the age of thirteen. "The court of England, however," says Hume, "always pretended, even in the memorials to the French court, that all the favourable conditions granted to the Catholics were inserted in the marriage treaty merely to please the Pope, and that their strict execution was, by an agreement with France, secretly dispensed with."*

Hume defends his Stuart against the murmurs of his fanatic subjects, for the disposition shown to give any toleration to popery ; and without seeming to be aware of the infamy which the validity of his apology would stamp on the king's character. A few pages further on he says: "The court, however, it must be confessed, always pretended, even in the memorials to the French court, that all the favourable conditions granted to the Catholics, were inserted in the marriage treaty merely to please the Pope, and their strict execution was, by an agreement with France, secretly dispensed with."†

The first remonstrance of the parliament to the king set forth the great grievance of popery, which had been tolerated and suffered to increase ; and complained bitterly of the many pardons which had been granted to recusants and priests, who by law were liable to be dealt with as traitors.‡

* Hume's History of England, Vol. vi. p. 155.
† Hume's History of England, Vol. vi. Chap. 50, p. 137. See also Franklyn, Rushworth, Kennet.
‡ Rushworth, 231.

The next session was ushered in with a similar remonstrance. The king wanted money, but the parliament was liberal only in complaints against popery. Instead of redressing the great grievance, however, by new persecution, the king compounded with the recusants for the penalties of their old offences against bigotry : he found the money of the Catholics more serviceable to him than their blood. Those compositions, however, in the next parliament, were declared by his faithful commons, " hurtful to God, full of dishonour and disprofit to his majesty, and extreme scandal and grief to his good people."*

Buckingham's unpopularity, which contributed so largely to his master's, was not altogether caused by his public or private misdeeds. The criminality of having a mother a professed Catholic, and a wife suspected of being one, and the guilt "of remitting the rigours of the penalties imposed on Catholics," were the chief causes of the hostility of the parliament to him, and eventually of his assassination by the zealot, Fenton. The parliament, however grateful to Providence for this manifest token of its goodness, proceeded in its pious course of remonstrating against popery. The king commanded an adjournment,which the speaker was not suffered to carry into effect before another remonstrance was framed, " declaring all Papists and Arminians capital enemies of the commonwealth."

The fury against papacy extended in a short time to episcopal protestantism ; and the whigs of that day lent themselves to all the fanatical measures of the puritans, whom in secret they despised and ridiculed.

Archbishop Laud (the precursor of Dr. Pusey) was accounted by the puritans a covert Catholic. All his leanings towards ancient ritual observances, were evidences of flat popery. The violence of their animosity to this eminent prelate begot violent measures on his part ; the puritanical zeal pushed on episcopal fervour to an unhappy extremity in Scotland, where the efforts of the archbishop to introduce the litany and canons of the Church of England, established completely the Presbyterian religion, made a great power of the Covenant, and brought a Scotch army beyond the English borders.

In 1629, in the midst of the strife between the king and

* Rushworth, 621.

the commons, and of the extraordinary occurrences which, in all similar remarkable conjunctures, call forth extraordinary energies, and bring on the public stage remarkable actors, "a young man, of no account in the nation,"* made his first appearance in the published accounts of the debates, "as complaining of one who, he was told, preached flat popery."†

The "young man of no account" was Oliver Cromwell. His debut was worthy of his character, and the drama in which he was destined *to play* the fanatic with such complete success.

Prynne, in his "Popish Royal Favourite," says, the number of convictions of recusants in twenty-nine English counties, was 11,970; even, in many instances, though the accounts were only up to the ninth year of the king's reign, and in some instances to the sixteenth. Browne makes mention of the parliamentary debates in 1640, in which, among the specified charges against Mr. Secretary Windebank, it was stated, "that he had granted seventy-four letters of grace to recusants within four years; that sixty-four priests had been discharged from the Gate-house within the same period, for the most part by him, and twenty-nine by his verbal warrant. With respect to the unfortunate priests, it appears that their denial of the pope's supremacy, and even their active endeavours to induce others to deny it also, availed them nothing in mitigating the spirit of persecution against them."‡

Respecting the condition of the persecuted Catholics, in a letter to the attorney-general, Archbishop Laud said: "They live more miserable lives, than if they were in the inquisition in many parts beyond the seas. By taking the oath of allegiance, and writing in defence of it, and opening some points of high consequence," he adds, "they have so displeased the pope, that if by any contriving they could catch them, they are sure to be burned and strangled for it. And if the placing our fellow creatures in this state of jeopardy and confinement, be not persecution, I confess I know not what is."§

"The proceedings of the Long Parliament, which began

---

* Hume, Vol. vi. 276.
† Ibid. Rushworth. Vol. i. p. 646.
‡ Rushworth, 243.
§ Brown's Penal Laws, p. 48.

its sittings in November, 1641, soon evinced what manner of men it was composed of. The commons ordered, of their own authority, that all images, altars, and crucifixes should be destroyed ; and so strictly were those orders executed, that Hume has observed, that they did 'not allow one piece of wood or stone to lie over another at right angles.' This was merely preparatory to a fresh requisition to the king, to seize on the two-thirds of the lands of recusants, to which he was by law entitled, and not, as he hitherto had done, to let them retain it on easy composi- tions. By one of their addresses they removed all popish officers from the army, insisted on the rigorous execution of the sanguinary laws against the priests, and even pro- cured one of these unfortunate beings, who was already in prison, to be condemned to suffer that ignominious death, from which he was saved but by the pressure of more impor- tant business on his persecutors.............

" In the celebrated remonstrance of the twenty-second of November, 1641, which the commons addressed as an appeal to the people, all the real and imaginary grievances which they could heap together, were, without the shadow of a' pretence, ascribed to the determined combination of the popish faction, which, according to their representa- tion, had ever governed the king. Soon after this declara- tion, on the single evidence of a journeyman tailor, who pretended that, when walking in the fields, he had over- heard some persons unknown, talking of the engagement of a hundred and eight bravoes to murder an equal number of noblemen and commoners, at the extravagant reward of ten pounds for each lord, and forty shillings for each com- moner,—these advocates of liberty, these opponents of tyranny and oppression, issued an order for the seizure of all priests and jesuits, to whom the plot, as a matter of course, was ascribed."*

In 1640, the queen-mother of France, who had sought refuge in England, was openly insulted in London by the populace on account of her religion. Her life was endan- gered ; application was made to parliament to cause these outrages to be suppressed. The commons admitted the royal lady was entitled to protection, but prayed that she might be desired to depart the kingdom, in which she had

<hr>

*. Brown's Penal Laws, p. 81, 82.

occasioned " great jealousies in the hearts of his majesty's well-affected subjects, by the use and practice of the idolatry of the mass, and exercise of other superstitious services of the Romish Church, to the great scandal of true religion."

The happy effects of the Reformation on the national character, were exhibited alike in the conduct of the brutal populace and the brutal commons, to a woman and a foreigner, the guest of the sovereign, the mother of the queen of England.

A clergyman of the name of Barnard, lecturer of St. Sepulchre's, London, poured forth a prayer before his sermon, with this passage: "Lord, open the eyes of the queen's majesty, that she may see Jesus Christ, whom she has pierced with her infidelity, superstition, and idolatry."*

" The queen, (Henrietta), after having been long subjected to the grossest insults, was threatened with a prosecution for exercising a mode of worship, secured to her by the faith of a public marriage treaty, and to save her life, as she thought (and, at least, not very improbably) was obliged to fly the kingdom."†

After the king's imprisonment, in violation of public faith and of all decency, by a vote of the Lords and Commons, it was declared that—" The Houses, out of their detestation to that abominable idolatry used in the mass, cannot admit of any such indulgence in any law as is desired by his majesty, for exempting the queen and her family out of such acts as are desired to be passed for a stricter course to prevent the hearing or saying of mass."‡

On the 2nd of December, 1641, we find that it was, "after a solemn debate, resolved by the Lords and Commons, that *they would never give consent to any toleration of the Popish religion in Ireland, or in any other of his majesty's dominions.*"

The Commons left no means untried, to make the No Popery cry, a great public clamour. Meetings were got up, petitions manufactured for them by their emissaries, the porters of London, to the number, it is said, of fifteen

* Hume, Vol. vi. Chap. 53, p. 297.
† Hume.
‡ Sir E. Walker's Copies of the Treaty, p. 71.

thousand,* professed themselves extremely alarmed for the
safety of the true religion, *against the attacks of papists and
delinquents.* " A petition was presented by many thousands
of the lower order of women, stating their fears of the commission of massacres, rapes, and the most dreadful outrages on their sex, by the abominable and wicked Papists."†
This address was interlarded with scriptural expressions,
they quoted the example of the women of Tekoah. Pym, a
leading member of the house, thanked this rabble for their
petition, and begged their prayers for the house, " against
the machinations of the Papists and other enemies of the
Lord and of the Church."‡

The emissaries of the Parliament thus stirred up the
people in various quarters to revolution. A proclamation was issued, calling on the people to take arms against
Papists and other ill-affected persons.§ A bill was passed
for making lieutenants and deputy-lieutenants accountable
only to their tribunal : the preamble of this bill makes
a piteous complaint of some, till then unheard of, design
against the House of Commons, which they believe had its
origin in the bloody councils of Papists. The king, with
good reason, refused his assent to the bill, and thus came
at last to open war with his faithful Commons. Civil war
ensued ; the chances of success were on the side of Parliament. It is needless to say, the king's friends were not
long on his.

There is one thing that ought to be borne in mind, in
considering the persecution of the Catholics in those
times —*All the Stuarts were averse to the furious measures of their Parliaments against Catholics.* They thought,
as Charles the First especially did, according to Hume,
" that a little humanity was due by the nation to the religion of their ancestors."

Extreme rage against Roman Catholics was, from first
to last, the true characteristic of Puritanism, we are told by
the same historian, and that rage was the only public
interest that could be said to be truly represented in any
Parliament of James, his son, or his grand-children.

The Puritans at length made an end of the monarchy

* 1 Clarendon, 322.
† 7 Harl. Misc. 367.
‡ Hume, Chap. 55. p. 78.
§ Nelson, p. 327.

and the monarch.   On the 30th of January, 1649, after a reign of twenty-four years, Charles the First fell a victim to the fury of faction and fanaticism, under the cloak of zeal for liberty and religion.

The arts of his enemies drove him to the commission of arbitrary and despotic acts.   But to his honour, it should be remembered, that all their remonstrances, menaces, and insolent addresses to him, succeeded only in two instances, in extorting his sanction to the enactment of English penal laws.   Cawley, in his collection of Penal Statutes, in the reigns of Elizabeth, James, and Charles, specifies no less than nine passed in the reign of Elizabeth ; five in the reign of James ; and *two only* in the reign of Charles I.   An act to restrain the sending of any children beyond the seas to be popishly educated, 3 Car. 1, cap. 2 ; and a supplemental act continuing for a time a temporary act of Elizabeth, 35, cap. 1, which compels non-conformists to abjure the realm.*

* This act after several revocations and revisals, was continued for three years by George II., and then expired.

CHAPTER XIII.

MEASURES OF THE COMMONWEALTH AND PROTECTORATE AGAINST
THE ROMAN CATHOLICS OF ENGLAND, FROM 1649 TO 1660.

WE are now truly come to the times,—

" When civil dudgeon first grew high,
    And men fell out they knew not why,
    When hard words, jealousies, and fears,
    Set folks together by the ears,
    And made them fight like mad or drunk,
    For dame Religion as for Punk,
    Whose honesty they all durst swear for,
    Though not a man of them knew wherefore:
    When gospel trumpeter surrounded,
    With long eared rout, to battle sounded,
    And pulpit drum ecclesiastic,
    Was beat with fist instead of a stick."*

The Presbyterians, in their great zeal for gospel liberty,
no sooner obtained power, than they forgot the wrongs
they had endured at the hands of Protestant intolerance ;
they became persecutors of all other sects and creeds, and
out-heroded Herod in the extravagance of their intolerance.
The Protestant clergy were ejected from their livings, not
only for refusing the Covenant, but for using the book of
Common Prayer, and for even signing the cross on chris-
tening a child, they were committed to prison.†
    Whitelocke, in his Memorials, p. 518, relates, that, in
December, 1650, a letter of advice was sent to the parliament, proposing that " *all those drunken, malignant, scanda-*

---

* Hudibras, Part 1. Can. 1.
    † By an ordinance of August 23, 1645, any person using the book of
Common Prayer, forfeited for the first offence five pounds, for the
second ten, and for the third suffered one year's imprisonment. Ministers not using the Directory, forfeited for each offence forty shillings,
and whoever disparaged any part of it, such sum as to those before
whom he is tried shall seem fit, provided it be not less than five, or
more than fifty pounds. And all Common Prayer Books in churches
or chapels, were ordered to be brought to the committee within a
month, under a forfeiture of forty shillings for each book.—4 Rushworth, 207.

lous, delinquent, ignorant, whoring, cursing, and profane ones, that go under the name of ministers, be put to work for their livings."

Dr. Walker, in his account of the sufferings of the Protestant clergy, p. 54, says, *" they were imprisoned in the holds of ships, where many of them died, and even a proposal was made for sending them to Algiers, to be sold as slaves to the Turks."*

It appears by a tract in the Harleian Miscellany, (vol. 2, p. 326), the number of the clergy in London and Westminster, deprived of their livings, amounted to 115; and "the most of them were plundered of their goods, and their wives and children turned out of doors." The tables were now turned on the persecutors,—the Puritans trampled on them, abolished their establishment, its episcopacy, its right and usages.

One ejected divine, in a "Petitionary Remonstrance," addressed to the Protector, in 1655, speaking of the distressed condition of "the sequestered ministers," says— " The vulture of famine, and all worldly calamities, must be ever preying upon the bowels of themselves, their wives, and children ; being only suffered to survive their miseries, as men hung alive in chains, *and forced, with their relations, either to beg, steal, or starve."*

. The acts of the parliaments assembled between the death of Charles I. and the Restoration, against Catholics, were in keeping with those of Elizabeth.

An ordinance of both houses, dated April 1, 1643, ordains the confiscation of two-thirds of all Papists' lands, rents, &c., and the same penalty for harbouring any Popish priest or Jesuit, or being present at mass, or suffering children, or grand-children, or others under their charge, to be brought up in the Roman Catholic religion : or refusing, being of the age of twenty-one years, to take the oath of abjuration and supremacy. The swearer whereof maketh oath, there is no truth in the doctrine of transubstantiation, purgatory, and no efficacy in worship offered up to crucifixes or images, and that salvation cannot be merited by works. .

On the 1st of January, 1654-5, " the house regulated the point of liberty of conscience upon the new plan, and agreed to give it to all who shall not maintain *Atheism,*

Popery, prelacy, profaneness, or any damnable heresy, to be enumerated by the parliament."

" In 1650, an act was passed, offering to the discoverers of priests and Jesuits, their receivers and abettors, the same reward as had been granted to the apprehenders of highway-men. Immediately officers and informers were employed in every direction : the houses of Catholics were broken open, and searched at all hours of the day and night : many clergymen were tried, and received judgment of death. Of these, only one, Peter Wright, chaplain to the Marquis of Winchester, suffered. The leaders shrunk from the odium of such sanguinary exhibitions, and transported the rest of the prisoners to the Continent."[*]

The ordinances for confiscating and sequestering Catholic property, however, were executed with unrelenting severity. In 1650, the annual rents of sequestered Catholic property, amounted to £.62,048, sterling.

The first important act of the Prince Charles, in the attempt to recover the throne of his father, was one of perfidy and baseness. He followed the example of his father respecting the powers of Glamorgan—he denied the commands he had given to the ill-fated Montrose, when the latter was defeated.[†] In 1650, " he bound himself to take the Scottish Covenant and solemn league, to declare null the peace with the Irish, and never to permit the free exercise of the Catholic religion in Ireland or any other part of his dominions."[‡]

On his arrival in Scotland, he was called on to make " an expiatory declaration in the name of the Parliament and the Kirk," in which he was called on to lament " his father's opposition to the work of God"—the Solemn League and Covenant—" his mother's idolatry;" " to detest popery and prelacy, idolatry and heresy, schism and profaneness."[§] The insulting declaration was at first indignantly refused, but at the expiration of three days, was signed by the young Prince. In a few days after, the Scotch troops in front of the English army, quitting the heights of Lammermoor and the Doon hill, were seen by Cromwell, when he exclaimed, " they are coming down, the Lord hath delivered them into our hands."

* Lingard's History of England, Vol. x. p. 399.
† Ibid. p. 307.   ‡ Ibid. p. 307.
        § Ibid, p. 313.

Having caused his regiments to sing the 117th Psalm—three thousand Scotchmen were slain, ten thousand taken prisoners, and all the artillery and stores of the army became the booty of the saints and Cromwell. The Scots attributed their defeat to their negligence in purging their army of malignant papists and other sons of Belial. The Prince's cause, in a word, was sacrificed to the bigotry of his supporters.*

" Cromwell," (says Lord Clarendon to one of his correspondents, on the 16th of November, 1652), "is solicitous enough to persuade them," (the Catholics, even at a time when *the priests and bishops are ignominiously murdered in cold blood, and after quarter given, as it falls out every day in Ireland*), " that they shall have a toleration for the exercise of their religion; whereas, whoever knows the temper of those people that govern the constitution of their army, and the humour of the rabble of England, who have now the power, must conclude that after they have lulled them asleep with these hopes, in a time when they might be of use towards their sovereign's restoration, they will no sooner find their fears abated, than they will exercise all imaginable rage and fury against the Roman Catholics, which shall not end, but with their utter eradication out of all the dominions subject to their tyranny."

In another letter, dated 10th October, 1653, he thus addresses himself to Mr. Secretary Nicholas : "Be confident, all that is done against the Catholics in England is real; not that I believe Cromwell would have it so, but *there is and always will be a senseless, violent, furious spirit* in such meetings, which in some particulars must be complied with *against prudence and reason of state, which hath never yet governed in that matter of the Catholics.*"†

By an "Ordinance for the ejection of scandalous, ignorant, and insufficient ministers and schoolmasters," passed on the 29th of August, 1654, it is enacted that such minis-

---

*After the defeat of the young prince at Worcester, Hume states, that the Catholics frequently sheltered the royal fugitive. He was concealed on various occasions by members of the proscribed faith, in what they termed the priest's hole. "Thus did those places of secretion, which the sanguinary laws of his ancestors had compelled a large body of his subjects to provide for the ministers of their religion, when hunted by the avaricious informers, or blood-thirsty zealots, who were seeking *their* lives, afford the king a refuge in his distress; when he, in his turn, was hunted by zealots as desirous of depriving him of *his.*"

† Clarendon's State Papers, p. 117.

ters and schoolmasters *shall be accounted scandalous in their lives and conversations, as have publicly and frequently read the Common Prayer Book*, or shall at any time hereafter do the same, or who maintain any of those *Popish opinions* required in the oath of abjuration to be abjured; such as do publicly and profanely scoff at and revile the strict profession or professors of religion or godliness, or do encourage or countenance, by word or practice, any *Whitson-ales-wakes, morris-dances, May-poles, stage-plays, or such like licentious practices.*

On the 1st of May, 1655, a proclamation was issued against Jesuits and priests, at the express recommendation of the Council of State, to the Lord Protector. And about the same time, we find it stated, as the opinion of Mr. Attorney General Prideaux, and Mr. Steele, the Recorder, on a question "whether the Lord Protector may not make a lease of the two parts of a recusant's estate which are under sequestration for recusancy only? that he may make such leases *for what time and what rent he pleaseth.*" .

. By the fifteenth article of the new fundamental governmental instrumental, the Catholics were deprived of the mere shadow of a political existence which they had hitherto retained; it being thereby enacted that *"persons who do or shall profess the Roman Catholic religion, shall be disabled and incapable for ever to be elected or to give any vote in the election of any member to serve in parliament."* This was a further extension of the disabilities to which Catholics were already subjected.

Lingard cites an original document, authenticated by the signatures of the parties concerned, which contains the names and fate of such Catholic priests, as were prosecuted in London by four servants of the Commonwealth, between the end of 1640 and the summer of 1651. The four prosecutors and priest-hunters had formed themselves into a kind of joint-stock company of traffickers in blood-money. In this document they boast of their great success in London,—"the like not having been done by any others since the reformation of religion." In their list of captured and prosecuted priests, there are the names of thirteen who had been executed, of ten who had been condemned to death, but were reprieved and died in prison, of four who were banished, and of several who were still in prison. Nearly all the executions took place in 1642 and 1643.*

These executions, deaths in jail, and banishments of priests, it is to be remembered, were the work of only four servants (messengers) of the Commonwealth, and their practice was confined to the capital. How many other practitioners may have been at work there and throughout the country, is unknown. One thing, however, is certain; that subsequently to 1643, the hangings and quarterings of Jesuits, and other ministers of religion, were "few and far between." Banishment was preferred by the men then in power, to bloodshed, and some of them, Sir Henry Vane amongst others, were opposed altogether to persecution.

In the time of the Protectorate, an old Catholic clergyman, who had been banished thirty-seven years before, and had returned in his old age to die in his own land, was dragged from his bed by Colonel Worsley, and cast into prison. On his trial, he admitted that he was a Catholic and in orders, and on his admission, judgment of death was pronounced, and Cromwell, notwithstanding the urgent solicitations of two of the foreign ambassadors, determined he should suffer. "It was not that Cromwell approved of sanguinary punishments in matters of religion, but that he had no objection to purchase the good will of the godly by shedding the blood of a priest."† The aged priest suffered the usual punishment of traitors, June 23rd, 1654.

For a year before Cromwell's death, "sleep had fled his pillow," fear possessed his soul, the dread of assassination continually haunted his imagination. September the 2nd, 1658, an awful tempest swept over the country. Trees were uprooted, houses unroofed; the parks of London were greatly injured. The cavaliers were of opinion that the fiends—"the princes of the air, were congregating over Whitehall, that they might pounce on the Protector's soul."‡

The following day Cromwell died. Thurloe communicated the intelligence to the Deputy of Ireland—"He is gone to heaven, embalmed with the tears of his people, and upon the wings of the prayers of the saints."

In the course of eighteen months, Charles II. was quietly seated on his throne.

* Lingard's History of England, Vol. x. p. 429.
† Ibid. Vol. xi. p. 25.   ‡ Ibid. p. 126.

CHAPTER XIV.

STATE OF THE ENGLISH CATHOLICS AND PENAL ENACTMENTS IN
THE REIGN OF CHARLES .II.   FROM 1660 TO 1685.

IN 1660 Charles II. was restored to the throne of his
ancestors. The kingdom had passed through one of the
cycles of civil strife and religious discord which the reformation was destined to make oft recurring epochs of its
history. The nation, wearied of turmoil, wished for rest
and concord. The Catholics expected toleration, but though
fanaticism had nearly burned itself out, in its own violence
and fury, the spirit of faction was not extinguished; the
parliament of the Restoration kept the nation in disquiet
and apprehension, and made the condition of the Catholics
worse than it had been since the death of Elizabeth. One
unsuccessful effort was made by one Venner, to revive the
old regime of "the Saints," but the day was gone by for
that species of spiritual insanity. The attempt resembled
very much in its fanaticism and its results, that of the
Canterbury apostle, Mr. Courtenay, in our own times.*

In 1661, Venner, a Millenarian preacher, of a conventicle
in Coleman Street, a furious zealot, at the head of about
sixty of his disciples, sallied forth with arms in their hands
into the streets of London,—an army of saints, in their
own idea, led on by the Lord of Hosts, against a king supposed to be popishly affected. They rushed unimpeded
from street to street, proclaiming the new reign of the
saints, killed many soldiers who dared to confront them,
retired in good order to Caen-wood, returned anew to the
city, terrified the citizens, and eventually intrenched themselves in a house, defended it, and refusing quarter a great
many were killed; those who were taken were brought to
trial and executed.

In 1660, Charles had married a Catholic princess, Cath-

* Strange to say, one of the former fanatics, whose violence was of a
similar kind to Venner's, but who had been imprisoned immediately
before his outbreak, was named Courtenay.

arine, daughter of John IV. of Portugal. This "Popish alliance" had a great influence on all the subsequent events of his reign.*

In July, 1661, the house of Commons, on the report of a committee appointed to enquire into the laws against heretics, Catholic priests, and their harbourers, resolved to abolish the writ, " De Hæretico Inquirendo, and to repeal all the statutes which imposed the penalties of treason on Catholic clergymen found within the realm, or those of felony on the harbourers of such clergymen, or those of premunire on all who maintained the authority of the Bishop of Rome."†

But this great measure of relief was frustrated by the animosity that was felt or feigned against the Jesuits: a motion made and carried, that members of that society should be excluded from the benefit of the new measure, led to discussions, strife, and vehement disputes, inside and outside the houses of parliament. The progress of the bill was suspended, the Jesuits were called on in several pamphlets and speeches by the friends of this measure of toleration, to resign their claims to the proposed benefits, and the bill, it was argued, though clogged with these exceptions, ought to be accepted.

The Catholic peers most unwisely requested the suspension of the progress of this measure of relief. It was suspended and renewed no more.

The Catholics, for their adherence to the royal cause in the late troubles, in conformity with the solemn engagement at Breda, had been promised by the king the free exercise of their religion.

On the 6th December, 1662, Charles, in virtue of his dispensing power, issued a declaration of indulgence, in which he said he would endeavour to procure an act from the parliament in cases of recusants, conducting themselves peaceably, to relax the rigour of the laws against non-conformity. A remonstrance of both houses was immediately presented against all indulgence to papists.

---

* Catharine resisted the efforts that were made after her arrival in England to dispense with the celebration of the marriage ceremony after the Catholic rite, according to the king's previous engagement. The marriage was celebrated in a private room at Portsmouth by the almoner of the princess, in the presence of six witnesses pledged to profound secrecy.—Lingard, Vol. xi. p. 255.

† Lingard, Vol. xi. p. 220.

Toleration, however, of any kind was now odious to all factions in England, and the people of the capital who are generally, though very falsely, supposed to represent the feelings of the nation, deriving their opinions solely from political leaders and from parliament, held every religion but their own as damnable and idolatrous.

At the opening of the next session (February 18th, 1663) Charles, to the astonishment of the Catholics, "demanded the enactment of new laws to check the progress of popery," but recommended the relaxation of those in force against dissenters.

This infamy was to vindicate himself from aspersions on the character of his protestantism.

An address from both houses followed, praying for a royal proclamation, "ordering all Catholic priests to quit the kingdom under penalty of death. After a faint struggle the king acquiesced."

The following July, an address to the king was presented, calling on him "to put in execution all the penal laws against Catholics, dissenters, and sectaries of every description."*

The parliament, in open defiance of the king, and avowed opposition to his known wishes, which he had not the manliness to make one vigorous effort to carry into effect, in the next session (May 17th, 1664) passed the outrageous act which declared "all meetings of more than five individuals, besides those of the family, seditious and unlawful conventicles," on a penalty for the first offence of £.5 or imprisonment for three months; for the second of double the amount and the time; for the third of £.100, or transportation for seven years. This intolerant act affected equally Catholics and dissenters. But the unworthy king gave "his reluctant assent" to it. It was carried most rigorously into execution; fines, imprisonments, terror in families, breaking into private houses, the employment of spies, and informers, and swearers, followed its enforcement. Lingard, who can use very carefully measured language when he has to do with great enormities, speaking of this atrocious measure says, "the world seldom witnessed a more flagrant violation of a most solemn engagement."†

* Lingard, Vol. xi. p. 267.
† Ibid, p. 271.

His restoration had been obtained on terms—toleration on one hand—the re-establishment of the protestant church on the other. The king basely violated the compact with the Catholics; instead of toleration, he gave the parties he contracted with persecution. The infamy of the act will rest on his memory while the history of his times is remembered.

Within a period of eighteen months after this persecution and violation of faith, many calamities had fallen on the nation ; the African slave-trade had been legalized by parliament, chartered by the king, and its nefarious interests were promoted at the expense of an unjust war with an ancient ally—the kingdom had been ravaged by the plague—two-thirds of the capital had been destroyed by fire.

"A striking instance of the bigoted aversion," says Brown, "to the professors of the Catholic religion which prevailed in the times of which we are treating, was afforded in 1666, the memorable year of the fire of London. This dreadful conflagration, without the shadow of a pretence, against the evidence of facts, against every surmise of probability, was most illiberally attributed to the machinations of the catholics. And though, after a most deliberate parliamentary investigation, it did not appear that there was any ground to suspect the existence of such a plot as the prejudices of men had conjured up to their imaginations,* I blush for the character of my countrymen, whilst I record that that part of the inscription on the monument, commemorative of this dreadful affliction, which ascribed its commencement to such a cause, though very properly removed by James, was restored at the revolution."† The charge, however, answered its purpose. Another proclamation was issued against popery and popish clergy.

Neither Hume nor Lingard have mentioned a fact that makes the infamous Bedloe an earlier actor and plot maker on the public stage than he is represented to have been in their pages.

Five months previously to the fire, in the month of April, it came out in evidence on the trial of some persons for high treason, that the latter had formed a plot to set

---

* Hume, c. 64.   † Brown's Penal Laws, p. 110.

fire to London, the 3rd of September following, with a view of creating confusion and overturning the government, and at two in the morning, on the 2nd of September, the fire in London burst out.

In 1656 a treatise had been advertised purporting to show from the apocalypse that in 1666 the Romish Babylon should be destroyed. (Burton's Diary, Mer. Pol. ap Lingard, vol. xi. p. 303.)

The No Popery interpreters of this prediction in the reign of Charles II., rendered "the Romish Babylon"—the Babylon of England, which had been desecrated by a king supposed to be popish in his tendencies. And accordingly they determined to accomplish the prediction in the predicted year, 1666.

The fact, to which reference has been made, occurred on the trial of Nathaniel Reading Esq., in the year 1679. Bedloe, under cross-examination by the prisoner, (a gentleman of high rank and character) was thus questioned by the latter: "Pray Sir, by the oath you have taken, did you not lay in provisions of coal and billets behind the Palsgravehead tavern, and hard by Charing Cross, in order to fire the city of Westminster?"[*] Mr. Bedloe made no answer. The lord chief justice objected to the question. If the witness had his pardon, it set him right against all objections.

In 1669, the Duke of York, shaken in his faith by the perusal of Dr. Heylin's History of the Reformation, announced to his brother "a conviction that it became his duty to reconcile himself with the church of Rome."

Charles, without hesitation, replied that he was of the same mind, and would consult with the duke on the subject in the presence of Lord Arundell, Lord Arlington, and his confidential friend, Lord Clifford.[†] "Arundell was a Catholic, the others had their church still to choose." "The meeting was held in the duke's closet, and Charles, with tears in his eyes, lamented the hardship of being obliged to profess a religion which he did not approve, and declared his determination to emancipate himself from this restraint."[‡] The means of doing this with safety, were suggested to him—the aid of the powerful monarch, Louis.

Lingard leaves it to be understood that this "most

* Hargrave's State Trials, Vol. ii. p. 891.
† Lingard, Vol. xi. p. 337.
‡ Ibid, p. 336.

accomplished dissembler in his dominions" had no other object in view but to deceive both his brother and the king of France. Certain it is the intimation of his intended conversion was conveyed to the French court by Lord Arundell, and money was solicited and obtained from Louis for the suppression of any tumults consequent on his change of religion.

Of the secret treaty concluded with France in the beginning of 1670, Dalrymple gives a draught,* from which the following is an extract.

"It is agreed, *that we shall receive two millions of livres tournois, to assist us in declaring ourself a Catholic*, and we declare and promise, that having received the two said millions, *we will give an acquittance as relative to the article of our being Catholic.*" On this singular treaty, which was conducted with all the regularity and nonchalance of the bartering transactions of the counting-house, Sir John† very justly remarks : "it is probable, that Charles, in his stipulations about declaring himself a Roman Catholic, *meant only to draw money from France at first and from Spain afterwards*, or at least to be very sure of his power at home before he took such a step. The shifts he fell upon to turn this part of the treaty to his own advantage, and to avoid performing it," continues this author, "make a true comedy in Colbert's dispatches. On the 21st of March, 1672, *he writes*, that Charles desired a theologian to be sent him, from Paris, to instruct him in the mysteries of the Catholic religion, but that *he desired this theologian might be a good chymist.*" On the 7th June, 1672, the same minister informs his court, that "*Charles had put off his conversion to the end of the campaign.*"

In May 1670, Charles entered into the secret treaty with Louis, the principal article of which Lingard states was, that the king of England should publicly profess himself a Catholic at such time as should appear to him most expedient.‡ On the 11th of March, 1671, Charles published a proclamation, in which he declared that "as he had always adhered against all temptations whatsoever to the true religion established, so he would still employ his utmost care and zeal in its maintenance and defence."

* 2 Dalrymple's Memoirs, p. 78.
† Memoirs, Vol. ii. p. 82.
‡ Lingard, Vol. xi. p. 345.

This proclamation was an echo to the no popery clamour that was then getting up in parliament.

Parliament was not satisfied with proclamations.—New penal laws were determined on.—A bill was introduced and went through both houses, but care was taken by the Duke of York's friends that some informality should be fatal to it. Another act, however, in spite of all efforts to defeat it, became the law of the land, the 25 Car. 11, c. 2. which excluded Catholics from all offices under government (with some few limitations to its operation) and share in its councils.

By this act it was ordained that all persons holding any office, civil, military, or naval—receiving fee or wages from the king, or being of his household, or that of the duke, at the next term or quarter sessions after his admission, must take the oaths of allegiance and supremacy, in open court, in the chancery or king's bench, or at the quarter sessions, and within three months must receive the sacrament in some open church on a Sunday. Of their compliance with this latter provision, they are required to deliver a certificate into court signed by the minister, churchwarden, and two respectable witnesses. In addition to this, they are commanded, at the same time, to make and subscribe a declaration against transubstantiation.

Refusal or neglect to make this declaration on the part of persons continuing in office, to be punished with a fine of £.500, and to be disabled from acting as guardians, or executors, or suitors, in any court of law. The act does not extend to pensions or lands granted by the king, nor to offices of inheritance (provided such offices being held by papists, are filled by conforming deputies) nor to persons under eighteen years of age, or married women, provided within four months after the death of their husbands, or their attaining the age of eighteen, they take the oaths and subscribe the declaration. Non-commissioned officers of the navy also, are only required to make the subscription. And constables, overseers, churchwardens, and like inferior civil officers, together with bailiffs of manors, keepers of forests, and persons in such private employments, are excepted from the operation of the statute.*

In February, 1673, the king in his speech to parliament,

* Brown's Penal Laws.

in allusion to his former declaration of his desire to relax the penal laws and those against dissenters, assures his faithful commons " he would stick to his declaration of indulgence."*

The commons, however, made so vigorous an opposition that he was at length induced to break the seals of his declaration in the presence of the council.†

As on all former occasions of any manifestation of the king's in favour of toleration, new clamour against popery resounded in both houses of parliament, and new measures of persecution were devised.

By a new act no person was allowed to instruct youth, even in a private family, without licence from the bishop or ordinary, on taking an oath that he would conform to the liturgy of the " Church of England," as it is now by law established.‡

The marriage of the Duke of York in 1674, with a princess of his own religious persuasion, caused a new protestant panic. " Charles partook of the common alarm" for the true religion, or rather the alarm common to him whenever his enemies pretended to be alarmed about religious matters. He refused his brother's wife the use of a public chapel which had been previously guaranteed to her, ordered all Catholics, or reputed Catholics, to be kept away from the palace or the royal presence ; " and by an order of council, forbade all popish recusants to walk in St. James's Park, or visit at the palace, and instructed the judges to enforce with rigour the laws against the Catholics."§

Parliament no sooner met than three addresses were presented to the king, to enjoin a public fast, and a national supplication to God, for the preservation of church and state against the undermining practices of popish recusants.

The undermining practices were those of the duke and the poor popish girl of fifteen, whom he had just married.

* "' I shall take it very ill to receive contradiction in what I have done. And I will deal plainly with you, I am resolved to stick to my declaration." King's Speech—Journals of the House of Lords, die Mercurii 5 die Februarii, 1672-3. Vol. xii. p. 522.

† Journals of the House of Lords, die Sabbati 1 and 8 diebus Martii, 1672-3. Vol. xii. p. 540-549. 2 Grey's Debates, 12—37, 48-69, 91-2.

‡ Hume, c. 63.

§ Lingard, Vol. xii. p. 38.

From that period to the close of the reign of Charles, parliament was indefatigable in its efforts to exclude the duke from the throne, to deprive him of all offices, to banish him from the council, from the court, and from the kingdom.   To effect these objects it was necessary to strike at all the Catholics in the kingdom, to get at the particular object of its aversion.

It would be useless to detail all the votes, addresses, remonstrances, and conferences, for this purpose.

In 1675, a royal proclamation was published, embodying six orders of the prelates assembled in council at Lambeth, ordaining that all natives in orders in the church of Rome should quit the realm in six weeks, on penalty of death; that every subject of the three realms who attended mass in the queen's chapel, or any chapel of a foreign ambassador, should be imprisoned for a year, pay a fine of 100 marks; that the laws against recusants should be carried into immediate execution; that any papist, or reputed papist, who should dare to enter a royal palace should, if a peer, be committed to the tower, or under that rank to a common jail, and that the laws for the suppression of conventicles, should be rigorously enforced.

In the same year, " in virtue of a royal mandate, the princess Mary (daughter of James) was conducted to church by the bishop of London, who conferred on her the rite of confirmation, in defiance of the authority of her father."*

. The first proposed test to be taken by members of parliament, privy councillors, magistrates, and all officers under the crown, was brought forward early in 1675, as a ministerial panacea for all the evils of the nation.†   This measure was truly designated by the Catholic peers, a dissettlement of the whole birthright of England.   The long discussion on this project led to a conflict with the lords, and furnished the king with a seasonable plea for a prorogation.

When parliament again assembled, a new test was ordained for members on admission, denying the truth of the doctrine of transubstantiation, declaring the invocation of saints, or adoration of the Virgin Mary, superstitious and idolatrous.

* Lingard, Vol. xii. p. 56.
† Ibid, p. 59.

Members of parliament not having taken this test, and all popish recusants, are forbidden to come into the presence of the king or queen, or into any house where they or their successors may be, without licence from the king or six of his privy council. And peers, or members of the house, violating any provisions of this act, are to be considered popish recusants, to be disqualified for any office, suing in any court, taking any legacy or deed of gift, or acting as guardian and executor: and liable also to a fine of £.500 for sitting or voting in parliament till they have conformed to its regulations.

This declaration to be subscribed by all servants of the royal family. The act, however, ends with a proviso, that nothing therein shall extend to the Duke of York.

On the discussion of one of the bills, concerning tests for members of parliament, much approbation was bestowed on the zeal of a member of the House of Peers, who thus expressed his aversion to popery: "I would not have so much as a popish man or a popish woman to remain here; not so much as a popish dog or a popish bitch; not so much as a popish cat to pur or mew about the king."*

In 1678, the commons refused the supplies they had promised the king to carry on the war they had urged him to enter on, "having discovered that a dozen Catholic priests existed in the counties of Hereford and Monmouth, and the laws against recusants were often evaded." "This was sufficient, the alarming intelligence awakened the fears of the godly and the credulous, and a resolution was passed that the house could not consistently, with its duty, lay any additional charges on the people *till the kingdom was secured*, and the dangers were prevented which might arise from the prevalence and the countenance given to the popish party."†

In a few days the king prorogued the parliament.

In the same year the princess Mary, daughter of James, was married to the prince of Orange, on which occasion the Duke of York said in the house of peers, "his consent was a proof that he meditated no changes in the church and state. The only change which he sought, was to secure

* Hume, c. 67.
† Lingard, Vol. xii. p. 121.

men from all molestation in civil concerns, on account of their opinion on religious matters."[*]

In the latter part of 1678, the godly men who had taken the interests of heaven and the protestant religion into their especial keeping—the virtuous Shaftesbury in the lords, and the leading tolerant christian patriots in the commons—prepared the parliament and the nation, by the increased fervour of their zeal against popery, for some impending evil that called for more than ordinary vigilance and violence of language and factious conduct to avert.

In the month of August, Dr. Titus Oates made his first appearance on the stage of Shaftesbury's theatre, in the character of "a Saviour of the Nation," introduced by another reverend performer, Dr. Tonge, rector of St. Michael's church in London. The piece for performance was "the popish plot;" the people applauded it highly—for two years it kept its ground.

The plot turned on the killing of the king, the overthrow of the protestant religion, (in England, Scotland, and Ireland,) and the substitution of the Duke of York, or some other Catholic prince, for the King Charles, and likewise of the popish religion, for the established faith. The king was to be taken off, either by poison administered by his physician, Sir G. Wakeman, or by being shot by a lay Jesuit brother, and another person named "honest William," or by two other sets of assassins, two Benedictine monks, and four Irishmen of names unknown. The plot was said to be originally contrived and so far put into execution by the order of the Jesuits. The provincial in England was the principal agent, and several Catholic noblemen his aiders and abettors.

"Oates," says Hume, "who, though his evidence were true, must by his own account, be regarded as an infamous villain, was by every one applauded, caressed, and called the saviour of the nation." Yet on his evidence alone both houses unanimously decreed, "that the lords and commons are of opinion that there hath been, and still is, a damnable and hellish plot, contrived and carried on by the popish recusants, for assassinating the king, for subverting the government, and for rooting out and destroying the protestant religion."

* Lingard, Vol. xii. p. 105.

It is not within the scope of this work to enter into a detailed account of the iniquitous conspiracy denominated the popish plot, fabricated by the unprincipled Shaftesbury and his infamous agents.

Its results require to be noticed, and the character of those who caused so much innocent blood to be shed on this occasion.

"Oates was the son of a ribbon-weaver, who, exchanging the loom for the bible, distinguished himself as an anabaptist minister during the government of Cromwell, and became an orthodox clergyman on the restoration of the ancient dynasty."* He officiated as curate in various places, and as chaplain on board a man-of-war. The infamy of his character drove him from his clerical employments. The odium, moreover, of two malicious prosecutions, in which his manifest perjuries were made evident to the juries, completed his ruin.

He sought assistance from Dr. Tonge, a fiery denouncer of popery, and periodical proclaimer of projected Romish massacres and rebellions.

The worthy Mucklewrath, rector of St. Michael's, and the man-of-war minister, Mr. Titus Oates, poor and hungry, but all the sharper in his zeal for true religion, entered into an arrangement for the concoction of a Jesuit conspiracy; and in June, 1677, in the execution of this plan, Oates renounced his religion, and was reconciled by a priest who gained him admission into the Jesuits' Spanish house, in Valladolid. After a trial of five months he was disgracefully expelled. By Tonge's advice he made a second application, and the repentant neophyte was received into the Jesuit college of St. Omer.

But even for the accomplishment of his diabolical purpose he could not control his unruly dispositions, and again, after a few months, he was expelled ignominiously.

While he remained in both houses, however, he learned that a congregational meeting of the English provincial and the principal members of the order, the usual triennial meeting of the order, was to be held in London, in April, 1768. Like all meetings of priests, it was necessarily held in secret, and imprudently enough in the Duke of York's

* Lingard, Vol. xii. p. 129.

palace at St. James's, and from thence appears to have
been adjourned to an inn in the Strand.

This meeting, whose object was the nomination of the
treasurer, and the transaction of the ordinary concerns
of the society, was transformed by Oates and Tonge into a
council of clerical assassins.

On this slight basis Oates and Tonge erected their monstrous structure of falsehood, aided and abetted by an able,
unprincipled politician.*

If James had to answer for no greater severity or injustice in his reign than the rigorous execution of the law
in the case of the sacrilegious murderous miscreant, who
disgraced the ministry of the established church, Dr. Titus
Oates, the odium would be little that rested on his memory.

One of the early acts of James's government, was to
prosecute, on two indictments, the perjurer on whose oaths
so much innocent blood had been shed in England.   The
wretch was convicted in 1785, and sentenced to a fine of
1000 marks on each indictment, imprisoned for life, to be
flogged twice through the city of London, and set in the
pillory five times in every year.   At the revolution he was
released by King William, a pension of £.400 settled on
him, and by a great number of persons he was treated with
the honours due to a martyr.

Bedloe, the compeer of Oates, came forward to obtain a
reward of £.300 for the murder of Godfrey, the magistrate,
who had received the first sworn informations of Oates.
He had been a stable boy, a menial in the household of a
Catholic peer; a courier on the continent, in the service of
many noble English families ; a swindler in various countries ; a convicted felon, on whom sentence of death had
been passed in Normandy.

"Godfrey," he said, "was murdered by two Jesuits, Le
Fevri and Walsh."   At first, this was all he knew of the
conspiracy ; but, day after day, his memory expanded, till
it comprehended the whole plot in all its ramifications. He
had the merit of first implicating the queen, Catharine, in
its guilt.   Oates, two days later, (November 28th, 1678,)
appeared at the bar of the House of Commons, and said in

---

* The services of Oates were rewarded with a pension of £1200. a
year, a lodging in Whitehall, and a guard for his protection.

a loud voice : " I, Titus Oates, accuse Catharine, queen of England, of high treason."

Mr. Bedloe having died in 1679, another miscreant of the name of Dangerfield was brought forward to sustain the declining credit of Oates and Dugdale, in 1680.   In a few years this young man had run through a long career of guilt. He had been repeatedly outlawed, prosecuted in several places for different crimes, fined, imprisoned, whipped, burnt in the hand, and set in the pillory.

The works of those infamous men, and still more infamous employers and supporters in high stations, were brought to a close in December, 1680, by the judicial murder of the virtuous and truly noble Earl of Stafford.

During the proceedings in parliament and the courts, Oates and Bedloe were frequently in communication with Shaftesbury.   One of the informers, Prance, subsequently repenting of his wickedness, confessed he had been instigated by one Boyce, " who had been several times with my Lord Shaftesbury and Bedloe, and had told him he would be hanged if he did not agree with Bedloe's evidence."* In the course of the trials it came out, on other occasions, that Shaftesbury and the informers were in close communication.

" Shaftesbury, who, after having alternately been the active supporter of the late king, the parliament, and the protector, soon after the Restoration became a leading member of the celebrated cabal, whose intentions certainly were the destruction of all civil liberty, and as it has been strongly, though perhaps somewhat erroneously suspected, of the re-establishment of the Catholic religion. When their measures, therefore, had driven the king to the choice of one or other of these extremities—either to govern without a parliament, or to yield to their remonstrances,— this subtle courtier, perceiving that Charles had not sufficient firmness to persist in his designs, or to screen his advisers from the impeachments which were suspended over them, again changed his party, and became the factious leader of the discontented multitude."†

Sir John Dalrymple, in his ' Memoirs,' thus speaks of the unprincipled whig lord : " Shaftesbury, who knew well the

* Lingard, Vol. xii. p. 165.
† Brown's Penal Laws, from 100 to 130.

power of popular rumours at times when popular passions are in ferment, framed the fiction of the popish plot in the year 1678, in order to bring the duke, and perhaps the king, under the weight of the national fear and hatred of popery." And in a note on this passage he further observes : " It has been much doubted, whether Shaftesbury contrived the popish plot, or if he only made use of it after it broke out. Some papers I have seen convince me he contrived it, though the persons he made use of as informers ran beyond their instructions. The common objection," continues he, " to the supposition of his contriving the plot, is the absurdity of its circumstances. When Shaftesbury himself was pressed with regard to that absurdity, he made an answer which shows equally the irregularity and the depth of his genius. An account of it is in North's Examen, p. 95. A certain lord of his confidence in parliament once asked him what he intended to do with the plot, which was so full of nonsense as would scarce go down with *tantum non* idiots ; what, then, could he propose by pressing the belief of it upon men of common sense, and especially in parliament. ' It is no matter,' said he, ' the more nonsensical the better ; if we cannot bring them to swallow worse nonsense than that, we shall never do any good with them.' "*

Hume, in speaking of Shaftesbury, whose apologist he may be considered, says of him : " Well acquainted with the blind attachment of faction, he surmounted all sense of shame, and relying on the subtlety of his contrivance, he was not startled with enterprises the most hazardous and most criminal."

In the latter part of 1678, the prosecution of the persons charged with being concerned in the popish plot commenced. The chief justice, Scroggs, who presided at most of those trials, was a monster, a judicial murderer, a man of profligate habits, of poor legal acquirements, but a great legal functionary in bad times for the perversion of justice and the purposes of faction.

The recorder, who assisted at some of them, was Sir George Jeffreys.

Of the conduct of the judges towards the prisoners and their witnesses the following specimens may be given. In

* Memoirs, Vol. i. p. 45.

the examination of Mary Tilden, a witness on the trial of
Green, Berry, and Hill, for the murder of Sir Edmonsbury
Godfrey,* we find Lord Chief Justice Scroggs thus address-
ing her.

L. C. J. "Pray what religion are you of? Are you a
papist ?"

Mary Tilden. "I know not whether I came here to make
a profession of my faith."

L. C. J. "Are you a Roman Catholic ?"

Mary Tilden. "Yes."

L. C. J. " *Have you a dispensation to eat supper on Saturday nights ?*"

To this question another of the judges added the following liberal and delicate insinuation.

Mr. Recorder. "I hope you did not keep him [one of
the prisoners] company after supper all night."

Mary Tilden. "No, I did not ; he came in to wait at
table at supper."

The witness to whom this language was addressed, was a
respectable, modest young woman, the niece of a clergyman.

The judges frequently intimated on these trials that no
papist was worthy of credit : " You may say anything to a
heretic for a papist ; *you come hither to say anything that will
serve your turn.*"†

Green, one of the prisoners, observed in his defence : "I
declare to all the world that I am as innocent of the thing
charged upon me as the child in the mother's womb. I
die innocent, I do not care for death, I go to my Saviour,
and I desire all that hear me to pray for me ; I never saw
the man to my knowledge, alive or dead."   To this solemn
protestation of innocence, the chief justice replied : " We
know that you have either downright denials, or equivocating terms for everything : yet, in plain dealing, every
one that heard your trial hath great satisfaction, and for
my own particular, *I have great satisfaction that you are every
one of you guilty.*"

He said to the jury, after passing sentence : " You have
done, gentlemen, like very good subjects and very good
christians, — *that is to say, like very good Protestants ;* and,"

* Published by authority of the Lord Chief Justice, &c. in 1679,
p. 53.
          † Trial of Hill, &c. p. 56.

(alluding to an alleged reward for assassinating the king) "much good may their thirty thousand masses do them."*

"Prosecutors," says Fox, "whether attorneys and solicitors-general, or managers of impeachment, acted with the fury which in such circumstances might be expected; juries partook naturally enough of the national ferment, and judges, whose duty it was to guard them against such impressions, were scandalously active in confirming them in their prejudices, and inflaming their passions. The king, who is supposed to have disbelieved the whole of their plot, never once exercised his glorious prerogative of mercy. It is said," remarks the right honourable gentleman, "that he dare not. His throne, perhaps his life, was at stake; and history does not furnish us with the example of any monarch with whom the lives of innocent, or even meritorious, subjects ever appeared to be of much weight, when put in balance against such considerations."†

The trials for the popish plot were introduced (Nov. 21st, 1678) by the prosecution of the Catholic banker, Stayley, for treasonable words against the king. The prisoner was convicted, sentenced to death, as in case of treason, and executed."‡

Nov. 27th, 1678, Coleman, § a gentleman, for high treason, convicted on Oates and Bedloe's testimony, sentenced to death, "as in high treason," and executed.

Dec. 17th, 1678, Ireland and Pickering, priests, and Grove, gentleman, for high treason, convicted on Oates's testimony, sentenced to death, "as in high treason," and executed.

Feb. 10th, 1678, Green, Berry, and Hill, labourers, for the murder of Sir Edmonsbury Godfrey, convicted on Bedloe's evidence, and sentenced to death, "as in high treason," and executed.

March 28th, 1679, Lewis, a Jesuit, for high treason,

* Trial of Ireland, published by authority, p. 78.
† Fox.—History of James, chap. 30.
‡ The charge was trumped up by the managers of the conspiracy. The only foundation for it, was a conversation of the prisoner in the French language with a Frenchman, on matters relating to his business.
§ Coleman was the son of a Protestant clergyman. He had embraced the Catholic religion, and filled the office of Secretary to the Duchess of York. He was the first victim of Oates.

being a priest, convicted, sentenced to death, "as in high treason," and executed.

June 13th, 1679, White, provincial of the Jesuits in England, Fenwick, procurator for the same, Gawen and Turner, "all Jesuits and priests," for high treason, convicted on the evidence of Oates, Bedloe, and Dugdale, and sentenced to death, and executed, "as in the case of treason."

June 14th, 1679, Richard Lang Horne, Esq. (an eminent lawyer,) for high treason, convicted on the evidence of Oates and Bedloe, sentenced to death, "as in high treason."

Nov. 30th, 1680, Viscount Stafford, for high treason, convicted on the evidence of Oates and Dugdale, and sentenced to death and executed.

This was the last victim of Oates and his colleagues and the managers of the popish plot.

In the preceding cases the prisoners were charged with complicity or agency in the popish plot. In the following, the only crime brought against them was—the being priests; but the issue was the same.

Aug. 14th, 1679, Brommich, for high treason, "being a Romish priest," convicted and sentenced to death, "as in high treason."

Aug. 13th, 1679, Atkins, "for high treason, *being a Romish priest,*" convicted and sentenced to death, "as in high treason."

Jan. 17th, 1679, Anderson, Parry, Starky, Carker, Marshall, "for high treason, being Romish priests," all convicted, sentenced to death, on the evidence of Oates, Bedloe, and Dangerfield.

The attorney-general in this case, stating the indictment, charged the prisoners with violating the 27th of Elizabeth, "and they were tried not only *quatenus* priests, but as ordained by the See of Rome, and coming into England, and abiding here."

The usual sentence was pronounced by the recorder, Jeffreys. It was especially worthy of him.

"The court does award it, that you and the several prisoners be conveyed on hurdles to the place of execution, where every one of you are to be severally hanged by the neck; that you be severally cut down alive; that your privy members be cut off, your bowels taken out, and be burnt in your view; that your heads be severed from your bodies; that your bodies be divided into four quarters, which are to be disposed of at the king's pleasure : and *the God of infinite mercy* have mercy upon your souls."*

Father Parry, when the sentence was ended, said :

" Te Deum laudamus : Te Dominum confitemur."

People of England, bear in mind this awful sentence was pronounced on ministers of religion, charged with no other crime but that of worshipping God according to the dictates of conscience, and officiating as ministers of a christian creed ; and when you read of this impious monster of a judge, in pronouncing the horrifying sentence which the sanguinary code of your country ordained—the mutilations of the still quivering flesh, the burning of the bowels, the severing of the head, and division of the quarters of those innocent men—daring to couple its iniquity with the name of " the God of infinite mercy," pray that the land may not be visited with His anger, in retribution of outraged justice and humanity.

Hume says : " Though the king scrupled not, whenever he could speak freely, to throw the highest ridicule on the plot, and on all who believed it, *he* yet found it necessary to adopt the popular opinion before the parliament : the torrent, he saw, ran too strong to be controlled ; and he could only hope, by a seeming compliance, to be able, after some time, to guide, and direct, and elude its fury."

Lord Clarendon, a contemporary writer, says : " Certain it is, that upon the strictest examination that could be made by the king's command, and then by the diligence of the house, that upon the jealousy and rumour made, *a committee that was very diligent and solicitous to make that discovery,* there was never any probable evidence that there was any other cause of that woful fire than the displeasure of God Almighty.".................."Yet *all the Roman Catholics found that their only safety consisted in keeping within doors, and yet some of them,*" says he, "*were taken by force out of their houses, and carried to prison.*"†

Speaking of this conspiracy, Mr. Fox, in his ' History of the earlier part of the reign of James II.,' says : "Although upon a review of this truly shocking transaction, we may

* Hargrave's State Trials, Vol. ii. p. 1106.
† Life of Lord Clarendon, continuation, pp. 348-353.

be fairly justified in adopting the milder alternative, and in imputing to the greater part of those concerned in it rather an extraordinary degree of blind credulity, than the deliberate wickedness of planning and assisting in the perpetration of legal murders ; yet the proceedings in the popish plot must always be considered as an indelible disgrace upon the English nation, in which king, parliament, judges, juries, witnesses, prosecutors, have all their respective, though certainly not equal, shares."

When the frenzy of the nation was sufficiently roused by the details of the plot in the parliament and the press, the Duke of York was removed from the council, deprived of all his offices, and ultimately compelled to quit the kingdom. In 1679 he was permitted to exchange his place of exile from Brussells to Edinburgh. A few months previously, the Lord Russell had taken a leading part in an attempt to implicate the absent Duke of York in a treasonable correspondence with the French king, with a view to the invasion of England. A resolution of the commons was sent to the lords by the Lord Russell for their concurrence, to the effect : "That the Duke of York being a papist, and the hope of his coming to the crown, had given the greatest encouragement to the conspiracies of papists."

"In 1680, the commons were preparing an act which would have operated severely against the Catholics, and even to re-introduce the obnoxious bill of exclusion, when the king came to the sudden resolution of dissolving the parliament. Of this intention it appears they had intelligence about a quarter of an hour previous to their being summoned to attend his majesty in the house of peers. Some violent resolutions were therefore passed in a manner little less tumultuary than those of the parliament which had been as unexpectedly dissolved by the late king. By one of these they resolved, ' That it is the opinion of this house, that the city of London was burnt in the year 1666 by the papists, designing thereby to introduce arbitrary power and popery into the kingdom.'* In fact, they were rapidly treading in the steps of their predecessors, in ascribing every evil of every description to the damnable and hellish plots of the papists. Nor could the compliance of

* Journals of the House of Commons, Lunædie 10 Januarii 1680, Vol. ix. p. 703.

the king with their bigoted prejudices, in causing several Catholics to be executed for the simple offence of being in priest's orders,* remove from him the imputation of a more than ordinary partiality to the proscribed faith.

"With the exception of the short session at Oxford, this was the last parliament that Charles ever assembled."†

In 1681, the Duke of York was presented by the justices of the Old Bailey as a popish recusant, on the affidavit of Dr. Oates, in which it was sworn that the duke had been seen by the deponent at mass. The proceedings were removed by certiorari to the King's Bench, where they were adjourned the 28th of March, 1681, and were no more heard of.‡ This was the last appearance in public, in his official capacity, of Dr. Oates.

The patrons of the plot derived no benefit from the death of Viscount Stafford. The general persuasion of his innocence gave the king courage to make a stand against Shaftesbury and the patriot lord, both of whom, in every stage of this infamous conspiracy against the Catholics, pushed on the subordinate agents to further excesses, supported their credit, and clamoured for the blood of their victims. The latter whig lord particularly distinguished himself in pressing for the execution of the convicted priests ; the former in sustaining the credit of the perjured witnesses.

The parliament being prorogued, a check was given to the machinations of the plotters. Shaftesbury and his followers proceeded to Oxford, when the next parliament assembled there, with many armed attendants, wearing round their hats a ribbon with the inscription, "No popery, no slavery."

Shaftesbury's reign, however, was over in October, 1681. He was indicted for subornation of perjury, and making warlike preparations, with the view of coercing the king at Oxford. The bill was ignored, and the earl was for a few days all triumphant. Two treasonable papers, however, were discovered, which deeply involved him. He skulked like a coward in various places, while he was urging Monmouth, Essex, and their friends to rise in arms ; and like a poltroon, terrified by fears for his own safety, he still endan-

---

* Hume, c. 68, § 14.
† Brown's Penal Laws.
‡ McPherson's State Papers, Vol. i. p. 141.

gered the lives of his associates by his counsels after he had effected his escape. He fled to Holland, and died there two months after his flight.

The whigs of 1682 sunk under the opprobrium of their leader and the machinations of their party. Their power and their places passed into the hands of the tories. The Duke of York returned in triumph to the capital. The clergy, however, were charged still by their prelates to present all recusant Catholics and others. But the king was now at liberty to follow his own inclinations. He remitted the sentence of death in the case of several priests convicted of taking orders in the Church of Rome, and sent them out of the kingdom.

The new government, however, plunged at once into the old excesses of intolerance. All nonconformists were anew warred against. Their tenets, opinions, and prejudices were outraged and insulted. The old spirit of persecution passed over to the side of power with its wonted instincts. The covenant, which the puritans believed dictated by the Holy Spirit, was burned by the hands of the common hangman, amidst the loud and continuous shouts of the same populace which had shouted for Cromwell and the other saints of "the Lord's army."

His majesty, moreover, did not forget the insulting terms he was compelled to subscribe to in Scotland, in respect to his father and his grandmother. He and his government, in opposition to the will of the whole Scotch people, proceeded to the re-establishment of episcopal Church government.

The 5th of February, 1685, Charles II. died. Having declined to receive the Sacrament from the Bishop of Bath and Wells, his brother, the Duke of York, knelt down, and asked him if he might send for a Catholic priest. "For God's sake, do," was the king's reply; "but will it not expose you to danger?" James minded not the danger. The priest Huddleston was brought to the king, and Charles died in the communion of the Catholic Church,* of the truth of which Hume states he had been previously convinced, as appeared from two papers left by him, and published after his death by James.

* Lingard, Vol. xii. p. 353.

CHAPTER XV.

STATE OF THE CATHOLICS IN ENGLAND, IN THE REIGN OF JAMES II., FROM 1685 TO THE END OF 1688.

JAMES II., succeeded to the throne in 1685, not only tranquilly, but "without a murmur." The second Sunday after his brother's death, he publicly attended the queen's chapel, and soon after on festivals went there in state, and on such occasions received the sacrament, some of his Protestant ministers usually accompanying him to the door. Within two months of his accession, he charged the judges to discourage prosecutions on account of religion, and ordered by proclamation the discharge of persons confined for non-conformity. The Presbyterians who were persecuted under the conventicle act were liberated, Catholics to the amount of some thousands, and Quakers of about twelve hundred.*

Though James had continued to conform to the Church of England till the year 1669, it is evident from a letter to him from his brother Charles in 1654, (at that time in exile,) that apprehensions were then entertained of his orthodoxy. The letter, taken from the Thurloe State Papers, is dated Cologne, Nov. 16, 1654.

" Dear Brother,

" I have received yours without a date, in which you mention, that Mr. Montague has endeavoured to pervert you in your religion. I do not doubt but you remember very well the commands I left with you at my going away, concerning that point, and am confident you will observe them. Yet the letters that come from Paris say, that it is the queen's purpose to do all she can to change your religion, which, if you hearken to her, or any body else in that matter, you must never think to see England or me

* Lingard, Vol. xiii. p. 9,

again ; and whatsoever mischief shall fall on me, or my affairs, from this time, I must lay all upon you, as being the only cause of it. Therefore, consider well what it is, not only to be the cause of ruining a brother that loves you so well, but also of your king and country. Do not let them persuade you, either by force or fair promises ; for the first, they neither dare nor will use ; and for the second, as soon as they have perverted you, they will have their end, and will care no more for you.

"I am also informed, that there is a purpose to put you in a Jesuit's college, which I command you, upon the same grounds, never to consent unto. And whenever any body shall go to dispute with you on religion, do not answer them at all ; for though you have the reason on your side, yet they being prepared, will have the advantage of any body, that is not upon the same security that they are. If you do not consider what I say to you, *remember the last words of your dead father, which were, to be constant to your religion, and never to be shaken in it ;* which, if you do not observe, this shall be the last time you will ever hear from your most affectionate brother,

CHARLES R.*

During his brother's reign, James had resolutely en-countered the malevolence of open hostility and secret intrigue on account of his religion, and now in power, he determined to set his face against persecution. The new king openly avowed the two great objects he had in view, were, to grant liberty of conscience and freedom of worship— the removal of religious tests, and the abolition of sanguinary and oppressive penal laws.†

The Bishop of London and the clergy became alarmed for the established Church ; toleration to them meant danger to Protestantism, the pulpits of the capital began to resound with declamations against popery. James remonstrated with the bishop, and his clergy were re-strained within becoming limits. The king and queen

---

* Thurloe's State Papers, Vol. i. p. 661.
† In a dispatch of Barillon, the French ambassador, to his master, (Feb. 19th, 1685, 2 Dalrymple's Memoirs, Appendix to Part 1. p. 104.) the latter states, James had told him "that he knew well enough he should never be in safety, till a liberty of conscience was established firmly in their (the Catholic's) favour in England: and that it was to this he was wholly to apply himself, as soon as he saw a possibility."

were crowned according to the Protestant ritual in February, and in May, Monmouth's unsuccessful ill-concerted rebellion broke out. On its suppression, the vengeance of the law had full swing. Jeffreys administered what was called justice, and three hundred and thirty executions manifested his zeal in the king's service. James triumphed over his enemies, but the triumph was too bloody to be permanently advantageous to him.

In 1686, the Catholic officers in his army were discharged from the penalties to which they were liable under the 25th of Charles I., by patents under the great seal, a mode of dispensing with law, sanctioned by Jeffreys, the Chief Justice Herbert, and some others.

Four of the judges, for refusing their concurrence, were punished with removal from the bench.

Several of the prelates complained loudly in the House of Lords of this proceeding.

Compton, Bishop of London, said in debate, " *he spoke the united sentiments of the episcopal bench, when he pronounced the test act, the chief security of the Established Church.*"*

This declaration is worthy of consideration ; the test act was founded on falsehood and forgery,—it had its origin in the machinations of Titus Oates.

In 1685, the revocation of the edict of Nantes, brought numbers of French Protestants to England. The press and the pulpit concurred in representing the Catholic religion as one that essentially was bloody, perfidious, and inhuman. The king in vain reprobated all kinds of religious persecutions. It was generally believed that a secret understanding existed between him and Louis ; " The people throughout the country called on their representatives to rally in defence of religion and their liberties."†

The Commons on the meeting of parliament, prayed the king to remove all Catholics who were officers in his army, in defiance of the laws. James reproved the Commons, and the result was a fierce conflict in both houses, between the king's party and the opponents of his religion.

In 1686, Compton, Bishop of London, was suspended during the royal pleasure, from the exercise of his episcopal functions. The prelate was looked upon as a martyr; at

* Lingard, Vol. xiii. p. 62.
† Ibid, p. 60.

the same time several Protestant clergymen of the Universities, became members of the Roman Catholic Church. The king allowed them to enjoy the benefits of their respective offices in College and in the Established Church, without taking the oaths or attending the Protestant worship. James defended his conduct on the ground of maintaining toleration in religious matters. He caused several chapels in which Catholic worship had been suppressed or privately performed hitherto, to be thrown open to the public. Four houses of the religious order, with his sanction, were re-established in London. While the king was thus acting, his opponents were tampering with his troops, calling on them "not to yoke themselves with bloody and idolatrous papists," nor to lend their support to "the setting up of mass-houses."

In 1687, James issued a proclamation, the crowning work of his grand object, "suspending the execution of all Penal Laws for religious offences, and forbidding the imposition of religious oaths or tests as qualifications for office;" and for the concurrence of both houses of parliament, he stated that he expected to receive it at the next meeting.

The illegality of the proclamation left it of little value, and it involved the king in a formidable contest with the courts of law and the universities. In April 1688, the king appended to his previous proclamation an additional declaration, securing to his subjects "freedom of conscience for ever;" which declaration, by an order of council, the bishops were enjoined to have read in the churches by their clergy. This step was the proximated cause of the king's ruin. It led to the prosecution and trial of the seven bishops for disobeying that order, to their triumph and his discomfiture. During their imprisonment, "the king was blessed with the birth of a son, the heir apparent to his crown," and advantage was taken of the public excitement to call in question the event. The party of the prelates took particular pains to prepare the people for a suppositious birth, for which there was no ground whatever, but their efforts were successful.

The prelates were no sooner acquitted, (for James, unlike some of his successors and their ministers in our own times, "never made an attempt to pervert the course of justice,"*)

* Lingard, Vol. xiii. p. 153

than the bishop of London associated himself with the Earls of Devonshire and Danby, Lord Lumley, Admiral Russell, and Sydney, in a conspiracy to subvert the throne. They subscribed an address to the Prince of Orange, offering him the crown of England, without a single condition for the liberties of the nation, and inviting him to send a foreign force into the kingdom to dethrone the reigning monarch, and to secure the crown for himself and his consort.

The revolution of 1688, which confirmed the reformation and established in England the Protestant religion, was effected by means so "perfidious, hypocritical, and un-principled," that it is difficult to conceive how any thing glorious or good could be expected from them. The chief actors in this revolution were the English prelates, "the same lords spiritual who," in the words of Sir James Mackintosh, "had preached passive obedience, and had sanctified orthodox atrocities during *a pious reign*, (that of Charles II.,) in which they enjoyed a monopoly of wealth, favour, power, and persecution. James invaded their exclusive privilege, he was guilty of the double sin of popery and toleration, and his tyranny to the nation could no longer be endured by the Church."[*]

"The party with whom the bishops acted," the same cool-headed historian tells us, "had no notion of religious toleration."

In September, 1688, the proclaimed purpose of the Prince of Orange to interfere in the affairs of England, and formidable preparations for the invasion of the kingdom of his son-in-law, filled James, notwithstanding his large military and naval forces, with serious apprehensions.[†]

In William's declaration to the States, (in October,) he said, "he had been invited to England by divers lords, both spiritual and temporal;" several of both orders were called on by the king to admit or deny the truth of the passage. Among the prelates, Compton, Bishop of London, distinguished himself by his equivocating mendacity.

The king had the folly to summon the bishops, whom he had lately prosecuted, to his councils in this emergency. He acquainted them with the dangers which menaced the

---

[*] History of the Revolution, p. 573.—American Edition.
[†] The fleet then consisted of thirty-seven men of war, and seventeen fireships. The army, (in England,) of forty thousand men.

kingdom, at the same time giving them plainly to understand, that the prelates were suspected of being parties to the designs of the Prince of Orange. The right reverend conspirators equivocated, shuffled, paltered in a double sense, and evinced great horror of the menaced invasion.

Mackintosh calls the result of the king's enquiry into the fealty of the bishops, "a great light by which to judge the spirit and genius of the Church, as a formidable power existing for itself by the side of the constitution, between the nation and the crown."

On the 16th of October, Mackintosh states, that the king commanded the attendance of the archbishop, and informed him of the designed invasion, and expressed his desire that the bishops should publish "An Abhorrence" of the designs of the invader. The archbishop replied, that his brethren had, for the most part, retired to their respective dioceses. This was an untruth; and the king stated as much in civil terms to the archbishop. The latter replied then with clumsy casuistry, that it was impossible so great a prince as James's son-in-law should entertain so execrable a design, and consequently it was unnecessary to express the proposed abhorrence.

Shortly after the king sent again for the Bishop of London. He was, or pretended to be, out of town when the summons came. He presented himself next day; and, on the king's reading the obnoxious passage about " the lords spiritual " in William's declaration, the right reverend father grossly equivocated.

" Sir," said he, " I am confident the rest of the bishops will as readily answer in the negative." (He had signed the invitation.)

James said, he believed them all innocent; but still required their subscription to the document above mentioned. The bishop begged time for reflection, and withdrew.

The next day, at another conference with his majesty, the archbishop and bishops of London, Peterborough, Rochester, Durham, Chester, and St. David's were present. The secretary of state having read the obnoxious passage, their disavowal of it was called for.

The archbishop protested his own innocence, and his belief in the innocence of his brethren.

The king questioned the Bishop of London. He replied, he had given his answer the day before, (confirming a falsehood he had already stated.) Of the lords spiritual implicated in this treason, the Bishop of Durham in his turn said, "I am sure I am not one of them." All the other bishops then repeated, "Nor I;" and at this very moment they were bound hand and foot to the invader.*

Here is falsehood, treason, perfidy, and equivocation plainly exhibited and had recourse to, not by ignorant priests or their deluded followers, but by the right reverend fathers in God, the prelates of the Church so recently "reformed." Such were the means which carried "the glorious revolution of 1688."

The king dismissed the bishops with an order to hold a general meeting of their body, and draw up a vindication of themselves, and to send it next day to him.

This meeting took place; the result of it was the adoption of a line of policy so scandalously dishonest, equivocating, and treacherous, that in the annals of revolutions nothing similar is probably to be compared to it.

The king having manifested much impatience at the procrastination of the bishops, a deputation from them, headed by the archbishop, came to Whitehall on the 6th of November. Here anew they protested their innocence, and the king affected to believe them. "But where is the paper," said he, "I desired you to draw up and bring me?"

The archbishop replied: "Sir, we have brought no paper, nor, with submission, do we think it necessary or proper for us so to do. Since your majesty is pleased to say you think us guiltless, we despise what all the world besides shall say."

"But," said the king, "I expected a paper from you. I take it you promised me one."

A long dialogue ensued, in which the archbishop, with extraordinary frankness, "has recorded the disingenuous artifices of dispute employed on his own side, and the prompt vigour with which he and his brethren were pressed by the king." The wary prelates sought refuge in a denial of the authenticity of the paper. "We assure

* History of the Revolution.

your majesty," said they, "that scarce one in five hundred believes it to be the prince's true declaration."*

"Then," said the king, vehemently, "your five hundred would bring in the Prince of Orange upon my throat."

"God forbid!" replied their lordships ; and the archbishop repeated the lie he commenced with. "So great a prince as the Prince of Orange would not proclaim a manifest falsehood."

"What," said the king, "he that can do as he does, think you he will stick at a lie ?"†

"Truly, Sire," said the bishops, "this is a business of state which does not properly concern us ;" and the archbishop followed up this cruel sarcasm by reminding his majesty they had been imprisoned for touching on matters of state.

"This, my lord," said the king, "is a 'querrelle d'Allemande,'—quite out of the way."

The king now pressed them hard for the required paper. At last they determined on a verbal disavowal, and a permission to the king to make it public.‡

"No," said the king, "if I should publish it, the people would not believe me."

"Sir," said the bishops, "the word of a king is sacred, and ought to be believed on its own authority ; it would be presumptuous in us to attempt to strengthen it ; the people cannot but believe your majesty in this matter."

"They," said the king, "that could believe me guilty of a false son, what will they not believe of me ?" (The very report which one of their body wilfully and wickedly propagated, knowing it to be false,—Bishop Burnet.)

The prelates in conclave said, that, as bishops, they could assist the king only with their prayers ; but, as peers, they were ready to serve him in parliament: and here ended the conference.§

The king's own account of these conferences differs nothing from the prelates'. Such was the jesuitical duplicity, sanctified perfidy, and covert treason of the mitred actors in the glorious revolution of men "attired in the vestments of a flimsy zeal," which, in the words of Mackintosh, "might be taken up by any knave or villain who violated the ordinances of God or man."

* History of the Revolution.
† Ibid.   ‡ Ibid.   § Ibid.

While these men were thus cajoling the king, the invited invader was in the kingdom, and one of their body, Bishop Burnet, was employed as a hackneyed scribbler, "to reconcile the invasion and the subject's duty of allegiance to the sovereign." He admitted, that the doctrine of non-resistance "was the constant doctrine of the Church of England ; but all general words, however large, have a tacit exception," he adds, "and a reserve in them, if the matter require it."

After this, let the clerical firebrands, who flare up periodically at Exeter Hall, declaim against the truculent, equivocating spirit of popery.

"But the real secret, if it be any longer a secret," says Mackintosh, "is, that the whigs of 1688 had no notion of freedom beyond their sect or party : that, with liberty in their lips, monopoly and persecution were in their hearts."

Such were the pious prelates and whig patriots from whom the Prince of Orange received an invitation to come to the deliverance of England from "popery" and its customary concomitants, "idolatry and superstition."

The memorable invitation to the Dutch prince bore but seven signatures. Compton, bishop of London, was one of the signers : he represented his wary brethren.

"It is a remarkable fact," says Mackintosh, "that not one great principle or generous inspiration escapes them in that document. Their invitation was a cold, creeping, irresolute address. The heart of one of the conspirators having failed him, he refused to sign the address,—Lord Nottingham. It was proposed in conclave by one of the seven subscribers of the invitation, to secure his silence by assassination."[*] The proposition was rejected, on the ground that the deed might not be necessary.

The most singular circumstance is, that these patriots, adopting the desperate resource of calling in a foreign power to assist them in the protection of their liberty—id est, immunity in persecuting their countrymen of a different persuasion—should never make a single stipulation for their country and constitution, but leave both at the absolute discretion of the invader they invited. Altogether, viewing the actors in this conspiracy, in their true light, one

* Mackintosh.—History of the Revolution.

cannot form too low an estimate of their patriotism, heroism, and wisdom.

In the words of Mackintosh, "viewing the revolution of 1688 at this distance of time, and with the lights of the present day, it is impossible to deny James a certain superiority in the comparison of abstract principles. His standard bore the nobler inscription. He proclaimed religious liberty, impartial and complete; and had he not sought to re-establish it by his own lawless will—had his proceedings been but worthy of his cause, posterity might regard him, not as a tyrant justly uncrowned, but as a beneficent prince who became the victim of an intolerable faction, an overweening hierarchy, and a besotted multitude."

The treachery of the prelates and principal whig nobility completely accomplished the king's ruin. He fled the kingdom the 23rd of December, 1688.

The fugitive king had no sooner taken his departure, than the friends of true religion and liberty gave vent to their pious and liberal feelings. The whig patriots paraded the streets with cries of "No popery;" and under pretence of searching for arms, they suffered the rabble to burst into the houses of the Catholics, to terrify the inhabitants, and to carry off everything valuable. Some houses were demolished, others given to the flames—the several Catholic chapels in Lincoln's Inn Fields, Lyme Street, St. John's, and Clerkenwell.* The night following, the citizens in every part of the metropolis were awakened simultaneously from their sleep by frightful cries of "The Irish are up and cutting throats." This deliberate attempt to provoke a massacre of the Catholics providentially failed.

Thus ended in a revolution an attempt in England to put a stop to persecutions on account of, or rather on pretence of, religion.

The prince who made that attempt is represented as a tyrant, a bigot, and an imbecile person; and the foreign prince, who drove him from his dominions, figures in our history as the champion of liberty, religion, and the British constitution. James was an austere, obstinate, injudicious man, not destitute, however, of many excellent qualities; he was upright, sincere, possessed great moral courage, aptitude for the business of state, and steadiness in his

---

* Mackintosh.—History of the Revolution, p. 199.

application to it: above all, in very bad times, and in very difficult circumstances, he was a defender of the great principle of freedom of opinion in religious matters.

Sergeant Heywood, referring to this subject in his 'Vindication,' says: "The MS. genealogy of the family of Lindsey, in the possession of the Earl of Balcarras, is a great authority upon this subject, and if James's most solemn declarations are to be credited, there can be no doubt that his designs in favour of the Catholic religion never extended to the destruction of the Established Church, or beyond a toleration sanctioned by law. The MS. says," continues the learned gentleman, that "when he became king, all his good qualities became defaced by a religion so detestable to his subjects. Yet he always protested, that he never meant to constrain the minds of any, and that all he wanted was toleration to his own religion. Certain it is, that some days before James died at St. Germain's, he brought all the foreign ministers into his room, and all his subjects of any rank who were there; took the Sacrament before them, and called the Almighty to witness, that he never intended to alter the laws or religion of his country, except that of toleration, for which he hoped for the concurrence of parliament."

Elsewhere we find evidence, in James's opposition to the Pope's nomination of Irish bishops, of a spirit of independence which is commonly supposed not to have belonged to him. The editor of the State Papers observes: "Notwithstanding the enthusiasm of this prince, and his submissive obedience to the See of Rome in spirituals, it appears that he never intended to acknowledge the Pope's supremacy in temporal concerns."*

This is a strange admission for a zealous advocate of this "glorious revolution" — the suitable result of an equally glorious revolt from the centre of religious unity.

* McPherson's State Papers, Vol. i. p. 57.

CHAPTER XVI.

STATE OF THE CATHOLICS IN ENGLAND FROM THE ACCESSION OF WILLIAM III. TO THAT OF GEORGE III., 1688 TO 1760.

THE Dutch invader having been seated by the whig lords, spiritual and temporal, on the throne of his father-in-law, the new king, who had been brought up in the principles of Calvin, soon showed himself favourably disposed towards the Presbyterians and other Dissenters from the Established Church. He became the patron of the Nonconformists, and by one of his first acts to facilitate their introduction into parliament, the oaths of supremacy and allegiance recited in 30 C. II. c. 2, so far as they relate to the qualification for members of either house, were repealed,* and substituted by a simple oath of allegiance and of abjuration of papal excommunications, and of papal authority, civil or ecclesiastical, in the realm.

In the same statute (cap. vi.) the new coronation oath is prescribed—whereby the sovereign is to be sworn " To the utmost of his power, to maintain the laws of God, the true Protestant profession of the gospel, and the Protestant reformed religion established by law. And to preserve unto the bishops and clergy of this realm, and to the churches committed to their charge, all such rights and privileges as by law do, or shall appertain unto them, or any of them."

The pious interpreters of this oath, (the one now taken by our sovereigns), religious men, scrupulous christians, persons of tender consciences, like the late Duke of York, and the old political theologian of the Court of Chancery, Lord Eldon—who held the sovereign bound by this engagement to persecute or to proscribe such of his subjects as worshipped God after the fashion of their fathers, of the faith of Augustine and of Alfred—seem to have forgotten another portion of the same coronation oath :—

* By 1 W. and M. ses. 1. c. 1.

Archbishop or Bishop.

"Will you, to your power, cause law and justice in mercy to be executed in all your judgments?"

King or Queen.

"I will."

There was no measure of a remedial kind passed to benefit the Dissenters in this reign, which did not inflict some new injury on Catholics. The 1 W. and M. sess. 1. c. 8, which repeals the oath of supremacy contained in 1 Eliz. c. 1, and that of allegiance in 3 J. I. c. 4, and all statutes relating thereto, as far as those oaths are concerned, requiring the oath of 1 W. and M. st. 1. c. 1, to be taken in their stead, under the penalties enumerated in those respective acts. It also contains a requisition for all commission and warrant officers in the king's service, by sea or land, to subscribe the declaration of 30 C. II. before they receive their commission or warrant.

By a provision of 1 Wm. and Mary, st. 1. c. 9, all persons are required to subscribe the declaration of 30 C. II., on its being tendered by any justice, and refusing to do so, if remaining within ten miles of the capital, shall be liable to the penalties of Popish recusants, with some exceptions in favour of artisans.

Persons refusing the declaration, by the fifteenth chapter, are forbidden to possess any arms or ammunition except with the permission of the Justices of Peace, by a regular order of Sessions. To these, magistrates power is given to authorize any persons, attended by a constable, to enter in the day-time the house of any Papist in search of arms, on the old penalty of three months' imprisonment and forfeiture of arms, and a further forfeiture of their value, to be levied on their goods for the informer's benefit, and of three times their value to go to the king.

The last provision of this atrocious act, likewise subjected Roman Catholics keeping a horse of above the value of five pounds, to the same fine, imprisonment, and loss of the property seized, as the concealment or unlawful retention of arms or ammunition, or resisting the delivery of the same. This was one of the early "gracious acts," sanctioned by "the champion of civil and religious liberty."

It is said, these intolerant measures were forced on the Dutchman. It is probable they were somewhat distasteful to him; but the power was not wanting to him, had he the moral courage that was requisite to refuse his assent to them.

By another act, (1 W. and M. s. 2. c. 1), refusal or neglect to subscribe the test declaration, on its being duly tendered, disqualified for the right of presentation to any benefice. "By this act, Catholics were deprived of a right which their ancestors might have purchased at a considerable expense, for no one reason that might not equally operate to the deprivation of a Dissenter, a Quaker, or a Jew; all of whom were nevertheless left in its full enjoyment."*

By another act, commonly called the Bill of Rights, (1. W. and M. s. 2. c. 1), papists, and persons marrying papists, are for ever declared incapable of enjoying the crown of these realms, and in the event of their succession, the subject is absolved from his allegiance, and the crown is settled on the next Protestant heir.

The literal construction of this act, would render the reign of the 4th George an usurpation. He had married "a papist" when Prince of Wales—and, like the beautiful Miss Palmer, in the Vice-regal court, in Lord Chesterfield's time—"a very dangerous papist." The letter of this law, moreover, would have been injurious to the right of succession of the Duke of Sussex to the throne, for he had likewise married a dangerous papist in his "days of nature."

In 1689, the tolerant spirit of the whig patriots in parliament, was shown in the impeachment of Sir Edward Hales, the Earls of Peterborough and Salisbury, and Obadiah Walker, for high treason, for having been reconciled to the Church of Rome. In the following sessions of parliament the impeachment was dropped.

In 1690, a detected conspiracy to restore James to his throne, in which the Earl of Clarendon, the Bishop of Ely, Lord Preston, William Penn, the celebrated Quaker, and several others of opposite principles in religion, were said to be implicated, showed the belief that was largely enter-

* Brown's Penal Laws, p. 165.

tained of James's sincerity in his declarations in favour of liberty of conscience.*

In the same year, an act was passed (3 W. and M. c. 2) by which it was ordained that all persons in Ireland, required by previous acts to take the oaths of allegiance and supremacy, were obliged to take the new oaths in lieu of them ; and also the declaration of 30 Car. 2, to be subscribed by all persons in office.

" By the same act, barristers, clerks, or officers in any of the courts of Justice, attorneys, or practisers of law or physic, practising before they have taken the oaths, and obtained a certificate thereof, are subjected to a fine of £.500, are disabled for ever from exercising their profession, from holding any office, from being executor or guardian, and from taking any legacy or deed of gift. By another provision, Catholics are for the first time rendered incapable to serve in parliament, as they are required by the fifth section to make the declaration of 30 C. 2, under similar regulations to those provided in England. This act, however, closes with an exception in favour of those who were in the garrison at Limerick, the 3rd of October, 1691."†

This closing provision, made only to save appearances, and never meant to be observed, like the Spanish edicts for the mitigation of slavery—in the terms of the accompanying instructions—to be " obecidos y non cumplidos," remains a lasting monument of the hypocrisy of those times, as the violation of it (to which fuller attention will be called in treating of the affairs of Ireland) will ever be a stain on the character of public faith in England.

In 1691, another "popish plot " was concocted in England, by the zealous friends of "true religion ;" and " this political engine," was anxiously laid hold of by the whig patriots, to promote their objects.

The scene of the new plot was laid in Lancashire, and the alleged actors in it, were the principal Roman Catholic gentry of that county. A resolution was moved in parliament and passed, to the effect that " a dangerous conspiracy against the king and government existed."

The Titus Oates of the day, was a prisoner in the King's-Bench, of the name of Fuller, on whose denunciations

---

* Smollett, ch. 3. s. 1.
† Brown's Penal Laws, p. 167.

a great number of Catholics were seized and cast into prison.

"The Popish conspirators" were prosecuted. The perjured witnesses broke down, the prisoners were acquitted, the impostor Fuller was convicted of perjury, and sentenced to stand in the pillory.

A conspiracy, however, in 1696, against the life of William, was discovered by an Irish Catholic of the name of Prendergast. Smollet gives it to be understood that many Protestants were implicated in this conspiracy, entered into to preserve unbroken the hereditary descent of the crown. Many Catholics also were said to be implicated in the plot, and the probability is that they were truly stated to have been so.

The new "No Popery" effort, albeit a failure, put parliament into a favourable disposition to gratify the wishes, perhaps to promote the interests, of some legal functionaries of the orthodox religion, to shut out Roman Catholics from the bar, to transfer the business of popish attorneys to solicitors who prayed to God, or. pretended to do so, in places of Protestant worship.

It was enacted by the 7 and 8 W. 3. c. 24, that all sergeants and counsellors at law, barristers, advocates, attorneys, solicitors, proctors, clerks, or notaries, practising in any of the courts without having taken the oaths of 1 W. and M. c. 8, and subscribed the declaration in 25 C. 2, shall incur the penalties and forfeitures of the statutes of Premunire.

By another act of this session, (7 and 8 W. 3. c. 27), persons refusing the oaths of William and Mary, (st. 1. c. 1), and declaration of the 25th year of Charles II., are to suffer as popish recusants ; but the penalties for refusing the oaths, may be pardoned by the king's writ of privy seal : and persons subscribing the above named declaration of Charles, are incapacitated to sit in parliament unless they also subscribe to a form or test agreed to by members of both houses of parliament, beginning with the words :— "Whereas there has been a horrible and detestable conspiracy formed and carried on by papists and other wicked and traitorous persons, for assassinating his majesty's royal person in order to subvert our religion, laws and liberty."

In 1697, the commons petitioned the king for the

removal of papists and non-jurors from London, and for the rigid execution of the penal laws. To procure this petition, Brown states, that rumours had been industriously circulated that some secret articles, favourable to the Catholics, had been entered into by the king at the peace of Ryswick, and it was even insinuated " that William was a papist in his heart."

By 10 and 11 W. 3, c. 12, the lieutenants of counties were empowered to appoint and determine such horse and foot soldiers as the estates of papists may be required to furnish, and to charge the cost of such appointment on their estates.

In the following session, by another act, (11 and 12 W. 3. c. 4), the old spirit of persecution was once more let loose. The private exercise of the Catholic religion was punished with enormous penalties. The prelates and pastors of that religion were delivered over to the tender mercies of a pack of ruffians, licensed by law to hunt them out like wild beasts, and amply rewarded for the successful chase.

By the 19th section of this act, persons refusing the new oaths, or affirmation of Quakers, were deprived of the elective franchise.

By this act, any person apprehending a popish bishop, priest, or Jesuit, saying mass, or exercising any clerical functions, was entitled to a reward of £.100, to be paid within four months' of conviction by the sheriff of the county.

By another clause, a penalty of £.100, was inflicted on any person sending a child beyond sea without license, and allotted entirely to the informer. By an act in the reign of James I., the same penalty being equally divided between the king, the poor, and the informer. By another clause, all Catholics over eighteen years of age, not taking the prescribed oath and declaration, are disqualified to inherit any landed property or tenements in England; but all such property to be enjoyed during the recusant's life, by the next Protestant heir: and all papists are further disabled to purchase or possess any manors, lands, profits, out-land, or tenements, within the kingdom of England.

This infamous law left no disposable property, except personal, to Catholic parents; it perverted the natural feelings and affections, it rent asunder the bonds which united the son to the father, and the child of a Catholic parent to the Church in which he was born and bred. It enabled any child of a Catholic, the youngest of his children it might be, on abandoning his Church and pretending to conform to the established one, to dispossess his father of the right of disposal of any landed property which he might possess, constitute himself his heir, and on filing a bill in chancery against his father, compel the latter to allow such maintenance till he came of age, as the chancellor might deem fit for a Protestant child.

This iniquitous act, and those of a similar kind which preceded, must ever stain the reign of William III. with the infamy that attaches to a persecuting era.

By 12 and 13 W. 3. c. 2, or act of settlement, it was provided (in the third clause) that whosoever should come hereafter to the crown of these realms, must join in communion with the Church of England.

The last penal act of this reign, renders it incumbent on members of parliament, all persons in office, lawyers, doctors, preachers, teachers, &c., to take the oaths of abjuration of the rights of the Pretender, under similar penalties to those incurred by refusing to subscribe the declaration of Charles II., c. 2.

The reign of " the glorious, pious, and immortal King William," was more calamitous in its effects and influence on the future destinies of England, than that of any former sovereign. He involved the kingdom for the sake of Holland in continental connexions. He introduced from Holland into England, the practice of mortgaging for present exigencies, the revenue of future years, to Jews and other money-jobbers. He originated state-borrowing on the security of anticipated taxes, and multiplied imposts on industry for means to pay interest on public debts and levies for a standing army, without whose bayonets the government of England henceforth was not to be propped up. He was destitute of moral courage, but not of the talents of soldiership; though naturally inclined to toleration in religious matters, he never made an effort worthy of a man of principle or ordinary firmness, to prevent his ministers following the footsteps of their predecessors of the times of Charles I. and II., in the career of persecution.

There was less excuse for it in the reign of William, than in that of either of those sovereigns. He possessed more power.   The persecuted people were far less formidable then to a Protestant government, than in any former reign.

Sir John Dalrymple* has published a curious official report of the number of Catholics in England in the reign of King William, found after his death in the iron chest of that vigilant monarch.   From this authentic document the following is an extract :—

" Number of Freeholders in England.

	Conformists.	Non-Conformists.	Papists.
Province of Canterbury,...	2,123,362	93,151	11,878
————— York, ...	353,892	15,525	1,978
	2,477,254	108,676	13,856

Conformists, ...	2,477,254
Non-Conformists, ...	108,676
Papists, ...	13,856
	2,599,786

According to which account the proportion of
    conformists to non-conformists is............ $22\frac{1}{4}$ to 1
Conformists to papists............................ .....$178\frac{19}{13}$
Conformists and non-conformists together to
    Papists .... $186\frac{3}{8}$"†

So much for the necessity of the severe measures against the Catholics in William's reign.

Anne, Princess of Denmark, ascended the throne in 1702, a weak narrow-minded woman, managed by the Duchess of Marlboro', through whose influence the husband of the latter maintained his faction against that of Rochester. The condition of the Catholics was never so low since the days of Elizabeth, as at the period of the death of William III.   One of the first acts of her reign, was a "no-popery measure," a new abjuration oath for the further security of

* Memoirs, Vol. ii. Appendix, part ii. p. 12, &c.
† Ap. Brown, p. 161.

her reign, and the succession in the Protestant line, and for extinguishing the hopes of the pretender.

The security of the church made it necessary to prevent any English Catholic from possessing property in Ireland. By the 1 Anne, c. 32., all Catholics are disabled from purchasing any of the forfeited estates in Ireland.

"The further security of the Protestant religion," the eternal plea for every imperial act emanating in ambition or avarice, the lust of domination or aggrandizement, seemed to make the union of the two kingdoms of England and Scotland, an essential obstacle at that period to the designs of France on the former country.   The act for appointing commissioners to consider the terms of a treaty for the proposed union, received the royal assent the sixth of May, 1702.

The tories, in this reign, affected extraordinary zeal for the church, and dread of dissenters. They brought in a bill against occasional conformity, which miscarried.   The whigs took the constitution under their especial patronage, and entertained no fears of it except from popery and toleration of papists.   The proceedings of the two houses of convocation in this reign, were analogous to those of the parliament.   High Church and Low Church polemics, were other phases of tory politics and whig opposition stratagems. The queen sided with High Church principles and tory politics.

The final settlement of the question of union between England and Scotland in 1706, and of that of the succession vested in the Princess Sophia, left the partisans of the son of James not altogether hopeless of success.

The people of Scotland, as they imagined, betrayed by their commissioners and choused out of their national independence, prepared, when it was too late, to defend their lost nationality.   While they were preparing for insurrection, a bill passed both houses of parliament, "for the security of the church of England," to be inserted as a fundamental and essential part of that treaty.*

Never was any thing so often secured, so frequently found wanting safety and stability, as the church of England.   The 4 Anne, c. 4, which naturalized the Princess

* Smollet's History of England, Vol. iv. p. 328.

Sophia, provided that this privilege should not extend to any one becoming a papist, then considered an alien.

The dominion of an insolent vulgar woman over a weak contemptible princess came to an end in 1707. The Duchess of Marlboro' was supplanted by Mrs. Masham, a kinswoman of the former, raised to a high rank in society from indigence and obscurity by the duchess. The whigs came into power. The preparations at Dunkirk for the expedition of the Chevalier de St. George, at this period, furnished parliament with another plea for a penal law. An act was passed making it obligatory on all persons to take the oath of abjuration on pain of incurring the penalties of convicted recusants.

A little later, Dr. Sacheverel was impeached for advocating in the pulpit " positions contrary to revolution principles."

And another rector, Mr. Hoadly, was recommended by parliament to the queen for preferment, for having advocated in his sermons physical force doctrines, and justified the principles which led to the late happy revolution.

Sacheverel was found guilty, prevented from preaching for three years, his objectionable sermons were burned by the hangman. So much for the opinion entertained of moral force doctrines in the reign of Queen Anne.

A new cry was now got up in England ; " The Church and Dr. Sacheverel." The latter made a progress through the country, that in splendour might vie with a sovereign's; the clergy rallied round him, the tories turned the religious excitement of the people to the good old cause of faction. The elections were carried by the new cry—the tories were reinstated in office, and the queen, in her speech at the opening of parliament, was made to declare her resolution " to support the Church of England," and likewise " to employ none but such as were heartily attached to the protestant succession in the house of Hanover."[*]

In 1711, an attempt to assassinate one of the members by a phrenzied desperado, a Frenchman, was followed, as a matter of course, by a cry in parliament against popery, and a proclamation ordering the laws to be strictly enforced against papists.

And in the same year the act against occasional confor-

* Smollet's History of England, Vol. iv. p. 374.

mity, 10 Anne, c. 2, finally passed into law. By another act of the same year, 10 Anne, c. 7, papists are debarred from presenting to any living in Scotland.

In 1713 the peers resolved, that all persons not included in the treaty of Limerick, who had not borne arms in France and Spain, should be incapable of employment, civil or military, or of sustaining the character of a diplomatic agent from any foreign power.

By the 12 Anne, st. 2, c. 14, further encouragement is given to discoverers of popish lands and trusts, and empower the Scotch authorities to punish Jesuits "and other trafficking papists."

It is to be observed, though the principle of toleration was recognized in the statute book in the reign of William, and in the tenth year of that of Anne, Catholics derived no benefit from them—they were formally excluded from the privileges conceded to the Scotch dissenters. In the act 10 Anne c. 2, it is provided, that nothing in the act "shall be construed to extend to give any ease, benefit, or advantage to any papist or popish recusant whatsoever."

The intolerance, however, of the high church party did not confine itself to Catholics. By the act 12 Anne, c. 7, keeping a school, or teaching youth as a schoolmaster, without subscribing the declaration of conformity to the Church of England, subjected the offender, of whatever creed he might be, to three months' imprisonment.

There was some abatement of persecution at the commencement of this reign, but not one glimpse of religious liberty for persons of the Catholic persuasion; nor was their condition bettered in any respect at the death of this sovereign, in 1714.

The German bigot, who succeeded the worthless daughter of James II.—George I., found the Catholics of his new dominions sunk in abject abasement; it was reserved for his reign to prove that a lower depth of degradation remained yet for them.

The son of James II. had been led to believe that his sister, the deceased sovereign, had contemplated his succession, and was favourably disposed towards that object. At her death he set about asserting his claim to the crown, and his supporters were by no means confined to persons of the Catholic religion.

The old policy that dictated in Rome the cry of "Christianos ad leones" in every panic, and got up the "no popery" clamour in every political crisis in England, prevailed on this occasion.

By 1 G. 1. st. 2. c. 13. every person refusing the oaths of allegiance and supremacy, contained in 1 W. and M. s. 1. c. 1. and that of abjuration, in 12 and 13 W. 3. c. 2. either in England or Ireland, and the oath of allegiance and assurance of abjuration (for in favour of the presbyterians the oath of supremacy could be dispensed with) in Scotland, is declared a popish recusant, and is of course made liable to the penalties of the acts against such offenders.

By the forty-seventh chapter of the same statute, persons having professed the popish religion, who, at the time of their enlisting for soldiers, do not produce a testimonial of their having publicly renounced it, or declare to the officer enlisting them, that they are papists, shall receive such corporal punishment, not extending to the loss of life and limb, as a court-martial shall inflict.

By a succeeding chapter of the same statute, papists not taking the oaths required by 1 G. 1, st. 2. c. 13, and subscribing the declaration of 30 C. 2, within six months after they come into possession of any lands, or if let on lease, of the yearly rent reserved to them, &c., must register such lands, and their value, under a penalty of £.40 and forfeiture. Two-thirds of all penalties to go to the king, and the other to any protestant that will sue. This infamous act was somewhat modified by the 3 Geo. 1, c. 18, which limited the time for commencing suits to two years after the offence; but provided that no lands, &c. should pass from papists by any deed unless enrolled within six months of the date of the deed or death of a testator.

By the 1 Geo. 1, st. 2. c. 50, entitled, "an act for appointing commissioners to enquire of the estates of certain traitors and of popish recusants, and of estates given to superstitious uses, in order to raise money out of their security for the use of the public," the commissioners are directed to enquire as to the estates of popish recusants, and whether they are registered.

In pursuance of this laudable method of raising money, by taxing people's consciences, the 9 G. I. c. 18, orders £.100,000 to be assessed on papists above eighteen years of age, over and above the double assessment by the land-

tax, to which they were already subjected. It provides,
however, that if the full sum charged be duly paid, they
shall be exempted from the forfeiture of the two-thirds of
their lands, and of all other penalties for recusancy. This
atrocious act was passed on pretence of defraying the
charges of suppressing the rebellion in Scotland. Thus
the Catholics were punished for the sins of the presbyterians.*

The Church, ever to be secured and never safe, appears
to have suffered from the same causes which affected the
credit of the nation. The south-sea scheme for enriching
the English people, was productive of habits of profligacy
and debauchery, which it was attempted to put a stop to by
an act of parliament, "against atheism, profaneness, and
immorality."

The Earl of Peterborough opposed the bill, "because he
was not for a parliamentary king, or a parliamentary religion, and would rather sit in a conclave of cardinals than
in one of peers of parliament on such principles as the
supporters of the bill seemed to lay down." Yet this peer
belonged to a parliamentary religion, the head of which
was a parliamentary king, (in virtue of the revolution of
1688) a foreign prince and pontiff too, imported from Hanover, to rule the church and state.

The suppression of the rebellion in Scotland, in 1716,
was followed by atrocities similar to those which disgraced
the reign of James II. after the defeat of the Duke of
Monmouth's attempt. Yet George I. met with little obloquy on account of his savagery on the former occasion.
The support of the church covers a multitude of sins in a
monarch, or a minister of state, in England.

George I. terminated his reign in 1727. To his memory
the Catholics of his dominions are little beholden.

George II. ascended the throne in 1727, and in a long
reign of thirty-four years, the Hanoverian bigot made no
effort to relax the rigour of the Penal Code, or to lighten
the heavy burdens of his Catholic subjects. Yet at his
death "a thousand pens were drawn to paint the beauties
and sublimity of his character in poetry as well as prose.
They extolled him above Alexander in courage and heroism,
above Augustus in liberality, Titus in clemency, Antoninus

* Brown's Penal Laws, p. 277, &c.

in piety and benevolence, Solomon in wisdom, and King Edward in devotion."*

The impediments thrown in the way of recruiting the land forces and marines by the absurdly impolitic measures of former reigns, rendered it necessary to frame an act, 30 Geo. 2, c. 8, exempting commissioners, churchwardens, constables, &c., discharging the duties assigned to them by that act, from the penalties imposed by certain statutes of Charles II. and William III. Yet making any commissioner thus acting, liable to a fine of £.200, for taking office without taking the oaths prescribed by two acts of William.

It is very singular that measures for the emancipation, or relief of the Jews, who denied the Christian faith in toto, never excited the rage of the "friends of true religion" in England to any extent, similar to that which any proposal to relax the rigour of the Penal Code under which Catholics groaned, was sure to do.

Why this distinction in the treatment of the Jews and Catholics should be made, it would be very difficult to say. By the 26 Geo. 2. c. 26, it is declared that Jews may be naturalized without receiving the sacrament, provided they have been members of the Jewish church or synagogue three years previously. But the English nation had not yet reached that degree of toleration which was requisite to suffer even an act of this kind to exist for any length of time.

In the succeeding session this act was repealed, because, says the preamble to 27 George II. c. 1, "occasion has been taken from it to raise discontents and to disquiet the minds of his majesty's subjects." A former act of this session, however, had naturalized such Jews as had been resident in the English colonies in America for seven years, on taking the oaths and subscribing the declaration of 30 C. 2, excepting in the oath of abjuration, the words "upon the true faith of a christian," which are omitted, because the Jews, say the parliament "may thereby be prevented from receiving the benefit of this act."

The only additional penal statute passed in the English parliament in this reign, was that which declared all grants of ecclesiastical promotions, or advowsons made by papists

---

* Smollet's History of England, Vol. vi. p. 156.

null and void, unless made to a bona fide protestant. This act, 2 Geo. 2, cap. 17, provided that popish owners of estates taking the oaths of allegiance, and subscribing the declaration of 30 Car. 2, and all protestants claiming under it for themselves or other protestants, are to hold such estates free from any incapacity, unless the persons interested take advantage of their disability, and recover in an action commenced six months before the conformity.

At the end of the reign of George II. the Catholics were nearly in as bad a condition as they were at its commencement.

CHAPTER XVII.

STATE OF THE CATHOLICS IN ENGLAND FROM THE ACCESSION OF GEORGE III. TO THEIR EMANCIPATION.—1760 TO 1829.

GEORGE III. ascended the throne in 1760. The five years succeeding his accession were disgraced by the enactment of several penal laws in England, which tended to increase their sufferings. But to the honour of this reign several of the most iniquitous of the infamous laws that have been noticed in the preceding pages were removed in it. Enough, however, of savagery and injustice were left in the remaining code, to try the patience of the Catholics, and to prove a curse to the peace of the whole kingdom for more than half-a-century to come.

The first penal statute in this reign, designed to conform and extend the system of persecution that had so long endured, was an act excluding Catholics from serving even as privates in the militia. By the 2 Geo. 3. c. 20, every man enrolled in the militia was obliged to take an oath of allegiance and conformity, in one part of which are the words, "And I do swear that I am a Protestant;" and by another clause of the same act, deputy lieutenants and all commissioned officers are required to take a similar oath, contained in the act 1 Geo. 1. c. 13, with the same objectionable clause, "And I do swear that I am a Protestant."

16

The second penal statute of this reign, was the 4 Geo. **3**. c. 2, which subjected papists over eighteen years of age, refusing or neglecting to take the oaths, (which, as Catholics, it was impossible for them to take,) to a double assessment of the land-tax.

The Regency Act, 5 Geo. 3. c. 27, disqualifies the person appointed regent of the kingdom, in the event of the crown descending to a minor, if he or she marry a papist. This important provision, which so seriously affected the rights of the Prince of Wales when he privately married Mrs. Fitzherbert, may be borne in mind by those who read with astonishment the solemn denial of Mr. Fox in the House of Commons of the fact of that marriage—his earnest protestations of ignorance of any nuptials of the prince. Nevertheless, the prince was married by a Roman Catholic priest, the chaplain of a foreign ambassador at the court of St. James.*

By annual acts of indemnity under George III., the operation of the Test and Corporation Acts had been partially suspended. The Catholics, who could not take the oath of supremacy, were debarred from their benefits. The Rev. T. Flanagan, in his recent work, 'The Manual of British and Irish History,' (page 793.) makes mention of so recent an enforcement of penal law as one in 1769, when James Talbot, the brother of the Earl of Shrewsbury, was tried for his life at the Old Bailey for saying mass, and was only acquitted on account of insufficiency of evidence. He cites Charles Butler's account of the "Single house of Dynely and Ashmall, attorneys in Gray's Inn Lane, having defended more than twenty priests under such prosecutions. Instances," he adds, "are on record, so late as 1782, of Catholic labourers being fined and distrained for refusing to attend the service of the Established Church."

No more atrocities of a legislative kind were added to the infamy of the penal code. But though, in the course of a few years, some of its most enormously unjust and sanguinary enactments were removed from the statute-book, the great body of oppression incorporated in those diabolical laws remained in being.

---

* All the circumstances of the marriage were known to an Irish Roman Catholic priest, who died in Naples a few years ago, possessed of considerable wealth; a person of no little notoriety in Southern Italy about twenty years ago—the eccentric Abbe Campbell.

The spirit of persecution from the fifth year of George III. waxed fainter and fainter every succeeding year: it only rarely, and at long intervals, raised its head in the English parliament.

The amelioration of the condition of the Catholics of Canada in 1774, was the first step towards toleration made in the British parliament. The 14 G. 3. c. 35, ? 5, enacts, that Catholics may enjoy the free exercise of their religion in Quebec, subject to the king's supremacy, and that their clergy may " receive and enjoy their accustomed dues and rights, in respect to such persons only as shall profess the said religion." The sixth section of the act reserves to his majesty the right of making a provision for Protestant ministers, otherwise than by compelling the Catholics to support them.*

The first dawn of toleration in England for English Catholics was in 1788, when Sir George Savile introduced a bill, which passed into law with little opposition, repealing certain laws of William and Anne inflicting severe penalties on Catholics for the exercise of their religion, which acts, in debate, he characterized as "disgraceful not only to religion, but to humanity."

By this measure, 18 Geo. 3. c. 60, an act of William (11 and 12, c. 4.) subjecting popish priests or schoolmasters to perpetual imprisonment for keeping school, and preventing papists inheriting or buying lands, was repealed. The priests or schoolmasters, it is provided, should take an oath of allegiance, to which no Catholic could reasonably object. By another act of relief, 18 Geo. 3. c. 61, the statute 1 Anne, c. 32. disabling papists from purchasing or inheriting forfeited estates, was repealed.

"The year 1780," says Browne, "will ever be memorable for the exhibition of a scene of as extended outrage as ever proceeded from the influence of bigotry and enthusiasm, in inflaming the passions of the multitude. The act, then known as Sir George Savile's, had been received in England, if not with favour, at least without opposition. The zealous presbyterians of the north, however, were alarmed, and raising their old war-cry of "No popery,"

* The 35 George III. c. 35, provides that all persons are eligible to be elected members of the legislative assembly of Quebec, except ministers of either of the Churches of England or Rome, or of congregations of Protestant dissenters.

they proceeded to demolish the Catholic chapels, by way of evincing their zeal in the 'good old cause,' which had so long appeared to have slumbered in an oblivion, that, it were to be wished, had proved eternal. These riots were, at length, in some measure tranquillized by a proclamation issued by the lord provost, assuring the good people of Edinburgh, 'that no repeal of the penal statutes would take place.' But notwithstanding this assurance, in imitation, I presume, of the memorable 'godly covenant,' they entered into that they termed 'The Protestant Association,'* of which Lord George Gordon, a fanatical enthusiast, who, perhaps, was a fit object for Bedlam, was an active member. This association soon diffused its fears and principles to the capital of England; and Lord George, at the head of 50,000 of the lower order of the people, with banners inscribed with the watchword of insurrection, 'No Popery,' presented a petition for the repeal of the slight concessions which had been granted to the Catholics, which had obtained, it is said, one hundred and twenty thousand signatures or marks."

Of these No popery riots Mr. Macaulay gives the following summary view :† "Without the shadow of a grievance, at the summons of a madman, a hundred thousand people rose in insurrection, and a week of anarchy commenced,—parliament besieged; your predecessor, Sir, trembling in his chair; lords pulled out of their coaches, bishops flying over the tiles [laughter]—a sight which he trusted would not be satisfactory to any of those who were the most unfavourable to the present measure [hear, hear]—at one time 36 fires blazing in different parts of London, the house of the chief justice sacked, the children of the prime minister taken out of bed in their night clothes, and laid upon the table at the Horse Guards—all these scenes were nothing but the effect of the ignorance of a population left like brutes in the midst of christianity, and savages in the midst of civilization."

In these riots, the chapels of the Sardinian and Bavarian

---

* Granville Sharpe, the zealous advocate of justice for African negroes, the President of one of the No Popery Associations called "the Protestant Union," took a leading part in the agitation against the Catholics, an agitation which led to murders, conflagration, and pillage.

.† Speech on the Education Question, April 29, 1847.

ambassadors were sacked and burned ; likewise the chapel at Moorfields and the houses of many Catholics. The houses of Sir George Savile, Lord Mansfield, and several other distinguished persons, were destroyed and pillaged ; Newgate was burned, and five of the six remaining prisons destroyed; Langton's distillery was likewise consumed by the defenders of Protestantism, and no inconsiderable quantity of the spirits that was found on the premises.

It was from this scene of terror on Holborn Bridge, that the infuriated rabble, maddened with drink, rushed at night-fall, and set fire to houses in various places, so that, at one time, thirty-six conflagrations were raging in the city.

"The month of June, 1780," Gibbon, an eye-witness of the no popery riots, well might say, "will ever be marked by a dark and diabolical fanaticism, which I supposed to be extinct, but which actually subsists in Great Britain perhaps beyond any other country in Europe."

That dark and diabolical fanaticism did not perish with Lord George Gordon in Newgate, and the twenty infatuated followers of the maniac lord, out of the fifty-nine capitally convicted, who were executed on that occasion.

The civil and the military power are now differently constituted to what they were sixty-seven years ago ; but the spirit of fanaticism has not undergone so great a change as might be hoped it would have done in that period in its stronghold, the middle class in England. In the upper ranks it never existed to any large extent; rapacity and the lust of power adopted the semblance of it, for their purposes. And as to the riddlings of society, the mere rabble of the large towns and cities, any cry against popery at any time, in any great political crisis, could be got up, if reasonable prospect of plunder could be presented, with as much effect as at the period when eighty-five " Christian Corresponding Societies" were affiliated to those of Edinburgh, were the police in the same state as to efficiency as that force was in 1780.

The worst scenes of 1666 were in process of renewal in 1780 in the capital, when the authorities began to think the friends of true religion were going too far. They had quietly looked on while the destruction of chapels only was being effected ; but when the prisons were broken open, the robbers and murderers who were their inmates let loose on the citizens, the persons of ministers attacked, and their houses pillaged and destroyed, the authorities then became alarmed, and caused five-and-twenty thousand troops to be brought against the rioters, and to attack them in various directions. Five hundred dead and wounded next morning lay in the streets, when order was restored, and the yells of "No Popery" had ceased to be heard in the late frightful scenes of pillage, bloodshed, and tumult, in the capital of "the most civilized country of the world."

The most important act of relief passed in favour of Catholics, was that measure deservedly styled the Toleration Act (31 Geo. 3. c. 32), which received the royal assent in 1791. By its provisions, Catholics taking the oath of allegiance, referred to in a former act, are exempted from prosecution as recusants for not resorting to Church, for being a papist or reputed papist, hearing or saying mass, being a priest, or deacon, or of any monastic order, or being present at or performing any religious rite. Places of Catholic worship to be certified at the quarter sessions, and the names of priests officiating therein to be registered in the books of the clerk of the peace. Catholics made eligible for the office of constable, churchwarden, or any parochial office by deputy, entitled to protection in the free exercise of their religion ; priests officiating in chapels with steeples excepted from the benefit of some provisions of the new act. Members of religious orders specially excluded from all Catholic schools, colleges, and academies. No Catholic duly registered to be punished for teaching youth, except in the case of a child of a Protestant father. No Catholic to be called on to take the oath of supremacy, or declaration of 25 Car. 2. c. 2, nor to be debarred from residing in London, nor to have his lands registered; barristers to be relieved from taking the oaths prescribed by an act of William III. ; and, finally, Catholic peers are declared no longer liable to the heavy penalties and disabilities incurred by coming into the king's presence without having signed the declaration of 30 Car. 2.

Catholics, however, remained till 1829 excluded from parliament, from office under government, and from corporate bodies. Their clergy were not allowed the celebration of their rites, without restrictions, by the act of 31 Geo. 3. c. 31. Schoolmasters of their persuasion could not take Protestant scholars. Catholics could not endow any

school or college for the education of children in their
faith. Catholic soldiers, by the Mutiny Act, refusing to
attend the Church of England worship, were liable to a
penalty of one shilling, for a second offence to the same
fine, and to be put in irons for twelve hours.* English
Catholics were moreover deprived of the elective franchise,
which privilege Irish Catholics possessed on producing a
certificate of having taken the oaths of 13 and 14 Geo. 3.
c. 35, and 33 Geo. 3. c. 21.

A great number of obsolete penal acts, moreover, still
remained on the statute book.

Lord Malmesbury's Diaries leave no doubt, that the second
attack of the disorder of the king's intellect was produced
by the constant state of excitement and mental disquietude
in which he was kept by Lord Eldon and two or three others
of his advisers on the subject of his coronation oath, and
the obligations it imposed on him to maintain the penal
code against Catholics, as the only safeguard for the Protestant religion.

In 1800, those groundless apprehensions of his majesty
caused the British government to violate the compact
entered into with some of the leaders of the Irish people,
which led them to support the union, in consideration of
the adjustment of the Catholic question solemnly promised
by Mr. Pitt.

In 1807, the poor deluded old king, alarmed at the
attempts of the ministry to relax the rigour of the penal
code, dismissed "all the talents," and gave occasion
throughout the country to get up another "No Popery"
cry for the new elections. Every wall was covered with
"No Popery" inscriptions; every old woman's imagination
was filled with terror of predicted plots and conspiracies;
and every house with blessings on the "good old king," who
had saved the Church from ruin and pillage. A stupid
lawyer, without character or practice, noted only for his
bigotry, Mr. Perceval, was made chancellor of the exchequer.

All the ancient calumnies against Catholics and Catholicity were now revived. There was no boldness in Eng-

---

* Catholic sailors on board British vessels of war, so late as 1841, to
the Author's own knowledge, were compelled to attend the Church of
England service performed every Sunday on board, and were subject
to punishment for refusing attendance.

land in the Catholic body to offer resistance to any injury. A few Catholics of the English aristocracy occasionally met in fear and trembling to make protestations of loyalty; to repudiate dangerous, blasphemous, murderous, or immoral doctrines, falsely attributed to them ; and declare unfeigned devotion to the house of Hanover.

In Ireland there was a Catholic committee, likewise of an aristocratic character, guided by Lords Kenmare and Fingal, which represented the interests and wishes of a few timid time-serving Roman Catholic lords and country gentlemen.

But the power and influence of the aristocratic Catholic body broke down, unable to resist opposition, when violently assailed and regularly assaulted, week after week, by an advocate of their claims of another school. A new Catholic power and influence sprung up. O'Connell made his appearance on the stage of Catholic politics, and he at once took entire possession of it. The celebrated Catholic Association of 1823 of his formation, was the fifth organized Catholic body that was called into existence for the agitation of this question.

The state of the Catholic question, from the year 1823 to that of 1829, has been admirably sketched by the able author of the ' Catholic History of England,' Mr. W. B. Mac Cabe, in his recently published Memoir of O'Connell. Scrupulously accurate and succinct in his details, Mr. Mac Cabe has brought to his task an intimate knowledge of the subject, and his opportunities of gaining it have been uninterrupted during the whole period in question.

With the kind permission of this gentleman, (whom the author is proud to call a friend,) the following extracts have been made from his valuable sketch :—

" The first meeting of the Catholic Association, as an organized body, took place on the 13th May, 1823.

" The position of the Roman Catholic body at that time was very peculiar. George IV., who had ascended the throne in 1820, visited Ireland in 1821, expressed a strong anxiety to see ' conciliation' prevail amongst all classes of his subjects, and led the Catholics to hope that their quiescence would ensure the favour of their sovereign, and ultimately the concession of their just rights. This was not distinctly promised, but it was permitted to be understood. O'Connell resolved that, on the part of the Catholics, no excuse should be afforded by violence or words, by agitation of any description, to permit the king or his advisers to have any pretext for continuing the persecution of the Roman Catholics.

"What followed from this quiescence? In a speech, in which he first suggested the formation of the Association, he observed, 'that much had been said in former times about the heat and intemperance of the Catholic 'leaders,' as they were called; but sure he was that no intemperance could have placed Catholic affairs in a more melancholy condition than that to which they were reduced at present. If the Catholics] looked back for years, he would confidently say, that they would find that they had not even the guilt of a mistake to answer for. They were, in fact, accused of no misconduct. If their names were mentioned in parliament, it was for the purpose of bestowing some approbation upon them. Yet, what was the reward of their conduct?—a state of things more degrading, if not more hopeless, than anything that has yet been witnessed in Ireland.' "—(Memoirs and Speeches of Daniel O'Connell, M.P., vol. ii. pp. 394, 395.)

They had followed the advice of their enemies—of Sir Robert Peel, for instance, who, in the debate on the Catholic Claims, March 1, 1813, said: 'If I were among the wavering friends of the Catholics, I would advise the postponement of the subject into which we are required to enter, until the first jealousies and suspicions of the Protestants might be somewhat allayed.' Which advice had been deliberately and purposely acted upon for the purpose of depriving bigotry and injustice of their old plea for perpetuating wrong, viz., 'the intemperance of some of their leaders.' The advice of their enemies was adopted, and what then was the conduct of *their friends?* In 1822, Mr. Canning was appointed governor general of India. He wished to make a fine speech on some subject. He chose the Catholic Question, and without condescending to consult the illustrious personages upon whom he volunteered to bestow his patronage, he moved on the 30th April, 1822, for leave to bring in 'a bill to relieve Roman Catholic peers from the disabilities imposed on them by the Act 30 of Charles II., with regard to the right of sitting and voting in the House of Peers.' Mr. Canning made a very brilliant speech upon this occasion—so particularly brilliant and beautiful, that he afterwards gratified the world with a corrected report of it; and he afterwards carried his motion by a majority of five! Even this small measure of relief was opposed in the Commons by Mr. (Sir Robert) Peel, and in the Lords it was rejected by a majority of *forty-two*. The Lords declined to meet in their chamber as *Peers*, the Duke of Norfolk, the Earl of Shrewsbury, Lord Petre, Lord Stourton, and other members of the ancient Catholic nobility—Lords of yesterday did not desire to see amongst them those whose names were identified with the bye-gone glories of England. ' It is to be observed, says Mr. Butler, ' that Mr. Canning acted on this occasion without any recommendation or suggestion from the Catholics.'—(Butler's ' Memoir of the Catholic Relief Bill,' 1829. See Cooke's ' History of Party,' vol. iii. p. 527.)

" The violent and unexpected death of Lord Londonderry conferred the seals of the Foreign Office upon Mr. Canning, but ' from this time,' to use the delicate phraseology of Mr. Butler, ' he apparently estranged himself from the Catholics, and desired this to be universally known.' At the same time other parliamentary advocates for emancipation, obtained power: but of the administration itself it was said, and justly, by a writer unfriendly to the Catholics :—

" ' The administration thus formed, although containing so strong a party in favour of the Catholic claims, *was their most strenuous opponent*. It was soon known that Canning and Plunkett, now attorney-general for Ireland, were less earnest in the cause.'—(Cooke's ' History of Party,' vol. iii. p. 527.)

" The lowest point of degradation had been reached on 17th April, 1823, when, upon the motion of Mr. Plunkett for a committee on the Catholic Claims, Sir Francis Burdett rose and said, with perfect truth, ' the annual discussion of the question had become a farce.'

" Never was a notorious fact uttered in a more plain phrase. The falsehood of professing friends, and the arts of cunning foes, had reduced a great principle, involving the rights of the poor and the privileges of the great, into a mere abstract question—such as might be speeched about by school-boys and talked of in a debating club—improving, as a display of oratorical talent; amusing, as helping to pass away an idle hour—meaning nothing, and leading to nothing. It was a farce—intended to be a farce—to delude and dazzle the ignorant, to be laughed at, jeered at, and thought of no more by those who were in the secret.

"The secession of Sir Francis Burdett, forced on the crisis it had been wished to avoid. The mock motion in favour of the Catholics was lost, and properly lost, in the mere question of adjournment.........

"The session of this year, 1823, witnessed an effort made to raise the English Catholics to *an equality with the Irish Catholics*. Both were degraded by the existing state of the law; but there were degrees in degradation, and the English Catholics stood on the lowest step. Amongst their members they could count the noblest in the land—amongst their members were the possessors of the largest landed property—amongst their members were men distinguished for their talents, their learning, and their virtues—amongst their members, with not a single exception, were those the most remarkable for the faithful performance of all the duties of life—as fathers, husbands, brothers, sons, citizens; and yet the odious laws with which kings identified the stability of their throne, Protestants the existence of their religion, statesmen the integrity of the Constitution, would not suffer one of these to exercise the franchise, to act as a magistrate, to hold the meanest office under the Crown; for *these* 'not even the lowest situation in the Excise could be had in Great Britain, without qualifying, by abjuring Popery.' (See Parliamentary Debates, New Series, vol. viii. p. 1133).

"On the 28th of May, 1823, when the cause of the Irish Catholics had been abandoned for the session, Lord Nugent (not having consulted the English Catholics on the subject) brought forward a motion for leave to introduce a bill which would place the Roman Catholics of England and Scotland in the same situation, with respect to civil rights and franchises, as those in Ireland. 'My object,' said Lord Nugent, 'will be to give them the means of qualifying for those offices only which would now be held by them in Ireland; and I pledge my word to the House, that to that standard I shall conform myself most strictly.'

"The spirit in which this Bill was met, was expressed by two Members of the Commons. Mr. Gooch said, 'He knew many Catholics, who were loyal and respectable men, but he must oppose the removal of the restrictions placed upon them.' A Mr. Butterworth, a Methodist, affirmed that he 'was a sincere friend to religious freedom, and therefore he opposed the Bill.' (Parliamentary Debates, New Series, vol. ix. pp. 1136-37). The reward which a Gooch would give for 'loyalty,' and 'respectability,' was a perpetuation of disabilities; and a Butterworth's love of religious freedom was proved by punishing men for conscience sake! The Catholics were then powerless, and they could be thus treated with impunity. As far as Parliament was concerned, it was manifest they were doomed to eternal degradation.

"It is unnecessary to pursue the history of the Bill further. Upon the proposal in the House of Lords of that portion of it which *conferred the franchise on English Catholics*, it was REJECTED *by a majority of seven!*

"In 1823, there was no hope of relief for the Catholics, no matter how gross might be the wrong done to them, or how afflicting their situation, from the working of the Penal Laws. The Legislature was tried in various ways, and in each was found to be obdurate in its determination to grant not the slightest relief, nor to make the smallest concession. The first peer of the realm was denied his rights because he was a Roman Catholic; whilst the humble man found that the Penal Laws invaded his home, that they cursed his marriage, that the woman who was united to him for life, by one of the most solemn sacraments of his Church, was, in the eye of the law—*the English Penal Law!*—regarded as the vilest of her sex, and that the children of his marriage, because he was a Catholic, were 'baseborn.' The law of God declared them the offspring of 'holy wedlock,' the law of man denounced them as 'bastards.' In this case, however, persecution brought its own punishment along with it, for the children of the Irish Catholic poor born in England, being *legally* 'illegitimate,' were chargeable on the respective parishes in which they were born, and were not removable with their parents, when the latter became paupers and were sent back to Ireland. A heavy burden was thus imposed upon English parishes, for illegitimacy gave a right to relief, as in former ages when villeinage existed, its proof entitled the supposed 'villein' to be declared a 'freeman.'

"In 1823, prejudice against Catholicism was too strong,

and the Catholics themselves too weak to obtain any re-dress for this grievous wrong, to which the attention of Parliament was called by the petition of a Roman Catholic Bishop, the Right Rev. Dr. Poynter, who prayed that ' the Roman Catholics in England might be placed on the same footing *as those in Ireland*, with respect to the performance of the marriage ceremony.' The arguments used in sup-port of this petition showed how much of selfishness there was in desiring this change.   Sir James Mackintosh spoke the opinions of others, and not of his own generous mind, when he referred to the petition of parish officers of a large and populous district, complaining ' of *the burden brought upon them*, and the injury to the country generally, in con-sequence of the law making the marriage of Roman Ca-tholics by their own clergymen unlawful. *The children were chargeable on the parishes from which they could not be removed by their parents.'*

"Upon this occasion, a complaint was made against the Catholic Clergy, by Mr. M. A. Taylor, which is deserving of being recorded. It is pregnant with reflections as to the degrading position in which Catholics and their Priests were placed in England in 1823.   This Mr. M. A. Taylor said, that ' he thought some legislative measure should be introduced to remedy the evil,' (that is, the burden !on the parishes), ' but many of the inconveniences complained of might be *attributed to the conduct of the Catholic Priests them-selves*, for they must know that such marriages were null and void, and *they ought, therefore, to refuse to perform the ceremony until the parties had first been married according to the rites of the Church of England.'*   (Parliamentary De-bates, New Series, vol. ix. pp. 965, 966, 967).

"So hopeless, so fallen, so low, and so degraded were the Catholics of England in 1823, that they were even threat-ened with a new persecution, if any attempt should be made to relieve them.   (See Parliamentary Debates, New Series, vol ix. p. 1536)......

"As the year 1824 advanced, the Irish Catholic Asso-ciation increased in strength, and the effects of its labours were nowhere more perceptible than in the proceedings of the Imperial Parliament. Those who had refused every-thing in 1823, made some important concessions in 1824. It is true that their language did not abate in violence,

but still they retreated. They blustered, bullied, but—
they shrunk back......

" The Catholics of this country felt particularly the beneficial effects of the bold operations of O'Connell and the
Catholic Association. Although measures proposing to
place them on an equality with Irish Catholics were not
successful, still bigotry had to yield to them on two points.
They were refused the franchise—they were denied the
eligibility to be nominated to offices of trust and honour ;
but there was in the 5th George IV. ch. 79, a concession
made to them. That Act permitted persons to hold any
office respecting the receipt of Customs, without taking any
oath, except that of allegiance, and the 5th George IV.
ch. 119, permitted the Earl Marshall and his deputy to exercise that office without taking the oath of supremacy, and
the declaration against transubstantiation.

" The ministry of Lord Liverpool was divided upon the
question of Catholic Emancipation, but there was a marvellous unanimity amongst its members when the Catholics
were to be persecuted. They had agreed in prosecuting
Mr. O'Connell, and in 1825 they were in ' one mind ' as
to the propriety of putting down the Catholic Association
by a new aggression on the liberty of the subject. The
enemies to the Catholic cause plainly perceived that the
refusal of Emancipation and the prolonged misgovernment
of Ireland, were alike incompatible with the existence of
the Catholic Association. This tyrannical proceeding was
recommended in the King's Speech at the commencement
of the session of 1825. The feeling in which it originated,
has long since been expressed by Tacitus. ' Nihil æquè
Tiberium anxium habebat quam ne composita turbaren-
tur.'—(' Ann.' lib. ii. s. 25). Upon this recommendation
of the United Cabinet, a bill was introduced by Mr. Goulburn, the foe to Catholic Emancipation, and supported by
Mr. Canning, the friend to Emancipation. On the part of
the Association, an attempt had been made, both in the
Commons and the Lords, to afford to its members the
opportunity of being heard against it at the bar. In the
House of Commons, the motion was rejected by a majority
of 123 ; in the Lords, by a majority of 46. On the 7th of
March, 1825, the Bill for Suppressing the Catholic Association, was read a third time ; and on the 9th of March, this

Bill, afterwards designated by O'Connell, 'the Algerine Act,' received the Royal assent......

"The events of the year 1825, are full of instruction to Catholics for all future time, and it is therefore necessary to dwell upon them. Some distinguished members of the Irish Hierarchy, Mr. O'Connell, Mr. Sheil, and other lay leaders of the Catholics, were at the moment in London— the former principally for the purpose of giving evidence before the Committees of both Houses, on the state of Ireland ; the latter mainly with the intention of opposing the Bill for the suppression of the Catholic Association. It was intimated to them, that the Act directed against the Association, might be compensated for in a Catholic Relief Bill, provided they were to offer no objection to — first, *the disfranchisement of the forty shilling freeholders,* and, secondly, *the pensioning of the Catholic Clergy.* What their enemies really desired, was to disembarrass themselves of the opposition to the Association Suppression Bill, which had excited a debate of four nights' duration, and then to destroy the hopes of the Catholics, even at the moment when they might have calculated upon their prosperous fulfilment. It was a vile policy ; but then it was successful, as it was vile.

" The opposition to the suppression of the Catholic Association—regarded as a useless measure—abated ; because Emancipation, it was supposed, was to be immediately agreed to. The passing of a Catholic Relief Bill was to be facilitated by the adoption of two other measures, hence designated 'the wings.' To these measures, Mr. O'Connell assented. It is the only portion of his political conduct which requires explanation."

(This subject requires a much more extended notice than Mr. Mac Cabe was able to give to it in the limits of a weekly journal. The subject, moreover, has a more particular reference to Irish Catholic affairs, and may be more appropriately considered in the volume which treats of the History of the Irish Penal Laws).

" The fate of 'the wings' was involved in the rejection of the Catholic Relief Bill in the House of Lords, where a majority ratified by their votes the oath of the Duke of York, that whilst he lived no such measure should be assented to. The destruction of such a plan—the pensioning of the Catholic clergy—was cheaply purchased in the postponement of emancipation. The bigotry of the enemies to Catholicity, prevented them from seeing the extent of power and influence, which the completion of such a project would have given to them. They fancied that in breaking faith with the Catholics, they were destroying the hope of emancipation for ever. Fools! They were flinging away an advantage, and losing an opportunity such as never again can be possessed by them.

"In 1825, O'Connell and the Catholics assented to 'conditional' emancipation. It was the last time that they did so. They were never again to seek for it, and they resolved never to accept it. Their terms had been rejected, and henceforth, when seeking for emancipation, they determined to demand not only that it should be 'full and unconditional,' but also to wage war open and avowed against those who had declared themselves as their enemies. The time for compromise had gone by, and O'Connell, finding that in England the existence of the rotten boroughs was made a pretext for refusing even the franchise to English Catholics, (see Parliamentary Debates, N. S., Vol. viii. pp. 1476 to 1490,) and that 'the safety of the Established Church in Ireland,' was an argument for the prolonged enthralment of his religion, he joined in the cry for 'reform,' and sought for the appropriation to state purposes of the temporalities of an institution, whose ministers and mitre-wearing professors, had been the inveterate enemies of religious toleration.

"If Catholic emancipation had passed in 1825, it would have left the masses comparatively unmoved. Their minds would have remained untouched by the violence of party strife; their feelings would not have been appealed to, and their passions would not have been stirred. Until the rejection of the bill of 1825, the struggle for emancipation might be compared to the manœuvres of a great general, who seeks to gain an advantage without committing his forces to the chances and dangers of a general engagement, but with the rejection of that measure, the time for skill and strategy had passed away. The cause and the leaders of the Irish Catholics were set at defiance, not only by the occupant of the throne, but by 'the presumptive' successor; and with their defiance had come treachery, deceit, and disunion. From the king, and prince, and parliament, the appeal was inevitable to the people. With them, and by them, the issue of the conflict was to be decided.

"A year was not permitted to pass away, until the enemies of emancipation were encountered and defeated, by those who were now, for the first time, brought into the conflict— the peasantry of Ireland. A general election took place in the year 1826, and for the first time since the franchise had been bestowed in 1793, the Catholics made use of it for their own benefit.

" In Ireland, the pro-Catholic candidates were every where successful. Far different was the result in England. The whigs had adopted the Catholic question as one of their party principles, and 'the general election accomplished but little for the whigs; these efforts in favour of the Catholics, formed a powerful topic against them.'—(Cooke's 'History of Party,' vol. iii. p. 534.) 'The prevailing tests,' says another authority, 'offered to the candidates on the hustings were, the Corn Laws, Catholic Emancipation, and the Slave Trade......In the city, a cry of ' No Popery' was raised against Alderman Wood."—(Wade's 'British History,' p. 804.)

" "O'Connell said that the elections in England had turned out so decidedly unfavourable to the Catholics, that there was no hope for the cause if he were to depend solely for success upon the votes of parliament. Instead of feeling daunted with the prospect before him, it only served to inspire him with fresh energy, and to impel him on to increased exertion. The elections of Ireland had proved that agitation was all-powerful, and that as it strengthened and extended itself, it must soon acquire a potency sufficient to enable him by whom it was created, guided, and controlled, to cope with parliament itself.

"On the fifth of January, 1827, the princely opponent of the Catholic claims, the Duke of York, expired; and on the 17th of February, 1827, the illness of the Earl of Liverpool, led to the dissolution of his administration. With the incompetency of Lord Liverpool, arose the necessity of forming a new government, and then for the first time, the Catholic question became a great embarrassment. Its debates had been 'a farce,' as long as the Catholics were content to leave its decision to the good will alone of their parliamentary friends. It had been 'a topic for discussion,' as long as the Catholics had quietly submitted to

17

the grievances imposed upon them; but when O'Connell
made them turn upon their enemies; when their persecutors were dragged to the bar of public opinion; when the
crimes of those adversaries were exposed—their sinecurism,
their peculation, their mean, shabby, and paltry tyranny—
and when O'Connell appealed to Europe and America to
pronounce a verdict against them, the Catholic question
assumed, at least sufficient importance to make and unmake
administrations.

"It is a fact, with respect to which there cannot be the
slightest doubt, that Mr. O'Connell and the Catholic Association of Ireland had given great offence to their opponents; but then they had, to use the language of one of
their most determined enemies, 'secured an unprecedent-
ed success to the party which favoured Emancipation,' and
when the necessity for forming an administration arrived,
their strength was felt, their power was feared, and their
demands were no longer to be trifled with for the conveni-
ence or advantage of individuals.

"The time for a great party struggle had arrived, and the
motion which Sir Francis Burdett submitted to the House
of Commons on the 5th of March, 1827, pledging the new
parliament to take 'into immediate consideration the laws
inflicting penalties on his Majesty's Roman Catholic subjects, with a view of removing them,' was regarded as a
contest for office—as if upon its decision were to rest whether the future Prime Minister of England should be favourable or adverse to the Catholic claims. The success
or defeat of these claims was interwoven with the struggle
of parties, and within their folds were at length clasped
faction and selfishness—to be crushed by those whom he
had provoked, to be strangled by those whom they had
irritated and defied :—

"Post ipsum auxilio subeuntem, ac tela ferentem
Corripiunt, spirisque ligant ingentibus."

"The Catholic claims had not merely 'paralyzed the
vigour of the executive government'—(Speech of Sir Robert
Peel, March 5, 1829,)—but they were now destined to
determine the whole course, policy, and constitution of the
government.

"The happiest and the best of the many great and wonderful displays made by Mr. Canning in parliament, was

his speech on the Catholic Question in 1827. A stronger proof of its excellence cannot be afforded, than the fact, that, whilst it demonstrates that he alone was worthy of the Premiership, it conciliated the Catholics and induced them to place their confidence in him, although there were many transactions in his past career for which neither justification or apology can ever be discovered. (See the Malmesbury Diary and Correspondence.) It proved that however he might have dallied hitherto with the question, however willing he had been to crush all efforts for its advancement to please the king, that now, at least, he was sincere—that now he had identified its ultimate triumph with his own fame, and that henceforward he might be trusted as its true, as he was undoubtedly its most able advocate.

"The Catholic Emancipationists and their opponents had made 'the question' the test of fitness for office, and it was not only debated with all the eagerness, anxiety, and zeal, of a party dispute, but every member who could be brought to London was required to give his aid in support of those that he most desired to see administering the affairs of England. The debate lasted, by adjournment, two days, and when a division was called for there were present 548 members. Of these 272 voted for Sir Francis Burdett's motion, and 276 against it. The motion was therefore rejected by a majority of four!

"The triumph was calamitous to the victors. It was the decision of a new House of Commons—a fresh defiance to O'Connell and the Catholics of Ireland, and to be consistent it ought to be followed up by a rigid system of coercion; but neither the king nor the tory party were prepared for that course. They knew that the elements of revolution were at that moment fermenting in France—that America was sympathising with the Irish Catholics—that even in despotic nations on the Continent there was a strong feeling roused in favour of men who were suffering persecution solely on account of their religion,—(see Wyse's 'Sketch of the late Catholic Association,' vol. i. pp. 307, 308)—and they were aware England itself had received a shock from the financial difficulties of 1825, from which she had not yet recovered. A more unfitting moment for civil war could not have been selected. They even trembled in the presence of their Catholic captive—Mr. Sheil

—the steadfast, eloquent, gifted, true friend of O'Connell from the commencement of the struggle for Emancipation by the Association, to its final triumph.

"The burst of indignation with which the announcement of this question in a new parliament was received by O'Connell and the Irish Catholics; the bold proposals that followed it, and among the rest that of seeking a Repeal of the Union—(See *Annual Register*, vol. lxix. p. 67)— terrified even those by whose exertions the hopes of the Catholics had been blighted. The necessity for temporising and deceiving was regarded as unavoidable by him to whom the awful sounds of the coming strife had penetrated, even in his Caprea at Windsor. The formation of a new ministry was entrusted to Mr. Canning, the king declaring that he was unconquerably hostile to the Catholic claims; but at the same time conceding to Mr. Canning that he was not only 'to have the substantial power of First Minister, but be known to have it.'—(Stapleton's 'Life of Canning,' vol. iii. p. 315.)

"The solitary—the routine favour of abandoning a prosecution—that directed against Mr. Sheil—was the only substantial advantage that the Catholics derived from the elevation of Mr. Canning to the Premiership. They believed that he intended to act honestly towards them, and seeing the difficulties that from the very first moment he took office were cast in his way, they resolved not to embarrass him by the agitation of their claims.

"The same means that Mr. Canning had in 1806 employed to drive the whigs from office were now used against himself—the latent bigotry of the country was excited against him; for it was said of him, as it had been said by himself of the Grenville and Fox Administration, that he was 'friendly to the settlement of the question,' and no confidence was to be reposed in a pro-Catholic Prime Minister. It was in vain that he endeavoured in his explanations in parliament to show that it had been his intention to have formed a cabinet, in which 'the Anti-Catholics should have a prepondering influence;' it was in vain that at his suggestion the king communicated to the assembled prelates, through the Archbishop of Canterbury and the Bishop of London, that 'his majesty was firm in his opposition to the Catholic claims, and that his opposition to the question was as strong as his father's had been.' (Parliamentary Debates, New Series, vol. xvii. p. 924.) It was in vain that these expedients were resorted to, for the fatuity of bigotry could not conceal from those most deeply affected by it, that the Catholics were waxing in strength—that their question was each day becoming more formidable, and that its power was magnified whilst its position was strengthened by the wisdom, the determination, the prudence, and beyond all other qualifications, the sincerity of him by whom it was now conducted.

"The opponents to the Catholic Question were conscious that the question itself was promoted, by there being placed at the head of the government a person who was disposed to its friendly settlement. Hence the unsparing, the unforgiving, the pitiless malignity exhibited against him. An entire party first forsook, and then assailed a single man! It was a piteous spectacle, and one more unworthy, or more unbecoming of Englishmen was never before so publicly displayed to the world. Mr. Canning, to the very last, defended himself with his usual courage, and his accustomed talent—but his struggle was a vain one against numbers; and at last he had to yield—his physical strength was exhausted, whilst his mental vigour remained unabated. Toryism triumphed over him—his party killed him—*he was harassed to death!*

"The elevation of Mr. Canning, as a pro-Catholic, to the supreme command of the empire, was an incident favourable to the advancement of the Catholic cause; but that cause had grown beyond the aid of any individual *except one*, and now by the demise neither of sovereign nor of minister could its progress be impeded nor its energies diminished. The Catholics lamented the death of Mr. Canning; for they believed, that he had been assailed with all the cowardly cruelty of a disappointed faction because he was supposed to be their friend. Mr. Wyse, in referring to the death of Canning, is correct in saying, ' the Catholics took his intentions for deeds, and lamented over his tomb, as if he had been their deliverer'—(' Sketch of the Catholic Association,' vol. i. p. 327.)—but Mr. Wyse falls into a mistake, when he affirms, that ' their grief was great, their despondency greater;' for it was immediately subsequent to that event that O'Connell and the Catholics determined on a course of action, the successful results of which belong to the year 1828.

"The death of Mr. Canning had been followed by the nomination of one of his colleagues to the Premiership. This was Lord Goderich (the Earl of Ripon), and it might be supposed that he would be agreeable to the Catholics—that they would be content and quiescent under his Premiership, as they had been with that of Mr. Canning; for Lord Goderich had been one of the supporters of the Catholic Question. There was, however, in the past career of Lord Goderich nothing to induce any man, or any party, to place reliance upon his firmness, his capacity, or his judgment. That keen observer, Lord Malmesbury, had said of him when he was in the very vigour of his youth, ' Frederick Robinson, doubtful, but with no good reason,' (' Diaries and Correspondence,' vol. iv. p. 380.); and ' doubtful, but with no good reason,' he appeared to be, alike to friends, if he had any, and to enemies, if mediocrity be capable of provoking enmity. No party relied upon him, and no party cared for him. He was a Premier, as Caius Caninius Rebilus had been a Consul—he filled up a gap—he occupied the space between one active ruler of the commonwealth and another—an unexpected death gave him a fugacious power, which he only nominally held and never really exercised. The Goderich government was a *Recess Government*. O'Connell saw that such a Premier as Lord Goderich would not, because he could not, aid the Catholic cause; and he therefore resolved to place the question in such a position that Lord Goderich could not, even if he would, resist it. O'Connell made arrangements calculated to master the imbecility of Lord Goderich should he remain in office, or to defeat the hostility of a more powerful and determined opponent.

"Experience had proved that the Catholic Question was to be carried *out* of parliament, and not *within its walls*—that the sole reliance of the Catholics must be on themselves—that the world should be convinced that ' Catholic Emancipation' was not the question of a faction, but of the multitude—not of a mere sect, but of an entire nation. Such was the feeling with which O'Connell animated the Catholics, and it was in accordance with it, and whilst it might be said that the Goderich Administration was in existence, that there was held on the one day and at the same hour, *a simultaneous meeting of all the Catholics of Ireland.*

" ' The simultaneous meetings'—they were the suggestion of Mr. Sheil—were held on the 21st of January, 1828. The Wellington Administration had not completed its arrangements until the 23rd of January.

" The appointment of the Duke of Wellington was regarded in Ireland as a declaration of civil war. He was the most illustrious opponent to Catholic Emancipation—he was an Irishman—had been secretary for Ireland, and in that capacity had proposed ' an Arms Bill,' and which, though it passed into law, had been declared by the celebrated Sheridan to be the 'worst, the foulest, and the foolishest measure that ever solicited the sanction of parliament.'— (See Parliamentary Debates, vol. ix. pp. 751, 971.) An attack on the part of the government was calculated upon, and ' a tremendous organization extended over the whole island. The Catholic gentry, peasantry, and priesthood, were all combined in one vast confederacy.'—(Cooke's History of Party,' vol. iii. p. 548.)

" The moment the formation of the Wellington ministry was announced, a resolution emanated from the association, pledging its members to refuse their suffrages to every individual who took office or gave his support to the duke's government. We forget whether or not this resolution was suggested by Mr. O'Connell. It was too important, however, to have been adopted without his being consulted upon and sanctioning it.

" Amongst the events of this year, of which O'Connell was most proud, was the aid he afforded to the emancipation of the Protestant dissenters. It is curious, that in the banquet which took place at which the Protestant dissenters celebrated their triumph, that fact seemed to be forgotten until the present Lord Denman—the now Chief Justice of the Queen's Bench—proposed ' Catholic Emancipation.'

" On the 8th of May, 1828, a resolution pledging the house to a favourable consideration of the Catholic claims was proposed, and after three nights' debate carried by a majority of *six!* Sir Robert Peel on this occasion saying of the Catholics, ' I am persuaded that the removal of their disabilities would be attended with a danger to the Protestant religion, against which it would be impossible to find any security equal to that of our present Protestant constitution.' (Debate on Removal of Catholic Disabilities,

May 9, 1828. See 'Opinions of Sir R. Peel,' by W. T. Haly, pp. 50, 51.)

"This resolution was communicated to the lords on the 16th of May, and on the 9th of June rejected by a majority of *forty-four*. The Duke of Wellington declaring 'that the securities which we now enjoy, and which for a length of time we have enjoyed, are indispensable to the safety of the Church and State.' (Parliamentary Debates, vol. xix. p. 1287.)

" The ministry of the Duke of Wellington had thus placed itself in open hostility to the Catholics of Ireland. It had aided in rejecting their claims, and yet ventured to bestow office on one of its devoted Irish supporters—Mr. Vesey Fitzgerald—who, elevated from the position of treasurer of the navy to that of president of the Board of Trade, had to appeal to his constituents to be re-elected.

" The Catholics of Ireland were pledged to oppose every member of the Wellington Administration, and Mr. Vesey Fitzgerald afforded them the first opportunity of testing their power. He had always voted for emancipation, but then he was the chosen minister of an adverse government, and he had made himself odious to O'Connell and the great body of the Catholics by the vote which he had recently given against the Protestant dissenters. Mr. Vesey Fitzgerald was the representative of a certain class—he was one of the false ' parliamentary friends' who, to render his return the more easy by a Catholic constituency, gave a useless vote for ' Emancipation,' whilst in aiding its foes on every other occasion he strengthened their power, and enabled them to defeat the great cause to which he professed to be attached.

" The period had come when it was to be determined whether the representative of Clare was to be a ' real' or a ' pretended' one of the Catholics. At first, the only thought that suggested itself to the mind of O'Connell—to the members of the Association—to the Catholics universally —was to nominate a Liberal Protestant—and there were many such in Ireland. All that was wished and looked for was, that their representative should be a man, who would not prefer the favour of the Sovereign, or the smiles of a Minister, to their just cause. They tendered the re-presentation of the county to many such Protestants— some, like Mr. Steele, refused it, because they would not subject themselves to the chance or probability of an imputation that in seeking to promote Emancipation, they were struggling to gratify their own ambition; others declined the offer, because they felt themselves under a personal obligation to Mr. Vesey Fitzgerald. At last, the noble idea was suggested to them of starting 'the foremost man' in Ireland—DANIEL O'CONNELL—a Catholic, a sufferer from the Penal Laws: to send him—the idol of Ireland—the elected of the people, to the House of Commons—*there* to prove the determination of the Irish—and *there* to exhibit to bigotry and intolerance, how glorious was the genius, how illustrious the virtues, and how transcendent the talents they excluded from the Imperial Legislature.

" It was a noble thought! but with whom did it originate? Not with a Catholic—not with a Liberal Protestant—but with an Orangeman—Sir David Roos—the then High Sheriff of Dublin. Despite the difference in their politics, Sir David Roos loved and revered O'Connell—as what good man did not, who ever came in personal communication with him? At the time that the Catholics were seeking for a Protestant candidate for Clare, this gentleman met Mr. P. V. Fitzpatrick, one of the most intimate friends of O'Connell, told him how his thoughts had been occupied for hours, with the notion that O'Connell ought himself to stand for Clare, and he added that he was going then to the house of the Liberator to urge him to do so. To Mr. Fitzpatrick the suggestion seemed providential; for, from his boyhood, he had been told by the once distinguished Irish Catholic, John Keogh, that 'the Catholics never would be emancipated, until they elected a Roman Catholic; that the iniquity of the Penal Laws which thus destroyed the rights of the constituency, would be made so apparent to the mind of every honest man in England and Ireland, that they would insist on the repeal of such laws.' This statement, repeated over and over again to the young Fitzpatrick, with the warning that he should always bear it in mind, produced its impression; but never, until the suggestion came from Sir David Roos, did he see the feasibility of carrying it into effect. The repetition of the conversation of John Keogh, following the suggestion of Sir David Roos, produced some impression on the mind of O'Connell; but it was not until he found that so strange an idea was sanctioned by the leading Catholic merchants of Dublin, that

he could be induced to go to the *Dublin Evening Post* office
—and there, in the presence of its truly learned and most
able Editor, Mr. Conway, and Mr. Fitzpatrick, he dashed
off in a hurry a few lines as his "Address to the Electors
of Clare," leaving it to them both to see it in print and
make in it what corrections they pleased.

"These facts, respecting one of the most important events
in Catholic history, we have deemed it right to insert here,
because we are aware they have never been generally
known, and because they were told to us, first by Sir
David Roos, in 1829, and very recently corroborated by
Mr. Fitzpatrick.

"O'Connell, the law-proscribed Catholic, to stand for
Clare! It was a noble thought; and once expressed in
O'Connell's Address to the Electors, it filled as with a new
fire the hearts of the people. It elevated their minds—inspired them with zeal—and diffused an enthusiasm that
defied every obstacle, and rendered defeat impossible.

"At the Clare Election, in 1828, the Cabinet of St.
James's was pitted against the Catholic Association of
Burgh Quay—the prize they contended for was the government of a kingdom—their rival champions were Mr. Vesey
Fitzgerald, the President of the Board of Trade, and
Daniel O'Connell, the creator of the Catholic Association—
the leader of the Irish people. It was a renewal of the
civil strife of Ancient Rome—of the Patricians and Ple-
beians. Here were the oligarchy, and on the other side—the
people. Here were power, influence, troops of clients, with
the superabundant riches and many iniquities of a political religion; and there were men worthy of freedom, subjected to unmerited disabilities, denied equality of rights,
but earnest, eager, determined and united together with
the firm purpose never to retire from the conflict until
they had won back that which was perfidiously withheld
from them.

"Never, assuredly, was there a spectacle beheld like to
that which the Clare election of 1828 exhibited. On the
one side, a candidate having at his command the army,
the police, and the Treasury—the means to overawe, and
the funds to corrupt. On the other, 'a simple, private
country gentleman,' with no friends but the priests of
a persecuted religion, and no supporters but an undisci-
plined multitude of humble, half-clothed, half-fed peasants,

And yet the words of that one man had in an hour inspired his followers with a discipline such as no regiment ever equalled, and with a self-control which, though regimental chaplains may have preached, they never yet have been able to enforce.   The temperance pledge of the Waterford election of 1826, was here renewed, and here as faithfully adhered to.   And then, what a wonderful man was that popular candidate at the Clare election in 1828!   Engaged, as he was daily engaged for more than thirty years of his life, on the previous Saturday—in his study before five amidst his briefs ; from ten to three in the Courts, in *all* the Courts, and every moment pleading in some one of them until four o'clock ; from four to seven speaking at the Catholic Association ; from eight to eleven again at his law cases : travelling on the following day from Dublin to Ennis, he enters the road lined with thousands—obliged to speak in every great town he passed through—and not in Ennis until three o'clock on the Monday morning.   In the Court-house at nine, facing his foes, and inspiring his friends by his presence, he had to reply to a most able electioneering speech from Mr. Fitzgerald—and he had to crush it.   Self-interest combined on this occasion with fanaticism—the hope of Government favours, and the enjoyment of unjust monopolies, were linked and banded together with that hatred of Catholicity which ' the gentry ' had inherited with the forfeited estates of Roman Catholics.   O'Connell had these with a most plausible advocate to expose—and in one of the most masterly displays of his eloquence he demolished them.   That speech never was fully reported.   One person attempted it—and from his imperfect copy whatever transcript may now be found of it was derived ; for such was the state of the Court-house— that heat and crowd combined together, exhausted the strength of every one within its walls, but one—that one was O'Connell.

" O'Connell laid bare the pretences of his adversary, exposed his selfish and his fanatical opponents, and then appealed to the people.   By them the appeal was fittingly answered.   The polling began on the first of July, and five days afterwards Mr. O'Connell was declared ' duly elected ' —the first Catholic returned to parliament by an Irish constituency, since the reign of the unfortunate James II.

The Clare Election in 1828, had decided the fate of the

Catholic Question. 'The events of the Clare Election,' said Sir Robert Peel, 'showed that matters could not long rest where they were ; that there must be either a settlement of the Catholic Question, or the elective franchise must be modified.' (Speech of Sir Robert Peel, December 17, 1831).

" ' The circumstances attending the Clare Election.' ' The circumstances that preceded and followed that Election.' (Speech of the Duke of Wellington on moving the second reading of the Catholic Relief Bill in 1829. Parliamentary Debates, vol. xxi. p. 42.)

" The Clare Election won Catholic Emancipation. It did so, because the Catholics acting under the advice of O'Connell, had treated with the scorn it deserved the insidious advice tendered to them by their foe, the Duke of Wellington. 'The public mind' was not 'suffered to be tranquil '—'the agitators of Ireland,' so far from allowing ' the public mind to be at rest,' (see Duke of Wellington's Speech, Parliamentary Debates, vol. xix. pp. 1287, 1292), in the very moment of their triumph, and when the entire physical strength of the country was rising up to support them ; when the army sent to overawe, was affected by the popular enthusiasm, and cheered ' the Catholic member for Clare,' even in the presence of their officers—(Parliamentary Debates, vol. xxix. p. 983)—at this very time they felt with O'Connell, that their victory over bigotry, toryism, and the oligarchy, was another Pharsalia—that it had broken the strength, tarnished the fame, but left merely unmitigated the hostility of their enemies.'

> ' Sparsit potius Pharsalia nostras
> ' Qam subvertit opes.' '"*

In the preceding notice of the Catholic question, from 1823 to 1829, from Mr. Mac Cabe's excellent article, the particulars of the passage of the Relief Bill through parliament, are not detailed.

February the fifth, 1829, in the king's speech from the throne, the following passages plainly announced the doom of the Penal Code.

" The state of Ireland has been the object of his majesty's continued solicitude.

* Memoir of O'Connell, by W. B. Mac Cabe.—Tablet, 29th of May, 1847.

" His majesty laments that in that part of the United Kingdom, an association should still exist which is dangerous to the public peace, and inconsistent with the spirit of the constitution......

" His majesty recommends that when this essential object shall have been accomplished, (the suppression of the Catholic association,) you shall take into your deliberate consideration the whole state of Ireland, and that you shall review the laws which impose civil disabilities on his Roman Catholic subjects."

The Duke of Wellington, immediately after the king's speech had been read, announced the intention of government " to propose a measure for the adjustment of what was called the Catholic question."

The Earl of Winchelsea, in reply to this announcement observed, that " from the moment Roman Catholics take their seats in either houses of parliament, the sun of Great Britain was set."

In the Commons on the same day, Mr. Peel, in reference to the intended relief measure said, " He pretended to no new lights on the Catholic question. He retained the opinions which he formerly expressed in reference to that question. He saw the dangers which he heretofore felt as connected with that subject, but he had no hesitation in saying, that the pressure of the present circumstances was so great, that he was willing to incur those dangers rather than in the existing state and situation of the country, to endure not only the continuance, but the aggravation of the present system."......" For the last twenty-five years, there had been a division in the king's council respecting the Catholic question.".....". No man could lament this more than he did, but he believed that the difference which existed on the Catholic question, had rendered it impossible to form an administration completely united."

Mr. George Dawson, brother-in-law of Mr. Peel, owned himself a recent convert to the views of government on this subject. " He had been recently in Ireland. He had seen the country on the eve of convulsion ; had seen its institutions ready to give way, public men opposed to the very members of their own families on this question—every thing gradually creeping down to the very brink of destruction ; that party feeling was raging in every direction ; that grand juries and magistrates, in short, every one partook of the same feeling, and that it was impossible for things to go on as they were.......

"He would confess that he had a fear, that he was not ashamed to own, for he trusted it was a fear that every loyal christian man should ever entertain, he feared to see a civil war and all its consequences follow such a state of things; he feared to see human blood spilled in the streets, and it seemed to him to be little short of such a consummation."

After a long debate, in which general confidence in the intentions of the government was expressed, the address was finally agreed to.

On the 19th of February, on presenting a petition against the proposed measure in the Lords, the Duke of Cumberland said, "the question undoubtedly in the present case, was neither more nor less than this : Is England to be a Protestant or a Popish country? For, my lords, the very moment we admit one Roman Catholic into this house or into the other house of parliament, I maintain that this ceases to be a Protestant parliament. I have carefully and attentively viewed this question, every way in which it has been considered, and the result is, that I will never give my consent either to a Roman Catholic peer sitting in this house or the other, or being a minister of the crown, or a Lord Lieutenant of Ireland, or any Roman Catholic holding any office that may give him power to injure the Established Church."

On the 23rd of February, the Duke of Clarence, on the presentation of another petition, made the most remarkably efficient speech he ever pronounced in the house, in which he said, in reference to the union which a noble lord had stated prevailed in the cabinet on this question, "That expression makes me now rise. *I wish, my lords, that the ministers had been so united in 1825.*" "It will be forty-six years next month, my lord, since I first sat in this house, and I have never given a vote of which, thank God, I have been ashamed; and never one with so much pleasure, as the vote I shall give in favour of Catholic Emancipation."

The Duke of Sussex concurred in the sentiments of his brother, the Duke of Clarence.

March the 30th, Mr. Peel moved the third reading of the bill, which passed the house at a quarter to four o'clock, for the third reading there being 320 votes, for the amendment, that it be read that day six months 142 ; majority 178.

The Forty Shillings Freeholders' Disfranchisement Bill was also read a third time and passed.

April the 2nd, the Duke of Wellington, (in a speech of upwards of an hour in delivery,) introduced the Bill into the House of Peers. He observed that the evils of Ireland were not to be put down by the suppression only of the Catholic association. "It was said, let them, (the Irish Catholics,) go into a civil war. But the people would not resist the laws so as to justify a civil war, and those evils might go on unremoved to the decay and ruin of the country. *He had spent the greatest part of his life in war, yet he would sacrifice his existence to prevent a civil war.* There was nothing which so completely rent asunder the bonds of society, and uprooted the prosperity of a nation."

The Archbishops of Canterbury, York, and Armagh, strenuously opposed the measure.

Lord Grey supported it in a speech of transcendent power.

At the division on the second reading in the Lords, the numbers were, contents present 147, proxies 70, total 217 ; not content 79, proxies 33, total 112. Majority for the second reading 105.

April the 8th, at the division on the third reading, the contents present were 149, proxies 64, total 213 ; not content present 76, proxies 76, majority 104.

The passing of the Bill in the House of Peers, was hailed with repeated cheers.

The Disfranchisement Bill was then read a third time and passed.*

On the 15th of May, 1829, O'Connell was introduced by Lord Duncannon, the late viceroy of Ireland, to the House of Commons, as member for Clare.†

---

* Before the last division, the Duke of Wellington, in reply to the several objections urged against the bill observed, "The introduction of securities into this bill, would really have done mischief to the Church. If the bill did not give securities, neither did it take any away. It did nothing more, in fact, than admit a few Catholic Peers and Commons into parliament." This indeed was perfectly true, eighteen years' experience has proved it to be so.

† The 15th of May, 1829, was a day of triumph to O'Connell. The 15th day of May, 1847, was the day of his death.

The speaker objecting to the return of Mr. O'Connell, having taken place " after the commencement of the act," declined tendering the Catholic oath. It was then discussed whether he should be heard at the table or at the bar, and it was decided that he should be heard at the latter. His short address produced conflicting opinions on the question of his right to a seat in the house ; the Solicitor General, however, moved " that Mr. O'Connell was not entitled to take his seat, until he had first taken the oath of supremacy," and his motion was carried.

On the 19th of May, O'Connell appeared at the bar, and was informed of. the resolution come to, which imposed the necessity of taking the customary oath against the leading doctrine of his Church, to be admitted to a seat in the house.

O'Connell demanded to see the oath. A copy of it was presented to him, and having slowly read those words of it, " the Pope neither has nor ought to have spiritual power or authority in this country," he fixed his eyes on the ministerial benches, and said in a clear sonorous voice, " I see in this oath one assertion as to a matter of fact, which I know is not true ; and I see in it another assertion as to a matter of opinion, which I believe is not true. I therefore refuse to take this oath."

Mr. O'Connell then withdrew, infinitely more triumphant than the short-sighted government and its partisans, who had excluded him for a few weeks from parliament, and for the sake of a miserable resentment, deprived a great remedial measure of those claims to gratitude, which might otherwise have been freely recognised by all the Roman Catholics of the Empire.

When one reflects on all the sufferings endured by the Catholics on account of their religion, on all the misery occasioned by the penal code—the profuse shedding of blood, the infliction of torture, the terrors inspired by the machinations of the Cecils, the Walsinghams, the Shaftesburys, and their imitators ; by the subordinate villany of their agents, the Oates, the Bedloes, the Dangerfields, and other traffickers in blood in those frightful times ; on the mockery of justice in the proceedings against Catholics, the violation of humanity, of every law of nature and principle of right in regard to them, credibility is startled, and we can

hardly bring ourselves to believe the matters of which
we read could ever have been realities in this land.

When, with violence to our feelings, we ponder on the
hunting of the proscribed clergy, the ransacking of the
houses of Catholics, suspected of harbouring ministers of
their religion, the insolent bearing of the ruffians who
tracked their victims from place to place — " the priest
catchers," the brutal " pursuivants," the truculent seekers
after proofs of the celebration of Catholic rites in
private dwellings ; the fines and forfeitures, the wreck of
property, the ruin of families, the sundering of all the ties
of nature among people of the same kith and kin, believers
in the same God, subjects of the same sovereign, children
of the same soil—on the wrongs, in fine, of every kind
inflicted by those laws of blood and rapine, in the holy
name of religion, the mind is appalled, and one needs all
the true philosophy of a strong faith in the unerring wisdom of an inscrutable Providence, to rise from the contemplation of those awful results with reason and religion
in accord, and our feelings in conformity with both, in
respect to all that has happened to the victims of this un-
hallowed code.

Have the people of England gained by this persecution
of nearly three centuries ?   Has the empire been benefited
by the Reformation, and the penal code devised to sustain
it ?   Has its interests been promoted abroad by the deadly
war waged against a religion which is that of two-thirds of
the people of the Christian world ?   Answers to those queries may be found in the eleven poor-laws of Elizabeth ;
the report of the poor-law commissioners in the reign of
William IV. ; the report of the Devon commission in that
of Victoria ; the smouldering fires of Chartism in England;
the animosities of classes ; the terrible competition in
trade, manufactures, and labour ; the spirit and soul-sub-
duing anxieties to procure a bare subsistence resulting
from that competition ; the growing hatred of the rich that
prevails among the poor throughout the land ; the want
of sympathy with the privations of the poor on the part
of the upper and, most especially, of the middle classes ;
the hardness of heart which wealth, and luxury, long continued commercial prosperity, and the pride of territorial
aggrandizement invariably bring with them, unsoftened by
the influences of a religion that has humanizing tendencies,

18

that enlists the affections on the side of salvation, makes men feel for others, and manifest their christian principles in human sympathies, as well as in solemn professions of belief and in formal observance of all the less . weighty matters of the law.

The legacies of two revolutions—a debt of 800 millions, taxation exceeding fifty millions a-year, a standing army considered a necessity of the constitution ; re-action of religious opinion on the law-established Church, whose security was declared on one memorable occasion by its prelates, dependant on the test acts that had their origin in fraud and forgery ; the position of a large portion of the clergy of that Church in our own times, holding the tenets of one Church and the emoluments of another ; the fierce spirit of bigotry and fanaticism that grew up with the legalized ascendancy of intolerance, discouraged and repressed of late years, but yet not dead nor dying ; the remains of old prejudices, stronger than new opinions—prejudices that have survived the laws of an infernal spirit which gave them birth; bitter rancours, class jealousies, and sectarian hatreds; divided interests, councils, and opinions; parties without principles, or earnest convictions, or belief in the reality of disinterested actions or patriotic motives ; and, finally, a people without veneration for their Church, a lively faith in their religion, and a restraining power in the influence of the latter : these, also, are matters far from irrelevant to the subject of the preceding enquiries.

And yet the chief evils arising from the abandonment and persecution of the old faith, are to be sought elsewhere —in the unavailing efforts to subvert it in Ireland, in the Protestant garrison government planted in that Catholic country; in the legislation for ages against its people for Protestant purposes ; in the effects of this policy—social strife and misery, evictions, agrarian outrages, murders, periodical famines, and the pestilence that walks at noonday in the sister kingdom, after centuries of dominion in that ill-fated land.

In foreign lands we find the same inordinate zeal for protestantizing Catholics, producing mischief to British interests.   In the colonies and dependencies of Great Britain, where the Catholic religion prevails, the efforts of this kind made by the agents, members, or encouragers of English proselytizing societies ; by injudicious, intemperate, and often unscrupulous persons, who make a living of the Bible, and whose proceedings are productive of the chief part of the difficulties of government. In foreign countries, too, weak-minded, well-intentioned English enthusiasts, or self-sufficient people, animated by a strong sense of the superiority of their nation and its character as a Protestant country, in all their intercourse with strangers of another faith, prominently and offensively exhibit in their supercilious deportment, their unconcealed scorn for the religion, the Church, and the clergy of the people amongst whom they may happen to sojourn, and by the cold reserve with which, even in society, they abstain from coming into terms of intimacy, nay, of common civility, or into contact at all with Catholic families,—prejudice in no slight degree British interests, by the mistaken notions which these absurdly arrogant proceedings and pretensions give rise to, by causing the people of such countries to confound the acts of such persons and agencies of such societies with the policy, the objects, or the influence of the British government. This observation is a reply to one question, whose importance can only be duly appreciated by those who have some knowledge of the Canadas, of Malta, and the Ionian Islands, as well as of the principal countries of southern Europe.

But of all the results of persecution in England, of all the evil consequences of the Penal Code, of its operation, the worst is the spirit of hypocrisy it gave rise to amongst persons in all public positions ; and which not only made the semblance of virtue a policy and a profitable practice, but eventually became a substitute for the former. Nay, that spirit of simulated zeal for religion crept into literature itself, and there came perpetually into conflict with truth and justice. Hypocrisy, in fine, served as a mantle for all kinds of ambitions before the world. It was adopted by patriots — alas ! by the earliest philanthropists of England ; by the banker, the merchant, the public dinner speaker, the public charity contributor, the dull bigot, the astute politician, the philosophic historian, the deist, and the disciple of Whitfield, the sitter in the high church and the low church ; the shopkeeper ambitious of being a vestryman, of becoming a churchwarden, of attaining the glory of that civic apotheosis which converts a mere man into a lord mayor ; the tradesman who aspired to the dig-

nity of a presidental chair at a club; the elderly lady
living on "a genteel income" in the suburbs, who looked
after the heathen in distant regions, or who took an interest
in the souls of benighted people nearer home;—one and all
found it necessary to wrap themselves up in that cloak of
sanctimonious respectability, which covers such a multitude
of sins in England. Like the old Spanish mantle adopted
in Ireland, that, according to Spenser, was suitable for all
sorts and seasons, this goodly cloak of sanctimony became
a pleasant vesture for the spring, a light covering for the
summer, a loose garment for the autumn, and a comfortable wrapper for the winter.

Oh, all-potent, mystic, self-complacent, specious, sanctimonious spirit of hypocrisy!

"Ore pius, mendax animo, nequitiam vultu tegens:"

how canst thou impose on the minds of great multitudes of
people—nay, even on the minds of men of genius and intelligence!

What solemnity of aspect canst thou assume—what
power of face canst thou command, when simulating the
forms of piety, of freedom and of liberality! By thy influence the atrocities that were committed in the reigns of
Elizabeth, James, Charles I., Cromwell, Charles II., William, Anne, George I., and his successor, are divested of
their horrors in all that our Humes, our Henrys, and our
Goldsmiths have written of those times; their wickedness
is lost sight of, and the perpetrators of those enormities,
who consented to them, or suffered them to be committed,
are held forth as the wise ministers or the good and gracious
sovereigns of a land of civil and religious freedom!

So much for the Reformation, and operation of the
Penal Code in England.

The second volume of this work will be confined ex-
clusively to the history of the sufferings of the Roman
Catholics of Ireland on account of their religion, the unsuccessful means adopted to suppress it, and to support the
Church it was in vain attempted to establish on its ruins.

APPENDIX.

No.
1. Suppression of the Monasteries.
2. Digest of proceedings in parliament on the Catholic question.
3. Protests against the Relief Bill of 1829.
4. Majorities and Minorities on divisions.
5. Petitions for and against the Bill.
6. English nobility and gentry benefited by it.
7. Spirit of the Penal Code existing in the British Colonies.
8. The Relief Bill of 1829.
9. Watson's rejected Relief Bill of 1847.
10. Outlawry of the Religious Orders in 1829.
11. The Education Question in 1847.

APPENDIX.

No. 1.

SUPPRESSION OF MONASTERIES.

" Whatever accusations may have been brought against the monasteries, it is an undoubted fact that they were seminaries of learning, and the schools of the nation. 'In *every great abbey*,' says 'Bishop Tanner, Monast. p. xxx,— xxxiii., 'there was a large room called the *Scriptorium*, where several writers made it their whole business to transcribe books for the use of the library. They sometimes, indeed, wrote the leiger books of the house, and the missals, and other books used in divine service, but they were generally upon other works, viz.: the Fathers, Classics, Histories, &c. John Wethamsted, abbot of St. Albans, caused above eighty books to be thus transcribed during his abbacy. Fifty-eight were transcribed by the care of one abbot, at Glastonbury ; and so zealous were the monks in general for this work, that they often got lands given, and churches appropriated, for the carrying of it on. In all the greater abbeys, there were also persons appointed to take notice of the principal occurrences of the kingdom, and at the end of every year to digest them into annals. The constitutions of the clergy in their national and provincial synods, and after the conquest even Acts of Parliament, were sent to the abbeys to be recorded......secondly, *they were schools of learning and education; for every convent had one person or more appointed for this purpose; and all the neighbours that desired it, might have their children taught grammar and church music without any expense to them. In the nunneries also young women were taught* to work, and to read English, and sometimes Latin also. *So that not only the lower rank of people who could not pay for their learning, but most of the noblemen and gentlemen's daughters were educated in those places.'*

" These places, then, were the schools of the kingdom, where rich and poor were educated together, and the latter free of all expense ; there the writings of antiquity were preserved from destruction, and the chronicles of our own history prepared. Let us now contrast what we have learned above were the duties, habits and employments, of the calumniated clergy of the Catholic Church, with the conduct of their calumniators, the so-called reformers. You have believed that the changes were all in favour of learning, and of a better and more enlightened order of things.

" It will be well, however, to have before us a summary of the foundations left by our Catholic forefathers for the benefit either of the poor, the sick, of learning, or religion, destroyed at the reformation, and though it differs slightly from some other accounts, I shall present the one drawn up by Burns.*

Of lesser monasteries whereof we have the
     valuation, ...   374
Of greater monasteries, ...   186
Belonging to the Hospitallers, ...   48
Colleges, ...   90
Hospitals, ...   110
Chantries and free chapels, ... 2374

                     Total,............ 3182

" The sum total of the clear yearly revenue of the several houses at the time of their dissolution, of which we have any account, seems to have been as follows :—

	£.	s.	d.
Of the great monasteries,...............	104,919	13	3¼
Of all those of the lesser monasteries of which we have the valuation, ...	29,702	1	10¼
Knights hospitallers' head house in London,.................................	2,385	12	8

* Eccles. Law. Art. Monasteries.

	£.	s.	d.
We have the valuation of only 28 of their houses in the country, ...	3,026	9	5
Friars' houses of which we have the valuation, ...	751	2	0¾
Total,............£.140,784	19	3¼

" And if we consider that there were many of the lesser monasteries and houses of the hospitallers and friars, of which no computation hath been found ; and that not one of the colleges, hospitals, and great number of chantries and free chapels are reckoned in this estimate ; and consider withal the vast quantity of plate and other goods which came into the hands of the king by the dissolution, and the value of money at that time, which was at least six times as much as it is at present, and also that the estimate of the lands was supposed to be much under the real worth, we must needs conclude the whole to have been immense.

" I will subjoin also the account given by the same author, of the number of persons driven from their homes by these flagrant acts.

Those of the lesser monasteries, dissolved by the 27 H. 8, were reckoned at about	10,000
If we suppose the colleges and hospitals to have contained a proportional number, these will make about	5,347
If we reckon the number in the greater monasteries, according to the proportion of their revenues, they will be about 35,000 ; but as probably they had larger allowances in proportion to their number, than those of the smaller monasteries, if we abate 5,000, upon that account, they will be	30,000
One for each chantry, and free chapel, ...	2,347
Total,............	47,694

" Now, was the reformation favourable to learning, or

was it its bitterest enemy? *Ninety colleges* at one fell swoop destroyed! and the only receptacles of the infirm, the hospitals, that might have melted a heart of stone to spare, the refuge of those whom God's hand has been heavy upon, the very visiting of which is a work so hallowed, *one hundred and ten* of these noble charities ruined at once! And this is the reformation: the heart sickens at the name, associated as it is with the destruction of every thing that religion, humanity, and reason, tells us is useful, instructive, and holy. Was it a change for the better to destroy so many hundred schools, where the poor were taught without cost, not merely their own language and the ordinary elements of learning, but even some of the more accomplished arts, as music? Was it a reformation to scatter, sell, and destroy some of the noblest libraries in the kingdom, collected at an enormous expense, and cherished as the best ornament of their houses by the religious, who, to increase their precious store, employed *several* persons to transcribe and preserve the elegant and precious productions of antiquity, thus guarding the springs from which learning was derived? Now, read the following accounts of the destruction of books and manuscripts, and judge whether it did not seem to be the object of the reformers to smother learning altogether, to plunge the nation into hopeless ignorance, or rather whether they cared what went to ruin, provided they could increase their plunder, and promote their own interests. 'Most of the learned records of the age,' says Collier,* 'were lodged in the monasteries. Printing was then but a late invention, and had secured but a few books in comparison of the rest. The main of learning lay in manuscripts, and the most considerable of these, both for number and quality, were in the monks' possession. But the abbeys at the dissolution falling oftentimes into hands who understood no farther than the estates, the libraries were miserably disposed of. The books, instead of being removed to royal libraries, to those of cathedrals or the universities, were frequently thrown in to the grantees, as things of slender consideration. Now these men oftentimes proved a very ill protection for learning and antiquity. Their avarice was sometimes so mean, and their ignorance so undistinguish-

* Collier, Eccl. Hist. Vol. ii. B. iii. p. 166.

ing, that when the covers were somewhat rich, and would yield a little, they pulled them off, threw away the books, or turned them to waste paper. Thus many noble libraries were destroyed.' Fuller, the church historian, declares* that ' *all arts and sciences*' fell under the common calamity. How many admirable manuscripts of the fathers, schoolmen, and commentators, were destroyed by this means? What number of historians of all ages and countries? *The holy scriptures themselves, as much as these gospellers pretended to regard them, underwent the fate of the rest.* If a book had a cross on't, it was condemned for popery ; and those with lines and circles were interpreted the black art, and destroyed for conjuring. And thus divinity was profaned, mathematics suffered for corresponding with evil spirits, physic was maimed, and riot committed on the law itself.' But listen to Bishop Bale, 'one of the most bitter enemies the monks ever had,' as Marsham calls him,† and learn to do justice to the calumniated religious, and to their barbarous enemies. Never had we been offended for the loss of our libraries, being so many in number, and in so desolate places, for the more part, if the chief monuments and most notable works of our most excellent writers had been reserved. If there had been in every shire of England, but one solemn library for the preservation of those most noble works, and preferment of good learning in our posterity, it had been somewhat. But to destroy all without consideration, *is, and will, unto England, be for ever, a most horrible infamy*, among the grave seniors of other nations. A great number of them which purchased these superstitious mansions, reserved those library books, some to serve their jakes, some to scour their candlesticks, and to rub their boots. Some they sold to the grocers and soapsellers, and some they sent over sea to the bookbinders ; not in small numbers, but at times *whole ships full*, to the wondering of foreign nations. Yea, the Universities of this realm are not all clear in this detestable fact. But cursed is that belly which seeketh to be fed with such ungodly gains, and so deeply shameth his natural country. I know a merchantman, which shall at this time be nameless, that bought the contents of two noble libraries for

---

* Fuller Ch. Hist. B. vi. p. 335.
† Pref. to Dugd. Mon.

forty shillings price: a shame it is to be spoken. This stuff hath he occupied instead of grey paper for the space of more than these ten years, and yet he hath store enough for as many years to come. A prodigious example this, and to be abhorred of all men, which love their nation as they should do. Yea, what may bring our realm to more shame and rebuke, than to have it noised abroad that we are despisers of learning? I judge this to be true, and utter it with heaviness, that neither the *Britons*, under the *Romans* and *Saxons*, nor yet the *English* people under the *Danes* and *Normans*, had ever such damage of their learned monuments, as we have seen in our time. *Our posterity may well curse this wicked fact of our age, this unreasonable spoil of England's most noble antiquities.*[*]

"'The monks,' says another writer, 'were formerly the greater part of Ecclesiastics, and the walls of convents were, for a long time, the fences of sanctity and the better sort of literature. From that seminary came forth those mighty lights of the christian world, Bede, Alcunius, Willebrord, Boniface, and others, worthy of much honour for their learning, and for propagating the faith. Were it not for the monks, we had certainly ever been children in the history of our own country. Many ill consequences attended the suppression of religious houses; but it is my design at present to take notice only of the great decay of learning that was like to ensue the dissolution: insomuch, that in parliament, held 2 and 3 Edward VI., there were bills brought in for encouraging men to give lands for the maintenance of schools of learning. And the loss of good books was irreparable, as Bale tells us.—Bale, one of the most bitter enemies the monks ever had, is forced to lament the great damage the learned world sustained at

---

[*] John Bale, Declaration in Leland's Journal, An. 1549. Fuller, C. H. B. vi. p. 335. Bale was bishop of Ossery. D'Israeli, after giving a summary of the above extract from Bale, adds, "the fear of destruction induced many to hide manuscripts under ground, and in old walls. At the Reformation, popular rage exhausted itself on illuminated books, or MSS. that had red letters in the title-page; any work that was decorated was sure to be thrown into the flames as superstitious. Red letters and embellished figures were sure marks of being papistical and diabolical. We still find such volumes mutilated of the gilt letters and elegant flourishes, but the greater number were annihilated. Many have been found under ground, being forgotten. What escaped the flames were obliterated by the damp."—Curiosities of Literature, Vol. i. p. 85.

this dissolution. Indeed, those well-furnished libraries, that were in most monasteries, plainly show, that we are too much prejudiced against the monks, when we rashly condemn them as idle, ignorant, or discouragers of learning; and that, on the contrary, we ought to esteem many of them to be learned and industrious, and promoters of several useful parts of knowledge. In every abbey there was a large room, called the Scriptorium, to which belonged several writers, whose business it was to transcribe books for the use of the public library of the house. There were no less than 1700 manuscript tracts in the library at Peterborough, and the catalogue of books belonging to the Priory of Dover, and the Abbey of St. Mary de la Pre, at Leicester, clearly evinced that those houses had no mean libraries, and those kept in very good order. Nay, so zealous were the monks for the encouragement of learning, that they very often got churches appropriated *ad libros faciendos*, for making of books; nor were they less careful of preserving the old. The British, Irish, and Saxon monasteries were, we find, the schools and universities of those times. They were not only cells of devotion, but also nurseries of learned men for the use of the church. The works of Bede are a sufficient argument of the knowledge the monks of those times had in all parts of learning. Their skill in the learned languages was so very eminent, that 'tis reported some of them understood Greek and Latin as well as their mother tongue. When the monks were rooted out by the Danish wars, an universal ignorance overspread the land, insomuch that there was scarce any one in England that could read or write Latin; but when, by the care of King Edward and Archbishop Dunstan, monasteries were restored, learning found its former encouragement, and flourished very much within the walls of cloisters. So that Leland, who was no great friend to the monks, often confesses, that in those old times there were few or no writers but monks.'*

"The injury done to education and letters, nay, their almost total overthrow by the men of the 'new learning,' may also be clearly seen from the state of the universities immediately on the suppression of the monasteries. 'The dissolution,' says the historian of Oxford,† 'completely

---

* Marsham, Preface to Dugdale's Monasticon.
† Literatorum studia tam penitus extinxit cœnobiorum eversio Abbates omnes suos monachos domum accersunt. Nobiles suos libe-

destroyed all learned studies.　The abbeys withdrew their youth, the nobility their children, the clergy their relations ; hence the number of scholars was sadly lessened, the liberal sciences were neglected, the halls abandoned. There is good reason to believe, that in Oxford there were formerly 300 halls at least, whilst now we have but eight.' The university libraries shared the same fate as those of the monasteries.　'Richard de Bury, bishop of Durham, who died 1345, very opportunely left all his books, "more than all the bishops in England had then in custody," according to Wood, to the end that the students of Dur- ham College and of the whole university might, under certain conditions, make use of them.　This was called "Angervyle's Library," and the books were kept in chests many years, under the custody of several scholars deputed for the purpose ; until the library being built in Durham College, tempore Hen. IV., as Wood states, when the col- lege was quadrangularly finished, about the same time with Rede's library at Merton, the said books were there de- posited in chains, in certain pews or studies.　Here they remained till the dissolution of that house, and for some years after, when King Edward's visitors, in their hasty and ill-directed zeal against superstition, issued injunctions for their removal, and though some are said to have found their way into the library of Balliol College, *yet these and all other libraries in Oxford were subject to the same inquisito- rial havoc and spoliation.*　By a decree of *Convocation,* Jan. 25, 1555-6, certain persons were appointed *to sell the very benches and desks of Duke Humphrey's library,* so that it re- mained empty till Bodley's time.　The value of these repo- sitories of ancient lore may be estimated by some inciden- tal notes taken of their contents by Leland, and preserved in his "Collectanea." '*

　　"Many similar lamentations over the barbarous war against books and knowledge might easily be collected, but

ros, presbyteri suos cognatos; sic minuitur scholasticorum numerus, sic ruunt aulæ nostræ, sic frigescunt omnes liberales disciplinæ, collegia solum perseverant.—Ad munera civilia, vel etiam mechanica sese con- verterunt.　*Wood. Antiq. Univ. Ox.* p. 262, 265.　Nam licet 300 olim, et adhuc plures, et fama constanti, et registrorum fide ductus, extitisse crediderim, ad 8 jam recidisse deprehendo.—Ibid. p. 265.

　　* Memorials of Oxford, by J. Ingram, D.D. Pres. of Trinity College. Vol. ii. Art. Bodleian Lib. 1837.

the above facts will suffice to show, that the 'men of the new learning' were the bitterest enemies to education and everything connected with it, that ever disgraced this nation ; that schools for the poor, libraries for the learned, the records and annals of our country, and the very word of God, the Holy Bible, were swept away in indiscriminate pillage and destruction, and this under the name of reformation. Ignorance, then, contempt of learning, and heedlessness of the improvement of the national mind, barbarian spoliation of whatever former and better times had founded and venerated as noble, charitable, and useful, have branded the change as hateful to God, and injurious and debasing to man.

"The consideration of these facts extorted from Gibbon the confession, that 'a single Benedictine monastery has produced more learned men than both our universities.' "*

No. 2.

CATHOLIC QUESTION.   DIGEST OF THE PROCEEDINGS IN PARLIAMENT SINCE THE UNION.

1805, May 10th, Lord Grenville's motion for committee. Lords 49 ay. 178 no.
" May 15th, Fox ditto.   Commons 124 ay. 336 no.
1807, March 5th, Lord Grenville's bill to open the army and navy to English Catholics.   King's opposition. Dissolution of parliament.   Grenville ministry broken up.
1808, May 25th, Grattan's motion for committee.   Commons 128 ay. 281 no.
" May 27th, Lord Donoughmore, ditto.   Peers 74 ay. 161 no.   Maynooth endowed this year.
1810, May 10th, Grattan's motion for committee.   Commons 101 ay. 213 no.
" June 6th, Lord Donoughmore, ditto.   Peers 68 ay. 154 no.

* Watterworth's Digest of the Penal Laws, pp. 33 to 39.

1812, April 20th, ditto, to consider the claims. Peers 102 ay. 174 no.

" April 23rd, Grattan, ditto. Commons 215, ay. 300 no.

" June 22nd, Canning, ditto, to consider claims next session. Commons 106 ay. 235 no.

" July 1st, Marquis Wellesley, ditto. Peers 120 ay. 12 no.

1813, February 23rd, Grattan's resolution for committee. Commons 264 ay. 224 no.

" May 11th, Sir J. C. Hippesley's motion for ditto. Commons 187 ay. 235 no.

1815, May 30th, Sir H. Parnell's motion for committee. Commons 147 ay. 228 no.

1816, May 21st, Grattan's ditto. Commons 141 ay. 172 no.

1817, May 9th, ditto, ditto, 221 ay. 245 no.

" In this session the Liverpool administration introduced a bill which passed both houses, opening the army and navy to English Catholics; by annual acts of indemnity, relieving Catholic officers from the penalty of not taking the oaths of supremacy, &c.

1819, May 4th, Grattan's motion for committee. Commons 241 ay. 243 no.

1821, February 8th, Plunkett, ditto, ditto, 227 ay. 221 no.

" Ditto. Bill brought in on third reading division. Commons 216 ay. 197 no.

" April 16th, Lord Donoughmore, ditto. Peers 120 ay. 159 no.

" April 30th, Canning, ditto. Commons for leave to bring in a bill for Catholic peers to sit in parliament, 249 ay. 244 no.

" April 30th, ditto, on third reading. Commons 248 ay. 227 no.

" June 22nd, Duke of Portland, ditto. Peers 129 ay. 271 no.

1823, April 28th, Mr. Plunkett's motion for a committee met by counter motions; division on amendment. Commons 313 ay. 111 no.

1824, Bills introduced in the Commons to enable Catholics to vote at elections, and act as magistrates, 101 ay. 139 no.

" Another division, 109 ay. 143 no.

" An act passed both houses to enable the Duke of Norfolk to execute the office of Earl Marshall.

1825, April 19th, Sir F. Burdett's Relief Bill, with the disfranchising and clergy pensioning wings. Commons, second reading, 268 ay. 241 no., third reading no division.

" May 18th, ditto. Peers, second reading, 130 ay. 178 no.

1827, March 5th, Sir F. Burdett's motion for committee. Commons 272 ay. 276 no.

1828, March 8th, ditto, ditto, 272 ay. 206 no.

" May 16th, conference with lords agreed to.

" May 19th, Duke of Wellington's motion for appointment of lords to confer.

" June 9th, Marquis of Lansdown's motion on Commons' resolution. Peers 137 ay. 182 no.

" Mr. G. Bankes's bill introduced and passed, relieving English Catholics from penalty of double assessment of land-tax.

1829, February 5th, Speech from the throne, recommending consideration of the propriety of removing civil disabilities in the case of Catholics, consistently with the interests of the established church.

" March 5th, Bill passed both houses unanimously, and received the royal assent for suppression of the Catholic Association.

" March 5th, Peel's motion for committee on the Catholic question. Commons 348 ay. 160 no.

" March 5th, ditto. Relief bill introduced for abolition of civil disabilities by repealing the oaths of supremacy and abjuration, and substituting an oath of allegiance; binding Catholics to defend the settlement of property as by law established, and not to injure the established church; rendering Catholics eligible likewise to all offices excepting the chancellorship, the lord lieutenant of Ireland, the regency and commissionership of the church of Scotland; excluding them also from the right of presentation to livings and offices in ecclesiastical courts and their establishments; their bishops also from assuming the titles of sees held by Protestant prelates, their priests from walking in processions or performing other public functions in their clerical robes outside their churches; laymen from wearing the insignia of civil office, such as the mace, alder-

19

manic gown, or dress of office, in any other than
a protestant place of worship.

1829, In the way of securities for the protestant church,
the forty shillings freeholders were to be abolished
and the monastic orders banned, subjected to penalties of fine and banishment for life—to the former
penalty, to the extent of fifty pounds a month, for
remaining in the united kingdom unregistered, and
to the latter penalty, for coming into this realm
" after the commencement of this act—and shall be
deemed and taken guilty of a misdemeanour," except where the parties are natural born subjects
previously in orders to the passing of this act, and
on their return to this United Kingdom register
their names; and for neglect or refusal to do so they
shall pay a fine of fifty pounds a month, and also,
except in cases of special permission, granted to any
persons in orders for periods not exceeding six
months by a protestant secretary of state, and being
revoked, within twenty days after revocation, on
pain of banishment for life, such parties to quit the
realm.

"   In case of members of monastic orders " admitting
any regular ecclesiastic, or brother, or member, &c.,
into any religious community or society, or be aiding
and consenting thereto," in England and Ireland,
they shall be deemed guilty of a misdemeanor, and
in Scotland, shall be punished by fine and imprisonment ; and the penalty of the guilt of any such misdemeanor, is declared banishment for life ; and the
penalty of refusal or omission to quit the realm three
calendar months after such sentence, transportation
for life.   Provided always that nothing in the clauses
against the monastic orders, shall extend to or affect
females bound by religious or monastic vows.

1847, February 10th, " A Bill for the further repeal of
enactments imposing pains and penalties upon her
majesty's Roman Catholic subjects on account of
their religion, prepared and brought in by Mr.
Watson, Lord John Manners, and Mr. Escott."
The preamble recites the existence of eight Penal
Laws against Catholics left unrepealed by the Relief
Bill of 1829, the further repeal act in the eighth

year the Queen Victoria, and the subsequent one in the tenth year of the same reign.

This bill contained a clause for the repeal of the provisions of 10 George IV. c. 7. prohibiting Roman Catholic ecclesiastics, or members of monastic orders, from performing the rites of their church, except within their churches, or wearing the habits of their orders; and also prohibiting laymen from being present in any place of worship other than that of the Established Church, wearing the insignia or any peculiar habit of their office.

The Bill was rejected by a majority of 39.

DIVISION ON THE ROMAN CATHOLIC RELIEF BILL.

HOUSE OF COMMONS, APRIL 14, 1847.

Order for committee read, motion made, and question proposed, "that Mr. Speaker do now leave the chair." Amendment proposed, to leave out from the word "That" to the end of the question, in order to add the words, "this house will, upon this day six months, resolve itself into the said committee," instead thereof :—Question put, "That the words proposed to be left out stand part of the question:" The house divided; Ayes, 119, Noes, 158.

MINORITY—AYES.

Adam, W.
Anson, hon. col.
Arundel and Surrey, earl of
Bannerman, A.
Baring, F. T.
Bentinck, lord G.
Bodkin, J. J.
Bouverie, hon. E. P.
Bowring, Dr.
Bright, J.
Brotherton, J.
Brown, W.
Browne, R. D.
Browne, hon. W.
Brownrigg, J. S.
Buller, C.
Buller, E.
Busfeild, W.
Byng, G. S.
Carew, hon. R. S.
Cayley, E. S.
Christie, W. D.
Clive, viscount
Colebrooke, sir T. E.
Collett, J.
Coote, sir C. H.

Craig, W. G.
Currie, R.
Dalmeny, lord
Dalrymple, capt.
Damer, hon. col.
Dawson, hon. T. V.
Dickinson, F. H.
Dodd, G.
Duncan, G.
Duncombe, T.
Dundas, admiral
Dundas, F.
Dundas, sir D.
Easthope, sir J.
Ebrington, viscount
Ellis, W.
Escott, B.
Evans, sir De Lacy
Ewart, W.
Fitzroy, lord C.
Forster, M.
Gill, T.
Granger, T. C.
Greene, T.
Grey, sir G.
Grosvenor, lord R.
Hatton, captain V.
Hay, sir A. L.
Hervey, lord A.
Howard, P. H.
Hume, J.
James, sir W. C.
Jervis, sir J.
Johnstone, sir J.
Labouchere, H.
Lambton, H.
Lascelles, hon. W. S.
Leader, J. T.
Lincoln, earl of
Macaulay, T. B.
Macnamara, major
M'Carthy, A.
M'Donnell, J. M.

Maitland, T.
Marjoribanks, S.
Marshall, W.
Mitchell, T. A.
Moffatt, G.
Molesworth, sir W.
Monahan, J. H.
Morpeth, viscount
Muntz, G. F.
Mure, colonel
Napier, sir C.
Nicholl, J.
O'Brien, C.
O'Connell, M. J.
Ogle, S. C. H.
Ord, W.
Paget, colonel
Parker, J.
Pattison, J.
Pechell, captain
Philips, M.
Plumridge, captain
Pulsford, R.
Pusey, P.
Rawdon, colonel
Rich, H.
Romilly, J.
Russell, lord J.
Russell, lord E.
Rutherford, A.
Sandon, viscount
Sheil, R. L.
Smith, B.
Smythe, hon. G.
Somerville, W. M.
Stansfield, W. R. C.
Strutt, E.
Tancred, H. W.
Thornely, T.
Towneley, J.
Trelawny, J. S.
Tufnell, H.
Vane, lord H.

Wall, C. B.
Warburton, H.
Ward, H. G.
Wawn, J. T.
Williams, W.

Wyse, T.
Yorke, H. R.

Watson, W. H.
Manners, lord J.

MAJORITY—NOES.

Ackers, J.
Adderley, C. B.
Alford, viscount
Allix, J. P.
Archdall, captain
Arkwright, G.
Austen, colonel
Baillie, H. J.
Baillie, W.
Barrington, viscount
Bateson, T.
Beckett, W.
Bennet, P.
Beresford, major
Blackburne, J. I.
Blackstone, W. S.
Boldero, H. G.
Broadley, H.
Broadwood, H.
Brooke, lord
Bruce, C. L. C.
Buck, L. W.
Buller, sir J. Y.
Burroughes, H. W.
Cabbell, B. B.
Carew, W. H. P.
Chandos, marquis of
Chapman, A.
Chelsea, viscount
Chichester, lord J. L.
Cholmeley, sir M.
Christopher, R. A.
Chute, W. L. W.
Clerk, sir G.
Codrington, sir W.

Colville, C. R.
Compton, H. C.
Copeland, Mr. Alderman
Cripps, W.
Deedes, W.
Denison, G. B.
Dick, Q.
Douglas, sir H.
Douglas, sir Chas. E.
Douglas, J. D. S.
Douro, marquis of
Duckworth, sir J. T. B.
Duncombe, hon. O.
Du Prè, C. G.
East, sir J. B.
Egerton, W. T.
Egerton, sir P.
Estcourt, T. G. B.
Feilden, W.
Fellowes, E.
Ferrand, W. B.
Filmer, sir E.
Finch, G.
Fitzroy, hon. H.
Forester, hon. G. C. W.
Fox, S. L.
Frewen, C. H.
Fuller, A. E.
Gladstone, captain
Gooch, E. S.
Gore, M.
Gore, W. O.
Gore, W. R. O.
Goring, C.
Goulburn, H.

Granby, marquis of
Gregory, W. H.
Hale, R. B.
Hall, colonel
Halsey, T. P.
Hamilton, W. J.
Hardy, J.
Harris, hon. captain
Heathcote, sir W.
Henley, J. W.
Hildyard, T. B. T.
Hope, sir, J.
Hornby, J.
Hotham, lord,
Hudson, G.
Hussey, T.
Ingestre, viscount
Johnstone, H.
Jolliffe, sir W. G. H.
Jones, captain
Kemble, H.
Knight, F. W.
Knightly, sir C.
Lawson, A.
Lennox, lord G. H. G.
Leslie, C. P.
Lindsay, C.
Lockhart, W.
Lowther, hon. colonel
Lygon, hon. general
Manners, lord C. S.
March, earl of
Marten, G.
Masterman, J.
Meynell, captain
Morgan, Octavius
Morgan, Sir C.
Mundy, E. M.
Newdegate, C. N.
Newry, viscount
Packe, C. W.
Palmer, R.

Palmer, G.
Peel, J.
Plumptre, J. P.
Polhill, F.
Pollington, viscount
Powell, colonel
Prime, R.
Rashleigh, W.
Reid, colonel
Rendlesham, lord
Repton, G. W.
Richards, R.
Rolleston, colonel
Round, C. G.
Round, J.
Ryder, hon. G. D.
Sanderson, R.
Seymer, H. K.
Sheppard, T.
Shirley, E. J.
Shirley, E. P.
Sibthorp, colonel
Smith, A.
Smyth, sir H.
Somerset, lord G.
Sotheton, T. H. S,
Spooner, R,
Stuart, H.
Stuart, J.
Taylor, J. A.
Thesiger, sir F.
Thompson, alderman
Thornhill, G.
Tollemache, J.
Tower, C.
Troubridge, sir E. T.
Turner, E.
Turnor, C.
Tyrell, sir J. T.
Verner, sir W.
Vyse, H.
Vyvyan, sir R. S.

Waddington, H. S.
Walpole, S. H.
Wellesley, lord C.

TELLERS.

Inglis, sir H.
Law, hon. C. E.

SUMMARY.

Majority (Tellers included) 160
Minority (Tellers included) 121
Majority against the Bill ....—— 39

No. 3.

PROTESTS AGAINST THE RELIEF BILL OF 1829.

Protests on the Journals of the House of Peers were entered for a great variety of reasons, all of which might be resolved into one conclusive and compendious reason,—the protesters thought it essential to the Protestant Church to oppress the Roman Catholics.

It would be doing an injustice to those enlightened persons to withhold their names in a work of this kind. Indeed, if it were possible to have them engraved on bronze or carved on granite, and placed in a conspicuous part of the monument that commemorates " the conflagration of London by the papists;" there—

"Where the tall bully lifts his head, and lies"—

the fame of those protesters against an act of tardy justice, and of the last expiring efforts of fanaticism and intolerance, should be perpetuated.

Thus stand, in the order of their signatures, the names of the Duke of Newcastle; Lords Kenyon, Howe, Malmesbury, Romney, Walsingham and Farnham, Brownlow, O'Neill; Lords Eldon, Winchilsea, Bexley, Mayo, Kinnoul, Mansfield, Sidmouth, Farnborough, Roden; Marquis of Ailesbury; Lords Romney, Lorton, Verulam, Thomond; Duke of Gordon; Lords Digby, Shaftesbury, Falmouth, Skelmersdale, Feversham, Bradford, Redesdale; Bishop of Bath and Wells; Lord Mountcashel.

No. 4.

MAJORITIES AND MINORITIES.

HOUSE OF LORDS.

DIVISION ON THE SECOND READING OF THE CATHOLIC RELIEF
BILL ON SATURDAY, APRIL 4.

Those marked thus * had heretofore opposed the claims,
either in the House of Lords or House of Commons.

CONTENT.—PRESENT.

*Duke of Clarence
Duke of Sussex
Duke of Gloucester
*Lord Chancellor
*Lord President
Lord Privy Seal
　　　　DUKES.
Brandon (Hamilton)
*Beaufort
Devonshire
*Leeds
*Manchester
*Rutland
Somerset
*St. Albans
*Wellington
　　　　MARQUISSES.
Anglesea
*Bath
Bristol
Bute
Camden
Conyngham .
Hastings
Lansdowne
Winchester
　　　　EARLS.
Albemarle

Amherst
Blessington
Chesterfield
Carlisle
Cowper
Clarendon
Carnarvon
Caledon
*Chichester
Cawdor
Denbigh
*Doncaster (D. of Buccleugh)
*Dartmouth
De la Warr
Dudley
Essex
Elgin
Ferrers
Fitzwilliam
Grosvenor
Gosford
Grey
Hardwicke
Hillsborough (Marquis of
　　Downshire)
Harrowby
Ilchester
Jersey

*Liverpool
Limerick
Minto
Morley
Oxford
*Powis
Radnor
Roseberry
Rosslyn
*Strange (Duke of Athol)
Somers
*Stradbrooke
Thanet
Tankerville
Vane (M. of Londonderry)
*Westmoreland .
Wicklow

VISCOUNTS.

*Beresford
Duncan
Gordon (Earl of Aberdeen)
Granville
Goderich
Hood
Leinster (Duke of)
Maynard
Melville
St. Vincent
Torrington

BISHOPS.

Chester
*Derry
Kildare
*Llandaff
*Lichfield and Coventry
*Oxford
Rochester
*St. David's
*Winchester

LORDS.

Auckland
Abercromby
Ailsa (Earl Cassilis)

Belhaven
Boyle (Earl of Cork)
Braybrooke
*Byron
Clifton (Earl of Darnley)
Carleton (Earl of Shannon)
Carteret
Calthorpe
*Carberry
*Clanwilliam (Earl)
Dacre
Dundas
De Dunstanville
Dunally
Durham
Foley
Fitzgibbon (Earl of Clare)
*Fife (Earl of)
Gower
Grantham .
Granard
Howard de Walden
Holland
Hill
King
*Ker (Marquis of Lothian)
Lyttleton
*Lilford
Lynedoch
Montford
*Montague
Mendip
*Meldrum (Earl of Aboyne)
Melbourne
Maryborough
Melros (Earl of Haddington)
Monteagle (M. of Sligo)
Napier
Ormonde (Marquis of)
Oriel
Plunkett
*Ravensworth
Ranfurly (Northumberland)

*Saltoun
Say and Sele
Sundridge (Duke of Argyle)
Suffield
Selsey
Somerhill (M. of Clanricarde)

Seaford
*Teynham
Wellesley (Marquis)
Wharncliffe
Willoughby d'Eresby
Yarborough

PROXIES.

DUKES.
Cambridge
Bedford
Buckingham
Grafton
Marlborough
*Northumberland
Portland

MARQUISSES.
Cleveland
*Hertford
Northampton
Queensberry
Stafford
Tweeddale

EARLS.
*Ashburnham
Belmore
Buckinghamshire
*Chatham
Charlemont
Derby
Errol
Fortescue
*Graham (Duke of Montrose)
Home
Harrington
*Harcourt
Kingston
Lucan
Mulgrave
*Orford
Rosse
Spencer

St. Germans
Suffolk
Waldegrave
*Warwick
Wilton

VISCOUNTS.
*Arbuthnot
Anson
Hereford
Hutchinson (Donoughmore)
*Strathallan

BISHOP.
Norwich

LORDS.
Alvanley
Barham
Berwick
Bredalbane (Earl)
Carrington
Clinton
Crewe
*Douglas
Downey (V. Downe)
*Dufferin
Ducie
Erskine
*Forester
Grenville
Howard of Effingham
*Hawke
Hopetoun (Earl of)
Lauderdale (Earl)
Lovell and Holland (Earl of
 Egmont)

Ponsonby (Earl of Besbo-
  rough)
*Ross (E. of Glasgow)
Sondes
Southampton
Sherborne

Stewart-Garlies (Earl of Gal-
  loway)
*Saltersford (Earl of Cour-
  town)
*Stuart and Rothsay)
*Wemyss (Earl of)

NOT CONTENT.—Present.

Duke of Cumberland

ARCHBISHOPS.
Canterbury
York
Armagh

DUKES.
Dorset
Newcastle
Richmond

MARQUISSES.
Ailesbury
Cholmondeley
Exeter
Salisbury
Thomond

EARLS.
Abingdon
Aylesford
Beauchamp
Bradford
Brownlow
Clancarty
Digby
Eldon
Enniskillen
Falmouth
Guildford
Harewood
Howe
Longford
Lonsdale
Malmesbury
Mansfield
Mayo

Morton
Mountcashel
Norwich (Duke of Gordon)
O'Neill
Onslow
Plymouth
Poulett
Romney
Shaftesbury
Stamford
Talbot
Verulam
Winchilsea

VISCOUNTS.
Lake
Lorton
Sidmouth

BISHOPS.
Bath and Wells
Bristol
Carlisle
Chichester
Durham
Ely
Exeter
Gloucester
Lincoln
London
Meath
Salisbury
St. Asaph

LORDS.
Arden
Bexley

Boston
Colville
Farnborough
Farnham
Grantley
Hay (Earl of Kinnoull)
Kenyon
Manners
Middleton

Redesdale
Rivers
Rodney
Rolle
Sheffield (Earl)
Sinclair
Skelmersdale
Tenterden
Walsingham

PROXIES.

EARLS.

Carrick
Cardigan
Charleville
Macclesfield
Manvers
Mount Edgecumbe
Nelson
Rochfort
Scarborough

VISCOUNT.

Exmouth

BISHOPS.

Hereford
Peterborough
Worcester

LORDS.

Baygot
Bayning

Churchill
Clanbrassil (Earl of Roden)
Colchester
Dalhousie (Earl)
Delamere
De Clifford
Dynevor
Faversham
Fisherwick (M. of Donegal)
Gambier
Gray
Loftus (M. of Ely)
Le Despencer
St. Helen's
Stowell
Wallace
Willoughby de Broke
Wodehouse

THE FOLLOWING PEERS VOTED ON THE THIRD READING, AND
NOT ON THE SECOND.

In the Majority—(*Present.*)—Lords Ducie, Gage, Glenlyon, Ranfurly (Northland.)—(*Proxies*)—Earls Cornwallis, Home, Lord Howard of Effingham.—(*Paired off*)—Duke of Manchester, Norwich, (Duke of Gordon.)

Minority.—(*Present*)—Viscount Gort, Lord Ribblesdale. (*Proxy*)—Lord Dynevor.

Thirteen peers who voted in the majority on the second reading, did not vote on the passing of the bill, and six peers who voted in the minority on the second reading, did not vote on the third.

PEERS WHO DID NOT VOTE ON THE SECOND READING.

MARQUISSES.
Abercorn (minor)
Townshend (in France)

EARLS.
Abergavenny
Beverley
Berkeley (will not take his seat)
Coventry
Cornwallis
Cadogan
Cathcart
Craven (minor)
Egremont
Harborough
Huntingdon (minor)
Lindsey (minor)
Pomfret
Portsmouth (lunatic)
Pembroke
Sandwich (minor)
Stanhope

VISCOUNTS.
Combermere (in India)
Courtenay (abroad)
Sidney

BARONS.
Audley
Androssan (Earl of Eglington, in Scotland) a minor
Bolton
Brodrick
Carysfort Earl of (lunatic)

Cowley
De la Zouch
Dorchester (minor)
Forbes
De Tabley (minor)
Glenlyon
Gage (too late)
Gardner (minor)
Harris
Heytesbury
Home (Earl of)
Moore (Marquis of Drogheda) a lunatic
Monson (minor)
Northwick (too late)
Penshurs (Viscount)
Ponsonby (of Imokilly)
Prudhoe
Ribblesdale
Scarsdale
Strangford (in Brazil)
Stuart, (Earl of Moray)
Tyrone (Marquis of Waterford) a minor
Thurlow
Vernon
Wigan (Earl of Balcarras)

BISHOP.
Bangor (Magendie)

IRISH PEERS.
Bandon Earl of (not taken his seat)
Headfort, Marquis of

HOUSE OF COMMONS.

DIVISION ON THE THIRD READING OF THE ROMAN CATHOLIC
RELIEF BILL IN THE HOUSE OF COMMONS, MONDAY, MARCH
30th, 1829.

Those who in 1827 voted against concession, and whose
names now appear in the majority on the third reading, are
marked (o.) The places not otherwise distinguished are
boroughs; (co.) signifies county, and (c.) city members.
This mark (*) denotes Irish members, and this (†) Scotch.

MAJORITY.

Abercromby, J. Calne
Acland, sir T. Devonshire
Alexander, J. Barnstaple
Althorp, lord, Northampton-
shire
Anson, sir G. Lichfield, c.
Anson, hon. G. Yarmouth
Apsley, lord, Cirencester
Arbuthnot, rt. hon. C. St.
Ives
(o) † Arbuthnot, hon. col.
Kincardinshire.
Archdeckne, A. Dunwich
(o) Ashley, lord, Woodstock
Baillie, col. Hedon
†Balfour, J. Anstruther
Barclay, D. Penryn
Baring, A. Callington
Baring, W. B. Thetford
Baring, F. Portsmouth
Beaumont, T. W. Stafford
*Bective, earl of, Meath, co.
Benett, J. Wiltshire
Bentinck, lord G. King's
Lynn
(o) Beresford, sir J. Northal-
lerton
(o) Beresford, lieut.-col. Ber-
wick, c.

*Bernard, T. King's co.
*Bingham, L. Mayo, co.
Birch, J. Nottingham,
Blake, sir F. Berwick-on-
Tweed
*Boyle, hon. J. Cork, co.
Bourne, rt. hon. L. Ashbur-
ton
Brecknock, earl of, Bath, c.
(o) Brogden, J. Launceston
Brougham, J. Truro
*Browne, J. Mayo
*Brownlow, C. Armagh, co.
*Bruen, H. Carlow, co.
Buller, C. West Looe
Burdett, sir F. Westminster, c.
Buxton, T. F. Weymouth
Burrard, G. Lymington
Byng, G. Middlesex
Calcraft, rt. hon. J. Ware-
ham
Calthorpe, hon. F. Bramber
Calvert, C. Southwark
(o) Calvert, J. Huntingdon
Calvert, N. Hertfordshire
(o)†Campbell, A. Glasgow, c.
†Campbell, W. Argyleshire
(o) † Campbell, J. Dumbar-
tonshire

*Carew, R. Wexford, co.
Carrington, sir C. St. Mawe's
(o) Cartwright, W. Northamptonshire
*Castlereagh, visc. Down, co.
*Caulfield, hon. H. Armagh, county. ⸗
Cave, O. Leicester
Cavendish, lord G. Derbysh.
Cavendish, C. Newtown
*Chichester, sir A. Carrickfergus, c.
Cholmondeley, lord H. Castle Rising
†Clerk, sir G. Edinburgh
*Clements, visc. Leitrim, co.
Clifton, visc. Canterbury, c.
(o) Clive, visc. Ludlow
(o) Clive, hon. R. Ludlow
(o) Clive, E. Hereford, c.
Clive, H. Montgomery
Cockburn, sir G. Plymouth
Cocks, J. Reygate
Colborne, N. R. Thetford
(o) Cole, sir C. Glamorganshire
(o) Cook, sir H. Orford
*Coote, sir C. Queen's co.
(o) Corbett, P. Shrewsbury, c.
Courtenay, rt. hon. T. Totness
Cradock, S. Camelford
Crampton, S. Derry, c.
*Dawson, A. Louth, co.
*Daly, J. Galway, co.
Denison, W. J. Surrey
Denison, J. Hastings
*Doherty, J. Kilkenny, c.
†Douglas, W. R. Dumfries, &c.
†Drummond, H. Stirlingsh
Ducane, P. Steyning
Darlington, earl of, Totness

*Duncannon, viscount, Kilkenny, co.
Duncombe, T. S. Hertford
Dundas, hon. G. Orkney, &c.
Dundas, hon. R. Richmond
Dundas, C. Berkshire
East, sir E. Winchester, c.
Easthope, J. St. Alban's
Eastnor, visc. Hereford
Ebrington, visc. Tavistock
(o) Eden, hon. R. Fowey
Elliot, lord, Liskeard
Ellis, hon. G. A. Ludgershall
Ellis, hon. A. Seaford
Ellison, C. Newcastle-on-Tyne
*Ennismore, visc. Cork, co.
Ewart, W. Bletchingly
(o) Fane, hon. H. Lyme Regis
Fane, T. Lyme Regis
Farquhar, sir R. Hythe
Fazakerley, J. N. Lincoln, c.
†Ferguson, sir R. Dysart
*Fitzgerald, right hon. M. Kerry, co.
*Fitzgerald, lord W. Kildare, co.
Fitzgerald, right hon. V. Newport
Fitzgerald, J. Seaford
*Fitzgibbon, col. Limerick, c.
(o) Foley, J. H. Droitwich
*Forbes, visc. Longford, co.
Forbes, sir C. Malmesbury
Forbes, J. Malmesbury
Fortescue, hon. G. Hindon
(o) *Foster, L. Louth, co.
Frankland, R. Thirk
Fremantle sir T. Buckingham
*French, A. Roscommon, co.
Garlies, visc. Cockermouth
(o) Gilbert, D. Bodmin
Gordon, R. Cricklade

(o) *Goulburn, right hon. R. Armagh

†Gower, lord F. L. Sutherlandshire

Graham, sir J. Cumberland

(o) Graham, marq. Cambridge

†Grant, right hon. C. Inverness-shire

†Grant, col. Elginshire

†Grant, R. Fortrose

*Grattan, J. Wicklow, co.

*Grattan, H. Dublin, c.

Grosvenor, gen. Stockbridge

Grosvenor, hon. R. Chester, c.

†Gordon, sir W. Aberdeenshire

Guest, J. Honiton

Guise, sir B. Gloucestershire

Gurney, H. Newport—(I. W.)

Hardinge, sir H. Durham, c.

†Hay, lord J. Haddingtonshire

†Hay, A. Peebles, &c.

Heathcote, sir G. Boston

(o) Herries, right hon. J. C. Harwich

*Hill, lord A. Down, co.

(o) *Hill, right hon. sir G. Derry, c.

Hobhouse, J. C. Westminster, c.

(o) Hodgson, F. Barnstaple

Horton, R. W. Newcastle-under-Lyne

Howard, H. Shoreham

Hughes, W. L. Wallingford

(o) Halse, J. St. Ives

†Hume, J. Aberdeen, &c.

Hurst, R. Horsham

Huskisson, rt. hon. W. Liverpool, c.

*Hutchinson, J. H. Tipperary, co.

*Hutchinson, J. Cork, c.

Howard, hon. G. Castle Rising

Ingilby, sir R. Lincolnshire

†Innes, sir H. Dingwall, &c.

*Jephson, C. D. Mallow

Jermyn, earl, Orford

Joliffe, col. Petersfield

(o) Kekewich, S. Exeter, c.

†Kennedy, F. Ayr, &c.

*King, hon. R. Roscommon

Knight, R. Wallingford

*Knox, hon. T. Dungannon

Labouchere, H. St. Michael's

Lamb, hon. G. Dungarvon

*Lambert, J. S. Galway, co.

(o)Langston, J. Oxford, c.

Lascelles, hon. W. East Looe

*Latouche, R. Kildare, co.

Lawley, F. Warwickshire

Lennard, T. B. Maldon

Leycester, R. Shaftesbury

†Lewis, rt. hon. T. F. Ennis

Lester, B. Poole

Liddel, hon. H. Northumberlandshire

†Lindsay, hon. H. Perth, &c.

Littleton, E. Staffordshire

Lloyd, Sir E. Flint

*Lloyd, T. Limerick, co.

Lockhart, J. Oxford, c.

Loch, J. St. Germains

Lumley, J. Nottinghamshire

Lushington, Dr. Tregony

Maberley, J. Abingdon

Maberley, lt.-col. Northampton

Mackintosh, Sir J. Knaresborough

†Mackenzie, Sir J. Ross-sh.

Maitland, visc. Appleby

†Maitland, hon. capt. Berwickshire

Marjoribanks, S. Hythe

Marshall, J. Yorkshire
Marshall, W. Petersfield
(o)Martin, sir T. B. Plymouth
Martin, J. Tewkesbury
†Maule, hon. W. Forfarsh.
*Maxwell, J. Downpatrick
Milbank, M. Camelford
Mildmay, P. Winchester
Milton, visc. Yorkshire
Monck, J. Reading
†Morrison, J. Bamff, co.
Morland, Sir S. St. Mawes
Morpeth, visc. Morpeth
Mostyn, Sir T. Flint
*Mountcharles, lord, Donegal, co.
†Murray, Sir G. Perthshire
(o) Northcote, H. Heytesbury
Nugent, lord, Aylesbury
Nugent, sir G. Buckingham, c.
North, J. Dublin University
O'Brien, W. S. Ennis
*O'Brien, L. Clare, co.
Ord, W. Morpeth
Owen, Sir J. Pembrokeshire
*Oxmanstown, lord, King's co.
(o) Palmer, C. F. Reading
(o) Palmer, R. Berkshire
Palmerston, visc. Cambridge University
*Parnell, sir H. Queen's co.
(o) Peel, rt. hon. R. Westbury
(o) Peel, W. Y. Tamworth
Peel, L. Cockermouth
Pendarvis, E. Cornwall, co.
Phillips, G. Steyning
Phillips, G. Wotton Basset
Phillimore, Dr. Yarmouth (I. W.)
Phipps, hon. G. Scarborough
Perceval, S. Newport, Hants.
Ponsonby, hon. F. Higham Ferrers

*Ponsonby, hon. G. Youghall
Ponsonby, hon. W. Poole
*Power, R. Waterford, co.
Powlett, lord W. Durham, c.
Poyntz, W. Chichester
(o) Prendergast, M. Gatton
Price, R. New Radnor
Pringle, Sir W. Liskeard
*Prittie, hon. F. Tipperary, co.
*Proby, hon. G. Wicklow, co.
Protheroe, E. Evesham
Pryse, P. Cardigan
Rae, right hon. sir W. Harwich
(o) Raine, J. Newport (Cornwall)
Ramsbottom, J. Windsor
Ramsden, hon. J. C. Malton
Rancliffe, lord, Nottingham,
Rice, T. S. Limerick, c.
Robarts, A. Maidstone
Robinson, sir G. Northampton
Robinson, G. Worcester, c.
Rowley, sir W. Suffolk
Rumbold, C. Yarmouth
Russell, lord J. Bedford
Russell, R. G. Thirsk
Sandon, viscount, Tiverton
(o) *Saunderson, A. Cavan, co.
Scarlett, sir J. Peterborough
Scott, sir W. Carlisle
†Scott, H. F. Roxburghshire
Sebright, sir J. Hertfordshire
†Sinclair, hon. major, Caithness
Slaney, R. A. Shrewsbury
Smith, G. Wendover
Smith, W. Norwich

(o) Somerset, lord G. Monmouthshire

*Somerville, sir M. Meath, co.

Stanley, lord, Lancashire

Stanley, E. Preston

*Stewart, A. R. Londonderry, co.

†Stewart, sir M. Lanark, co.

Stuart, lord J. Cardiff

*Stuart, H. V. Waterford, co.

Sykes, D. Hull

Sugden, E. B. Weymouth

Talmash, hon. F. Grantham

Talmash, hon. L. Ilchester

Taylor, M. A. Durham, c.

Taylor, sir C. Wells

Tennyson, C. Bletchingly

(o) Thompson, W. London, c.

Thompson, P. B. Wenlock

Thompson, C. P. Dover

Thynne, lord J. Bath, c.

Thynne, lord W. Weobly

Thyne, lord H.

Tierney, right honourable G. Knaresboro'

(o) Tindal, sir N. Cambridge University

Tomes, J. Warwick c.

Townshend, hon. J. Whitchurch

Trench, col. Cambridge

Tufton, hon. H. Appleby

Tunno, E. Bossiney

Twiss, H. Wotton Basset

Valletort, lord. Lostwithiel

*Van Homrigh, P. Drogheda

Vernon, G. Lichfield, c.

Villiers, T. H. Hedon

Waithman, R. London, c.

Wall, C. Wareham

Walpole, hon. C. King's Lynn

Warburton, H. Bridport

Warrender, Sir G. Westbury

(o) Webb, E. Gloucester, c.

*Westenra, hon. H. Monaghan, co.

Western, C. C. Essex

Whitbread, S. C. Middlesex

Whitbread, W. Bedford

*White, S. Leitrim, co.

*White, col. Dublin, co.

Whitmore, W. Bridgnorth

Wilbraham, G. Stockbridge

Williams, O. Great Marlow

Williams, T. P. Great Marlow

Wilson, sir R. Southwark

Winnington, sir F. Worcestershire

Wodehouse, E. Norfolk

Wood, M. London, c.

Wood, C. Preston

Wortley, hon. J. Bossiney

Wrottesley, sir J. Staffordshire

Wynn, sir W. W. Denbighshire

Wyvill, M. York

(o) Yorke, sir J. Reigate

TELLERS.

(o) Dawson, G. Londonderry, co.

Planta, J. Hastings

PAIRED OFF IN FAVOUR OF THE BILL.

Bouverie, hon. B. Downton

*Colthurst, sir N. Cork, c.

*Clarke, hon. C. Kilkenny, co.

†Dundas, right hon. W. Edinburgh, c.

Davies, col. Worcester, c.

Davenport, E. Shaftesbury
Heron, sir R. Peterborough
Howick, lord, Winchilsea
(o) Lethbridge, sir T. Somerset
Marshall, J. Yorkshire
*Newport, sir J. Waterford, c.
Owen, H. Pembroke
*O'Hara, J. Galway, co.

Sefton, earl of, Droitwich
Smith, hon. R. Buckinghamshire
Somerset, lord R. Gloucestershire
Stewart, J. Beverley
Tavistock, marquis, Bedfordshire
Talbot, R. W. Dublin, co.

MINORITY.

Antrobus, G. Plympton
*Archdall, gen. Fermanagh, co.
Arkwright, R. Eye
Ashurst, W. Oxfordshire
Astley, sir J. D. Wiltshire
Baker, E. Wilton
Bankes H. Dorchester
Bankes, W. Marlborough
Bankes, G. Corfe Castle
Bastard, E. Devonshire
Batley, C. Beverley
Beckett, sir J. Haslemere
*Belfast, earl of, Belfast, c.
Bell, M. Northumberland
Blandford, marquis, Woodstock
Borrodaile, R. Newcastle-under-Lyne
Bradshaw, capt. Brackley
Bright, H. Bristol, c.
Brydges, sir J. Kent, co.
Buck, L. W. Exeter, c.
Burrell, sir C. Shoreham
Buxton, J. Bedwin
Capel, J. Queenborough
Cawthorne, J. Lancaster
Cecil, lord T. Stamford
Chichester, sir A. Millborne Port
*Cole, hon. A. Enniskillen

Cooper, R. B. Gloucester, c.
Cooper, E. S. Dartmouth
*Corry, visc. Fermanagh, co.
*Cory, hon. H. Tyrone, co.
Cotterell, sir J. Herefordsh.
Curteis, E. J. Sussex
Cust, hon. capt. Clitheroe
Cust, hon. E. Lostwithiel
Davenport, E. Shaftesbury
Davis, R. H. Bristol, c.
Dawkins, col. Boroughbridge
Dick, Q. Orford
Dick, H. G. Maldon
Dickenson, W. Somersetsh.
Dottin, A. Southampton
†Downie, R. Stirling, &c.
Drake, T. Amersham
Drake, W. Amersham
Domville, sir C. Oakhampton
Dugdale, D. Warwickshire
Dowdeswell, J. Tewkesbury
Dundas, R. A. Ipswich
Egerton, W. Chester, c.
Estcourt, T. Oxford University
Encomb, viscount, Truro
Estcourt, T. H. Marlborough
*Farquhar, J. Portarlington
Fellowes, H. Huntingdonshire
*Fetherston, sir G. Lonford, co.
Foley, E. Ludgershall

Forestor, hon. C. Wenlock
Fyler, T. B. Coventry, c.
Gascoyne, general, Liverpool
Gordon, J. Weymouth
Grant, sir A. Lostwithiel
Greene, T. Lancaster
Gye, F. Chippenham
Hastings, sir C. Leicester
Heathcote, sir W. Hampshire
Holdsworth, A. H. Clifton, &c.
Hodson, J. A. Wigan
Hotham, lord, Leominster
Inglis, sir R. Oxford University
Keck, G. A. Leicestershire
Kemp, T. Lewes
Kerrison, sir E. Eye
King, sir J. D. Wycombe
*King, hon. H. Sligo, co.
Knatchbull, sir E. Kent
Legge, hon. A. Banbury
Lott, H. B. Honiton
Lushington, col. Carlisle
Lowther, visc. Westmoreland
Lowther, hon. colonel, Westmoreland
†Lowther, J. H. Wigton, &c.
Lucy, G. Fowey
Luttrell, J. Minehead
Lygon, hon. col. Worcestersh.
Mackinnon, C. Ipswich
Malcolm, N. Boston
Mandeville, lord, Huntingdonshire
Manners, ld. R. Leicestersh.
Macleod, J. N. Sudbury
*Maxwell, H. Cavan, co.
*Meynell, captain, Lisburne
Morgan, sir C. Monmouthsh.
Munday, G. Boroughbridge
Mundy, F. Derbyshire
Miles, P. J. Corfe Castle
*O'Neil, hon. general, Antrim

O'Neil, A. J. Hull
Palk, sir L. Ashburton
Pallmer, C. N. Surrey
Peachey, general, Taunton
Pearse, J. Devizes
Peel, colonel, Norwich, c.
Pelham, J. C. Shropshire
Pennant, G. New Romney
†Pigot, col. Kinross-shire
Petit, L. H. Ripon
Peach, N. W. Corfe Castle
Powell, col. Cardigan, co.
Powell, A. Downton
Price, R. New Radnor
Rickford, W. Aylesbury
*Rochfort, G. Westmeath, co.
Rose, rt. hon. G. Christchurch
Rose, G. P. Christchurch
Ryder, rt. hon. B. Tiverton
Sadler, M. T. Newark
St. Paul, sir H. Bridport
Scott, hon. W. Gatton
Scott, hon. W. Newport (I.W.)
Spence, G. Ripon
*Shirley, J. C. Monaghan, co.
Sibthorp, col. Lincoln
Smyth, sir G. Colchester
Sotheron, adm. Nottinghamshire
Strutt, col. Oakhampton
Taylor, G. Devizes
Thompson, G. Halesmere
Tapps, G. W. New Romney
Trant, W. Dover
Trevor, hon. G. Carmarthenshire
*Tulamore, lord, Carlow
Uxbridge, earl of, Anglesea
Vyvyan, sir R. H. Cornwall, co.
Wells, J. Maidstone
†Wemys, capt. Fifeshire
West, hon. F. Denbigh
Wetherell, sir C. Hastings

*Wigram, W. New Ross
Willoughby, H. Newark
Wilson, R. F. Yorkshire
Wilson, col. York, *c.*
Wyndham, W. New Sarum

*Wynn, O. Sligo
TELLERS.
Chandos, marq. of, Buckinghamshire
*Moore, G. Dublin, *c.*

PAIRED OFF AGAINST THE BILL.

Bastard, J. Dartmouth
Blackburne, J. Lancashire
Chaplin, C. Lincolnshire
Chaplin, T. Stamford
Carmarthen, marq. Helston
Duncombe, hon. W. Yorksh.
*Evans, H. Wexford, *c.*
Gooch, sir T. Suffolk
Houldsworth, T. Pontefract

Harvey, sir E. Essex
*Handcock, R. Athlone
Lennox, W. G. Chichester
Lowther, sir J. Cumberland
Morgan, G. Brecon
Noel, sir G. Rutland, *co.*
Nicholl, sir J. Bedwin
Whitmore, T. Bridgnorth

Irish members absent.—Croker, right hon. J. W. Dublin University, (indisposed); Macnaghten, E. Antrim, *co.*; Kavenagh, F. Carlo, *co.*; Collett, E. Cashel; Dawson, J. M. Clonmel; Maxwell, J. W. Downpatrick; Russell, J. Kinsale; Knox, hon. J. Newry; King, hon. W. Cork, *co.*; Denny, sir E. Tralee; Stewart, W. Tyrone, *co.*; Tuite, H. M. Westmeath, *co.*; Stopford, lord, Wexford, *co.*

. *The following members, who had heretofore opposed the claims, voted in favour of the bill on previous divisions.*—Ashley, lord, Woodstock; Arbuthnot, hon. col. Kincardineshire; Bradshaw, capt. J. Brackley; Jones, J. Carmarthen; Irving, J. Bramber; King, hon. W. Cork, *c.*; Lindsey, col. Wigan; Norton, G. Guildford; Owen, sir E. Sandwich; Paget, lord W. Carnarvon; Somerset, lord E. Gloucestershire; Vivian, sir H. Windsor.

No. 5.

PETITIONS PRESENTED TO THE HOUSE OF LORDS DURING THE DISCUSSION OF THE RELIEF MEASURE OF 1829.

Against the Bill, ... 2521
In favour of it, ... 1014

PRESENTED TO THE HOUSE OF COMMONS.

Against the Bill, ... 2013
In favour of it, ... 955

THE PRESS.

Of 238 newspapers in the United Kingdom, in 1829, as computed in the *Atlas* newspaper of April 19, that year, there were 107 in favour of Emancipation, 87 against it, and 44 neutral.

No. 6.

ENGLISH CATHOLICS NOBILITY, AND GENTRY, BENEFITED BY THE RELIEF BILL.

Eight entitled by right to take their seats in the House of Peers:—the Duke of Norfolk, Earl of Shrewsbury, Barons Stourtown, Petre, Arundell, Donner, Stafford and Clifford.

The Roman Catholic baronets of England were sixteen. (Scotch, one; Irish, five. Peers of the latter country, eight.)

No. 7.

THE SPIRIT OF THE PENAL CODE IN SOME OF THE BRITISH SETTLEMENTS.

In Bermuda the Roman Catholic clergyman is not allowed to see the members of his flock who may be priso-

ners in jail, without the permission of the Protestant clergyman, or magistrate.

The Roman Catholic clergyman is not allowed to see the
members of his flock who may be convicts on board the
Hulks, without permission of the Protestant clergyman.

The convicts obliged to attend Protestant service and
Protestant schools, and in case of refusal, punished.

Three Protestant clergymen are paid for attending the
soldiers in the Island, a very large number of whom are
Catholics. An application to the military authorities was
recently made for the appointment and payment of one
Roman Catholic clergyman for the Catholic soldiers, and
refused.

No. 8.

A BILL INTITULED AN ACT FOR THE RELIEF OF HIS MAJESTY'S
ROMAN CATHOLIC SUBJECTS.

WHEREAS by various acts of Parliament certain restraints
and disabilities are imposed on the Roman Catholic subjects of his majesty, to which other subjects of his majesty
are not liable : and whereas it is expedient that such restraints and disabilities shall be from henceforth discon-
tinued : and whereas by various acts, certain oaths, and
certain declarations, commonly called the declaration
against transubstantiation, and the declaration against
transubstantiation and the invocation of the saints, and the
sacrifice of the mass, as practised in the Church of Rome,
are or may be required to be taken, made, and subscribed
by the subjects of his majesty, as qualifications for sitting
and voting in Parliament, and for the enjoyment of certain
offices, franchises, and civil rights ; be it enacted by the king's
most excellent majesty, by and with the advice and consent
of the lords spiritual and temporal, and commons, in this present Parliament assembled, and by the authority of the
same, that from and after the commencement of this act,
all such parts of the said acts as require the said declarations, or either of them, to be made or subscribed by any
of his majesty's subjects, as a qualification for sitting and

voting in Parliament, or for the exercise or enjoyment of any office, franchise, or civil right, be and the same are (save as hereinafter provided and excepted) hereby repealed.

And be it enacted, that from ·and after the commencement of this act, it shall be lawful for any person professing the Roman Catholic religion, being a peer, or who shall after the commencement of this act be returned as a member of the House of Commons, to sit and vote in either House of Parliament respectively, being in all other respects duly qualified to sit and vote therein, upon taking and subscribing the following oath, instead of the oaths of allegiance, supremacy, and abjuration.

" I, A. B., do sincerely promise and swear, that I will be faithful, and bear true allegiance to his majesty King George the Fourth, and will defend him to the utmost of my power against all conspiracies and attempts whatever which shall be made against his person, crown, or dignity, and I will do my utmost endeavour to disclose and make known to his majesty, his heirs and successors, all treasons and traitorous conspiracies which may be formed against him or them. And I do faithfully promise to maintain, support, and defend, to the utmost of my power, the succession of the crown, which succession, by an act entitled— ' An Act for the further limitation of the crown, and better securing the rights and liberties of the subject,' is, and stands limited to the Princess Sophia, Electress of Hanover, and the heirs of her body, being Protestants ; hereby utterly renouncing and abjuring any obedience or allegiance unto any other person claiming or pretending a right to the crown of this realm. And I do further declare, that it is not an article of my faith, and that I do renounce, reject, and abjure the opinion, that princes excommunicated or deprived by the Pope, or any other authority of the See of Rome, may be deposed or murdered by their subjects, or by any person whatsoever. And I do declare, that I do not believe that the Pope of Rome, or any other foreign prince, prelate, person, state, or potentate, hath, or ought to have, any temporal or civil jurisdiction, power, superiority, or pre-eminence, directly or indirectly, within this realm. I do swear, that I will defend, to the utmost of my power, the settlement of property within this realm as established by the laws ; and I do hereby disclaim, disavow, and solemnly abjure any intention to subvert the present church establishment, as settled by law within this realm ; and I do solemnly swear, that I never will exercise any privilege to which I am or may become entitled, to disturb or weaken the Protestant religion or Protestant government, in the United Kingdom ; and I do solemnly, in the presence of God, profess, testify, and declare, that I do make this delaration, and every part thereof, in the plain and ordinary sense of the words of this oath, without any evasion, equivocation, or mental reservation whatsoever.   " So help me God."

And be it further enacted, that wherever in the oath hereby appointed and set forth, the name of his present majesty is expressed or referred to, the name of the sovereign of this kingdom for the time being, by virtue of the act for the further limitation of the crown, and better securing the rights and liberties of the subject, shall be substituted from time to time with proper words of reference thereto.

Provided always, and be it further enacted, that no peer, professing the Roman Catholic religion, and no person, professing the Roman Catholic religion, who shall be returned a member of the House of Commons after the commencement of this act, shall be capable of sitting or voting in either House of Parliament respectively, unless he shall first take and subscribe the oath hereinbefore appointed and set forth, before the same persons, at the same times and places, and in the same manner as the oaths and declaration now required by law are respectively taken, made, and subscribed : and that any such person, professing the Roman Catholic religion, who shall sit or vote in either house of Parliament, without having first taken or subscribed in the manner aforesaid the oath in this act appointed and set forth, shall be subject and liable to the same penalties, forfeitures, and disabilities, and the offence of so sitting or voting shall be followed and attended by and with the same consequences as are by law enacted and provided in the case of persons sitting or voting in either house of parliament respectively, without the taking, making, and subscribing the oaths and the declaration now required by law.

And be it further enacted, that it shall be lawful for

persons professing the Roman Catholic religion to vote at
elections of members to serve in Parliament for England
and for Ireland, and also to vote at the elections of representative peers of Scotland and of Ireland, and to be elected
such representative peers, being in all other respects duly
qualified, upon taking and subscribing the oath hereinbefore appointed and set forth, instead of the oaths of allegiance, supremacy, and abjuration ; and instead of the
declaration now by law required, and instead also of such
other oath or oaths as are now by law required to be taken
by any of his majesty's subjects professing the Roman
Catholic religion, and upon taking also such other oath or
oaths as may now be lawfully tendered to any persons
offering to vote at such elections.

And be it further enacted, that the oath hereinbefore
appointed and set forth shall be administered to his majesty's subjects professing the Roman Catholic religion, for
the purpose of enabling them to vote in any of the cases
aforesaid, in the same manner, at the same time, and by
the same officers or other persons as the oaths for which it
is hereby substituted are or may be now by law administered ; and that in all cases in which a certificate of the
taking, making, or subscribing of any of the oaths, or of
the declaration now required by law is directed to be
given, a like certificate of the taking or subscribing of the
oath hereby appointed and set forth, shall be given by the
same officer or other person, and in the same manner as
the certificate now required by law is directed to be given,
and shall be of the like force and effect.

And be it further enacted, that in all cases where the
persons now authorized by law to administer the oaths of
allegiance, supremacy, and abjuration, to persons voting at
elections, are themselves required to take an oath previous
to their administering such oaths, they shall, in addition to
the oath now by them taken, take an oath for the duly
administering the oath hereby appointed and set forth, and
for the duly granting certificates of the same.

And whereas in an act of the Parliament of Scotland,
made in the eighth and ninth session of the first Parliament
of King William the Third, entitled, " An act for the preventing the growth of popery," a certain declaration or
formula is therein contained, which it is expedient should
no longer be required to be taken and subscribed ; be it

therefore enacted, that such parts of any acts as authorize
the said declaration or formula to be tendered, or require
the same to be taken, sworn, and subscribed, shall be, and
the same are hereby repealed, except as to such offices,
places, and rights, as are hereinafter excepted ; and that
from and after the commencement of this act, it shall be
lawful for persons professing the Roman Catholic religion
to elect and be elected members to serve in Parliament for
Scotland, and to be enrolled as freeholders in any shire or
stewartry of Scotland, and to be chosen commissioners or
delegates for choosing burgesses to serve in Parliament for
any districts or burghs in Scotland, being in all other
respects duly qualified, such persons always taking and
subscribing the oath hereinbefore appointed and set forth,
instead of the oaths of allegiance and abjuration as now
required by law, at such time as the last mentioned oaths,
or either of them, are now required by law to be taken.

And be it further enacted, that no person in holy orders
in the church of Rome shall be capable of being elected to
serve in Parliament as a member of the House of Commons, and if any such person shall be elected to serve in
Parliament as aforesaid, such election shall be void ; and
if any person being elected to serve in Parliament as a
member of the House of Commons shall after his election
take or receive holy orders in the church of Rome, the seat
of such person shall immediately become void ; and if any
such person shall in any of the cases aforesaid presume to
sit or vote as a member of the House of Commons, he shall
be subject to the same penalties, forfeitures, and disabilities
as are enacted by an act passed in the 41st year of the
reign of King George the Third, intituled " An act to
remove doubts respecting the eligibility of persons in holy
orders to sit in the House of Commons," and proof of the
celebration of any religious service by such person according to the rites of the church of Rome shall be deemed
and taken to be *prima facie* evidence of the fact of such
person being in holy orders within the intent and meaning
of this act.

And be it enacted, that it shall be lawful for any of his
majesty's subjects, professing the Roman Catholic religion,
to hold, exercise, and enjoy all civil and military offices,
and places of trust or profit under his majesty, his heirs,
or successors, and to exercise any other franchise or civil

right, except as hereinafter excepted, upon taking and subscribing at the times and in the manner hereinafter mentioned, the oath hereinbefore appointed and set forth,
instead of the oaths of allegiance, supremacy, and abjuration, and instead of such other oath or oaths as are or may
be now by law required to be taken for the purpose aforesaid by any of his majesty's subjects professing the Roman
Catholic religion.

Provided always, and be it enacted, that nothing herein
contained shall be construed to exempt any person professing the Roman Catholic religion from the necessity of
taking any oath or oaths, or making any declaration not
hereinbefore mentioned, which are or may be by law required to be taken or subscribed by any person on his
admission into any such office or place of trust or profit as
aforesaid.

Provided always, and be it further enacted, that nothing
herein contained shall extend, or be construed to extend, to
enable any person or persons professing the Roman Catholic
religion, to hold or exercise the office of guardians and justices of the United Kingdom, or of regent of the United Kingdom, during the absence of his majesty or his successors,
under whatever name, style, or title such office may be
constituted ; nor to enable any person, otherwise than as he
is now by law enabled, to hold or enjoy the office of lord
high chancellor, lord keeper, or lord commissioner of the
great seal of Great Britain or Ireland ; or the office of lord
lieutenant, or lord deputy, or other chief governor or governors of Ireland ; or his majesty's high commissioner to the
general assembly of the church of Scotland.

And be it enacted, that it shall be lawful for any of his
majesty's subjects professing the Roman Catholic religion
to be a member of any lay body corporate, and to hold any
civil office or place of trust or profit therein, and to do any
corporate act, or vote in any corporate election or other
proceeding, upon taking and subscribing the oath hereby
appointed and set forth, instead of the oaths of allegiance,
abjuration, and supremacy ; and upon taking also such
other oath or oaths as may now by law be required to be
taken by any persons becoming members of such lay body
corporate, or being admitted to hold any office or place of
trust or profit within the same.

Provided also, and be it further enacted, that nothing

herein contained shall be construed to affect or alter any of the provisions of an act passed in the 7th year of his present majesty's reign, intituled—" An act to consolidate and amend the laws which regulate the levy and application of church rates and parish cesses, and the election of churchwardens and the maintenance of parish clerks in Ireland."

Provided nevertheless, and be it further enacted, that nothing herein contained shall extend to authorize or empower any of his majesty's subjects professing the Roman Catholic religion, and being a member of any lay body corporate, to give any vote at, or in any manner to join in, the election, presentation, or appointment of any person to any ecclesiastical benefice whatever, or any office or place belonging to or connected with the united church of England or Ireland, or the church of Scotland, being in the gift, patronage, or disposal of such lay corporate body.

Provided also, and be it enacted, that nothing in this act contained shall be construed to enable any persons, otherwise than as they are now by law enabled, to hold, enjoy, or exercise any office, place or dignity, of, to, or belonging to the united church of England and Ireland, or the church of Scotland, or any place or office whatever, of, in, or belonging to any of the ecclesiastical courts of judicature of England and Ireland respectively, or any court of appeal from, or review of, the sentences of such courts, or of, in, or belonging to the Commissary Court of Edinburgh, or of, in, or belonging to any cathedral, or collegiate, or ecclesiastical establishment or foundation ; or any office or place whatever, of, in, or belonging to any of the universities of this realm ; or any office or place whatever, and by whatever name the same may be called, of, in, or belonging to any of the colleges or halls of the said universities, or the colleges of Eton, Westminster, or Winchester, or any college or school within this realm ; or to repeal, abrogate, or in any manner to interfere with any local statute, ordinance or rule, which is or shall be established by competent authority within any university, college, hall, or school, by which Roman Catholics shall be prevented from being admitted thereto, or from residing or taking degrees therein. Provided also, that nothing herein contained shall extend, or be construed to extend,

to enable any person otherwise than he is now by law
enabled to exercise any right of presentation to any ecclesiastical benefice whatsoever, or to repeal, vary, or alter
in any manner the laws now in force in respect to the right
of presentation to any ecclesiastical benefice.

Provided always, and be it enacted, that where any
right of presentation to any ecclesiastical benefice should
belong to any office in the gift or appointment of his
majesty, his heirs or successors, and such office shall be
held by a person professing the Roman Catholic religion,
the right of presentation shall devolve upon, and be exercised by, the Archbishop of Canterbury for the time
being.

And be it enacted, that it shall not be lawful for any
person professing the Roman Catholic religion, directly
or indirectly, to advise his majesty, his heirs, or successors, or any person or persons holding or exercising the
office of guardians of the United Kingdom, or of regent of
the United Kingdom, under whatever name, style, or title,
such office may be constituted, or the lord lieutenant, or
lord deputy, or other chief governor, or governors of Ireland, touching or concerning the appointment to, or disposal of, any office or preferment in the united church of
England and Ireland, or in the church of Scotland; and
if any such person shall offend in the premises, he shall be
thereof convicted by due course of law, be deemed guilty
of a high misdemeanor, and disabled for ever from holding
any office, civil or military, under the crown.

And be it enacted, that every person professing the
Roman Catholic religion, who shall after the commencement of this act be placed, elected or chosen in or to the
office of mayor, provost, alderman, recorder, bailiff, town-
clerk, magistrate, councillor or common councilman, or in
or to any office of magistracy or place, trust or employment, relating to the government of any city, corporation,
borough, burgh, or district, within the United Kingdom of
Great Britain and Ireland, shall within one calendar month
next, before or upon his admission into any of the aforesaid
offices or trusts, take and subscribe the oath herein before
appointed and set forth, in the presence of such person or
persons respectively as by the charters or usages of the
said respective cities, corporations, burghs, boroughs, and
districts, ought to administer the oath for due execution

of the said offices or places respectively, and in default of such, in the presence of two justices of the peace, councillors, or magistrates of the said cities, corporations, burghs, boroughs, or districts, if such there be, or otherwise in the presence of two justices of the peace of the respective counties, ridings, divisions or franchises wherein the said cities, corporations, burghs, boroughs, or districts are, which said oath shall either be entered in a book, roll, or other record to be kept for that purpose, or shall be filed amongst the records of the city, corporation, burgh, borough, or district.

And be it enacted, that every person professing the Roman Catholic religion, who shall after the commencement of this act be appointed to any office or place of trust or profit under his majesty, his heirs, or successors, shall within three calendar months next before such appointment, or otherwise shall, before he presumes to exercise or enjoy, or in any manner to act in such office or place, take and subscribe the oath hereinbefore appointed and set forth, either in his majesty's High Court of Chancery, or in any of his majesty's Courts of King's Bench, Common Pleas, or Exchequer, at Westminster or Dublin, or before any judge of assize, or any court of general or quarter sessions of the peace in Great Britain or Ireland, for the county or place where the person so taking and subscribing the same shall reside; or in any of his majesty's courts of session, justiciary, exchequer or jury court, or in any sheriff or stewart court, or in any burgh court, or before the magistrates and councillors of any royal burgh in Scotland, between the hours of nine in the morning and four in the afternoon; and the proper officer of the court in which such oath shall be so taken and subscribed, shall cause the same to be preserved amongst the records of the court; and such officer shall make, sign, and deliver a certificate of such oath having been duly taken and subscribed, as often as the same shall be demanded of him, upon payment of two shillings and sixpence for the same, and such certificate shall be sufficient evidence of the person therein named having duly taken and subscribed such oath.

And be it enacted, that if any person professing the Roman Catholic religion, shall enter upon the exercise or enjoyment of any office or place of trust or profit under his majesty, or of any other office or franchise, not having in the manner and at the times aforesaid taken and subscribed the oath hereinbefore appointed and set forth, then and in every such case such person shall forfeit to his majesty the sum of two hundred pounds; and the appointment of such person to the office, franchise, or place so by him held, shall thereupon become altogether void, and the office, place, or franchise shall be deemed and taken to be vacant to all intents and purposes whatsoever.

Provided always, that for and notwithstanding anything in this act contained, the oath hereinbefore appointed and set forth shall be taken by the officers in his majesty's land and sea service, professing the Roman Catholic religion, at the same times and in the same manner as the oaths and declarations now required by law are directed to be taken and not otherwise.

And be it further enacted, that from and after the passing of this act, no oath or oaths shall be tendered to, or required to be taken by, his majesty's subjects professing the Roman Catholic religion, for enabling them to hold or enjoy any real or personal property, other than such as may by law be tendered to and required to be taken by his majesty's other subjects; and that the oath herein appointed and set forth being taken and subscribed in any of the courts, or before any of the persons above mentioned, shall be of the same force and effect, to all intents and purposes, as, and shall stand in the place of, all oaths and declarations required or prescribed by any law now in force for the relief of his majesty's Roman Catholic subjects from any disabilities, incapacities, or penalties; and the proper officer of any of the courts above mentioned, in which any person professing the Roman Catholic religion shall demand to take and subscribe the oath herein appointed and set forth, is hereby authorized and required to administer the said oath to such person; and such officer shall make, sign, and deliver, a certificate of such oath having been duly taken and subscribed, as often as the same shall be demanded of him, upon payment of one shilling; and such certificate shall be sufficient evidence of the person therein named having duly taken and subscribed such oath.

And whereas the Protestant episcopal church of England and Ireland, and the doctrine, discipline, and government thereof, and likewise the Protestant Presbyterian church of Scotland, and the doctrine, discipline, and government thereof, are by the respective acts of union of England and Scotland, and of Great Britain and Ireland, established permanently and inviolably.

And whereas the right and title of archbishops to their respective provinces, of bishops to their sees, and of deans to their deaneries, as well in England as in Ireland, have been settled and established by law; be it therefore enacted, that if any person after the commencement of this act, other than the person thereunto authorized by law, shall assume or use the name, style, or title of archbishop of any province, bishop of any bishoprick, or dean of any deanery in England or Ireland ; he shall for every such offence forfeit and pay the sum of one hundred pounds.

And be it further enacted, that if any person holding any judicial or civil office, or any mayor, provost, jurat, bailiff, or other corporate officer, shall after the commencement of this act resort to or be present at any place or public meeting for religious worship, in England or in Ireland, other than that of the united church of England and Ireland, or in Scotland, other than that of the church of Scotland, as by law established, in the robe, gown, or peculiar habit of his office, or attended with the ensign or insignia, or any part thereof, of or belonging to such his office ; such person shall, being thereof convicted by due course of law, forfeit such office, and pay for every such offence the sum of one hundred pounds.

And be it further enacted, that if any Roman Catholic ecclesiastic, or any member of the orders, communities, or societies hereinafter mentioned, shall after the commencement of this act exercise any of the rites or ceremonies of the Roman Catholic religion, or wear the habits of his order, save within the usual places of worship of the Roman Catholic religion, or in private houses ; such ecclesiastic or other person shall, being thereof convicted by due course of law, forfeit for every such offence the sum of fifty pounds.

Provided always, and be it enacted, that nothing in this act contained shall in any manner repeal, alter, or affect any provision of an act made in the fifth year of his present majesty's reign, entituled " An act to repeal so much of an act passed in the ninth year of the reign of King William III. as relates to burials in suppressed monasteries, abbeys, or convents in Ireland, and to make further provision with respect to the burial in Ireland of persons dissenting from the established church.

And whereas Jesuits and members of other religious orders, communities, or societies of the church of Rome, bound by monastic or religious vows, are resident within the United Kingdom; and it is expedient to make provision for the gradual suppression and final prohibition of the same therein. Be it therefore enacted, that every Jesuit, and every member of any other religious order, community, or society of the church of Rome, bound by monastic or religious vows, who, at the time of the commencement of this act, shall be within the United Kingdom, shall within six calendar months after the commencement of this act, deliver to the clerk of the peace of the county or place where such person shall reside, or to his deputy, a notice or statement, in the form and containing the particulars required to be set forth in the schedule to this act annexed; which notice or statement, such clerk of the peace, or his deputy, shall preserve and register amongst the other records of such county or place, without any fee, and shall forthwith transmit a copy of such notice or statement, to the chief secretary of the lord lieutenant, or other chief governor or governors of Ireland, if such person shall reside in Ireland, or if in Great Britain, to one of his majesty's principal secretaries of state; and in case any person shall offend in the premises, he shall forfeit and pay to his majesty, for every calendar month during which he shall remain in the United Kingdom without having delivered such notice or statement as is hereinbefore required, the sum of fifty pounds.

And be it further enacted, that if any Jesuit or member of any such religious order, community, or society as aforesaid, shall, after the commencement of this act, come into this realm, he shall be deemed and taken to be guilty of a misdemeanor, and being thereof lawfully convicted, shall be sentenced and ordered to be banished from the United Kingdom for the term of his natural life.

Provided always, and be it further enacted, that in case any natural born subject of this realm, being at the time of the commencement of this act a Jesuit, or other member of any such religious order, community, or society as aforesaid, shall, at the time of the commencement of this act, be out of the realm, it shall be lawful for such person to return or to come into this realm, and upon such his return or coming into the realm, he is hereby required, within the space of six calendar months after his first returning or coming into the United Kingdom, to deliver such notice or statement to the clerk of the peace of the county or place where he shall reside, or his deputy, for the purpose of being so registered and transmitted as hereinbefore directed; and in case any such person shall neglect or refuse so to do, he shall, for every such offence, forfeit and pay to his majesty, for every calendar month during which he shall remain in the United Kingdom without having delivered such notice or statement, the sum of fifty pounds.

Provided also, and be it further enacted, that notwithstanding any thing hereinbefore contained, it shall be lawful for any one of his majesty's principal secretaries of state, being a Protestant, by a licence in writing, signed by him, to grant permission to any Jesuit or member of any such religious order, community, or society as aforesaid, to come into the United Kingdom, and to remain therein for such period as the said secretary of state shall think proper, not exceeding in any case the space of six calendar months, and it shall also be lawful for any of his majesty's principal secretaries of state to revoke any licence so granted before the expiration of the time mentioned therein if he shall so think fit; and if any such person to whom any such licence shall have been granted shall not depart from the United Kingdom within twenty days after the expiration of the time mentioned in such licence, or if such licence shall have been revoked, then within twenty days after notice of such revocation shall have been given to him, every person so offending shall be deemed guilty of a misdemeanor, and being thereof lawfully convicted, shall be sentenced and ordered to be banished from the United Kingdom for the term of his natural life.

And be it further enacted, that there shall annually be laid before both Houses of Parliament, an account of all such licences as shall have been granted for the purpose hereinbefore mentioned, within the twelve months next preceding.

And be it further enacted, that in case any Jesuit, or member of any such religious order, community, or society as aforesaid, shall, after the commencement of this act, within any part of the United Kingdom, admit any person

to become a regular ecclesiastic, or brother, or member of any such religious order, community, or society, or be aiding or consenting thereto, or shall administer or cause to be administered, or be aiding or assisting in the administration or taking any oath, vow, or engagement, purporting or intended to bind the person taking the same to the rules, ordinances, or ceremonies of such religious order, community, or society, every person offending in the premises, in England or Ireland, shall be deemed guilty of a misdemeanor, and in Scotland shall be punished by fine and imprisonment.

And be it further enacted, that in case any person shall after the commencement of this act, within any part of this United Kingdom, be admitted or become a Jesuit, or brother, or member of any other such religious order, community, or society as aforesaid, such person shall be deemed and taken to be guilty of a misdemeanor, and being thereof lawfully convicted, shall be sentenced and ordered to be banished from the United Kingdom for the term of his natural life.

And be it further enacted, that in case any person sentenced and ordered to be banished under the provisions of this act, shall not depart from this United Kingdom within thirty days after the pronouncing of such sentence and order, it shall be lawful for his majesty to cause such person to be conveyed to such place out of the United Kingdom, as his majesty by the advice of his Privy Council, shall direct.

And be it further enacted, that if any offender who shall be so sentenced, and ordered to be banished in manner aforesaid, shall, after the end of three calendar months, from the time such sentence and order hath been pronounced, be at large within any part of the United Kingdom, without some lawful cause ; every such offender being so at large as aforesaid, on being thereof lawfully convicted, shall be transported to such place as shall be appointed by his majesty, for the term of his natural life.

Provided always, and be it enacted, that nothing herein contained, shall extend or be construed to extend in any manner to affect any religious order, community, or establishment consisting of females bound by religious or monastic vows.

And be it further enacted, that all penalties imposed by

this act shall and may be recovered as a debt due to his majesty, by information to be filed in the name of his majesty's attorney-general for England or for Ireland as the case may be, in the Courts of Exchequer, in England or Ireland respectively, or in the name of his majesty's advocate-general in the Court of Exchequer in Scotland.

And be it further enacted, that this act, or any part thereof, may be repealed, altered, or varied at any time within this present Session of Parliament.

And be it further enacted, that this act shall commence and take effect at the expiration of ten days from and after the passing thereof.

SCHEDULE REFERRED TO IN THIS ACT.

Date of the registry.	Name of the party.	Age.	Place of birth.	Name of the order, community, or society whereof he is a member.	Name and usual residence of the next immediate superior of the order, community, or society.	Usual place of residence of the party.

No. 9.

A BILL FOR THE FURTHER REPEAL OF ENACTMENTS IMPOSING PAINS AND PENALTIES UPON HER MAJESTY'S ROMAN CATHOLIC SUBJECTS ON ACCOUNT OF THEIR RELIGION, 10TH FEB. 1847, 10 VIC.

Whereas by an act passed in the eighth year of the reign of her present majesty, intituled, "An act to repeal certain penal enactments made against her majesty's Roman Catholic subjects," the several penal acts, and parts of penal acts made against Roman Catholics, and thereinafter mentioned or specified, were, from and after the passing of that act, repealed :

And whereas by another act passed in the tenth year of the reign of her said majesty, intituled, " An Act to relieve

her majesty's subjects from certain penalties and disabilities in regard to religious opinions," certain other penal
acts, and parts of penal acts, made against Roman Catholics, and thereinafter specified, were (amongst other acts),
from and after the commencement of the said last-mentioned act, repealed :

And whereas, notwithstanding the provisions of the said
acts, her majesty's Roman Catholic subjects do still continue to be liable for, or on account of their religious
belief, practice or profession, to sundry punishments, pains,
penalties, and disabilities, ordained and enacted by certain
acts made and passed by the parliament of England, the
parliament of Great Britain, and the parliament of Great
Britain and Ireland respectively, and to which punishments, pains, penalties, and disabilities, none other of her
majesty's subjects are liable :

And whereas it is expedient that all such punishments,
pains, and penalties, as aforesaid shall be for ever repealed
and taken away :

And whereas it is likewise expedient that all such and
so many of the aforesaid disabilities shall be in like manner
repealed and taken away as do not in anywise relate to the
holding of offices, collegiate or ecclesiastical, or whereunto
collegiate or ecclesiastical preferment or patronage is incident, or to the presenting to ecclesiastical benefices, or as
do not in any other manner tend to the better securing
and strengthening the present church establishment, and
the present civil government, and the settlement of property within this realm ;

Be it therefore enacted, by the Queen's most excellent
Majesty, by and with the advice and consent of the lords,
spiritual and temporal, and commons, in this present parliament assembled, and by the authority of the same, that
from, and after the *passing of this act*, the several acts hereinafter mentioned, or so much and such parts of any of
them as are hereinafter specified, shall be repealed ; (that
is to say) so much of an act passed in the first year of the
reign of Queen Elizabeth, intituled, "An Act to restore to
the crown the ancient jurisdiction over the estate, ecclesiastical and spiritual, and abolishing all foreign powers
repugnant to the same," whereby it is enacted, "That if
any person or persons dwelling or inhabiting within this
your realm, or in any other your highness's realms or

dominions, of what estate, dignity, or degree soever he or they be, after the end of thirty days next after the determination of this session of this present parliament, shall, by writing, printing, teaching, preaching, express words, deed or act, advisedly, maliciously, and directly affirm, hold, stand with, set forth, maintain, or defend the authority, pre-eminence, power, or jurisdiction, spiritual or ecclesiastical, of any foreign prince, prelate, person, state or potentate whatsoever, heretofore claimed, used, or usurped, within this realm, or any dominion or country being within or under the power, dominion, or allegiance, of your highness, or shall advisedly, maliciously, and directly, put in ure or execute anything for the extolling, advancement, setting forth, maintenance or defence, of any such pretended or usurped jurisdiction, power, pre-eminence and authority, or any part thereof, that then every such person and persons so doing and offending, their abettors, aiders, procurers, and counsellors, being thereof lawfully convicted and attainted according to the due order and course of the common laws of this realm, for his or their first offence shall forfeit and lose unto your highness, your heirs, and successors, all his and their goods and chattels, as well real as personal; and if any such person so convicted or attainted shall not have or be worth of his proper goods and chattels to the value of twenty pounds at the time of his conviction or attainder, that then every such person so convicted or attainted, over and besides the forfeiture of all his said goods and chattels, shall have and suffer imprisonment by the space of one whole year, without bail or mainprise," (so far as the same relates to or in anywise concerns Roman Catholics); also the whole of an act passed in the thirteenth year of the reign of the said Queen Elizabeth, intituled, "An Act against the bringing in and putting in execution of bulls, writings, or instruments, and other superstitious things from the See of Rome," (so far as the same relates to or in anywise concerns Roman Catholics); also so much of an act passed in the thirteenth and fourteenth years of the reign of King Charles II., intituled, "An Act for the uniformity of public prayers and administration of sacraments, and other rites and ceremonies, and for establishing the form of making, ordaining, and consecrating bishops, priests, and deacons, in the church of England," as in any

way relates to the offence of willingly and wittingly hearing
and being present at any other manner or form of common
prayer, of administration of the sacraments, of making of
ministers in the churches, or of any other rites contained
in the said book than is therein mentioned and set forth,
(so far as the same in anywise relates to or concerns Roman
Catholics) ; also, the whole of an act passed in the twenty-
fifth year of the reign of the said King Charles II., intituled, " An Act for preventing dangers which may happen
from popish recusants ;" also, the whole of an act passed
in the second session of parliament in the thirtieth year of
the reign of the said King Charles II., intituled, " An Act
for the more effectual preserving the king's person and
government, by disabling papists from sitting in either
house of parliament ;" also, the whole of an act passed in
the seventh and eighth years of the reign of King William
III., intituled, " An Act requiring the practisers of law to
take the oaths and subscribe the declarations therein mentioned ;" also, so much of an act passed in the thirty-first
year of the reign of King George III., intituled, " An Act
to relieve, upon conditions and under restrictions, the
persons therein described, from certain penalties and disabilities to which papists or persons professing the popish
religion are by law subject," as makes it a condition precedent to any relief or benefit being had or taken under
or by virtue of the said last-mentioned act, that the oath
thereby appointed shall have been previously taken and
subscribed by the party desiring such relief or benefit, or
that his or her declaration and oath, or name or description, shall have been previously recorded in any of his
majesty's courts of chancery, king's bench, common pleas,
or exchequer at Westminster, or at any quarter or other
general session of the peace for any county or other division or place ; also, so much of the said last-mentioned act
whereby it is provided and enacted, " That all uses, trusts,
and dispositions, whether of real or personal property
which, immediately before the twenty-fourth day of June,
one thousand seven hundred and ninety-one, shall be
deemed to be superstitious or unlawful, shall continue to
be so deemed and taken, anything in this act contained
notwithstanding ; and also so much of the said last-mentioned act, whereby it is provided and enacted, " That no
benefit in this act contained shall extend or be construed

to extend to any Roman Catholic ecclesiastic permitted by this act, who shall officiate in any place of congregation or assembly for religious worship permitted by this act, with a steeple and bell, or at any funeral in any church or churchyard, or who shall exercise any of the rites or ceremonies of his religion, or wear the habits of his order, save within some place of congregation or assembly for religious worship permitted by this act, or in a private house where there shall not be more than five persons assembled besides those of the household; also, so much of an act passed in the tenth year of the reign of King George IV., intituled, "An Act for the relief of his majesty's Roman Catholic subjects," whereby it is enacted, "That if any Roman Catholic ecclesiastic, or any member of any of the orders, communities, or societies, hereinafter mentioned, shall, after the commencement of this act, exercise any of the rites or ceremonies of the Roman Catholic religion, or wear the habits of his order, save within the usual places of worship of the Roman Catholic religion, or in private houses, such ecclesiastic or other person shall, being thereof convicted by due course of law, forfeit for every such offence the sum of fifty pounds;" also, so much of the said last-mentioned act as imposes penalties upon any person holding any judicial, civil, or corporate office, who shall resort to or be present at any place of worship in England or Ireland, other than that of the United Church of England and Ireland, or in Scotland other than that of the Church of Scotland as by law established, in the robe, gown, or other peculiar habit of his office, or attend thereat with the ensign or insignia, or any part thereof, of or belonging to such his office; and also so much of the said last-mentioned act as relates to the gradual suppression and final prohibition of Jesuits and members of other religious orders, communities, or societies of the Church of Rome, bound by monastic or religious vows, and resident within the kingdom, and the coming and returning of Jesuits, or members of any such religious orders, communities, or societies into this realm, and the registration of Jesuits or members of any such orders, communities, or societies, and the admittance of persons to become Jesuits or regular ecclesiastics, or brothers or members of any such religious orders, communities, or societies, and the administering or taking of any oaths, vows, or engagements, purporting or intending to bind the persons taking the same to the rules, ordinances, or ceremonies, of any such religious orders, communities, or societies, and the granting of licenses in writing signed by any one of his majesty's principal Secretaries of State being a Protestant, and the several misdemeanors in the premises respectively created or enacted or declared by the said act, and the fines or forfeitures of monies, pains, and penalties of banishment, and transportation beyond seas for term of life, and all other the forfeitures, pains, penalties, punishments, and disabilities, thereby respectively in that behalf enacted against all persons respectively offending in the premises, or otherwise provided or enacted, or ensuing, for or in respect of or as incidental to the same.

No. 10.

THE OUTLAWRY OF THE RELIGIOUS ORDERS IN 1829, CONFIRMED IN 1845.

The re-enactment of one of the most offensive of the penal laws in 1829, against the religious orders, and the confirmation of that odious outlawry of the regular clergy in 1845, merit more attention than has been given to them by the people of England and Ireland. It is a shame and a reproach that such an egregious wrong should have been committed with impunity and hardly remonstrated against; that this renewal of penal law barbarity, directed against a large body of the Catholic clergy of those countries, should have been tamely endured and acquiesced in by them. One of the body aggrieved by this outlawry of his order, and justly indignant at the recent confirmation of it, has placed in my hands a letter of his in reference to the wrong inflicted on him and his brethren, which I willingly avail myself of, with the view of putting the matter of which he so ably treats fully and fairly before the public. This letter is the production of a minister of religion—a scholar—a christian gentleman—a man of the highest sense of honour—of unfeigned piety and indefatigable zeal in doing good, who, if he dared, to-morrow without the sanction of the government, to set his foot on his native soil, might be seized as a felon, banished or transported, for *the crime* of belonging to a monastic order.

This letter is addressed by a member of one of the outlawed monastic orders to his fellow-countrymen and Christians, without distinction of creed or class.

Protestants! you never bent your necks to the yoke of servitude; you are unaccustomed to insult or slight, and not likely to tolerate either patiently. There was a time when you considered yourselves as the only rightful children of your own land; and you loved her with an ardent proud attachment. When dominant you were keenly jealous of her rights, and zealous in defence of them.

Protestants of England and Ireland, the wrong done to us concerns you. The religious orders were banned to conciliate and cajole you. You are proud but you are not mean nor wantonly vindictive. Will you accept the implied insult, that crying outrage and tyrannical injustice wantonly and uselessly inflicted on a few of your fellow-countrymen, is pleasing to you?

Presbyterians! you are a stern and stubborn race, and you have been factious and ungovernable in your choler sometimes. They sought to impose a religious yoke upon you in Scotland, and you flung it from you with a shout and a blow. But you still had disabilities, and they weighed heavily on you until, by the help of your Catholic brethren, you were emancipated.

Catholics of England and Ireland; slaves by birth and sons of slaves, your limbs are at last free; the members of the proscribed monastic orders were never unfaithful to you, their fidelity contributed to the bursting of your bands. With a bad grace, at the last hour, while the king wept and the lords stormed, when you were allowed to rise from slavery your leaders suffered us to have new chains forged for us.

That Sunday morning, that brought the glad tidings of emancipation to Ireland, was a memorable day. I was present that day at a charity sermon in aid of the brothers of the Christian Schools. The aisles, sanctuary, and galleries, of the extensive church were thronged. The good and benevolent Protestant shared in the quiet triumph of his Catholic countrymen. The hearts of all throbbed with feelings too happy for utterance. A small, pale, but intellectual man, a member of a religious order, ascended the pulpit. He saw the joy flashing from the eyes of the multitude. His clear ringing voice, in thrilling accents, hailed and congratulated the enfranchised people. He reminded them of what they had been, that they might feel with more keen pleasure what they were. Their country, the loveliest spot on earth, upon which God had poured such abundant natural beauties and advantages, but over which for three hundred years hung the darkness of slavery. Its inhabitants for ages groaning in hopeless bondage; shut out from every honourable pursuit, the bench, the bar, the army, and the navy, ignominiously closed against them; too low and degraded to merit a representation in either house of parliament.

But now, changing the picture in language too vivid to be remembered or imitated, he described the bursting of the morning of liberty upon them. The darkness and shame that so long hung over their island rolling away— the gyves falling from their limbs—the portals of the constitution opening for their admission, and honours, and dignities, brought within their grasp.

But the look of that pale face became one of shame and mental agony, with a voice sunk almost to a whisper, yet painfully distinct in every part of that vast church, he spoke these words: "There is in this assembly one upon whose limbs the chain yet clanks, upon whose brow still burns the ignominious band of slavery. The bill that gave freedom to you forged new fetters for him. You go forth to liberty and joy, and he is thrust back into all the horrors of his old condition. This bill banishes him and his from their native land. Your country is no longer his country; for they have made him an outlaw and a slave."

It was formerly said, that any one touching British soil was free. That boast is now false. Any member, since 1829, of the religious orders, by landing in the British dominions in violation of the terms of this law, loses his liberty; he may be seized on, and at the will of the British ministry can be forcibly and ignominiously banished from the British dominions, or transported to a distant land.

This fact intimately concerns you, free and high-minded Protestants, because this foul and wanton wrong, this hideous abuse of power, this banishment of innocent persons, was avowedly perpetrated to conciliate you. They feared that you would be exasperated at the emancipation of the millions, and they fettered and branded us to appease your supposed anger at their deed. Protestants, did they not malign you? Your vanity may have been mortified to feel yourselves stripped by friendly hands of your long possessed civil superiority, and to see the Catholic serf raised to an enjoyment of all your privileges. But is it true, that you could be gratified with the cruelly ignominious and tyrannical treatment of a few pious and literary recluses? Did you accept their banishment from Sir Robert Peel and the Duke of Wellington, as a peace-offering or a substitute for the lost power of intolerance?

Does it not concern and move you, sturdy, honest Presbyterians? Do you love oppression for conscience' sake? Would they dare do this to you and to your pastors? They dare not. They should seek your pastors in the midst of your armed bands, and reach them over your dead bodies.

It concerns you, anti-slavery philanthropists. You make the ears to tingle with your earnest and impassioned invectives against black slavery in America and Brazil. Slavery beyond the Atlantic, or below the Equator, is, of a certainty, a foul and hideous thing. But do you hear no chains clanking nearer home, even in your own land? Look here on slavery. You will find on the statute-books new laws only of fifteen years' existence, and renewed within but a few months, re-enacting bondage for a portion of your fellow citizens, and treating them when caught as proscribed criminals; and yet, good Sirs, those men have natural rights and immortal spirits, though the former are not pagans, and the latter are lodged in tenements of an aspect and complexion that do not differ from your own. But they are Catholics, Englishmen and Irishmen; ministers of the religion of their countrymen, monks:—these are accidents of creed of country, and results of the exercise of christian will, which chooses the mode of serving God most suitable, as they think, to the aim, end, and object of their devotion, but which are very obnoxious to our rulers.

Advocates of freedom and of justice, I remind you that, if you acquiesce by your silence in this foul oppression, that your denunciations against slavery are a mockery and a delusion.

If we are criminals, let us be fairly convicted by a jury of our countrymen. But. before all England, I here indignantly and loudly protest against the wanton injustice of singling a small class out of millions, and passing laws to banish them from their native land, because they are pleased to use their natural, free-born right of bending before their God in the manner that they are sure will please Him well.

Our degradation above all concerns you, Catholic people of Ireland. Who are we, that you should permit us to be treated thus? Have we no claims of gratitude on your protection? Are we not so inseparably bound up with you, that you must consider our shame as your own dishonour? There was a time, in your days of bitter distress and abandonment, when our love for you made us patient of fatigue, cheerful under privations, and fearless of the scaffold and the pile. Much did they hate us, and keenly did they pursue us, and remorselessly butcher us. But like the men of the bridge of Athlone, group of us succeeded mowed-down group. We hung over your wounded bodies on the battle-field; we moistened your lips, and soothed your aching brows in the pest cabin or tent. We cheered and filled you with hope in your reverses, and followed you to bog, and mountain, and sea-side cavern to celebrate the divine mysteries for your consolation. One thing we never did, and that was to desert you.

O' Sullivan Beare, in his Latin History, vol. iv., book i,, page 229, writing in the year 1615, says: "The more they are ordered to quit the kingdom, the more resolutely they remain and flock to it; and that they may not be known to the English, some, clothed as secular persons, affect to be merchants or physicians; others, girt with a sword or dagger, affect to be knights: thus some assume one profession, others another.

"But it surpasses credibility (fidem superat) how fearlessly the priests do their duty, and resist the enemy. Above all others, the religious of St. Dominick labour much. Formerly they possessed many noble establishments in Ireland; and yet they now are as zealous to succour her in her distress, as when they were masters of those same mansions. The children of the seraphic

Francis are held in the highest veneration in Ireland, and surpass all the other religious in number; nor do the fathers of the society of Jesus yield in merit to any others: they consider it their duty and province to withstand the deadly gaze and raging onset of the enemy. Other religious are not so numerous at present in Ireland. The members of the sacred order of St. Augustine are few." Though he does not, he says, know the full number of the priests then in Ireland, yet "I am not ignorant that the names of 1160 religious and secular priests, their relatives, and protectors, have been sought, and are known to the English; and they are sought for no other purpose than that the priests and their protectors should be destroyed by every possible means."

Burke, in his 'Hybernia Dominicana,' chap. xvii., page 556, gives the names, residences, and modes of martyrdom for their faith and country, of fifty Dominican friars within the space of sixteen years—that is, between the years 1641 and 1657. From other parts of his curious work, I find that the Dominicans, when hunted from their smoking houses of study, founded three extensive colleges on the continent; one at Rome, another at Louvain, and a third at Lisbon. At chap. xii. page 419, he tells, that the latter (that of Lisbon) was shortly after its foundation called the "Seminary of Martyrs," because, within a couple of years, so many as seven of its earliest students were, on their return home, seized in various parts of the country, and suffered death for you.

If the Dominican Order poured out its blood so lavishly, rather than abandon you in your straits, what must not the more numerous and equally zealous Franciscans and Jesuits have done? Oh, the religious orders were found in the midst of you, when most you needed them—men on whose heads was set a price, and against whose entrance into Ireland the most ruthless proclamations issued periodically from jealous kings and parliament! But the more they were ordered to quit, the more they clung to you. Such was their devotion. "He is indeed the true shepherd, who lays down his life for his flock. Greater love than this no man hath, than that a man lay down his life for his friends." Try by this test the religious orders, fifty of whose children were martyred for you in sixteen years. That order has not at present, I imagine, forty members in all

Ireland. Will you allow a vindictive and relentless policy to rob and banish from among you this small remnant of the successors of your martyred saints?—will you, O Catholic people of Ireland? Alas, alas! how can I hint the bitter shame and the painful doubt that is forced on me by the memory of the past? They gave you liberty in 1829, because they dared not keep it longer. And when we, who defied the scaffold and the pile to succour you in your woe, went struggling forwards to share in your triumphs, you saw them singling us out from your victorious millions, and vindictively and ignominiously thrusting us back. You murmured—oh, how faintly! and then, as if your consciences were satisfied, you crossed your hands, and, for fear of injuring yourselves by any effort to save us—did we calculate so in the old times?—you allowed them to bind and brand us, and to send us forth among you, as a type of your old condition, and as a sort of perpetually clanking proclamation, that you would be, but for England's generosity, what we are now,—slaves worse than slaves, proscribed criminals.

People of England and Ireland, does it not concern your national character to prove to the world, that you do not repay by cold neglect and heartless abandonment the faithful services of a remnant of those religious bodies, whose members, during 300 years of persecution and affliction, in peril, in pestilence, and famine, stood fast by your forefathers, consoled, and cheered, and guided them.

A Member of one of the Outlawed
Religious Orders.

No. 11.

EDUCATION.

In debate on the Education Question, on the 19th of April, 1847, Lord J. Russell in the house of commons said: "It has been asked if Roman Catholics are to be included? To that I answer, that in the minutes of August and December, 1846, the question was not entered into—it was not then before us, and it does not arise on those minutes. There certain rules are laid down in conformity with the original intentions of the framers, that the sum of money to be expended should be laid out in aid of the National Society's and other schools, but the question does not arise on those minutes as to the omission of Roman Catholic schools; and on referring to the minutes of 1839, I find that these minutes are confirmed, for the minutes of 1839 confine the grant to the schools in which the scriptures are read daily, and, as I have already stated, I believe that by the word scriptures is intended the version which is usually used in this country, namely, the authorized version. Then the question comes, if a desire were expressed on the part of the Roman Catholics to have schools for Catholics, and Catholics only —if such a desire were entertained, I would be in favour of it; but the greatest care should be taken in dealing with this subject, and I think, for example, that it would not do to support monastic schools, which might be set up in connection with monasteries for the education of Roman Catholics; and I must also say that I think schools which Protestant children might attend, and at which no opportunity would be afforded for reading the Bible daily, would be highly objectionable. The question as to the Roman Catholics was not, as I have remarked, raised in the minutes of 1839 or 1846, and having stated that the authorized version is the version of scriptures which was alluded to, it would not be desirable now, indeed, it would be hardly expedient, to expend any of the £.100,000 in aid of the Roman Catholic schools. I believe, that of all the half-million which has been already spent under the direction of the Treasury, and in accordance with the minutes of council on education, not one shilling was given in aid of the Roman Catholic schools, and I do not see the advantage of placing this question now merely as a stumbling-block in the way of our coming to a decision on the subject before the house."

On presenting a petition in the House of Lords the same night, Lord Brougham "doubted whether the exclusion of a particular class of schools was so well understood as the noble marquis seemed to think. And if government had no doubt themselves on the point, why, he would ask, was their answer to recent applications for aid from Roman Catholic schools, that they would consider the question of

giving aid to them? He, for one, thought that the word
'scripture' ought to include every regular version of the
sacred writings, whether of the Roman Catholic or of the
Protestant church, and he was never more astonished in
his life than he was to find that any doubt ever existed as
to the propriety of educating Roman Catholic children.
They all knew that in England there were very few Roman
Catholic schools of a class requiring government aid. Such
schools were confined to one or two places, such as Liverpool, and Glasgow, in Scotland. In Ireland, where the
great bulk of the population was Roman Catholic, no such
exclusion was possible, or was attempted [hear, hear]. He
could not allow the opportunity to pass, without expressing
the sorrow he felt that, not in 1447 or in 1547, but in the
year 1847, they should find, as appeared from what was
going on elsewhere, the great question of education
mixed up with all the embroiling of sectarian violence and
bigotry.'

Roman Catholic children were finally excluded from any
participation in the grant of £.100,000 a-year, that formed
part of the government scheme of education brought forward by Lord John Russell.

INDEX.

RICHARDSON AND SON, PRINTERS, DERBY.